THE TRANSPAREN

THE TRANSPARENCY FIX

Secrets, Leaks, and
Uncontrollable Government Information

Mark Fenster

STANFORD LAW BOOKS
An Imprint of Stanford University Press
Stanford, California

Stanford University Press
Stanford, California

Printed in the United States of America on acid-free, archival-quality paper

Library of Congress Cataloging-in-Publication Data

Names: Fenster, Mark, author.
Title: The transparency fix : secrets, leaks, and uncontrollable government
    information / Mark Fenster.
Description: Stanford, California : Stanford Law Books, an imprint of
    Stanford University Press, 2017. | Includes index.
Identifiers: LCCN 2017001368 (print) | LCCN 2017003719 (ebook) |
    ISBN 9781503601710 (cloth : alk. paper) | ISBN 9781503602663 (pbk. : alk. paper) |
    ISBN 9781503602670 (e-book)
Subjects: LCSH: Transparency in government--Law and legislation--United
    States. | Freedom of information--United States. | Official
    secrets--United States. | Government information--Law and
    legislation--United States. | Leaks (Disclosure of information)--United
    States.
Classification: LCC KF5753 .F46 2017 (print) | LCC KF5753 (ebook) |
    DDC 352.8/80973--dc23
LC record available at https://lccn.loc.gov/2017001368

Cover design: Christian Fuenfhausen
Typeset by Bruce Lundquist in 10/14 Minion

For Ruby, and for Rachel

Table of Contents

Acknowledgments

This project is the product of my separate academic training in law and cultural studies, and I continue to be indebted to faculty and colleagues from graduate and law school. I received incredibly helpful comments during the decade I've spent on this project from Steven Aftergood, Clare Birchall, Lars Thøger Christensen, Nick Cullather, Mikkel Flyverbom, David Fontana, Lyrissa Lidsky, Bill Page, David Pozen, Rachel Rebouché, Larry Solum, and Trysh Travis. Many thanks to students at the University of Florida who helped with research over the past decade, including Ariane Assadoghli, Stephen Bagge, Joe Cordova, Tara DiJohn, Jennifer Kent, Grace Kim, Lauren Milcarek, Sam Morris, Rob Norway, Joey Posey, and Michael Thomas. Finally, I'm grateful to Stanford University Press, and especially to my editor Michelle Lipinski, for guidance and support in moving this project from manuscript to book.

Some of the material in this book is adapted from previous works published in the past decade. I have shortened and updated the borrowed material, with a focus on making it more readable for a general academic audience and part of a more organic whole. Parts of the Introduction and Chapter 4 are adapted from "Seeing the State: Transparency as Metaphor," *Administrative Law Review* 62, no. 3 (2010): 617–672. Parts of Chapters 1 and 3 are adapted from "The Opacity of Transparency," *Iowa Law Review* 91, no. 3 (2006): 885–949. Parts of Chapters 1 and 2 are adapted from "The Transparency Fix: Advocating Legal Rights and Their Alternatives in the Pursuit of a Visible State," *University of Pittsburgh Law Review* 73, no. 3 (2012): 443–503. Chapter 7 is adapted from "The Implausibility of Secrecy," *Hastings Law Journal* 65, no. 2 (2014): 309–363. Part of Chapter 8 is adapted from "Disclosure's Effects: WikiLeaks and Transparency," *Iowa Law Review* 97, no. 3 (2012): 753–807. I thank the journals and their editors for their hard work in helping edit the manuscripts and check citations, as well as for granting permission to use the adapted materials in this book.

Introduction

The Transparent State We Want But Can't Have

Early in his memoir *Secrets*, Daniel Ellsberg recalls the moment he first sur-reptitiously accessed top-secret government information. Then a young, rising Pentagon bureaucrat, Ellsberg had been hired away from his previous position as a research analyst at Rand, a private think tank consulting for the Defense Department's efforts in fighting the Vietnam War. At the Pentagon he worked for an assistant secretary of state for international security affairs who regularly received classified documents that Ellsberg, with limited security clearance, could not read. The binder in which those documents were filed sat on a rolling bookstand in his boss's Pentagon office that Ellsberg was supposed to wheel into a secure, locked closet. Ellsberg explains how, having found himself alone in the office one night, he surrendered to the documents' temptation:

> The office was dark; the light was coming from inside the closet. I was in the process of putting the rolling stand away for the night. I looked inside the thick binder and riffled through the contents. It was like opening the door on Ali Baba's treasure. . . . At a glance I could see that what I held in my hand was precious. Reading just a few paragraphs here and there was, for me, like breathing pure oxygen. My heart was pounding.[1]

Up to this point in his career, Ellsberg had found himself in a somewhat inner circle within the Pentagon's extended bureaucracy. But this circle was not inner enough for a Harvard Ph.D. who had produced widely cited academic papers at a tender age and proven himself one of the best and brightest. The paper records that he was forbidden to view commanded his attention by promising entry to an even-more privileged position from which he could catch a glimpse of some greater truth. They offered him the "oxygen" an ambitious analyst needs in order to survive and prosper. His desire for secret, forbidden information pained Ellsberg, a pain that only access could relieve with its promise of deep satisfaction and pleasure.

Ellsberg's longing for greater access met one of the criteria for entry into *the inner circle*: He recognized the value of receiving clearance to view protected information as both a resource and a commodity of distinction—a "treasure," as he described it, access to which requires sacrifice. As he recently observed, "The invitation [to join a group], and the acceptance of the promise of secrecy, is the result of co-optation, often after a process of initiation, . . . after which one has been judged worthy of having one's promise of secrecy believed."[2] Secrecy divides the knowledgeable from the ignorant, at once bestowing authority and providing the basis for it. To be an informational hub in what Jana Costas and Christopher Grey have described as secrecy's "architectural properties" is to operate at an organization's center, while to be disconnected from information's flow is to sit on a branch, away from the action.[3] To gain access, Ellsberg also needed to prove willing to withhold information from those on the outside. Excluding the wrong people is as important to maintaining informational elite status as is including the right ones.[4] The German sociologist Georg Simmel called this the "aggressive defensive" process of hiding and masking information. It creates a property right that grants a "position of exception" to those who hold it.[5]

Ellsberg's Ali Baba moment bore special significance, then, for both the zealous bureaucrat that Ellsberg was and for the dissident leaker that he would soon become. The successive stages of information access produce tension, expectation, and release, with the ecstasy of surreptitious revelation promising a movement from dusky ignorance to the radiant high of information access. Ellsberg would acquire fame and infamy for illegally copying and releasing to congressmen and newspapers the Pentagon Papers—a treasure trove of documents akin to those he had craved when he longed for that access. He epitomized the political trajectory of his cohort of "Defense intellectuals" recruited to the Cold War military project who then joined the movement opposing the Vietnam War.[6] His whistleblowing ultimately led to his ouster from the information-rich world he had inhabited. The Nixon administration even initiated a covert campaign to discredit him—surely as frightening a prospect as an individual could face, and as great a badge of honor as any American dissident of his generation could garner.

By violating the law that prohibited him from viewing the documents, Ellsberg crossed both the legal line and the physical boundary that placed the binder beyond his view. His heroism, to those many who see him as a hero, began when he traversed that well-guarded (but not well-guarded enough!) threshold into the sacred space where the most privileged information is secured. Only then could he imagine freeing that information from its physical constraints. Only then could he envision educating the public about the policies and actions that were being undertaken in its name. And only then could he become the famous whistleblower and secret-slayer of the left, the role he has occupied since.

The Transparency Fix

Ellsberg's trajectory—from relative outsider to insider to banished exile—illustrates many of the basic legal, administrative, social, and cultural issues bound up in the informational ideal of a truly democratic representative government. Although he named his memoir *Secrets*, Ellsberg's purpose in telling his story was to inspire readers to join his nearly career-long fight to destroy government secrecy. As he explains in the book's preface, "telling the truth, revealing wrongly kept secrets, can have a surprisingly strong, unforeseeable power to help end a wrong and save lives."[7] For Ellsberg and those committed to the expansion and strict enforcement of open government laws, there is a singular truth about disclosure: Greater access to government information can remedy the wrong of excessive state secrets and can also initiate necessary and significant political change. Enough collective Ali Baba moments will surely lead the public to demand permanent and complete access to secret information.

Ellsberg tied his justification for disclosing what he viewed as precious, secret documents to his commitment to popular democracy. The public must view the state and its key documents; indeed, the term that contemporary advocates frequently use to describe the government they envision is "transparent," a metaphor invoking a window that enables one to see inside from outside and vice versa, despite their separation.[8] In the context of open government laws and norms, the metaphor presumes a problem and suggests its logical solution: The distant, invisible state must be revealed to the public. It provides the foundational logic for laws protecting a "right to know" by mandating "open government." I characterize the logic—which aims to solve government secrecy—as the *transparency fix*. It works as follows.

The government is large, faceless, bureaucratic. It operates at a remove from the public, enforcing countless complex laws while enjoying the enormous authority to impose criminal and civil sanctions on those who disobey it. It holds the awesome power of waging war and negotiating with foreign nations. Even those who support the majority of government programs and decisions fear an unbridled, unaccountable state. To be held accountable and to perform well, government institutions and officials must be visible to the public.

But in the normal course of their bureaucratic operation, public organizations create institutional impediments that obstruct external observation. Sometimes they do so inadvertently, sometimes willfully; sometimes with good intent, but sometimes with unethical or illegal intent. Their doing so is inevitable. As Max Weber wrote, "[b]ureaucratic administration always tends to exclude the public, to hide its knowledge and action from criticism as well as it can."[9] Government agencies and officials enjoy and zealously protect the greater access to information, or the information asymmetry, that they enjoy over the public and over their rivals.

There is a solution, however. A transparent state removes the obstructions that keep the government hidden and the public imperfectly informed. This solution does not occur naturally because the state will not reveal itself willingly. The public needs a powerful external mechanism to force the state bureaucracy to make itself visible. Commonly, such instruments are administrative laws, enacted by legislative bodies and enforced by the judiciary, and constitutional protections against excessive secrecy developed and enforced by courts, which impose obligations upon government entities and officials to make their work more visible.[10] These laws establish mandates for government entities to release documents and open their operations to public view.[11] Their proponents claim that these laws can fix the secretive state.

Law is not the only fix, of course. Law's failure to fully reveal the state has led to other solutions—some institutional and some technological. But no matter the different means that transparency proponents espouse, advocates claim that prohibiting or at least limiting secrecy can eradicate all of the obstacles that keep citizens from seeing the state.

Legal, institutional, and technological transparency fixes build on, and gain persuasive influence from, the powerful metaphor of the legitimate visible state and the illegitimate concealed one. The visibility metaphor performs an enormous amount of work for transparency advocates, constituting the problem as obvious, almost commonsensical, and its solution as essential to democracy. Advocates, judges, and legislatures frequently invoke it when they campaign for transparency, adjudicate disclosure disputes, and limit secrecy by statute. When he decried the corrupt corporate trusts of the early twentieth century, for example, Louis Brandeis famously contended that "sunlight" or "sunshine" must perforate darkened, secretive places to act as a "disinfectant."[12] The quotation is a frequently cited chestnut for advocates, and even the names of laws and transparency nongovernmental organizations (NGOs) draw the stark contrast between the sunlight of disclosure and secrecy's darkness.

But it is not the only metaphoric flourish. "Democracies die behind closed doors," a federal appellate court declared when finding that the First Amendment prohibits the government from closing immigration hearings to the public and the press without an individualized showing of justification.[13] Nor is visibility the only metaphor. Congress declared in the title of the Freedom of Information Act (FOIA) that information must be set "free" from its bureaucratic constraints, assuming that information that is freed from the federal government automatically becomes visible.[14]

The transparency fix predicts that vision will lead inexorably to knowledge and to power. Information seen is information gleaned. It enables and, in some conceptions, even *creates* political reform through communication, cognition, and action. Legal fixes to government secrecy work by forcing the government to communicate information to its citizens. Whether by requiring state actors to make documents and data publicly accessible or to open their meetings and operations to the public, open government laws place the state in the position of sending messages to its citizenry. The public cannot act properly without this information; the state will not act properly without disgorging the information that it hoards.

Transparency thus promises to breathe life into a failing political order by allowing information to flow from the state. It does so by assuming that this communicative process necessarily has important dynamic effects on both actors in this transaction. Forced to communicate accurate and complete information about its plans and actions to the public, the state will act more responsibly to its citizens and explain its decisions and actions; able to understand and hold its representatives accountable, the public will act as an authentic, deliberative polis, in the classically democratic sense of a citizenry that capably governs itself. A truly democratic state transparently and perfectly communicates its actions to its truly democratic, engaged citizens.

Transparency thus represents a normative, achievable goal. It inspires legal, institutional, and technological reform and stands as a powerful metaphor that drives and shapes the desire for a more perfect democratic order. If secrecy is the problem, transparency is the solution. It promises to fix the state.

Transparency as a Problem

Excessive secrecy can threaten democracy and act as its antithesis. And transparency laws no doubt cure some excessive secrecy, as do institutional and technological reforms. But they don't seem to stop the government from hoarding information. Consider the nation's most important secrets, referred to within the military, intelligence, and diplomatic bureaucracies as "classified"—as in, documents that are classified at some level of secrecy. The ever-expanding universe of classified information remains hidden from the public, despite mandated but underfunded efforts to force agencies to declassify documents. Since 1956, blue ribbon commissions and congressional committees have regularly and uniformly decried overclassification, issuing official reports and proclamations that have had minimal effect, comparable to the impact of a tsk-tsk sermon delivered by a beat cop to a publicly inebriated alcoholic.[15] This is because few of the normal legal and bureaucratic checks and balances exist that would otherwise obstruct or discourage the system's expansion.

Classification is easier than declassification. Declassifying usually requires the review of multiple officials and agencies, including risk-averse classification authorities who would prefer to knowingly overclassify than to mistakenly underclassify. Also, the classification process begins in the executive branch, and Congress has shown little interest in taking on the responsibility of legislating the practice or even of challenging the president's prerogative to oversee the process. And courts generally defer to presumably expert judgments by agency personnel about the dangers posed by information disclosure. Although classification and declassification policies change incrementally from president to president and in response to national security crises (or their absence), the general trend holds steady, and the pool of classified documents simply remains unfathomably large.

Consider too the expectations that met the Obama administration upon taking office after a campaign that pledged to remove the veil of secrecy of the George W. Bush administration. President Obama attempted to make good upon his campaign promise in some of his first official acts after his inauguration, and by the beginning of his second term, in February 2013, he declared that his was "the most transparent administration in history."[16] Let's assume that candidate Obama meant to fulfill his campaign promises and that President Obama firmly believed his 2013 claim, which he made despite widespread complaints about his administration's secrecy not only from his political opponents but also from transparency advocates.

By late spring 2013, Obama and his administration fought scandals of various degrees of merit and import in which Republican legislators and activists denounced his administration's actions and, worse, its efforts to cover them up: the National Security Agency's domestic surveillance; the Internal Revenue Service's secret targeting of Tea Party groups' tax exempt status; the Department of Justice's secret subpoena of phone records of reporters in order to chase down the sources of national security leaks; and the response by the State Department and Central Intelligence Agency to the fatal attack of the U.S. Embassy in Benghazi, Libya.

Without agreeing about the substance of these scandals (or even their status as scandals), transparency advocates and Republicans compared what they characterized as the administration's coverups to those of the Nixon administration, perhaps the most scandalously secretive presidency of all. In 2014, more lawsuits were filed against the Obama administration under the FOIA than in any year since 2001, suggesting that the administration was willing to be hauled into court rather than disclose information to those who request it.[17] By late spring 2014, a majority of White House press correspondents responding to a poll from the web publication *Politico* did not view the administration's transparency policies any more favorably than they did those of his predecessor.[18] Scholars and transparency advocates generally agreed with this assessment.[19]

It is not clear when the government "jumped the shark" with its secrecy, as the advocacy group Electronic Frontier Foundation had complained as early as 2011 about the government's disclosure and classification performance, but some meaningful marker of containment has clearly been left behind.[20] To transparency advocates, secrecy's recurring triumph—even in the administration of a liberal, former constitutional law professor—represents a failure of leadership and institutional will. Perhaps the right leader—overseeing the correctly sized, ethical bureaucracy—could avoid the lure of information control.

Perhaps, too, we are merely awaiting the proper implementation of the transparency fix. Indeed, transparency advocates have initiated important, incremental legal reforms that have allowed the state to be seen and that have informed the public (or at least parts of it) on many topics. But they have not been able to make the state transparent. Advocates concede as much, as they regularly season their confident prophecy that the promised land of visibility will soon surely come with a strong measure of outrage at the state's continued opacity. They begin with the assumption of a solvable problem but then inevitably face the limits of their own ability to impose their solution on a recalcitrant, unwieldy state.

Part of the problem is structural, at least in the United States. The Supreme Court has held that there is no individual right to government information in the U.S. Constitution. As recently as 2013, the Court declared that information access laws are "of recent vintage" and are not "basic to the maintenance or well-being of the Union," and that the right to information that access laws establish is neither part of, nor equal to, the foundational rights of speech and assembly.[21] Elected officials therefore establish and define the political rights of public access to information and the state's obligation to disclose government information. Their commitment to such rights and obligations always seems to waver and is limited by their own self-interest. The FOIA, for example, extends only to the executive branch. Notably, Congress has not extended the law's obligations to itself, nor to the judiciary.

The problem also appears to be permanent. Notwithstanding occasions of openness, government seems eternally resistant to disclosure.[22] This was most obvious in the Bush administration's efforts to control the flow of information from the executive branch post–September 11, out of concern that government information disclosure might breach homeland security.[23] But as the Obama administration's transparency controversies illustrate, government opacity is entrenched.[24] The notably secretive Bush administration occasionally expressed its commitment to openness,[25] as do most courts when they have reviewed challenges to government agencies' refusals to disclose information.[26] But when executive officers and agencies routinely refuse to release information about the government's inner workings on the grounds that some exception or other privilege overrides a statutory disclosure requirement, and when agencies at all levels seem resistant to comply with open government mandates, transparency becomes more of a distant, deferred ideal than an existing practice.[27]

The endemic frustration with secretive governments no doubt emanates from some combination of official malfeasance and nonfeasance, and from the constitutional distribution of power and sedimented institutional structures. But the unresolvable political, legal, and social conflicts embedded within the concept of transparency itself cause this frustration. Transparency is only one means to achieve the end of a more responsive state that more effectively achieves democratically agreed-upon ends. The fear of a secret, remote government—like the hope for a visible, accessible one—heightens transparency's salience at the cost of obscuring the limits of its enforceability as an administrative norm. Overinvestment in transparency as a metaphor leads open government advocates to lament ineffective administrative laws and other measures that inevitably fail to make the state permanently and entirely visible. Transparency's symbolic pull, its ability to grab the public's imagination with the image of Ali Baba's treasure trove of secrets, leads us to fetishize means without fully considering the ends they are intended to reach and without attempting to grapple with the question of why these means always prove unsatisfactory.[28] The many ongoing campaigns to open the state have not led us to the promised land of good, legitimate governance.

The Transparency Fix Meets the Secrecy Privilege

At the same time that transparency never seems to fix the state, the state itself claims that it requires and enjoys the right to keep secrets. As Gilbert Schoenfeld argued in *Necessary Secrets*, secrecy represents "one of the most critical tools of national defense" in the state's battle to protect itself from terrorist attacks and constitutes "a basic precept of warfare."[29] Secrecy advocates like Schoenfeld push in the opposite direction on the basis of the state's unquestionable need to control information so that it can advance diplomacy and protect national security, law enforcement, personal privacy, and other widely cherished concerns. Like transparency, the state's interest in protecting its information also enjoys enormous symbolic salience. Officials continually and successfully invoke this interest before legislators, courts, and the general public. Such pressure sometimes negates transparency's influence, forcing it to give way to state claims for the need to protect its information for the public safety and good. The secrecy privilege offers a mirror image to the transparency ideal, constituting a conceptual ideal that helps explain the systematic transparency problem we face.

To understand the relationship between the transparency fix and the secrecy privilege, consider two alternative ways of understanding transparency—a strong form, which seeks a means to fix the secretive state, and a weaker one, which concedes the existence of a secrecy privilege. In its strong form, the transparency ideal represents the precise basis and measure of a state that purports to be democratic. Government doors should *never* be closed, and *all* government information should be available to the public as it is created or collected.[30] The state should be *as perfectly visible as possible.*

From the moment of its emergence in the public eye, WikiLeaks, the website publisher that distributes purloined documents and protects the leaker's anonymity, claimed it would serve as the preeminent proponent and enforcer of this ideal. It would make available the universe of secret documents held by those public and private institutions that govern our lives. WikiLeaks' innovative threat to the state comes from the complete nature of its disclosures, the government's lack of control over their release and distribution, the site's seeming statelessness and resistance to the interests of the nation whose secrets it is revealing, and the theoretical possibility that it could distribute a nearly limitless amount of documents. At the apex of its apparent power, WikiLeaks claimed the ability to cure the state of its ills by making it fully visible against its wishes.

WikiLeaks' position makes it an outlier. More advocates of transparency subscribe to a weaker ideal that views the unexpurgated, perfectly visible state as excessively open in a way that renders it vulnerable to its enemies and incapable of operating deliberatively and effectively. They are willing to concede the need, or at least the advisability, of asking complex questions: When is transparency most important as an administrative norm? To what extent should an agency be held to that norm? When must secrecy bend to transparency, and when must transparency give way to secrecy? These challenging but necessary questions typically lead many transparency proponents and open government laws to concede a set of exceptions to disclosure that are just as broad and opaque as the transparency norms themselves.

This requires the transparency fix to stare down its powerful mirror image—the secrecy privilege. Administrative laws generally balance transparency's beneficial effects and normative value against the state's need to withhold a limited amount of information, the disclosure of which would cause identifiable harm. This commitment to a balance reduces the transparency fix to a line-drawing exercise between information that can be safely disclosed and that which must be kept secret. Some government documents and meetings must remain privileged, but the precise scope of that privilege in hard cases remains hazy and contested.

Once an effort to fix transparency relies upon drawing a line between defensible and indefensible secrecy, transparency becomes one among many values vying for legal and administrative predominance. It is subject to all of the different means by which policymakers and courts resolve conflicts among competing visions of the good—situational distinctions among the kinds of actions in which government agencies engage; rank-ordering based on political commitments to democratic norms; cost–benefit analysis; the separation of powers among the executive, legislative, and judicial branches; and the like. Transparency emerges from this process as something less than an essential fix and more as one among many tools available to regulate the administrative state. Thus, the state might prefer secretive deliberations (or privacy), or it might prefer immediate, efficient decision making (such as national security or law enforcement concerns) over transparency. Once open government laws begin to recognize exceptions to disclosure, the exceptions in turn threaten to unravel the ideal of transparency by vesting broad discretion about whether and how much to disclose in the very state actors that have claimed the exceptions in the first place.

Divining when transparency must give way because disclosure would harm the public good is a complex task, one that leads to frustrating debates and ritualistic political and legal struggle over abstract democratic ideals and deeply held anxieties. "Transparency" thus becomes a term of concealment and opacity that promises more than it can deliver. Used in its strongest and most abstract form in the context of open government, it presents an impossibly simple ideal of the state as a holder and potential conduit of information that can be made available in real time, whether or not officials agree. Used in its weaker form, as it more typically is, transparency represents merely one value among others but nevertheless requires privilege and priority that it often does not receive. And however it is viewed, transparency appears to fail ultimately to further its stated end of a better, more responsive, and truly democratic government.

Thus transparency itself constitutes a problem. Notwithstanding the enactment of open government laws and presidential commitments to make the executive branch transparent, the state remains distant, and members of the public and opposition politicians regularly complain about an excessively powerful, secretive government. Too often, the government fails to meet its citizens' expectations that it act in a manner that is visible, accessible, and above all *communicative*. And too often, the public appears incapable of acting like the democratic public that transparency assumes must exist. We long for a state that we can see and know, but we never seem to get it. We long for a public that can process and act on information fully and accurately, but it rarely seems to emerge. Meanwhile, the state seems incapable of holding onto its information— creating another problem for the state if secrecy proponents are correct in predicting that some portion of the state's information is essential to keep private for national security.

Some Realism About Information Control

Despite the best efforts of many smart and powerful people, the efforts to bring about transparency while maintaining necessary secrecy have often failed, sometimes spectacularly. Rather than abstract normative claims and rhetoric that establish essential but mutually exclusive goals, we need some realism about the possibility of imposing transparency and secrecy, as well as their costs and benefits—for the public, for the government, and for the relationship between the public and that government that efforts to do so create.[31] To that end, this book describes and critiques the informational ideals that transparency and secrecy represent. It claims that while both the democratic, populist will to transparency and the state's desire for secrecy are legitimate in the abstract, they share an assumption that make both improbable as goals to impose on the contemporary state: They assume that someone—either internal or external to the state—can control the state's flow of information.

The first part of this book describes the history and specifics of this debate. Chapters 1 and 2 chronicle the development of the concepts of a "right to know," "freedom of information," and "transparency." U.S. press advocates developed the first two terms as ways of describing first the American ideal of freedom of the press and then, increasingly, the best means to curb Cold War secrecy. The press's success in persuading Congress to establish juridical rights to government information marked the high point of open government activism in the United States—activism that has been exported abroad since late in the previous century by an international freedom of information (FOI) movement. These legislative efforts, which Chapter 1 explains and analyzes, have failed to create the fully visible, trustworthy, non-corrupt state that had been envisioned. Frustration with the law's shortcomings has provoked the development of new movements that advocate transparency as a means to solve public corruption, to deliver government information via new information technology, and to enforce the human right to information via the vigilante leaking of stolen state documents. Chapter 2 introduces and critiques these individual movements. All of them, including traditional FOI advocacy, have presented transparency as both a morally unimpeachable, paramount virtue for the state and as a universal fix to bureaucratic failures.

Chapter 3 presents the inevitable counter to transparency's push: the state's need to control its information for a variety of its functions, with an emphasis on its role in protecting the nation and effectively administering public bureaucracy. The theoretical justifications for transparency themselves concede the limitations necessary for the state to operate; meanwhile, secrecy's defenders offer a set of affirmative arguments on secrecy's behalf—based on the Constitution's structural balance of powers, on the cost to the public fisc, and on the burden on effective and efficient government operations that disclosure imposes. The result of this often-persuasive counterargument is a balance between a government that is open to the public and the state's privilege to withhold certain information. As the chapter explains, this balance can be difficult or even impossible to strike; even if attained, the elusive balance does not succeed in forcing the full disclosure of information, producing a fully informed and participatory public or stopping the revelation of secrets. Laws, technology, political activism, massive public and private investment, and high-profile international NGOs cannot control the state's information by making it either public or secret.

The book's second part introduces what I characterize as the cybernetic conception of the state that forms the basis for the transparency and secrecy ideals and then pulls that conception apart to reveal its inadequacies. Transparency and secrecy advocates both view disclosure as the transmission of information from state to public. Transparency advocates assume that transmission will banish public ignorance, magically transform public discourse, and allow the true public to appear and triumph. Secrecy advocates assume the opposite—that government information can be dammed and that the dam's proper construction will inevitably secure the state and make it more functional.

Both transparency and secrecy proponents thus assume the existence of an identifiable, bounded state that produces information and that the information flow can either be opened or closed. They also assume the existence of government information as a thing that self-evidently reveals state action and official decision making. This information can be captured and preserved and can in turn either be disclosed or kept safe from disclosure. Both transparency and secrecy advocates rest on the notion that information (or data) communicates something of value and can be controlled. Both imagine that a perfect system can fix the disclosure problem that they identify. They also view the public as able and motivated to understand disclosed messages and their significance. The public awaits revelation of the state's actions so that it can act upon it, using the proper channels of public discourse and democratic voice; or, the public and particularly some members of it would misinterpret or misuse state information and act in ways detrimental to public safety, to national security, to democratic politics, and ultimately to the state and its citizens.

But this cybernetic view of the state is wrong. The state's large, organizationally and physically dispersed public bureaucracies perform an assortment of functions and make a staggering number of decisions of varying importance, not all of which can be viewed before the fact or easily reviewed later. As I explain in Chapter 4, the state is too big, too remote, and too enclosed to be either the open or closed entity that transparency and secrecy advocates imagine. Chapter 5 describes how "government information" constitutes an elusive object; the totality of that information constitutes only a hypothetical archive rather than an object that can easily be controlled by law, technology, and organizational discipline. Chapter 6 then critiques the assumption that an audience necessarily exists for disclosure—either a nascent public that can respond to information in predictable and rational ways within democratic institutions, or a set of existing or potential enemies of the state who will use disclosed information in ways that will harm the nation and its citizens. Although these chapters are grounded in law, they pull together legal, political, and social theories, as well as accounts of government information's production and handling, from a wide range of sources and disciplines.

Part III carries forward this schematic critique of the cybernetic model with case studies that illustrate the mistaken ideal of the informational state. Chapter 7 notes the many different informal ways by which information seeps out of the state through various kinds of leaks, mistakes, and simple public observations. The chapter presents a series of case studies that reveal the difficulty that officials—including Vice President Dick Cheney, the Voldemort of secrecy for transparency advocates—have faced in trying to hold onto documents, selectively erase them by redaction, and keep secret covert actions. In each, the state's most aggressive efforts to control information by using legal means to stop disclosure, by blacking out information, and by attempting to restrict access to history ultimately give way.

To test the claim that such disclosure has the impact that its proponents and opponents claim, Chapter 8 evaluates the effects of the two most famous recent "megaleaks": WikiLeaks' release of the Iraq War Logs and State Department cables that Chelsea Manning purloined and Edward Snowden's liberation of NSA documents. Reviewing widely available open source reports, the chapter finds no single answer—itself a rebuke to both transparency and secrecy advocates. It is fairly clear that WikiLeaks' only significant political impact, itself contested, was on some of the nations that participated in the so-called Arab Spring—a great distance from the nation whose secret information had been leaked and whose laws had been broken in the process. The Snowden leaks more clearly had an impact on political debates and on parts of the information technology industry, although, again, their positive and negative effects are not nearly as clear and direct as the cybernetic theory would predict.

This book's project is critical, rather than normative, and it does not offer any particular solution to the problem that it argues cannot in fact be fixed. The Conclusion restates and extends this point by considering the perfectly transparent presidential administration that the television series *The West Wing* presented. Nevertheless, I consider modest ways to reform the state through institutional mechanisms that can help the government investigate and disclose information about itself; I also suggest pre-commitments to mechanical time limitations on secrecy and timely investigations conducted prior to key governmental decision making. I consider these reforms to constitute a tinkering with the state rather a fix for the state's informational issues. The Conclusion thus returns the book to its central argument about the transparent government we desire but cannot have. A brief Epilogue, written as the book went to press, explains how the 2016 presidential campaign and its surprising result confirm the book's central argument.

Managing the Informational State

A final introductory word on the book's assumptions and purpose before I proceed. I believe that bureaucracy is necessary to execute the tasks required in a complex society and economy. As the public administration scholar Donald Kettl has argued, "society has yet to discover anything better in coordinating complex action" than public bureaucracies.[32] The public must certainly know about the government's operations, but obtaining that information has a price, and the public's willingness and ability to act on it cannot be assumed. Simplistic understandings of the state's operations and the potential of imposing equally simplistic understandings of transparency and secrecy can lead to imperfect, costly measures to disclose and hoard information. As the social theorist David Beetham has explained, any proposals to achieve openness "are likely to prove insufficient when they take no account of the pressures causing secretiveness in the first place," pressures that arise from the bureaucracy to which we delegate a vast array of tasks as part of a wide and contested social and political agenda.[33]

Abandoning transparency in its broadest conceptual form does not require abandoning a commitment to open government and democracy. Rather, recognizing transparency's limits forces us to recognize the practical limits of imposing open government requirements on a bureaucratic state to which we delegate significant authority. We must instead ease our impossibly high expectations and abandon the quest for a magical solution to a complex endeavor of governance. Secrecy is one of many problems that affect government performance, but it occupies too much of our political imagination.

At the same time, we must recognize and concede that extensive, long-lasting state secrecy is improbably difficult to achieve. Exhortations to perfect information control and transparency are not new, and they have not transformed administrative, legislative, and judicial practice; a nickel deposited into a bank account that compounds the interest for every such proposal made against secrecy since the American Revolution, or even since the Cold War, would likely make a sizable dent in the federal deficit. At its core, this book's project is to identify, describe, and consider the implications of that latter concession—to help lead us to recognize that no perfect means to control information exists. So long as we have a state to which we delegate significant responsibility to protect the nation and its inhabitants and to provide for their social welfare, we will have imperfect secrecy and frustrated calls for transparency. That imperfection is the state with which we must live.

I   TRANSPARENCY, SECRECY, AND THE DREAM OF INFORMATION CONTROL

1 Liberating the Family Jewels

*"Free" Information and "Open" Government
in the Post-War Legal Imaginary*

The concepts of "freedom of information" and the "right to know" carry the weight of the transparency advocacy movement, and their historical and theoretical development therefore deserve close consideration. The concepts assumed their current meanings in a highly influential campaign engaged in by press organizations and a government committee to fight against government secrecy, but they emerged first in response to two related issues facing the press as World War II wound down: concern about the availability of foreign markets for American news gathering and distribution and the U.S. media industry's desire to define and export American free press and liberal democratic ideals. This initial campaign established an understanding of the state, information, and the press that remain key elements of access to information law today—understandings that themselves rely upon broader theoretical justifications developed in modern political theory. In their development and deployment, the two concepts reveal transparency's symbolic meaning, as well as its emphasis on the state as an entity defined by its information. I begin this chapter with a parable about a fantastic but real cache of government documents and then offer a history of early transparency advocacy and its relationship to prevalent theories of democracy.

The Family Jewels

Imagine yourself an investigative journalist meeting a confidential, high-level government source. Fearful of detection and eavesdropping, your source schedules meetings in locations like darkened parking garages late at night or a crowded public park in broad daylight. She tells you about a massive, unprecedented collection of documents nicknamed the "Vandamm File," commissioned by the director of the CIA and produced for the president and his closest advisors. It documents a long history of illegal or questionable CIA activities, including coups in far-flung countries, successful and failed assassinations of foreign leaders, friendly relations with very bad people in troubled nations, and illegal domestic activities, including the surveillance of American citizens. These files will never come to you except through illegal means—indeed, the mere fact that you know of their existence puts your source, and even you, in legal and possibly physical danger. These are the most significant secrets of a government you have come to see as filled with politicians, spies, soldiers, and bureaucrats who expend enormous effort to conceal their incompetent and nefarious acts behind a veil of secrecy and lies.

Their acts are wrong, as is their secrecy—indeed, for a reporter, the latter sin is anathema to you, your editors, and, you presume, your readers. In the absence of legal authority to require their disclosure, you view it as your obligation to bring the file's contents to light. Despite the threat that the CIA and perhaps the entire federal government will come after you and your source, your commitment to exposing the file outweighs the personal and professional costs of doing so.

The Vandamm File is surely the stuff of fantasy—the dream of every investigative journalist and a narrative MacGuffin for a summer film blockbuster.[1] If it did not actually exist, any novelist or screenwriter with a decent imagination would have devised it as a means to kick-start a ripping yarn.

But it *did* exist. In 1973, Director of the CIA James Schlesinger had ordered production of a compendium of documents, later nicknamed the "Family Jewels," that detailed the CIA's actions since 1959 that had broken laws or at least exceeded CIA authority under the National Security Act of 1947. The results of this classified internal investigation began to leak soon thereafter. On the front page of its December 22, 1974, issue, the *New York Times* published a story by investigative journalist Seymour Hersh based largely on leaks from whistleblowing CIA officials about Operation CHAOS, an intelligence program to spy on domestic dissidents, especially those in the anti-war movement. Coming four months after President Richard Nixon's resignation, the article revealed that the Nixon administration's secret abuses of power constituted more than the wiretapping of Democratic Party headquarters and the dirty campaign tricks that the Watergate scandal revealed.

The treasure trove of secrets that Nixon (and his predecessors) had sought to maintain also extended beyond the secret bombing of Cambodia, which had initially become public knowledge via a leak in the *New York Times* five years earlier and which was the subject of congressional hearings and part of Nixon's proposed impeachment earlier that year.[2] Hersh had established his reputation as an investigative journalist by reporting on the covered-up massacre of Vietnamese civilians by U.S. Army soldiers at My Lai, but the scope of this new leak made My Lai's savagery seem historically insignificant by comparison. Although Hersh did not receive the full Family Jewels from a single source, and his investigation had begun before Schlesinger had even commissioned their collection, his story provided a glimpse of the CIA's secret history.[3]

Hersh's reporting set in motion a series of events and political conflicts that culminated in unprecedented congressional investigations. The Church Committee in the Senate and the Pike Committee in the House of Representatives exposed an untold number of unknown or forgotten operations, programs, and events. The disclosure influenced elections, the intelligence community, and the media for at least the remainder of the decade. In the wake of the reports and with the vocal support of the press, Congress enacted legal checks on executive branch secrets and developed new institutional checks on the intelligence community.

Hersh's role as an influential public figure—and especially the celebrity that attached to the *Washington Post* reporters who broke the Watergate story—inspired investigative reporting in the mainstream and emergent alternative press; soon, especially in the wake of the movie adaptation of *All the President's Men*, the lone investigative journalist took on the role of folk hero. But, of course, the congressional investigations were not universally beloved; an increasingly prevalent counternarrative, which gained significant political traction during the Reagan presidency, viewed them as excessively critical and harmful to American national security by stripping the presidency of essential powers and prerogative, and especially by curbing the use of covert action.

For transparency advocates, as well as for those who warn about disclosure's dangers, the Church and Pike committees continue to symbolize transparency's importance and promise. The committees' purpose was in large part prescriptive, and their prescriptions were in large part informational. To perform their essential constitutional role, the committees concluded, Congress needed to investigate and disclose the CIA's previously secret actions. The Church Committee's final report on abuses by the intelligence agencies declared:

> Abuse thrives on secrecy. Obviously, public disclosure of matters such as the names of intelligence agents or the technological details of collection methods is inappropriate. But in the field of intelligence, secrecy has been extended to inhibit review of the basic programs and practices themselves.
>
> Those within the Executive branch and the Congress who would exercise their responsibilities wisely must be fully informed. The American public, as well, should know enough about intelligence activities to be able to apply its good sense to the underlying issues of policy and morality.
>
> Knowledge is the key to control. Secrecy should no longer be allowed to shield the existence of constitutional, legal and moral problems from the scrutiny of all three branches of government or from the American people themselves.[4]

The Church Committee declared transparency's basic premise: The public needs to learn about past and future abuses because ignorance of the government's illegal actions threatens democratic ideals and allows government malfeasance. In doing so, it articulated a vision of democracy focused on making the state visible. It offered legal and institutional reforms that would lead the nation to meet that standard. The committee's vision and programmatic reforms seem commonsensical—of course government transparency and an informed public are foundational democratic principles, and of course law is the tool for establishing and ensuring those principles.

The episode demonstrates the ongoing dynamics of transparency and secrecy in the United States: first, the disclosure of confidential state information; then, public outrage at both the substance of the information and its having been kept secret; followed by legal reform to solve the secrecy problem; and, later, the revelation of new scandalous covert actions in the teeth of these new reforms. Slightly more than a decade after the Church Committee, the news broke about the Reagan administration's secret money channel to the Nicaraguan Contras via Iran in violation of federal law, beginning the cycle all over again.

Revelation, reaction, reform, retrenchment. This cycle began, as the following sections discuss, in the post–World War II era, when the American press, promoting the modern norms of independent, professional journalism, bridled at the expansion of the national security state during the Cold War and of government secrecy at the federal, state, and local levels.

Editors as Advocates: Press Freedom
and Rights After World War II

The movement for open government had historical antecedents and contemporaries in the United States and elsewhere. If one views transparency advocacy as a subset of more general campaigns for good government, then it emerged in the United States during the Progressive era of the late nineteenth and early twentieth centuries, when a social and political movement led the charge for reforms to eradicate bureaucratic corruption, especially at the municipal level.[5] Louis Brandeis's famous claim that sunlight is "the best of disinfectants," made as part of his campaign as a Progressive trustbuster, dates from this period.[6]

These efforts were themselves not the first to appear in the West; Anders Chydenius, a priest and legislator, led Sweden to adopt the first freedom of information law in 1766, although that law neither established a general public right to information, nor augured a significantly more open domestic state, nor inspired imitation abroad.[7] But two decades before enactment of the Freedom of Information Act in the United States in 1966, few publicly advocated the public right to government information. Secrecy and its cure had not yet become the defining administrative issue it is today. And notably, Brandeis's famous statement about sunlight focused on secrecy's role in enabling large banking trusts to amass private power, rather than on the public's right to view the state itself.

Free Press and Free Markets

In the period just prior to the U.S. entry into World War II, the mainstream American press was more concerned with its access to markets and news abroad than with government secrecy. When the war ended, the American wire services, which extended around the world to supply international and national news to local newspapers, faced journalistic and economic constraints in attempting both to collect news in other countries and to export their products around the world. A century earlier, a cartel of major European news agencies—which included Reuters (Great Britain), Agence Havas (France), and Wolff (Germany) as its original members—had divided the world among themselves for purposes of newsgathering. They conspired to respect territorial constraints for their individual businesses and to publish international news only from the cartel's members.[8]

The U.S.-based Associated Press (AP) had joined the cartel in 1887 but later bridled at the cartel's constraints on its newsgathering operations abroad. AP asserted that the cartel artificially limited its ability to expand its newsgathering into new territories. Its immediate concern was with its domestic competitor—the United Press agency (UP) (founded in 1907)—which was unconstrained by the cartel agreement.[9] The AP found itself in an increasingly uncomfortable and disadvantageous role as junior member of a state-affiliated, anti-competitive cartel whose restraints on AP's activities had come to cost more than the benefits they created.

The fascist governments that began to take over state-controlled presses produced propaganda that was decidedly uncomplimentary to the United States and limited the AP's access to news in other countries. In reaction, the AP freed itself from the cartel in 1934.[10] The fight against the Axis powers and then against the Soviet Union led American news organizations to view themselves as upholders of emergent ideals for a free press, and they took responsibility for developing entrepreneurial, independent news media around the world.[11] In the decades that followed, AP and the American press would wage a political and ideological struggle to free the global press from state controls and censorship, gaining both institutional authority and self-confidence that would drive the post-war fight against post-war secrecy.[12]

The AP's fight with the cartel was also a commercial effort to take advantage of expansion opportunities that allowed it to compete with UP, as American press companies hoped to seize market share and gain influence in the post-war period through the distribution of news and propaganda to western Europe and developing countries.[13] When the AP and UP continued to expand and began to coordinate as well as compete, the United States, the only nation with multiple news services, seized a leading position in the global competition over news and media content.[14] And the global crisis provided these private companies with increased profits.[15]

The British weekly magazine *The Economist* criticized AP's aggressive efforts to expand its market throughout the world, complaining that Kent Cooper, AP's outspoken general manager,

> experiences a peculiar moral glow in finding that his idea of freedom coincides with financial commercial advantage. In his ode to liberty there is no suggestion that when all barriers are down the huge financial resources of the American agencies might enable them to dominate the world. . . . [D]emocracy does not necessarily mean making the whole world safe for the A.P.[16]

In a response published in *Time*, Cooper suggested that perhaps *The Economist* wanted the British to control world communications.[17] Five years later, in his book *Freedom of Information*, Herbert Brucker explicitly defended the confluence of free press and enterprise and asked, "Suppose there is opportunity for commercial gain in striking down the barriers that block nation off from nation—is it not still a good idea?"[18] Whether a good idea or not, the AP's work preeminently served the commercial interests of American media industries that sought to export their products abroad via their wire services and to open foreign markets to American reporters for newsgathering.[19]

This ideological and commercial battle had moral overtones. In its 1944 convention, the American Society of Newspaper Editors (ASNE), the most active trade group representing news editors and journalists, announced a campaign to protect "the right of the people" against censorship and to advocate for "freedom of information" around the world.[20] The campaign included several key components. The press collaborated with the Truman administration to spur development of an international press industry that would adopt the American model of the profession.[21] Three prominent newspaper editors undertook a world tour with the assistance of the State Department during the waning days of the war to review the state of the press in other nations; the tour included Ralph McGill, who would later become a key liberal voice against segregation in the *Atlanta Constitution* and in a nationally syndicated column.[22] Press organizations also coordinated efforts on behalf of international rights for a free press in the new United Nations.[23] Press representatives ultimately played key roles in the Subcommission on Freedom of Information created by the UN's Human Rights Commission in 1947, and, alongside prominent Harvard constitutional law professor Zechariah Chafee, served as delegates to the Conference on Freedom of Information held in Geneva in 1948.[24]

Exporting the U.S. Model

For leaders of the American press, the ideal press was private, independent, and capable of objectively reporting on events. It should enjoy and help to enforce liberal democratic rights. In a 1949 article, Erwin Canham—editor of the *Christian Science Monitor*, officer of the American Society of News Editors, and member of the American delegation at the Geneva conference[25]—surveyed journalistic practices around the world and ranked them against the preeminent work of the American media in supporting the preeminent American democratic model. "[D]espotisms of various degrees will finally end," Canham declared, "when the people really know what is happening to them—

when they learn the facts of international and national life—and thus throw off their chains." Facts made available by the press would produce the public's freedom—they "will ultimately bring tyranny down," in Canham's terms—and "the efforts to lower barriers will ultimately produce conditions that will bring about a truly free press everywhere."[26]

The specter of tyranny Canham identified was the Soviet Union, the principal Cold War threat, which used the press as a propaganda organ rather than allowing it to serve as a true fourth estate. During the Cold War, scholars and journalists noted that different approaches to press freedoms existed, that nation states generally adopted one of them and disdained the others, and that the theories for justifying each approach rested on the political system underlying each nation's regime. The American model was decidedly "libertarian" or classically liberal, and it distinguished itself from competing models: the authoritarian model of press control, the Soviet communist model (which scholars differentiated from the authoritarian model), and the "social responsibility" model of western Europe's social democratic states.[27] In parsing these theories, the emerging academic field studying journalism provided an intellectual basis for the press's Cold War struggle. This struggle assumed that it was up to the United States and its press institutions to spread the word about democracy and the role of the fourth estate and to counter the Soviet state as both a political force and a model for others.

At the same time, and consistent with its civil libertarian focus, the American press was not necessarily comfortable with any government, including its own. Still smarting from the federal government's role as an official censor during World War I and its aftermath, advocates viewed journalism as the essential private bulwark against state oppression, even when imposed by a democratically elected one.[28] For the newspaper editors who sought its support in their international campaign, the state constituted a grave threat to the crucial role of the press in reporting news objectively and thoroughly, a conflict that arose from the importance the press placed on its independence from the state. Newspaper publishers tended to be quite conservative during this era and generally disliked President Roosevelt, the Democratic Party, and the New Deal.[29] But their concerns were not unique to newspaper owners and executives. Pendleton Herring, a prominent Harvard professor of government, complained about the Roosevelt administration's use of "public relations" professionals in its attempt to manage publicity and the press, while the preeminent progressive public intellectual John Dewey worried that the "publicity agent" had become "the most significant symbol of our present social life."[30] Government propaganda was not just a European phenomenon.

The resolution to this conflict lay in the press's emerging conception of journalism as a free, independent, and objective enterprise staffed by full-time, well-trained, professional journalists.[31] The Commission on Freedom of the Free Press, a private, widely heralded group of leading academics and government officials (nicknamed the "Hutchins Commission" in honor of its convener Robert Hutchins, the University of Chicago's president), had declared in its 1947 final report that the press bore the social and professional responsibility to provide "full access to the day's intelligence" and a "truthful, comprehensive, and intelligent account of the day's events in a context which gives them meaning."[32]

Objectivity took on an increasingly central role in journalism practice and in journalists' self-conception during the twentieth century; it defined the bureaucratic practice of journalism, the training of those who wished to enter the profession, and the evaluation of what constituted good versus bad reporting.[33] The objectivity ideal justified the press's explicit right to be free from government constraint, as well as its position as an independent institution of civil society—one just as important to the protection of individual rights and democratic institutions, the press asserted, as an independent judiciary. In this vision, the state must protect civil institutions and contribute to a liberal international order in which the press could flourish. Premised upon the existence of an objective press that operated free from government constraint, the American model of journalism needed to be exported abroad after World War II.

The Development of "Freedom of Information" and the "Right to Know"

The movement for international press freedom would evolve into a movement for open government, and in the process it redeployed the terms "freedom of information" and the "right to know" that press freedom advocates first used to connect the issue of access to state information to established ideals of the democratic state. Franklin Roosevelt used the term "freedom of information" in a presidential press conference in 1940 to refer to the flow of uncensored news, identifying it as one of the key principles of democratic government and the unenumerated freedoms that the Constitution set in motion.[34] President Truman used it similarly in a message to Congress in 1947, reporting on U.S. participation in the United Nations.[35]

At the same time, news editors adopted the phrase as part of the broad ideal of press freedom. The ASNE established a Freedom of Information Committee to press for international speech liberalization, and Herbert Brucker, one of that committee's chairmen during the early post-war period, appropriated the term as the title for his 1949 book on the need for press freedom.[36] Brucker's own definition of the term rejected anything less than complete fealty to the professional norms of objective reportage: "[F]reedom of information for newspapers and related media will have not only the historic sense of freedom from government but also include *freedom from any attachment, direct or indirect, to any class, political party, economic group, or other fraction of society.*"[37]

The embryonic international human rights movement appropriated it as well. At its first meeting in 1946, the United Nations General Assembly issued an official declaration that called for recognizing and protecting the freedom of information as a fundamental, "touchstone" human right. It defined the concept quite broadly: "Freedom of information implies the right to gather, transmit and publish news anywhere and everywhere without fetters."[38] These broad definitions proposed an institutional freedom for the press from external interference of any kind, including both the state and private interests.

The idea of a "right to know" came later than "freedom of information." AP general manager Kent Cooper called for it as early as 1945 and would later title his 1956 book on the general topic of press freedom *The Right to Know.*[39] Cooper defined the right both affirmatively, as the right of individuals to have access to full and accurate news reporting, and negatively, as prohibiting the government from interfering with the relationship between the press and its public. "It means," he wrote, "that the government may not, and the newspapers and broadcasters should not, by any method whatever, curb delivery of any information essential to the public welfare and enlightenment."[40] Newspapers, which he considered the preeminent means both for spreading news and for communicating "facts to the mind" of the public, should be free from government control as well as from political or private subsidy, free to gather news, and free from any tariffs that a government might impose.[41]

Cooper also offered a modern revision to the Constitution's First Amendment: "Congress shall make no law . . . abridging the Right to Know through the oral or printed word or any other means of communicating ideas or intelligence."[42] In Cooper's understanding, the right to information belongs to the public; the state has the legal duty to disclose and is prohibited from restraining the press; and the independent commercial press serves as the essential go-between with an ethical duty to ferret out and present information. Leveraging its related, longstanding, and well-entrenched constitutional First Amendment right, the press would protect the public's right to information by transforming data into knowledge. With the press's assistance, the reading public could and would act rationally, as the democratic citizens they were capable of becoming.

The two terms—"freedom of information" and "right to know"—have endured as often interchangeable phrases in the movement for open government. They invoke several concepts. First, although they have long implied more than simply access to *government* information, the terms identified and sought to protect a natural right that would limit the state's control of information flows. Growing out of the immediate post-war concern about international press freedoms, they belong to a classically liberal conception of a limited state checked by the press, composed of private entities whose professional norms provide it the legitimacy to stand as a fourth estate capable of protecting the public's interest. Second, the terms conceptualized the state as something distinct from the public—as an entity that represents and governs its citizens but is distant from them. The right to receive information and to "know" can protect the public from the state's natural tendency to amass power and use propaganda to obscure itself. Third, the terms assume that information—in its raw and cooked forms as data, news stories, and opinion—constitutes a truth to which the public must have access in order to gain knowledge and act as citizens.

And finally, at least in its American version as defined by Kent Cooper and Herbert Brucker, the terms contemplate a free and independent press as the public's agent in protecting the right to know and in delivering the information that should flow freely. Rights (to know) and freedoms (of information) simultaneously enable the press to report objectively, without the constraints of excessive state or private interest, and allow that independent pillar of civil society to play its crucial role in a functional democracy. As the institution capable of mediating between the public and a distant, increasingly complex state, the press had come by midcentury to view itself as the community's representative and enforcer of public rights. Only the press could unveil and criticize the state.[43] "The right of the individual to know," Cooper asserted, is "coordinated with the right of his newspaper to tell him all the news, except what the government [is] guilty of withholding and suppressing."[44] The goals of the original FOI campaign were to transform the inchoate notion of wrongfully excessive information control into an illegal act and to transform the abstract ideal of a "right" into an enforceable cause of action for the individuals to whom it belonged.

These concepts—invoking a natural public right to information and free information flows, with the press serving as the public's representative and intermediary—remain at the core of transparency advocacy. Recall the Church Commission's rhetoric that secrecy enables abuse by preventing the public review of government performance. The public can only exercise its "good sense" when it is "fully informed," when "the American people themselves" can scrutinize the state. Hence, the public must have a "right to know"; hence, information must be "freed" from state constraints. And the press, whose investigatory work played a key role in motivating Congress to review the intelligence community, could deliver the informational goods to the news markets it served. These core concepts, merely abstract and notional before World War II, emerged later as ideals that would drive a domestically focused political reform movement.[45]

The Legal Fix: The Political Enactment of Legal Informational Rights

Frustrated in its efforts to formalize press freedoms in international law, ASNE's Freedom of Information Committee turned its attention in the late 1940s to press freedom in the United States and to one particular issue—government secrecy—which ASNE viewed as expanding at all levels of government and which seemed less defensible during the Cold War than censorship imposed during World War II.[46] *Louisville Courier-Journal* editor James Pope's term as FOI Committee chair, which started in 1950, proved integral in shifting the organization toward an explicitly political fight against federal, state, and local government secrecy.

Pope's committee began by organizing state-level committees—both to help provide legal advocacy and defense on behalf of local newspapers and to serve as the basis for an effort to change federal policy.[47] Pope recruited Harold Cross, a retired media lawyer and journalism professor at Columbia, to serve as the committee's legal advisor.[48] Cross's monograph *The People's Right to Know* (1953) both summarized the patchwork of existing constitutional and administrative laws regulating government secrecy and advocated for reforms to strengthen the public's access to information.[49] "Enlisted as an adviser," Pope gushed in his foreword to *The People's Right to Know*, Cross "became our leader" in a movement that Pope characterized as an "agent of the people" to enforce the right of access to information.[50] Although it was not the sole book on the subject—James Russell Wiggins, a former ASNE FOI Committee chair,

published *Freedom or Secrecy* in 1956 and joined Cross in advocating on behalf of an enforceable right to know—*The People's Right to Know* would prove,
along with its author, to be the most influential legal authority in the campaign
for government transparency.[51]

The title of *The People's Right to Know* echoed the concept of rights from the
press's earlier advocacy of press freedoms abroad, while the term also framed
the problem of secrecy as one of insufficiently enforced legal rights. The book
resembled a legal brief that sought to implant the concept of rights into intellectual and legal opinion. It opened with a series of declarations emphasizing the most prominent terms from the earlier free press campaign: "Public
business is the public's business. The people have the right to know. Freedom
of information is their just heritage. Without that the citizens of a democracy
have but changed their kings."[52] "Rights" against the state, along with the ideal
of "freedom" from state barriers to access, served as the logical way for a legal
advocate like Cross to champion transparency. But the prevailing law of access to government information, Cross complained, was a mess: It existed only
"where you find it," in a "welter of varying statutes, conflicting court opinions
and wordy departmental regulations [that] present the problem as a veritable
Chinese puzzle."[53] The resulting information access law could not confront and
control the expansion of Cold War secrecy. Access to information was "a neglected constitutional right," Cross noted; citing a range of historical and contemporary figures for support, he advocated for it to be encompassed within
First Amendment protections.[54] As Sam Lebovic has argued, press advocates
had appropriated the classical liberal ideal of press freedom from the Cold
War ideological struggle against the Soviet Union to the fight against excessive state secrecy, using the First Amendment both as a negative right against
state censorship of the press and as an implied affirmative right of access to
information.[55]

But Cross lamented what he presciently viewed as the dim prospects of that
right's judicial recognition. He instead advocated federal legislation as an alternative to the elusive enshrinement of a federal constitutional right to know. In
the decade prior to World War II, Congress and lobbyists on behalf of regulated
parties had sought to establish a uniform set of legal procedures that would
rein in an increasingly active federal bureaucracy. Their efforts led to the Administrative Procedure Act, enacted in 1946, which imposed some procedures
that force agencies to process and disclose information regarding the regulatory
process but was not the sweeping law that would encompass the full range of

government information for which Cross and others advocated.[56] Specifically, it established no enforceable public right to information with judicial review of a government entity's refusal to disclose information.[57] Cross urged Congress to "begin exercising effectually its function to legislate freedom of information for itself, the public, and the press" by creating a legal right to know.[58] Better a statutory right than no right at all.

Soon after the publication of Cross's book, the ASNE committee finally found in California Representative John Moss an effective legislative partner for establishing the legal rights that Cross described.[59] In November 1954, a new Democratic majority had wrestled control of the U.S. House of Representatives back from a small Republican majority that had ridden Dwight Eisenhower's coattails in his 1952 election to a first presidential term. Although Eisenhower's moderate conservatism held at arm's length both Senator Joseph McCarthy (whose prominence was fast receding by 1954) and Vice President Richard Nixon, politics was ultimately partisan, and Democrats resented having lost the presidency for the first time since Franklin Roosevelt's initial election in 1932. Moreover, the executive branch's expansion during the New Deal and the president's administrative prerogative over executive branch secrets following the end of World War II constituted a source of political conflict. Even with a moderate war hero in the White House and a common enemy in the Soviet Union, Congress viewed its role both as a principled, institutional opposition to the presidency and the branch he controlled and as a political opposition to a Republican electoral foe. To that end, the House of Representatives' Government Operations Committee, chaired by Democratic Representative William Dawson of Illinois, established a Special Subcommittee on Government Information with Moss as chair, in order to investigate executive branch secrecy.[60]

ASNE leaders and prominent newspaper editors played key roles in spurring the Subcommittee on Government Information (referred to popularly as "the Moss Committee") into action.[61] The press provided personnel, with former journalists dominating the committee's staff, while prominent editors helped devise its aggressive strategy of investigating federal agencies that kept information secret from the press and public.[62] ASNE introduced Cross to Moss and his subcommittee, and the author of *The Right to Know* would play a key role as the committee's legal advisor until his death in 1959.[63] The press also provided publicity through newspapers around the country that promoted the subcommittee's work and especially its hearings and investigations.[64] And the press helped frame the issue as one of insufficiently recognized and enforced legal rights. In James Pope's words when he testified at the Moss Committee's first hearing, "freedom of information is not a political issue. . . . The right to know is the right of the people."[65]

After an amendment to existing law failed to change bureaucratic norms,[66] the Freedom of Information Act—a statute whose very title was apparently appropriated from the title of ASNE member Herbert Brucker's 1949 book[67]—finally gained sufficient legislative support in 1966, cleared Congress's procedural hurdles, and was enacted despite President Lyndon Johnson's publicly expressed ambivalence and privately expressed hostility.[68] According to Bill Moyers, his press secretary at the time, Johnson "had to be dragged kicking and screaming to the signing ceremony. He hated the very idea of the Freedom of Information Act; hated the thought of journalists rummaging in government closets; hated them challenging the official view of reality."[69] It is no wonder that Johnson disliked it so much, as it represented a significant incursion into what had long been executive and bureaucratic prerogative. The FOIA's version of a right to know and pledge to protect the informational freedom was, from a president's perspective, a pain in the ass.

In its original enactment and in subsequent amendments, Congress has continually recognized and proclaimed the crucial role that the right to know and informational freedom play in a democracy, stating in the original FOIA statute that "[a] democratic society requires an informed, intelligent electorate, and the intelligence of the electorate varies as the quantity and quality of its information varies."[70] Courts have consistently restated such legislative declarations when reviewing claims filed under the FOIA.[71] The statute recognized an individual right to information and granted broad private rights to "any person" to seek judicial enforcement of those rights—rights that were themselves balanced against the state's need to keep some information from the public eye.[72] FOIA not only placed certain procedural burdens on agencies but created a private right of action for aggrieved individuals. It empowered the federal judiciary to scrutinize agency decisions not to disclose with a higher level of scrutiny than courts usually apply in administrative law.[73] Utilizing this new right, the press could serve as a private attorney general to hold the government accountable and inform the public.

Congress has regularly attempted to strengthen and extend FOIA through amendment and additional legislation. It first expanded FOIA in 1974 in response to the revelations about Nixonian secrecy that the Watergate scandal revealed.[74] It enacted the "electronic FOIA" amendments of 1996 to reflect the increasing digitization of government documents.[75] And it expanded the "freedom of information" and "right to know" logic that FOIA first enacted beyond agency documents through the Government in the Sunshine Act (which requires executive branch agencies to hold open meetings),[76] the Federal Advisory Committee Act (which places open government requirements on certain types of committees created by the executive branch),[77] and the Presidential Records Act (which requires the president to retain records and make them available to the public after he or she leaves office).[78]

Each statute imposes a particular openness requirement on a limited universe of entities, most typically those defined by the respective statutes as agencies. Operating together, along with the APA, which provides transparency of agencies in their rulemaking processes, these statutes constitute a significant commitment to open government.[79] State governments have their own FOI legislation, some of which are enshrined in state constitutions and are stronger than the federal statute, while some localities have imposed even stronger mandates than the states in which they are located.[80] The campaign to conceptualize transparency as a public right, initiated by the institutional press and shaped by Harold Cross and Congressman John Moss, appears to have enjoyed enormous legislative success, even if it has never gained the constitutional anchor that advocates have sought.

Rights, Freedoms, and the Transparency Norm in Political Theory

In their quest to fight Cold War secrecy, Cooper, Cross, Moss, and the institutional press intuitively sought to develop a legal solution using existing legal tools and political ideals. Those ideals and tools had emerged from longstanding traditions of democratic political theory that had considered how and to what extent secrecy can threaten democracy and how the imposition of transparency can address that threat. This theoretical underpinning drives and justifies transparency on the ground that a liberal, functional democracy works not only by the dispersal of power but also by the distribution of state information. The circulation of government information itself constitutes a form of democratic practice, insofar as it is the basis for the public's effective exercise of its authority. It does so in three distinct ways: by supporting and instilling democratic values in a representative political system; by allowing direct popular self-rule; and by producing effective, efficient, non-corrupt governance.[81] Each of these threads appears in the discourse of transparency advocacy; separating them, as I do below, allows us to see the breadth of transparency's premiere position in modern conceptions of governance.

Transparency and Democratic Theory

To varying degrees and in different contexts, the classical liberals John Locke,[82] John Stuart Mill,[83] and Jean-Jacques Rousseau;[84] the utilitarian Jeremy Bentham;[85] and the moral philosopher Immanuel Kant[86] all made classic and, in some instances, quite famous statements in support of publicity and transparency. Mill's *Considerations on Representative Government* listed publicity as a key part of the "machinery" that constitutes the "goodness of government"— in its absence, Mill asked, "how could [the public] either check or encourage what they were not permitted to see?"[87] Bentham developed the most extensive concept of state publicity in his work. By facilitating communication between the state and the public, he argued, publicity creates a more informed electorate and secures the confidence of the governed in the legislature.[88] With its knowledge of the government's operations, the public can play its proper roles as enlightened tribunal and collective decision makers whose "national intelligence," trust, and attention lend "confidence and security" to "open and free policy."[89]

Twentieth-century retrospectives on this tradition have celebrated its role in the development of modern governance. In the sociologist Edward Shils's account, "publicity" of the state's political and administrative actions, political theory's precursor term to "transparency," played as crucial a role in the liberal democratic movement as the franchise and constitutional restraints on state action.[90] Jürgen Habermas's narrative of modern democratic development emphasizes publicity's role in the development of a rational, deliberative public sphere, thereby playing a key role in the shift from a state run by a monarchical sovereign's will to a representative state that rules by legislative reason.[91]

These ideals established deep roots in the United States, especially among American constitutional framers who stressed the importance of an informed electorate to the new republic.[92] In his "Dissertation on the Canon and Feudal Law" (1765), John Adams asserted that the people "have a right, an indisputable, unalienable, indefeasible, divine right to that most dreaded and envied kind of knowledge, I mean, of the characters and conduct of their rulers."[93] Exercise of that right to know enables "the people," as the founders understood the term and as it was repeated in the opening sentences of the Declaration of

Independence and Constitution, to effectively exercise their authority to revoke the power they bestow upon their rulers.

In a private letter written in the 1820s that has since become one of transparency advocates' favorite quotations, James Madison declared, "A people who mean to be their own governors must arm themselves with the power that knowledge gives. A popular government without popular information or the means of acquiring it is but a prologue to a farce or a tragedy or perhaps both."[94] Madison wrote the letter in response to a Kentucky professor who sought Madison's support for state funding of public school education. Although he likely intended "popular knowledge" as a general exhortation rather than a specific call for transparency,[95] the idea of an informed public, as the historian Richard Brown has chronicled, has long permeated American political culture; it has swept together access to government information as well as the free press, the postal service, and a publicly provided education.[96]

Madison's idea encompassed two justifications: a republican one that viewed the collective gain for a revolutionary and fledgling democracy that comes from a knowledgeable, engaged citizenry; and an individualist one that was increasingly promoted during the antebellum decades that asserted that each citizen could enrich himself and his spiritual life through access to information and learning.[97] The public's knowledge of the state and its workings served as a key ideal of American democracy. Though dissimilar from the contemporary ideals of informational freedom and rights, the tradition served as a key precursor in their emergence.

This tradition continues in contemporary political theory, which appropriates information as a concept that offers broader justifications for democracy. Liberal philosophers who assume that the state's legitimacy rests on a contractual relationship between government and its citizens presume that access to government information enables individuals to grant their informed consent to be governed. John Rawls's original position, for example, identifies publicity as a necessary condition for the creation of a just society because it allows individuals to choose, in a rational and knowledgeable manner, the principles for a society with which they would agree to associate.[98]

Formal notions of the rule of law, whether they emphasize a Rawlsian just state or a Hayekian minimalist one,[99] require self-enacting, publicly accessible, comprehensible legislation that facilitates the private ordering of individual behavior and can limit and confine all exercise of public authority.[100] Proponents of deliberative democracy share the contractarians' commitment to publicity, even if their concern is with communitarian, collaborative process rather than with individual choice. John Dewey viewed publicity as essential for the communication that would build the great public community he envisioned;[101] more contemporary deliberative democrats assert that transparent reasoning and decision making by a representative body enable public discussion, broaden citizens' and officials' moral and political perspectives, clarify the nature of moral disagreement, and allow citizens and officials to understand, discuss, and change their minds.[102] Publicity creates the conditions for the functional, democratic public sphere that the early Habermas sought to prescribe by promoting rational, critical public debate and unrestricted communication.[103] Information thus pervades democratic theory.

Transparency, Populism, and Self-Rule

But for some advocates and theorists, informational access does more than simply enable the public to rationally exercise its rights to choose its representatives and engage in rational debate. Transparency empowers individual and collective self-rule, while its absence facilitates perfidious, conspiratorial control of the state. This highly charged, affective understanding of transparency's significance requires the full unveiling of the invisible state to achieve democracy's perfection and holds that secrecy of any form represents democracy's opposite. The people will surely see the truth when it is made visible to them, and they will rule themselves fairly and well. Transparency's ideal of a visible state and fear of a hidden one thus issues not only from an affirmative embrace of deliberative democratic ideals, but also from a fear of concentrated power. Information enables opposition to a faceless bureaucratic state or a secretive authoritarian regime, and it can prove to be a means to create and mobilize a popular will.

With its promise of a more visible, proximate state, transparency advocacy mobilizes popular discontent with the state and constitutes a specifically populist rhetoric by offering a stark, symbolic dichotomy between the "people" at one pole, an identifiable collective "we," and the concentrated, hidden interests that hold power at the other.[104] Populism drifts left and right, with no necessary connection to an institutional party or ideology, at times mobilized by conservatives (as in the anti-communism of the 1950s and early 1960s and in contemporary anti-immigration rhetoric) and at times by liberals and the left (in the civil rights movement of the 1960s and in the more recent Occupy Wall Street protests).[105] Populist and Progressive-era reforms of political and administrative institutions focus on how to make popular control over a representative democracy more direct and authentic and how to close the inevitable gap between voters and elected officials. Direct democracy, expanded ballot access, term limits, campaign finance regulation, judicial elections, and jury nullification all further what James Morone has characterized as the "democratic wish" for a state that responds more readily and directly to the popular will and can prove impervious to elite manipulation.[106]

Transparency advocacy may play only a secondary role in populist movements, but its rhetoric and aims are consistent with populism's concerns about popular control over the state.[107] Consider, for example, WikiLeaks' description of itself as an institution that "relies upon the power of overt fact to enable and empower citizens to bring feared and corrupt governments and corporations to justice." It goes on: "We propose that authoritarian governments, oppressive institutions and corrupt corporations should be subject to the pressure, not merely of international diplomacy, freedom of information laws or even periodic elections, but of something far stronger—the consciences of the people within them."[108] Presenting itself as an essential and preeminent tool for popular sovereignty, WikiLeaks claims a stateless existence free of the political or economic burden associated with a person or media organization subject to the state's police powers; it claims to have the ability to represent only the people in their collective efforts to throw off the chains of secretive, authoritarian power. Secrecy obstructs the people's rule; the spread of information enables it.

Transparency and the Effective, Non-Corrupt State

A third justification for transparency focuses on its material and behavioral consequences rather than on the political order that it helps bring about, what Frederick Schauer has characterized as an "efficiency" argument as opposed to an epistemological one.[109] Secrecy produces a government prone to corrupt and wasteful acts; a government that is more transparent will function in a more effective and efficient manner by limiting the opportunity for public officials and private interests to exploit state power for illegal ends or personal advantage.[110] A nation with a functional, open government will be better able to reap the benefits of public information's free flow. This consequential justification is also rooted in the beginnings of modern liberal democratic theory, from Bentham's utilitarian claims for publicity's beneficial consequences to Mill's argument that robust publicity enables the citizens of a representative democracy to check the bad behavior and decisions of their leaders and to encourage the good.[111]

This contention rests on two distinct claims about transparency's consequences. The first is an affirmative one. A public that knows what the state is doing will demand better performance from the government, hold officials accountable for their actions, and in turn respond more rationally to the government's actions and signals.[112] Transparency allows government to monitor itself both within and across levels of bureaucracy and enables nations to verify one another's compliance with international agreements and standards.[113] Access to information that the government produces and collects also benefits individuals who will use it in countless personal decisions concerning their wealth, health, and safety.[114] Information is a public good, one that in some contexts might be insufficiently produced and circulated because it can be difficult to profit from doing so. Government is better situated to bear the costs of information production and distribution (for example, of information that will aid public health, product safety, and environmental degradation) if the diffusion of that information would create significant benefits to the entire population; it can then spread the costs of making that information available among all taxpayers.[115]

The second claim about transparency's beneficial consequences emphasizes its ability to stop corruption. Chapter 2 discusses the influential transnational nongovernmental organizations that focus on fighting bribery and other corrupt practices, whose work rests on the fundamental belief that disclosure serves the instrumental role of changing officials' behavior. The anti-corruption movement has successfully placed transparency on the agenda of both international financial institutions and the diplomatic community as a policy reform that can assist in state modernization and development; then-Secretary of State Hillary Clinton declared in a widely publicized 2011 address that open government and anti-corruption policies produce a "government [that] is, in the modern world, far more likely to succeed in designing and implementing effective policies and services."[116] Forcing government actors to speak and meet openly can make them less selfish and immoral; it can keep them from taking unrepresentative positions and from justifying their positions with selfish, immoral, or unrepresentative arguments, or later changing their position behind closed doors.[117] Transparency thus produces better officials and a non-corrupt bureaucracy, and, as a result, a better, more open, and more prosperous society.

. . .

All of these propositions—broad democratic theory, the full-throated embrace of populist self-rule, and the consequential focus on accountability, corruption, and the private benefits that flow from government information's production and circulation—in fact run together. An open democratic regime that enables informed individual choice not only provides means for citizens to monitor and participate in government decisions, enhancing democratic representation and self-rule, but it also enables an open society that encourages productive public and private investment, as well as good relationships with other nations.[118] Each disclosure of a government secret enables a more legitimate, consensual, and honest state that will function more democratically and effectively; and a truly democratic state will prove more willing to expose its workings to the public that it represents and serves.

An Endless, Necessary Campaign

The American FOIA's enactment inspired a modern, international movement championing open government laws, enshrining in law the theoretical ideal of the modern, functional democratic state. The domestic crusade to expand and strengthen freedom of information laws in the United States continues with every amendment to FOIA and the outraged response to every new secrecy-related scandal, illustrating how Cooper, Cross, and Moss's campaign has never ended. NGOs continue to play prominent roles and largely continue to view the press as the institution most capable of taking advantage of these legal rights in order to inform the public.[119] ASNE remains quite active in the field, especially during "Sunshine Week," an annual event it created in 2005, when newspapers, press-related foundations, and nongovernmental organizations publicize the existence of freedom of information laws and loudly lament government's failure to comply with them.[120] Meanwhile, advocates continue to argue for the judicial recognition of a constitutional right of information access.[121]

The United States is not alone in hosting these legal reforms. Nations on every continent—including especially those emerging from colonial and authoritarian governments for whom transparent governance was out of the question—have also enacted constitutional and/or statutory rights to government information. Although inspired and sometimes even patterned on U.S. law, these new laws have frequently extended those rights beyond the American model.[122] The activists who have taken up these struggles have relied on the same set of legal concepts of rights and freedoms as those developed by advocates of the American press, tied specifically to contemporary ideals of human rights.[123]

Civil society NGOs have connected a human right to information to Western ideals of liberalism, individualism, and free markets in order to press for the same juridically defined and recognized rights that prevailed in the United States after a long struggle.[124] Internationally, the human rights organization Article 19 "works so that people everywhere can express themselves freely, access information and enjoy freedom of the press."[125] Private foundations—including George Soros's Open Society Foundations, with its Freedom of Information program—also provide significant financial support for these organizations.[126] The struggle for informational access differs in every nation, subject to specific political, social, and historical contexts, but the basic thrust is similar everywhere: With transparency comes a more democratic system and a more functional society.[127]

2 Supplementing the Transparency Fix

Innovations in the Wake of Law's Inadequacies

The results of the freedom of information (FOI) campaign, while considerable, have not fully solved the problem that it sought to address. As I noted in the Introduction, the Obama administration stands as the symbol of transparency's hope and frustration: Having campaigned against the Bush administration's penchant for secrecy, critics excoriated the administration for carrying on and in some ways expanding its predecessor's efforts to control executive branch information. Advocates' disappointment and frustration with the legal fix for government secrecy have in turn spawned innovative transparency campaigns in the past twenty-five years that engage in a constant search for better, more effective means to unveil the state than legal rights. This chapter describes three of them.

The first campaign I discuss is the anti-corruption movement, exemplified by the nongovernmental organization (NGO) Transparency International. These anti-corruption activists view transnational and domestic lobbying for freedom of information laws and gathering and distributing information about governmental performance as essential weapons in the larger battle to identify and stigmatize venal states and unscrupulous officials. The movement insists that transnational NGOs can use the information they obtain from and about the state to lobby, pressure, and shame government into operating more accountably.

The second campaign is the digital transparency movement, which champions the use of information technology and networked communication to solve government secrecy and to create a more participatory, collaborative state. For its advocates, technology can and will open the state by freeing its information, unleashing a wave of entrepreneurial uses of data that government collects and produces.

The third campaign claims that the technological ability to distribute liberated government documents over the Internet will disrupt and overturn the existing political order and usher in a newly transparent one. WikiLeaks, the movement's first major entrant, in particular views itself as a radical but politically neutral entity that can enforce the public's natural and internationally recognized human right to government information through extralegal means—and, if necessary, illegal ones.

Law is not the answer to secrecy, these campaigns imply, or at least not the only solution. Each of them offers a combination of some innovative institutional arrangement or technology—foreign NGOs, hackers, or the digital techies who use open source computer code to handle Big Data and make it widely available—which will augment or supersede the imperfect legal fix that the FOI movement initiated. Nevertheless, each shares with the older freedom of information movement an evangelical commitment to the concept of transparency.[1] These new campaigns illustrate how transparency not only inspires but requires concerted political advocacy by organized efforts of private actors to impose a perfect and technically enforceable transparency. They may share the ideal of a visible state, but they depart from one another, as well as from the FOI movement, in both how they envision the state and what they identify as the best policies to make it transparent. In so doing, they reveal that the nearly universal embrace of transparency as a normative good masks irreconcilable substantive disagreements over what the newly visible state should look like— primarily protective of foreign investment for some, minimal and data-driven for others, or protective of the rights of citizens above all for still others. In the respective strengths and weaknesses of their distinct approaches, they reveal transparency's attraction as a norm as well as the difficulty of imposing it.

The Administrative and Institutional Fix:
Anti-Corruption as Transparency

Prominently incorporating the term in its name, Transparency International (TI) was founded in 1993 under the leadership of former World Bank executive Peter Eigen.[2] TI has expanded in the decades since to include nearly one hundred accredited national chapters that lobby and pressure public decision makers to adopt corruption control instruments in the many countries in which it operates.[3] It defines corruption as "the abuse of entrusted power for private gain"[4] and views corruption's prevalence as a central cause of the post–Cold War era's political and market failures in the developing world.[5] Part of a "transnational advocacy network" akin to those developed by human rights, labor, and feminist activists,[6] TI and organizations formed in its wake have prompted prominent human rights NGOs with agendas that look beyond anti-corruption, such as Amnesty International, to promote transparency campaigns to end human rights abuses and corruption.[7] The network has also succeeded spectacularly in persuading international financial institutions (IFIs) to adopt anti-corruption measures as part of their institutional commitment to further the financial integration of developing nations within global capitalism.[8]

TI's most prominent project is to collect and publicize information about corrupt practices in its Corruption Perception Index (CPI), the organization's signature product and a key element of its brand identity.[9] Quite different from the FOI movement's efforts to liberate pre-existing documents or government meetings from a recalcitrant bureaucracy, the CPI is an "aggregate indicator" that uses assessments and business opinion surveys to gauge the extent of a nation's corruption and of its anti-corruption efforts in the public sector. It then scores each nation on a 10-point scale that allows comparisons across countries.[10] TI publicizes nations' relative corruption in order to lead citizens, the international community (via the United Nations and the World Bank), other nations, and corporations and foreign investors to pressure government officials to enact and enforce anti-corruption measures. The CPI has proven exceptionally influential, inspiring new entrants in the anti-corruption field to use similar analytic approaches to protect developing nations from corrupt practices in the extractive industries (where corruption is often endemic),[11] or to offer an index of laws and government practices that competes with and complements Transparency International's CPI.[12]

Transparency thus enjoys special status among the package of good government reforms that the anti-corruption movement promotes.[13] In doing so, the movement shifts the emphasis on transparency from furthering formal democratic norms to promoting economic development. To be sure, the broad anti-corruption network hopes to extend transparency as the term is broadly construed, and TI's website states that it "supports the international efforts to have the right of access to information recognised and respected." Its focus, however, is above all on allowing citizens to hold the state and its officials accountable.[14] In advancing this proposition, TI positions the public right that enables public accountability within its fight against corruption rather than as part of an effort to further popular sovereignty or representative democracy. It privileges the economic and administrative consequences of transparency over transparency's relationship to political rights and democratic institutions.

The anti-corruption movement is more profoundly suspicious of the state and of law's ability to control state officials than the earlier FOI movement—which, in its own civil libertarian emphasis, is also skeptical of state power. If the state is corrupt, it will not enact laws to force the state to disclose information; and if the corrupt state has such laws, it will under-enforce them. Like other transnational NGOs, TI thus attempts to work *around* the state rather than through it by helping to construct an institutional network of organizations to shape international law and governance norms. International laws and norms will, TI asserts, in turn force national and local governments to disclose information and, as a result, reject bribery, nepotism, and all of the corrupt practices that harm the nation and its citizens.[15]

With local chapters and a complex, franchise-like structure—as well as strong relationships with influential IFIs, developed nations, and private firms—TI relies for reform on a far more complex set of institutional actors than the administrative procedures and judicial review that the traditional FOI movement envisions. It hopes to further a transnational ideal of non-corrupt governance without necessarily seeking to impose a transcendent constitutional and human right of public access to information that should allow no national variance. It works both above and below the state, serving as a watchdog that can go over and under state actors.

TI's fights against corruption and on transparency's behalf have not gone unchallenged. Critics argue that despite its seemingly precise, quantitative, and unambiguous calculation of corruption, Transparency International's CPI and the similar indices that other NGOs produce rely on imprecise perceptions and flawed sampling and survey methodologies.[16] But more than suffering from imprecision, some critics have argued, TI's technocratic focus masks its deeply ideological project to further Western, neoliberal conceptions of governance and of a minimal state.[17] When applied in the nations that the CPI identifies as corrupt, anti-corruption programs hope to shrink the size of government and limit its functions while expanding accountability regimes whose standards and practices impose external norms of fiscal responsibility.[18]

If we view transparency predominantly as an administrative tool to fight corruption, and we define corruption narrowly as rent-seeking behavior by public officials, then privatization and deregulation—reform strategies that can apply in any setting—can simultaneously reduce the potential for corruption and make the state ostensibly more transparent by making it smaller.[19] Smaller states can in turn be held accountable to a neoliberal Western model cognizable to NGOs and IFIs and be more attractive to direct foreign investment.[20] In the process, seemingly universal ideals of good government, developed and promoted by Western NGOs funded by Western governments and foundations, are imposed on distinct political, economic, and social systems of individual nations. These prescriptions prioritize anti-corruption over—and perhaps even at the expense of—popular democracy accountable to its citizens and effective, legitimate policy for the entire nation, while the pursuit of these ideals limits the range of political issues that voters and their elected representatives can decide.[21] The CPI thus acts as a disciplining technology, one whose seeming neutrality and basis in the administrative norm of transparency constitutes a form of unelected "organized governance" on states and their agencies while it hides its more normative, programmatic functions.[22]

Transparency International's distinction from the FOI movement reflects the distinct historical context from which the anti-corruption movement emerged. The Cold War had ended when TI began, removing world communism as the specter that threatened the developing world and reshaping the bipolar geopolitics that the West and East had embodied. Corruption plays an analogous role to TI in post-communist, failed, and developing states to the role of the Soviet threat among ASNE and free press advocates in the immediate post-war world. The anti-corruption movement has replaced the democratic development of FOI laws with economic development of an open, non-corrupt administrative state as its preeminent concern; it promotes administration and governance that can attract foreign capital and loans and investment from IFIs to serve the role that legal informational rights and a free press played and continue to play for the FOI movement.

The Technological Fix: Digital Transparency

Digital transparency advocates view the informational problem that freedom of information and anti-corruption advocates attempt to address primarily as one of data access and flow that can be solved through information technology. In their telling, code and networked communication can augment, if not wholly substitute for, the legal rights and duties that officials routinely ignore and that courts insufficiently enforce. Some digital transparency NGOs attempt to further the more traditional aims of the FOI movement, and some leading digital transparency thinkers evoke the rights concept upon which the original FOI advocates focused.[23] But the movement's innovation lies in its distinct efforts to use technology to free government data and allow information to move freely between state and public. Technology can overcome the costs, delays, and uncertainties that arise in attempts to enforce judicially enforced rights.

Digital technology advocates deploy a confident rhetoric to forecast and explain their optimistic vision, continuing a tradition established in the writings that heralded the emergence of digital information technology and especially of cyberspace.[24] The classic example is John Perry Barlow's popularization of Stewart Brand's claim that "information wants to be free," which viewed all forms of information control, including but not limited to intellectual property protections, as unable to stem the inexorable march of digital technology's progress.[25] An important essay collection advocating this position in the transparency context envisions an emerging state that

> opens its doors to the world; co-innovates with everyone, especially citizens; shares resources that were previously closely guarded; harnesses the power of mass collaboration; drives transparency throughout its operations; and behaves not as an isolated department or jurisdiction, but as something new—a truly integrated and networked organization.[26]

The new state will be leaner and more efficient than the modern bureaucratic state; moreover, as it "co-innovates," "shares resources," "drives transparency," integrates, and networks, digital governance will also act in a less hidebound, formally bureaucratic way. These ideals parallel and at times explicitly draw from those espoused by the open source code movement, as advocates urge government to adopt open, simple programming standards, design information technology to foster participation, and enable end users to mine and aggregate data the state collects to increase the state's visibility and ability to collaborate with the public.[27] Evoking the treasured technophilic ideals of open design and collaborative process, popular theorists of a digital political future now adopt the prevailing lingo in such concepts as "open-source democracy,"[28] "open-source politics,"[29] and "next generation democracy."[30] For former San Francisco mayor and California's lieutenant governor Gavin Newsom, writing in his book *Citizenville*, "[t]he future is sharing—open data, open participation, open source, open everything," that will lead to "the strengthening of our commonwealth."[31]

"Open everything" departs from the traditional open government ideal by replacing mere visibility with two-way communication—a much broader and bolder vision than the FOI movement's more restrained idea that the public's right to know, enforced by the traditional press, will increase government accountability and improve bureaucratic performance. Before, information needed to be freed to the public by newsgathering institutions; now, usable data can move *from* the state as well as *to* it when the public both pulls information from the state and pushes its data and opinions back.[32] A digital world should enable unmediated, interactive communication between state and citizens, an ideal that digital technology leaders and NGOs embrace in their invocation of "crowd-sourced" information made available to a "networked citizenry" that allows for a "networked age of politics."[33]

The Obama administration's Open Government Initiative (OGI), which the president announced soon after his January 2009 inauguration, linked open government to participation and collaboration in addition to transparency.[34] According to Beth Noveck, a legal academic who served as the OGI's first director, open government data can further a "collaborative vision of democratic theory" and enable the development of a "Wiki government" with egalitarian, democratic participation via information technology.[35] American municipalities that have aggressively adopted information technologies to make their data available have implemented this project most clearly and effectively.[36] In the process, the newly networked state will become more than simply a reformed, more accountable government. Citizens can finally act as informed users of government services and active participants in democratic politics, shifting, in Yochai Benkler's terms, "from passive couch potato to active participant in collaborative practices for making one's own information universe, [which] opens the opportunity for a more robust, sustainable level of involvement by citizens in the governance of their society."[37]

At their most exuberant, digital transparency advocates assert that the collaboration and data flows between public and private can shrink the state, if not make it wither away altogether. Digital "technologies of collaboration," Kevin Kelly argued in his book *What Technology Wants*, will enable the triumph of the free market over centralized state planning.[38] An "open civic system" carried over and through public and private networks allows everyone, from app designers to the wisest of crowds, to solve the problems that bureaucrats formerly struggled with behind the government's closed doors.[39] As a consequence, the state need no longer act as the "first mover of civic action," the leading technology publisher Tim O'Reilly has claimed, but instead as a "platform" and "the manager of a marketplace" for private and government interaction.[40] While it might continue to provide key public services and public goods like information highways and pothole-free city streets, the state can recede into a more constrained role once it builds out infrastructure.[41] Having made the data it collects and produces available, the state can allow individual entrepreneurs to aggregate and utilize it for commercial gain,[42] bloggers and websites to crowdsource and make sense out of it,[43] and software designers to "mash [it] up" to make it more user friendly for mobile computing devices like smartphones.[44] In its most emphatic, utopian form, then, digital transparency imagines a transformed state whose main if not sole purpose is to allow the distribution of information in order to stimulate private economic and civic development.[45]

These ideas and the terms upon which they rely are notably vague and ambiguous, banking on information's magical effects for a return on the state's financial investment in technology and advocates' affective investment in it.[46] The FOI movement, which shared this magical thinking about information, began with the assumption that its advocates—the institutional press and then Congress—would serve the essential role as mediator for the public to understand the traditional state. Digital transparency advocates' interest in the state lies less in the political realm of institutions and power and more in the informational traces that the state creates.[47] Whereas the traditional FOI approach seeks to open a window onto state activity, allowing the public to peer in, digital transparency offers to plug the state into existing data flows and to connect government, which it reconceives largely as a data repository, into part of a seamless web of information.[48]

Significant by its absence in this conception is government's more traditional, broader, and politically contested role in enforcing laws and regulating private activity, as well as its role in deciding whether and how to redistribute wealth. The digital state provides services and information; it eschews anything smacking of coercion and paternalism—old-style forms of governance that appear outdated when compared to shiny new technology—in favor of data flows, collaboration, and negotiation.[49] It is a state nearly drained of politics, one that avoids difficult questions over which individuals and groups fundamentally disagree, including the allocation of scarce resources, taxation, moral controversies (like abortion and drug prohibition), environmental regulation, law enforcement and policing, the military, and so on.

The digital transparency movement replaces the difficult and disputed issues that pervade politics either by ignoring them (for information distribution cannot solve them, and they are less interesting to technologists than the problems that can be solved) or by assuming that collaboration among fully informed participants can solve them.[50] While it is not surprising that the movement runs parallel to the minimal-state libertarianism that pervades information technologists, its vision of IT's promise could render digital advocacy incapable of separating the wired totalitarian state from the wired anarchic one.[51] It offers a vision that Dave Eggers mocks in *The Circle* (2013), his fictional representation of a near-future in which the endless, totalizing triumph of information technology, social media, and transparency allows citizens to easily, continually, and self-destructively voice their preferences with a click.[52]

The Vigilante Fix: WikiLeaks and Transparency

Along with its offshoots and followers, WikiLeaks represents a different kind of transparency agent: an organization and media outlet with the means to receive important government files, distribute them widely in electronic form, and protect their sources' anonymity.[53] WikiLeaks launched in 2006 and began releasing documents that proved embarrassing to some governments and private entities, including evidence of corruption in the Kenyan government; operation manuals of the Guantánamo Bay detention camp; secret manuals from the Church of Scientology; and documents that revealed self-dealing by the owners of Kaupthing Bank, whose collapse hastened Iceland's financial downfall.[54] Small and somewhat anonymous (besides the celebrity status of its founder and spokesperson Julian Assange), it presents itself as a transnational NGO "with a long standing dedication to the idea of a free press and the improved transparency in society that comes from this." As its website declares, "The broader principles on which our work is based are the defence of freedom of speech and media publishing, the improvement of our common historical record and the support of the rights of all people to create new history."[55]

WikiLeaks achieved its greatest fame in 2010, when it began to release the products of a cache of massive classified files that had been stolen from the U.S. Departments of Defense and State by Chelsea Manning.[56] All of the documents were unavailable to the public prior to their release by WikiLeaks,[57] although none was classified above "secret"—a classification that applied to 15,000 of the 250,000 documents WikiLeaks obtained.[58] Commentators have debated the extent of the documents' significance and how much they have revealed (an issue I consider in Chapter 7), but there can be no question that WikiLeaks' disclosures of state documents have increased public knowledge about recent American military campaigns and the nation's diplomatic relations with other countries.[59]

WikiLeaks combines elements of the rights-based and digital transparency advocacy movements. Assange has identified the state's ability to control and hoard information as a core political problem and offers a technological transparency fix: correcting state actors' under-enforcement or blatant disregard of the public's basic right to view government information.[60] The site describes its project in broad, world-historical terms:

> Article 19 [of the Universal Declaration of Human Rights] inspires the work of our journalists and other volunteers. It states that everyone has the right to freedom of opinion and expression; this right includes freedom to hold opinions without interference and to seek, receive and impart information and ideas through any media and regardless of frontiers. We agree, and we seek to uphold this and the other Articles of the Declaration.[61]

WikiLeaks enforces this right, it claims, by allowing readers to evaluate the truth of an objective news story via access to the original document on which the story was based. "That way," Assange has explained, "you can judge for yourself: Is the story true? Did the journalist report it accurately?"[62]

The site has played two significant, distinctive roles as a transparency advocate and enforcer. First, by establishing its own powerful brand identity as a technologically sophisticated service capable of distributing purloined data anonymously, it has proven the viability of an anonymous, online channel for leaks, a model that others have tried to adopt.[63] By mid-2015, hundreds of different websites offered WikiLeaks-like distribution, and varying levels of identity protection for whistleblowers have begun in WikiLeaks' wake.[64]

Edward Snowden's leaking of documents he stole from the National Security Agency followed the WikiLeaks' model more than Daniel Ellsberg's leaking of the entire Pentagon Papers, with the journalist Glenn Greenwald serving the Assange-like role of assisting Snowden in his negotiations with the news media over the documents' release. (Greenwald had previously championed WikiLeaks' disclosures and defended Assange against attack.) Snowden's willingness to identify himself while he sought asylum abroad made the anonymity that WikiLeaks promises unnecessary. But it is difficult to imagine Snowden and the carefully orchestrated release of the documents he stole—or, for that matter, the anonymously leaked Panama Papers cache of documents stolen from a law firm—without WikiLeaks (and the military prosecution of Chelsea Manning) as an immediate predecessor.

The site's practice of what it calls "principled leaking" actively ignores FOI and classification laws.[65] As Assange told one interviewer about the Manning leaks,

> Cablegate was not born from the citizen's rights to access information: if this was the case[,] Cablegate would have come from FOIA requests. Rather it was born from people who presumably worked for the US government feeling the information they saw showed wrongdoing that the public should know about.[66]

Media outlets, editors, and reporters to whom information is leaked face the threat of prosecution as the state attempts to obtain their source's identity. But the WikiLeaks' approach enables a leaking website to protect itself from prosecution—either by remaining ignorant of the source of its documents or by strategically locating its servers and personnel in a friendly jurisdiction. Such protection faces limits, as Assange's long exile in the sanctuary of the Ecuadorian Embassy in London makes clear. However, by using information technology to receive and distribute state secrets while it lowers if not eliminates risk to itself, its readers, and most importantly its sources, WikiLeaks need not rely on legal reform nor on the judicial enforcement of existing laws.

This may look superficially like a technological fix to secrecy akin to that proposed by the digital transparency movement. But WikiLeaks does not appear to share digital transparency advocates' technophilic view of social media and collaboration, and Assange himself is as disdainful of the market and of corporate entities as he is distrustful of the state.[67] He has explicitly disparaged the collaborative technological mechanisms that the digital transparency advocates embrace—blogs, crowdsourcing, and the like—in the distribution of information.[68] WikiLeaks had at first depended on the blogosphere and online communities to publicize its releases and provide further investigation into their significance and context, a hope that ultimately proved unavailing.[69] As a result, the site began to collaborate directly with major international newspapers for its Afghanistan, State Department, and Guantánamo releases, embracing the old media whose predecessors sponsored the first wave of transparency advocacy and whose role as information gatekeeper the digital advocates hoped to render obsolete.[70] Edward Snowden, too, began his leaks of NSA documents via a coordinated campaign with the existing institutional press, especially the UK-based news website *The Guardian*; his documents in turn helped initiate the founding of *The Intercept*, a traditional but fiercely independent news website coedited by Snowden's collaborators Glenn Greenwald and Laura Poitras to provide a platform for the NSA files and then for additional investigative journalism.

WikiLeaks also advocates a complex, conflicting conception of transparency that aspires to transform the state in more radical ways. Its critique of the state's tendency toward secrecy, as well as Assange's formative years in the cypherpunk community and his pre-2010 writings, bespeak a political program that views disclosure primarily as a means to discipline and limit the modern state's authority over its subjects and its dealings with other nations.[71]

One of Assange's essays, posted online in the period just prior to WikiLeaks' launch, sets forth his justification for and theory of deploying transparency as an almost revolutionary weapon against what he describes as the pervasively autocratic, secretive nature of contemporary states.[72] When faced with the threat that all of its internal correspondence will be leaked, a powerful, secretive regime will find itself unable to communicate with the agents it needs to oversee and instruct in order to operate. It must therefore either reform itself and act ethically—in which case transparency has in fact performed its reformist function—or collapse. Transparency, then, serves not merely to improve the state but to pose a fundamental challenge to its operations.[73] WikiLeaks cares less about the *content* of any disclosure and its effect on a democratic polis than about the disruptive effect that the threat of mass disclosure will have on the state's operations and ability to suppress dissent.[74] It views its technological capabilities as the spark to ignite a collective political uprising that can result in popular sovereignty, whether via democratic or revolutionary means. This distinguishes it (and even its most important source Chelsea Manning) from Edward Snowden, whose leaks were orchestrated and targeted to spur reform to a particular government program rather than create a more radical change to state structure and operations.

Leaks could cause reform or radical change, then, depending upon how each audience reacts. Assange's seemingly conflicting reformist and radical theories constitute what Finn Brunton has called a "two-tier strategy" that combines a Habermasian ideal of the public's capacity to engage in rational action and logical speech with a more radical, technological threat to disrupt the authoritarian state.[75] Disclosure and its effects serve as the catalyst for both approaches. The state WikiLeaks hopes to call forth is neither the traditional one that the FOI movement promotes nor the anti-corruption movement's international NGOs that are in turn tied to networks of global capital. Nor is it the participatory, collaborative (or minimal) market-oriented one that digital advocates espouse. Instead, WikiLeaks advocates for a small, left-libertarian state that fully meets its international human rights obligations—obligations that WikiLeaks will define and enforce if no one else will. A state that fails to meet these transparency obligations will suffer the revolutionary consequences.

Its weakness as an agent of transparency that can bring about these revolutionary political reforms comes from the fact that it operates not in a digital vacuum, but in a social and institutional field—one that has seen the winnowing of journalism, especially of the investigative sort, as well as the consolidation of websites and Internet advertising, all of which blunt the impact of WikiLeaks' content and threaten the site's financial health.[76] It also must rely on whistleblowers' bravery and hackers' abilities, as well as the laxity of the government's information security.

The United States turned with a vengeance on the site—first by threatening prosecution of Assange and indirectly forcing him to seek asylum in the Ecuadorian Embassy in London to avoid extradition to Sweden on sexual assault changes (which, in turn, would make him vulnerable to extradition to the United States), and then by persuading corporations that handled contribution payments to WikiLeaks to refuse to handle transactions.[77] Chelsea Manning's prosecution and incarceration and Edward Snowden's exile also make plain the high costs that leakers pay when they provide such sites access to secret government information. Nor did the website's distribution of a cache of Democratic National Committee documents and e-mails from the Hillary Clinton campaign, obtained via Russian hackers and released on the eve of the Democratic Party's 2016 convention and the presidential election—and rumored in the aftermath to be part of a Russian government operation intended to affect the U.S. presidential election—help WikiLeaks' reputation as a neutral conduit.[78] When its practice is embodied in real human beings subject to state laws, and in institutions that require financial sustenance, then the Internet's apparent statelessness and freedom cannot entirely protect the site and its content providers.[79]

Transparency in Search of a Fix

The varied transparency advocacy campaigns of the past six decades envision a bounded, tamed state whose relationship to the public (and, for anti-corruption and digital transparency advocates, the market) makes it more functional. The resulting state some of them envision may shrink—indeed, perhaps it will no longer exist in its present form—but it will certainly operate more efficiently, more effectively, and, most importantly, in a more publicly account-able, more democratic manner. The original FOI movement first stated this ideal clearly; all of the subsequent campaigns, in their own way, have restated and built upon it. The more recent campaigns work within and extend prevail-ing political, economic, and ideological shifts away from the post-war admin-istrative state and toward one or more other ends: the globalization of capital, popular sovereignty, the diffusion of digital technologies and networks, and a smaller, more modest role for the state in private markets and activities.

Like the earlier FOI movement, then, the newer campaigns are political ac-tors, deploying transparency to meet prescriptive, normative goals that extend beyond seemingly neutral principles. There is, of course, nothing wrong with the political nature of transparency advocacy; as the original FOI campaign made specific and as Transparency International and other anti-corruption NGOs carry forth in the countries in which they work, the very nature of trans-parency requires advocates to petition government officials and persuade the public about transparency's necessity. They also are alike in identifying similar or identical technological and institutional tools that could create a transparent state—all of the movements, including contemporary FOI advocates, rely to varying degrees on nongovernmental organizations to organize their activism and envision information technology as a key means to make the state visible.

But as this chapter has illustrated, transparency is not a single or neutral administrative norm, despite efforts to advance it as such, and the normative visions that advocates offer are quite different. The anti-corruption movement and WikiLeaks operate in separate spheres of influence and social networks, and their shared vision of a world without corruption belies the distinct politi-cal states that each would prefer to see emerge out of corrupt ones. Interna-tional financial institutions are largely uninterested in the popular sovereignty that Julian Assange espouses and are likely scared to death of it. FOI advocates continue to envision the institutional press as a key user of freedom of infor-mation laws; digital transparency advocates view the institutional press as an outmoded, entrenched interest that will be swept away in the tsunami of data flows. Embedded within such disagreements, in sum, are contested political ideas about the state and the means to unveil it. Transparency thus reveals itself to be a deeply political norm. And, as the next chapter explains, not everyone subscribes to it.

3 Transparency's Limits

Balancing the Open and Secret State

The case for transparency seems so commonsensical as a matter of political theory and good governance that it can be difficult to see a reasonable countervailing position. As soon as I offer the following hypothetical, however, the case for secrecy too will seem commonsensical. Consider this:

A reporter meets a source with direct access to classified information about a mole (or double agent) the United States has planted in an unfriendly nation. The reporter cultivates the source, encouraging him to provide details and documents for a story she is writing. She promises to protect the source's identity. The source gives her unredacted documents that do not disclose the mole's identity but provide some identifying personal information. The documents are marked in a manner that clearly identifies their top-secret classification. Based in part on those documents and information provided by the source, the reporter writes "Mole in the Hole," an investigative article that appears in a major national newspaper and does not reveal any personal details about its subject.

The CIA is enraged. The director of Central Intelligence maintains that by revealing the mole's infiltration, the article has not only damaged the agency's operations but places the mole at great risk of exposure. The State Department complains that the unfriendly nation will act in a more belligerent manner toward the United States because it now knows of this hostile act of espionage. The White House argues that the classified information included in the article has done little to inform the public, especially when compared to the damage that the leak has done to national security and international relations. Defending themselves and the story, the reporter and her editor claim that the story helps citizens understand and evaluate the work that the president and national security agencies are doing on the public's behalf. But their arguments do not move the president or his supporters, who continue to express outrage in the media. The day after the story's publication, the president directs the FBI to begin an investigation into the leak. He recommends that the Department of Justice prosecute the leaker and consider prosecuting the journalist if it proves necessary to find her source.

Patterned on events that occurred during the Obama administration,[1] the case raises two key issues that this chapter begins to explore. First, how far does the transparency norm extend? Does it *require* the state to disclose the mole's existence? Should the government be obliged to inform the press and public of all of its actions on the nation's behalf? Was the CIA wrong to run a *secret* intelligence program? As the enormous popularity of spy novels, films, biographies, and histories makes clear, a significant segment of the public is keenly interested in this kind of information.[2] National security stands as one of the most important factors that voters use in deciding whom to support in an election. It also constitutes 16 percent of the federal budget, costing $602 billion in 2015.[3] Perhaps, then, citizens should be able to evaluate the government's efforts to protect them with as much information as possible.

But only the strictest view of the transparency norm would hold that the state must disclose a secret intelligence program. The Julian Assange/ WikiLeaks' vision of vigilante transparency—deeply skeptical of the nation-state and almost entirely unwilling to allow a government to keep anything from not only its citizens but the world—does not have many adherents. Most open government advocates instead agree that the transparency norm allows the state to keep this information secret. American law follows suit by explicitly allowing the government to classify such information as secret and to regulate its circulation, as well as by criminalizing an individual's intentional, unauthorized release of classified information.

If we resolve the issue of whether transparency should be limited in any way by agreeing that the state may keep secrets when, for example, the secret concerns an important, ongoing intelligence program against an unfriendly regime, then we face a second, more difficult issue: Assuming the state is not required to disclose everything but instead enjoys some privilege to control information, what are the limits of that privilege? What kind of legal or political obligation can be placed on the state in order to limit its ability to control such information, and who will enforce it? Or is the state free to hoard any such information that it deems too dangerous to disclose? In the case of the "Mole in the Hole," for instance, could the state *suppress* publication of the mole's existence? If the state cannot do so because its action would constitute a form of unconstitutional prior restraint of publication, or if it chooses not even to try, can it successfully prosecute the reporter and newspaper after the story's publication?

And even if it can, should it? After all, the threat of suppression will deter the press from publishing other stories and will inhibit reporters' efforts to find and use sources for classified information, which in turn will limit the public's knowledge. If there are limits on secrets the state can keep, then by what authority do courts and Congress enforce them and impose some degree of transparency on a recalcitrant president? To recast the question as a problem— which is the purpose of this chapter—once we concede that the transparency norm is not absolute, we must resolve how and to what extent the norm limits the executive branch's ability to staunch the flow of information, whether by forcing it to disclose or by limiting its ability to control information that has left its custody.

This chapter takes up the critiques of transparency and justifications for secrecy that support a broad privilege for government to keep secrets. It begins with the work of political philosophers and theorists who offer justifications for the state's ability to protect information and who propose some principles for exercising that authority. The chapter also outlines the ideas of those who advocate affirmatively for the state's authority to keep secrets and who are deeply skeptical of transparency as a prevailing administrative norm. The longstanding, widely accepted notions that transparency must have limits and that state secrecy is essential for the state's functions have led to a body of law and group of norms that enable and even encourage the state to control information—laws and norms that the chapter outlines briefly.

By the chapter's end, the answer to the first question will be clear (if it isn't clear already): The state can and must be allowed to keep some secrets. As the final part of this chapter notes, however, arguments on behalf of transparency and secrecy result in a conflict at the heart of government information law and policy. The conflict is between the need to make the state visible and the need to keep parts of it closed, at least some of the time. The imperfect resolution to this conflict follows from the contested boundaries between transparency's reach and secrecy's limits. This unresolvable contest in turn drives the chase for an elusive balance between disclosure and privilege, one that can produce both a vibrant democracy with an informed electorate as well as a secure nation and functional state.

Conceding Transparency's Limitations

Many of the same political theorists and philosophers who have explained transparency's significance admit that complete transparency would impede some of government's most important operations and would infringe on the privacy interests of individuals who give personal information to the government.[4] Jeremy Bentham's classic work on the concept of publicity exemplifies this concession. He began his essay "Political Tactics" by placing publicity at "the head" of regulations for an ideal assembly that hopes to secure the public confidence and meet its publicly stated purposes. But he also identified those practices to which publicity should not extend: when it would assist an enemy and when it would either injure the innocent or assist the guilty. He ultimately admitted that "[i]t is not proper to make the law of publicity absolute," particularly in anticipation of the "trouble and peril" that might befall a nation if it committed itself to a complete unveiling of the information it produces and holds.[5]

The structure of Bentham's qualified embrace helped set a pattern that contemporary political theorists and transparency advocates follow. The case they typically make for transparency persuasively explains the concept's advantages and enumerates examples of secrecy's costs and dangers, only to concede that transparency cannot be absolute. In his influential Oxford Amnesty Lecture, the Nobel laureate economist Joseph Stiglitz helped place transparency at the top of the international finance community's agenda by asserting, among other things, that "there is, in democratic societies, a basic right to know, to be informed about what the government is doing and why." Like Bentham, however, Stiglitz provided a long list of exceptions—even longer than the one Bentham offered—adding exemptions for the deliberative process in policymaking to the well-established exceptions for privacy and national security.[6]

Sissela Bok's masterful consideration of the ethics of secrecy conceded a similar exception for necessary bureaucratic deliberation along with the state's need to control information to enforce criminal laws and to protect individual privacy.[7] Although she worried that an excessive privilege for national security would envelop all military information within it, Bok conceded the state has justifiable needs for keeping secrets to protect the nation from its enemies.[8] Deliberative democrats, who as I noted in Chapter 1 support the transparency norm because it enables reasoned public debate of important political issues, also assert that in some circumstances secrecy will protect the state's deliberative process from intrusive publicity.[9] Dennis Thompson, coauthor of a seminal work of deliberative democratic theory, has argued that democratic accountability does not require full transparency and that secrecy can be defensible and even justifiable within a framework for *accountable* secrecy—secrecy whose existence is made public and regulated by democratic procedures that allow the state to be held democratically accountable for the secrets it keeps.[10]

Political theorists thus recognize a dilemma, one that Thompson summarizes in this way: "[D]emocracy requires publicity, but some democratic policies require secrecy."[11] Of course, stating the dilemma is much simpler than resolving it. But in stating it, political theorists who otherwise value transparency concede its limits.

Transparency's Constitutional Threat

These theoretical cautions about excessive transparency were very much part of the founders' emphasis on the autonomy of the executive branch in certain spheres of government activity. The focus of their concern was national self-preservation—Bentham's worry, and one that the revolutionary generation understood well. The Federalist Papers are replete with clear statements that the executive needs the authority to act with "decision, activity, secrecy, and dispatch" in the conduct of war and, by implication, in the conduct of those key tasks delegated by the Constitution to the president; and the president should have the sole power to negotiate foreign treaties because of his ability to maintain secrecy.[12] James Madison warned of the "impetuous vortex" of the "legislative department" and of the relative vulnerability of the other departments, particularly the executive.[13] To protect himself and his power from the "more powerful" members of government, therefore, the president must enjoy control over information essential in performing the tasks that the Constitution delegated directly to him. This was not simply a philosophical matter for the framers; the executive branch and president would have authority over the post-revolutionary nation's most important relations with potentially hostile external forces.

In his recent monograph *Secrets and Leaks*, the political theorist Rahul Sagar unearthed significant evidence of the framers' cautious but nevertheless fulsome embrace of state secrecy from their reading of the historical record of Athenian and Roman republics, republican theorists in Renaissance Italy, the aftermath of the English civil war, and more recent literature in eighteenth-century Europe.[14] When the framers crafted a constitution that delegated authority to separate branches and dictated a republic of elected representatives, they understood the power that it distributed to control not merely the state's actions in certain areas but also its information. Sagar provides copious support for his claim that the framers viewed the state's ability to control information in the pursuit of "statecraft"—the conduct of foreign affairs and war, most significantly—as an essential executive power.[15] Sagar's account is unlikely to persuade transparency advocates to depart from their own understanding of disclosure's importance in constitutional history and theory, but it clearly supports the claim that the nation was not founded on the concept of a free, unexpurgated flow of state information to the public. At most, the constitutional framework strikes a balance between democratic debate about the state's performance and goals on the one hand and a functional government that could best preserve the nation's security and further its interests abroad on the other.

The framers' affirmative case for secrecy provides support for transparency's more vocal skeptics—those who embrace state secrecy but as an essential prerogative of a secure nation and functional government rather than as an exception to transparency's rule. Indeed, to question transparency's assumptions—as then-Professor Antonin Scalia did in an influential 1982 article titled "The Freedom of Information Act Has No Clothes"—is to challenge the notion that a lack of explicit disclosure requirements represents a threat at all.[16] According to Scalia, the Constitution's tripartite system of government provides sufficient disclosure of government information in its normal operations. The Constitution empowers Congress, within limits, to check executive discretion through the legislative process, to inquire into the president's actions through oversight committees, and to manage the executive branch indirectly by funding agencies and their programs or withholding money from them. The judiciary can force disclosure by reviewing constitutional and statutory challenges to executive action. And the public can communicate its displeasure with the president (as well as with Congress) and with excessive secrecy during every election cycle. Any effort to change these institutionalized checks and balances of a constitutional representative democracy—whether created by an overreaching Congress, as in the FOIA as it was amended in 1974, or by an excessively active, intrusive judiciary enforcing that statute or interpreting constitutional provisions—would upset the careful balance that the Constitution struck.[17]

Dick Cheney's career within the executive branch and especially as vice president under George W. Bush best translated Scalia's justification for secrecy into practice.[18] As chief of staff to President Gerald Ford, Cheney came to bridle at post-Watergate statutes like FOIA that curbed executive power by forcing the executive branch to disclose information. His first explicit endeavor to expand presidential discretion over executive branch information began as a member of the House of Representatives from Wyoming two years after Ford's defeat in the 1976 election. He was the ranking House Republican on a select congressional committee investigating the Reagan administration's efforts to covertly arm the Nicaraguan Contra rebels, and he oversaw drafting of the "Minority Report to the Report of the Congressional Committees Investigating the Iran-Contra Affair" (1987), an influential document that called for expanded executive branch power and an informational privilege to withhold information about executive action.[19] As its title suggests, the "Minority Report" dissented from the committee majority's report (authored by its Democratic members) that was critical of the Reagan administration. It excoriated congressional meddling in presidential policymaking in those areas where the executive branch can claim constitutional autonomy, and it serves in Cheney's biography as the text from which his work on executive prerogative and privilege within the Bush White House can best be understood.[20]

The "Minority Report" extensively discussed why the president must be free from invasive congressional oversight that would require the executive to disclose certain types of information to Congress.[21] The president's power is an essential element of the constitutional scheme, the "Minority Report" claimed, because the executive branch is better suited than Congress to take the decisive action that foreign policy often requires.[22] It therefore needs to exercise the "decision, activity, secrecy, and dispatch" that the Federalist Papers had prescribed in order to conduct diplomacy and engage in foreign affairs.[23] Every president from George Washington to Jimmy Carter, the "Report" argued, sponsored covert action against other nations to achieve an important objective of foreign policy.[24] Its claim neither ties the president's informational prerogative to a particular, well-defined legal doctrine, nor limits the reach of that prerogative to trump only particular legislative enactments.

In response to the contention made in the majority congressional report on Iran–Contra that the Reagan administration's failure to consult with Congress illegitimately circumvented congressional authority in the constitutional separation of powers,[25] the "Minority Report" quoted Madison's warning that the separation of powers doctrine existed in large part to protect the president from being "drawn ... into the legislature's 'vortex.'"[26] Further, it argued that the president has the inherent power to take certain foreign policy actions (such as international negotiations, "minor" projections of U.S. power, and intelligence and covert actions) without congressional approval or, in some cases, notification.[27] Using an amorphous ideal of separate powers and a particular reading of political history, the "Minority Report" tautologically asserted that the president has the authority to withhold information because he is the president.

The "Minority Report" did concede limits to the president's powers over foreign policy.[28] Congress can use its sole authority over appropriations to show its displeasure with executive action, so long as it does so without depriving the president of his inherent constitutional powers.[29] It can therefore withhold funds to the executive branch unless the president discloses information to support his request for appropriations. The political cost of keeping secrets also limits the executive's ability and willingness to hoard information. The "Minority Report" characterized President Reagan's decision to withhold notification to Congress of his administration's covert actions in the Iran–Contra scandal as legally permissible but one that forced him "to pay a stiff political price."[30] In sum, the "Minority Report" asserted that although the Constitution formally protects the president from the unwelcome intrusions of Congress into the operations of the executive branch and into the information that the executive branch produces and holds, congressional use of its own authority to sanction the president as well as the discipline of elections and political popularity limit the president's freedom to fully enclose himself from external scrutiny.

Just as transparency advocates impute bad motives to those who advocate government secrecy—surely they must have something corrupt or authoritarian to hide!—secrecy advocates view strong transparency advocacy as a form of puerile populist excess that is blind to the brilliance of America's constitutional structure. Like Cheney, Scalia viewed FOIA and similar efforts to force open government as part of an overwrought response to Watergate and its aftermath. Those singular events created an obsessive belief "that the first line of defense against an arbitrary executive is do-it-yourself oversight by the public and its surrogate, the press."[31] The period after Nixon's fall was an "extraordinary era ... when 'public interest law,' 'consumerism,' and 'investigative journalism' were at their zenith, public trust in government [was] at its nadir, and the executive branch and Congress [were] functioning more like two separate governments than two branches of the same."[32] Claiming the public learned of the Nixon administration's corruption and overreach because of the internal dynamics of the American constitutional system, Scalia argued that the 1970s-era good government movement dangerously misread history as well as the Constitution and that the nation and executive branch had been weakened as a result.[33]

Scalia's historical claim is largely without merit. Although he correctly noted that Watergate, the FBI's secret COINTELPRO (Counterintelligence Program), and the CIA's secret programs did not come to light via the FOIA, their revelation was the product of the investigative journalism and political activism that he dismissed. Congressional oversight organized more systematic investigations, but agents external to the state initiated disclosure, disrupting anti-democratic acts of governmental secrecy that sought to hide information about the progress of the war in Southeast Asia and about illegal acts taken by those within the executive branch or with ties to the president.[34] What Scalia viewed as the detritus of a misbegotten era was in fact a necessary response to a corrupt *ancien régime*. Transparency advocates had every reason to push for disclosure because the American constitutional system did not by itself solve the problem of bureaucratic information hoarding. The Nixon administration may have proved exceptional in the extent of its perfidious use of secrecy, but its effort to control information—and its temporary success in doing so—was not especially anomalous.

Although they overstated the case for secrecy, Scalia and Cheney's arguments reflect a powerful vein in constitutional limits on transparency. In *United States v. Nixon* (1974), for example, the Supreme Court rejected President Nixon's claims of executive privilege as a defense against the release of documents and tapes relating to the Watergate break-in and its coverup, but at the same time established that the executive branch's "supremacy . . . within its own assigned area of constitutional duties" provides a constitutional basis for the confidentiality of presidential communications.[35] In *United States v. New York Times* (1971), a six-justice majority ruled that the press's First Amendment prohibition against prior restraint outside very narrow circumstances trumped the government's broad claim that disclosure of the Pentagon Papers would harm national security.[36] But in his separate concurrence, Justice Stewart (joined by Justice White) emphasized the executive's need and constitutional duty to absolute secrecy "in the area of basic national defense."[37] Viewed in its strongest form, as the George W. Bush administration advocated more forcefully than its recent predecessors,[38] the Constitution's textual commitment of, among other authorities, the "Executive Power," grants the president a "zone of autonomy" from congressional intrusion.[39]

This steroidal view of executive privilege may not have the full force of law, but it is not far from the prevailing practice in high-stakes constitutional disputes. Courts tend to defer to executive branch claims or avoid potential constitutional conflicts with the executive branch by construing statutes narrowly.[40] This deference has two parallel effects[41]: It appears to offer "an oblique invitation to the President to throttle judicial review by presenting a claim of executive privilege in the cellophane wrapper of 'national security,'" as William Van Alstyne characterized it,[42] while it expressly invites endless political struggles over information between the executive and legislature in the absence of judicial interference.[43] These "endless political struggles" benefit the president, at least in the short term. The absence of judicial review grants the president time to limit the flow of information in advance of a key deadline—for example, in the dispute over intelligence about whether Iraq possessed weapons of mass destruction in advance of congressional authorization for the use of force.

In these instances, the fight over disclosure becomes a political struggle either between Congress and the president or between an agency and private actors (like the press), and sometimes between the president and all of his political opposition. The status quo favors the president and executive branch, who have possession of the information, and allows them to use their legal and political position to suppress information, even if only temporarily.

Secrecy advocates view the Constitution as creating a uniquely powerful, functional system of governance but worry that it is a uniquely vulnerable one—an anxiety shared across both sides of the transparency/secrecy divide, as each view characterizes the shift of an inch in the opposite direction as a disastrous foreboding of the system's imminent doom. This quite abstract, theoretical understanding of constitutional structure allows secrecy advocates to assert, often persuasively, secrecy's necessity while avoiding precise consideration of how much secrecy is tolerable.

Transparency's Costs

Secrecy advocates also worry about what they consider to be the enormous unintended consequences of disclosure requirements—consequences that flow in part from the threat transparency poses to the constitutional order.[44] The most often invoked costs are the increased risks to national security that the constitutional threat creates. Forced disclosure provides evildoers and those with interests adverse to the nation greater access to executive branch information that could be used to threaten the health and safety of the public. The "Mole in the Hole" scenario captures this fear—while the public might gain some small benefit from learning of the existence of an American double agent placed abroad, the unfriendly nation gains much more benefit from learning of the infiltration.

Bentham had expressed anxiety about this consequence long ago, and the anxiety continues in contemporary times, especially during periods when the nation faces a specific or seemingly existential threat. The Iran–Contra "Minority Report" echoed these concerns by noting that more harmful leaks occur when more officials have access to information.[45] Indeed, the "Report" claimed, members of Congress in the 1970s and 1980s regularly leaked classified information,[46] while even classified testimony presented to the congressional committee investigating the Iran–Contra affair was leaked to the press and public.[47] Accounting for these risks proves quite difficult, and the government takes advantage of that uncertainty before courts that hesitate to challenge the state's assessment of the threat that disclosure creates. But the consensus among transparency advocates that the state deserves some authority to keep certain kinds of secrets concedes that these costs are real, even if inflated.

Compliance Costs

These are not the only costs that disclosure mandates impose, however. Disclosure laws exact immediate and tangible compliance costs for government entities subject to them. In fiscal year 2015, federal agencies received more than 713,000 FOIA requests, a slight decrease from the previous year but an increase of nearly 10 percent from 2012 and of more than 25 percent from 2009.[48]

Processing requests is a complex enterprise because agencies must review the requested documents: In 2015, for example, only 22.6 percent of requests were granted in full, while 40 percent were granted in part and denied in part, 4.9 percent were fully denied, 16.9 percent were denied because no records responsive to the request were found, 5.1 percent were denied because the request was improperly made or the requested documents were improperly described, 1.2 percent were referred to another agency, and 2.3 percent were requests for documents that were not agency records under the statute. With this range of possible dispositions (and I have not included all of them), the internal review process for FOIA requests requires labor and judgment by government officials. In 2015, the federal government employed 4,122 "full-time FOIA staff" (a figure that includes full-time professionals and the cumulative time spent by government personnel who work on FOIA as a part of their duties), and the government spent \$480,235,967.62 on all FOIA-related activities (a 4 percent increase over the 2014 fiscal year, of which 5 percent was spent on litigation). Although agencies can charge fees for processing requests, they collected less than \$4.5 million in 2012, or less than 1 percent of their costs.[49]

According to studies performed in 2006 and 2015, a majority of the requests at certain agencies come from private commercial entities who resell the information they collect to firms eager for details about patterns of regulatory enforcement or about their competitors (or from the firms themselves, who seek directly to gather the same information), while a minority of the requests are made by public-interested journalists or individuals curious about government performance.[50] The state's effort to manage its informational system, especially given the extraordinary costs of operating the classification system, are well above zero and have climbed steadily since Congress's 1974 amendments to FOIA, which broadened the statute's scope.[51]

Even if we agree that FOIA successfully makes the state more visible in some meaningful way, we have no way to evaluate whether that progress is worth its cost. Perhaps even raising the question of value misconstrues the nonmonetary value of transparency to establishing and maintaining a democratic system of government.[52] But the compliance costs of the open government statutes—including not only FOIA but the Government in the Sunshine and Federal Advisory Committee acts, as well as the general statutory requirements included in the Administrative Procedure Act—are not an insignificant part of agency budgets, even if the costs are a defensible and necessary part of operating a democratic state. The judiciary too must bear the increased workload caused by litigation filed by private individuals and entities who complain that agencies wrongly refused to comply with statutory mandates to release information.[53]

State courts and state and local agencies are subject to analogous state open government laws and face similar administrative and adjudicatory costs, but they lack the resources and taxing authority enjoyed by the federal government. As part of California's efforts to address its budget crisis in 2012, for example, the state legislature suspended parts of its open meetings law in order to relieve the state of its obligations to cover local governments' costs of compliance.[54] The resulting controversy raised, but did not settle, the issue of how much it costs California's many public entities—including not only its state entities but also its cities and counties and more obscure governing bodies like water districts and school boards—to comply with the state's Public Records Act and open meetings law. No good estimate of those costs exists; California's Legislative Analyst's Office, a nonpartisan advisor to the legislature, has only described the costs for non-state entities as "likely in the tens of millions of dollars a year."[55] Although transparency advocates argued that fiscal concerns were a ruse to enable government actors to act secretly, they could not plausibly deny that compliance with these statutes is free.[56] Instead, debate over the suspension focused on the extent of compliance costs and the value of transparency, and it was resolved through political campaigns organized by transparency advocates, as well as by the ebb of the fiscal crisis that initially justified the suspension.[57]

The breadth of public disclosure requirements increases open government laws' compliance costs. Anyone can request information under FOIA's expansive mandate that agencies make all records that are not otherwise excepted available to "any person,"[58] for example, no matter the reason. Although a few states limit the right to request information under their open records acts to their own citizens, such limitations are unlikely to drastically lower compliance costs for their state and local agencies because an outsider need only find a citizen of the state to submit a request to work around the limitation.[59] In addition to the commercial information resellers—who make the majority of requests at some regulatory agencies—other categories of frequent requestors include individuals seeking personal and family records from the Social Security Administration for genealogical research and litigants attempting to circumvent discovery rules in suits against the government.[60] These requests may be legitimate inquiries that provide the requester personal satisfaction, edification, or material gain and therefore may serve some utilitarian purpose without directly harming anyone else. But such requests are not directly related to the classic normative ends of democratic accountability and popular sovereignty that transparency advocates claim as the laws' main justification; nor do they necessarily contribute to some larger public good.

Privacy Costs

Transparency requirements may also harm or hamper private individuals and corporations. As Bentham conceded, disclosure can harm individuals' privacy interests, especially as individuals regularly provide personal information both willingly in response to conditional government grants of licenses and benefits and unwillingly in response to government demands made under criminal and civil law.[61] Included in the pool of data that the state holds about individuals is information about their demographics and lineage, their property and finances, and their criminal record.

Although private information no doubt has some interest for the public and some market value for private entities, especially when the information is aggregated within databases, private information's disclosure is likely to feel intrusive to those who might have unknowingly or unwillingly given up their ability to control it. This concern has prompted several legislative efforts to curb the disclosure of private information. Most prominently, the Privacy Act, which the Department of Justice characterizes as a "code of fair information practices," attempts to protect against the dissemination of personal information that the federal government holds.[62] FOIA itself has two prominent privacy exceptions: a general one that exempts documents that include "personnel and medical and similar files the disclosure of which would constitute a clearly unwarranted invasion of personal privacy" and a narrower one that exempts law enforcement information, the disclosure of which "could reasonably be expected to constitute an unwarranted invasion of personal privacy." Neither of them is controversial, although transparency advocates complain that the government overuses them as an excuse to keep secrets it would otherwise be forced to disclose.[63]

The same concern applies to private firms contracting with the government or satisfying regulatory disclosure requirements. For example, environmental laws require firms to provide information about the composition of potentially hazardous products like insecticides, the disclosure of which can make a company's trade secrets vulnerable to its competitors. Concerns about disclosure of such valuable information could lead firms to withdraw from their relationships with government or make regulatory programs more difficult to administer.[64] A similar dynamic occurs with government or government-funded researchers who fear that disclosing data at an early stage of their studies will lead to premature use or criticism of their work.[65] Political activists have increasingly used open records requests as a means not only to learn more about scientists and academics who receive government funding or are employed by state universities but also to harass them.[66]

Governance Costs

As deliberative democratic theorists in particular have noted, transparency can also impinge on the state's ability to perform its functions in a thoughtful, effective manner. Government officials sometimes need to discuss policy matters outside of the public eye while they consider various options, some of which might appear controversial or difficult. Closed deliberations enable policymakers to make more thoughtful consideration of the available information and the relative advantages of alternatives, to engage in more fulsome and substantive debate over the most popular and unpopular alternatives regarding even the most controversial public issues, and to bargain openly in order to reach a widely acceptable and optimal result, without the inevitable pressure that accompanies public scrutiny.[67] The threat of later disclosure may inhibit a president and agency decision makers from receiving candid, objective, and knowledgeable advice from subordinates, who would shy away from full and honest communication if they fear later publicity of their advice. Coupled with limitations on officials' informal discussions with one another, open meeting requirements may foreclose the potential for unofficial, open debate in planned or random meetings held in private.[68]

Anecdotal complaints about open meeting laws suggest that agencies subject to them hold fewer meetings, engage in constrained, less informed dialogue when they meet, and are vulnerable to greater domination by those who possess greater communication skills and self-confidence no matter the quality of their ideas. One recent study of the language used in discussions by the Federal Reserve's Federal Open Markets Committee before and after its commitment to release transcripts of its meetings concluded that later disclosure appeared to make some members more disciplined and deliberative but seemed to instill greater conformity and inspire less freewheeling debate.[69] As disclosure requirements become more rigorous, then, the quality of decision-makers' deliberations does not necessarily improve, while the quantity and quality of information available to and considered by them can shrink. Making closed deliberations transparent, in sum, does not necessarily make them better and may make them worse.

Indeed, it sometimes makes sense to keep the public in the dark about information that the state knows and could disclose. Public health officials might be unwilling to share information about the risks of a vaccine because vaccinating the entire population offers great societal benefits, even if an individual might irrationally or even rationally be unwilling to participate.[70] The field of international relations is full of similar dilemmas: Full disclosure about diplomatic relations and negotiations might not only harm the negotiations themselves, but might increase national rivalries; full disclosure of relative military capabilities can encourage aggression against weaker states; and full disclosure of the conditions of other nations can assist international human rights organizations and civil society activity but can also have negative consequences by aiding or inflaming terrorist networks.[71]

For transparency skeptics, as well as for those who affirmatively advocate on secrecy's behalf, disclosure obligations can only extend so far. The state needs to protect against the uncontrolled circulation of certain types of information. Public officers and agencies need some privilege to keep information secret, at least temporarily, in order to perform their jobs properly. And, more broadly, transparency must be limited in order to allow a functioning democracy. Skeptics sometimes articulate these concerns in the broadest of terms—Francis Fukuyama, for example, has recently asserted that transparency reforms are part of broader democratizing reforms that have perversely led to advanced democracies' increasing dysfunctions.[72] They may not reject transparency per se, but secrecy advocates challenge the moral and political force of transparency as an administrative norm and advocate strict limits to its reach.

Balancing Transparency and Privilege

The thrust of transparency's claims—on behalf of its moral superiority, its essential connection to and necessity for democracy, and its beneficial consequences—thus faces the parry of secrecy's claim that the privilege to control information is essential to a functioning state. As with most administrative norms, any legal rules that would impose transparency requirements or extend a privilege to keep secrets must attempt to draw lines between essential openness and essential secrecy.[73]

Open government laws and secrecy privileges attempt to reconcile this conflict by striking a balance between the competing norms. Courts applying the constitutional doctrine of executive privilege, for example, have attempted to balance protection for the president and his advisors against a criminal defendant's need for allegedly privileged information to mount his defense,[74] and they have weighed the public benefits of preserving former presidents' archival materials for legitimate historical and government purposes against the claim that those materials are privileged.[75] Statutory disclosure requirements proceed in similar fashion. In crafting FOIA, for example, Congress sought to legislate a "general" or "broad" philosophy of openness while respecting "certain equally important rights" and "opposing interests" which are difficult but "not . . . impossible" to balance.[76] "Success lies," the Senate Report to FOIA concluded, "in providing a workable formula which encompasses, balances, and protects all interests, yet places emphasis on the fullest responsible disclosure."[77] Congress imposed these limits most explicitly in a series of enumerated exemptions to disclosure requirements to address precisely the concerns secrecy advocates have identified,[78] versions of which are part of state open records and meetings acts.[79]

The balance struck between transparency and secrecy promises both sufficient stability to provide a sense of continuity in public rights and government practices and sufficient flexibility to allow somewhat diverse approaches over successive presidential administrations and historical periods. At least as a theoretical construct, the balance enables transparency as an administrative norm to transcend political partisanship. And fears of political secrecy have proven inherently partisan. Political parties' regular role reversal—advocating executive branch openness except when they hold the White House—is reflected in public polling, which finds respondents stating that the administration they dislike is, among other things, excessively secret. A 2006 poll found that 79 percent of Democrats agreed with the statement that George W. Bush's administration "has been too secretive about things the public should know," while 66 percent of Republicans said it was not; a 2013 poll, by contrast, found that 66 percent of Democrats considered the Obama administration the "most transparent ever" while 81 percent of Republicans disagreed.[80] A similar shift in concern about secrecy had occurred in the transition from the Clinton administration, which Republicans decried for its efforts to hide scandals, to the Bush administration, whose penchant for secrecy Democrats decried even before the 9/11 attacks.[81]

This partisan dichotomy regarding secrecy tracks the partisan disagreement about the underlying substantive issue that disclosure reveals. Polls taken following the release in late 2014 of the U.S. Senate Intelligence Committee's report on the use of torture in Iraq and the so-called global war on terror found a significant partisan split regarding the question of whether the report should have been released to the public, with large majorities of Republican-identified respondents stating that the disclosure excessively endangered the nation and Democrats expressing more support for the report's release.[82]

The seemingly unprincipled, partisan nature of the transparency/secrecy duality is not the only conflict in public opinion about disclosure. Polls taken in the wake of both the Pentagon Papers disclosures in 1971 and the NSA disclosures in 2013 reveal a consistent split of opinion across decades regarding the unauthorized leak and publication of classified national security documents. A 1971 Harris poll taken soon after newspapers had begun publishing the Pentagon Papers found that a majority of respondents thought it wrong for a newspaper to knowingly publish a top-secret document without first seeking permission from the government. A majority also worried that publication of such documents would affect how officials communicate. At the same time, a majority agreed with the statement that, "In a democracy such as ours, it is necessary to tell the people the truth about how we got into the war in Vietnam, even if it means printing 'top secret' documents, as long as they are not about today's situation there."[83]

A Gallup poll taken around the same time found that a majority of respondents thought the government kept too many secrets and disapproved of government efforts to stop publication of the Pentagon Papers, but also were more worried about the effects of their disclosure on national security than on the freedom of the press.[84] Polling about the 2013 NSA revelations had similar findings. Respondents expressed considerable worry about the government's attempt to keep the NSA surveillance program secret, and a strong majority of respondents asserted that the public has a right to the information Snowden revealed.[85] But even in the polls that found the strongest support for the disclosures, half of those expressing an opinion disapproved of Edward Snowden's actions and supported his prosecution. The public seems to want an open government but worries about the consequences, and while the public does not necessarily support the leakers and media who expose closely held state secrets, they generally support the disclosure of those secrets.

The public's ambivalence and partisanship regarding transparency suggest that a balance between secrecy and openness might offer the best *political* as well as legal solution to a difficult issue. Viewed in this light, complaints that shift among partisans about the excessive secrecy of a present administration might demonstrate both the necessity and success of the balance struck in information disclosure laws. When this shift occurs, we could conclude that the balance between disclosure and privilege has produced a sufficient quantity of government information to allow a functioning, competitive democratic system—albeit one that produces a significant quantity of fulminating rhetoric regarding excess secrecy, corruption, and conspiracy. And public embrace of the open government ideal, even if tempered by ambivalence about leaks, might similarly suggest that a proper balance between transparency mandates and essential secrecy could enable a functional open government. A balance struck between secrecy and transparency through laws, government structure, and bureaucratic practices could stymie any effort either to excessively disclose secrets or excessively keep them.

And yet, the balance that law, practice, and policy currently attempt to strike between transparency and its risks and bad effects appears not to be working. This is clearly the conclusion of those who focus professionally on the disclosure or nondisclosure of government information. As this and the previous chapters have shown, advocates find the current efforts to strike such a balance to be utterly dysfunctional, if not dangerous to the state of the political order and the nation itself. But it also seems intuitively true that the state is simultaneously too secretive and too leaky. That which the public needs to hold state officials accountable and to act as productive, engaged citizens remains secret for too long. At the same time, state information leaks out to the press, to the nation's enemies, and occasionally to the public against the wishes and best efforts of state officials. We have a government that engages in rampant overclassification and holds terrible secrets from the public, and we also have the "Mole in the Hole" and Edward Snowden.

Why do transparency and its other—secrecy—continually frustrate everyone who wants one or the other, as well as those committed to striking an effective balance between them? The book's next part attempts to answer that question with a broad critique of the foundational assumptions shared among those who engage in the debate about open government and that pervade the laws, policies, and norms driving efforts to both open and secure the state's information. The distance between ideal and reality is not solely the consequence of a failure of public will, nor is it a reflection of government officials' lack of moral character. Nor is it a failure to develop, calibrate, and roll out the right sets of laws, institutions, and technology. Rather, it is a failure to understand the state and its information. The three chapters that follow pull apart the individual components of transparency's model of communication and information— the state as information producer and repository, the state's information as a message that could be liberated, and the public who would receive that message—in order to reveal the broad misconceptions upon which the model relies.

II DISENTANGLING
THE CYBERNETIC DREAM

4   The Uncontrollable State

The Story So Far

Transparency and secrecy advocates share certain assumptions about government information. Put schematically, these assumptions look like this:

1. *Government* constitutes a producer and repository of information, and it can be made to control that information.

2. *Government information* constitutes a message that can be isolated and disclosed.

3. *A receiver*—the public for transparency advocates or, for secrecy advocates, existing or potential enemies of the state or bad actors—awaits disclosure of government information and is ready, willing, and able to act in predictable, informed ways in response to the disclosure of state information.

Transparency and secrecy thus presume the inevitability of a communicative act—one that advances in a direct line as information, which constitutes a message that moves from the state to the public. It is a classic, linear model of communication that posits a simple process of transmission from a source to an intended audience via the medium of a message.[1]

The most famous such model, deriving from the late 1940s work of the engineer Claude Shannon and his coauthor Warren Weaver, sought to evaluate communication technology's ability to transmit information efficiently and effectively. It defined the formal components of communication as an information source that selects a message to send; a transmitter that changes the message into a signal to be sent over a communication channel to a receiver; and a receiver that transforms the transmitted signal back into a message.[2] Its simplicity and generality have made Shannon and Weaver's model the exemplary conception of communication in both engineering and social science.[3] The emerging field of mass communications research adopted it as the basis on which it would develop its own models to conceptualize the processes and effects of the mass media.[4] The model also wove through the field of public administration, where it served as another means to understand and theorize bureaucratic decision making.[5] It offered a universal intellectual answer to post-war inquiries about technology and society. With the proper transmission of information would come peace, prosperity, and a response to the Soviet specter that lurked behind the Iron Curtain.[6]

The Shannon and Weaver model recast communication as a problem not of meaning but of "reproducing at one point either exactly or approximately a message selected at another point."[7] It explicitly disavowed any interpretive process, viewing the transmission of information as an engineering problem to be solved by a new theorem—and the technologies that would develop from it—that reconsidered the process by which information can be moved via electronic channel. Shannon and Weaver conceded that the technical problem that engineers and scientific theory faced was merely one in a group of three problems—a group that also included the semantic problem of communicative meaning and the behavioral problem of communication's effects. Each needed attention for a message to be perfectly transmitted.[8] But the technical problem framed their discussion as well as their solution for how to move information from point to point.

As I explained in Chapter 1, transparency similarly emerged as a primary administrative norm during the midcentury Cold War era in the United States when press and trade groups used the phrases "freedom of information" and a "right to know" to advocate for technical legal requirements that would make the state's workings more visible to the public. Transparency proponents argued then, and continue to argue today, that communication can occur, and therefore stronger democracy can emerge, once the state is pried open and its information set free. To the extent that the movement has offered a theory to explain its model, it is one based on the necessity, practice, and effects of making information available. Excessive secrecy represented a technical problem of moving information from the state to the public, one that required a legal solution. The press would help make meaning out of this information once it could gain access to it. During the mid–twentieth century high point of journalism's status as a neutral arbiter of news, the press's authority to report self-evident facts in an objective and clear manner seemed secure and went largely unquestioned. Once state information flowed to the public, the right behavioral effects—the emergence of a truly democratic state, especially in relation to the totalitarian regimes against which the United States was in competition—would surely follow.

This concept of the state as bearer of information has survived, even as the geopolitical world, state bureaucracies, and information technology have changed considerably.[9] Setting aside the question of whether the cybernetic model of government information ever accurately described the state, government information, and the public, the model is not only flawed as a present foundation for law, policy, and practice, but it is misbegotten. It reduces the very political nature and dynamics of the state and its relationship to the public to transmission and effects. It views the divide between public and private as essential and functional. And it imagines a noiseless communication cycle that allows an engineering solution to the problem it identifies and frames[10]—again, whether the model provides the basis for transparency advocates or secrecy proponents. This reductive impulse ignores the multiple roles that communication plays in establishing complex relationships among the parties to the communicative act.

The seemingly neutral engineering model posits the space between state and subject as a problem to conquer and control. Its application by transparency proponents suggests that citizens can only loosen their subjugation to the state by wresting control of the state's information and by gaining a new political subjectivity as information is transmitted through the auspices of some medium (print or electronic) and some mechanism (law, the press, a website). Secrecy proponents instead worry that the state's visibility will allow enemies to defeat it, and they argue that the state must go to unending, exorbitant lengths to stop that from occurring. But by conceptualizing the political as communicative and communication as transmission, transparency and secrecy advocates equally ignore human communication's interactive, responsive, and iterative social process.[11] If we view government information in this way—as contingent upon its bureaucratic, political, and social context—neither transparency nor secrecy can be imposed in a manner in which the outcome is certain, where the state becomes visible as a result of the release of its information. The behaviors that information disclosure is presumed to produce will not follow inevitably in its wake.

The three chapters that follow dismantle the cybernetic model piece by piece. This chapter unbundles the ideal notion of "the state," isolating the problems of identifying, in contemporary governance, where the state is, who composes a state actor, and how difficult it is to tame. Chapter 5 performs a similar unbundling of the ideal of "information," and Chapter 6 questions the ideal of a "public." The purpose of this extended critique, which I take up in Part III of the book, is to demonstrate that in battling over transparency and secrecy, we are missing the difficulty of controlling the government and its information.

Anonymous Leakers in a Sprawling Bureaucracy

Edward Snowden did not work for the federal government when he absconded to Hong Kong with a huge digital cache of files that he had stolen from the National Security Agency, and his résumé did not suggest that he would have either the access or experience necessary to blow the whistle on the NSA's highly classified, controversial surveillance programs. After his discharge from the U.S. Army Reserve Special Forces as a 20-year-old, Snowden had only worked directly for the government for three years, as an information technology specialist focusing on cybersecurity for the CIA. Snowden left that position for a job with the computer company Dell, where he served as a contractor for the NSA. He worked for the defense contractor Booz Allen Hamilton before he left for Hong Kong, although the extent to which this position gave him new work responsibilities is not entirely clear. In all, Snowden worked via contract for the NSA for only three years.[12] He exposed the most secretive agency in the intelligence community without ever working directly for it.

Snowden thus was not a typical government bureaucrat in the sense of being in its direct employ. Nor was he a typical leaker. Indeed, the journalist Glenn Greenwald had assumed before he met Snowden that the man who had anonymously offered him these files would be a senior national security official; Greenwald describes finally meeting the young man in person as "one of the most disorienting experiences of my life."[13] He worried that this kid—Snowden was not yet 30 years old when he reached Hong Kong—was a fraud. Or maybe he was a spy, as longtime investigative journalist Edward Jay Epstein asserted in the *Wall Street Journal*.[14] Perhaps he was spying for the Russians, numerous commentators (including a senator, a congressman, and the former NSA director who departed the agency after Snowden's disclosures) speculated.[15] Or maybe for the Chinese, one author implied in *Newsweek*.[16] Who was this guy, and what was he doing with access to all this government information?

Snowden's curious path was not too far removed from that taken by Chelsea Manning, WikiLeaks' most famous source. Like Snowden, Manning was quite young; she was also an anonymous, low-level employee with IT skills. Unlike Snowden, Manning was actually employed by the federal government as a private first-class with the U.S. Army. But she too leveraged her security clearance and relatively anonymous position inside the enormous Department of Defense to download enormous quantities of files not only from the military but also from the State Department. She was stationed in Iraq when she downloaded the files she would release to WikiLeaks, and she ultimately sent material to the site while on leave in the United States. Her low-level position provided her invisibility and limited the control the military could exercise over her use of information, while her physical distance, coupled with the ease with which she could move large quantities of digital data, made control that much more difficult.

The majority of government leaks may emanate from high-level officials,[17] but Manning and Snowden's relative anonymity illustrates the state's dazzling complexity. Like Manning, Snowden appeared unconstrained by employers (or by the NSA) and was in Japan and Hawaii while a contractor for the NSA, far removed from the agency's Maryland headquarters.

Both of them thus reveal how difficult it is for an increasingly diffuse and privatized state to control information. They demonstrate not only why the state faces such a difficult task in stopping leaks but also why it proves so difficult to impose transparency on the state. The same anonymity that Manning and Snowden had enjoyed within the enormous military and security bureaucracies also provides the ability to keep information hidden from outsiders and even from their superiors. This chapter considers the state as a set of logically but loosely organized bureaucratic institutions that occupy vast geographic and physical space. The contemporary state's size and complexity resist the kind of informational controls that transparency and secrecy require as administrative ideals. These ideals presume the existence of a singular entity capable of communication, understood as "sending" the message of government information to a receiver or preventing itself from doing so by choosing to be uncommunicative. But the state cannot both serve as the producer and repository of information that controls that information's flow *and* act as a unified, intentional communicator. It sprawls too much geographically and organizationally to perfectly send or keep itself from sending its information as a message.

Organizing the Visible State

From its post-revolutionary beginnings, the new United States faced a dire organizational problem: whether and how to address the popular demand for a
direct, accessible state by creating a federal government out of a disparate set
of colonies spread over a large territory. The effort to do so spawned anxious
commentary from proponents of the new Constitution and angry condemna-
tions by their critics. In *Federalist No. 37*, James Madison worried about the
"arduous" task facing the Constitutional Convention in "marking the proper
line of partition between the authority of the general and that of the State governments," and suggested that the issue was so complex, and its solution so
difficult to derive, that the resulting lines drawn in the Constitutional Convention were the necessary result of human estimation and political compromise.[18]

The Anti-Federalists, meanwhile, characterized the task as impossible rather
than merely arduous and dismissed the resulting Constitution as fatally flawed.
Writing as Cato in *The New-York Journal* in 1787 (in a letter later collected
as part of the "Anti-Federalist Papers"), New York Governor George Clinton
warned against the "consolidation or union" of states into "one great whole"
because "[w]here, from the vast extent of your territory, and the complication
of interests, the science of government will become intricate and perplexed,
and too mysterious for you to understand and observe," then "a monarchy, either limited or despotic" would surely result.[19] Clinton worried that the sprawling, distant federal government would threaten the public's ability to observe
and understand it.

In response to such arguments, Alexander Hamilton conceded that those
who lived closer to the seat of power would enjoy greater access to the state
than those who lived far away. But the proper institutional design of government, coupled with the development of an active civil society and independent
press, would produce a functional, accountable state.[20] The Hamiltonian belief
that organization can correct the structural problems caused by a large territory
and complex federal system has remained prevalent throughout the twentieth
century, most notably in repeated efforts to reorganize and tame what are seen
as fragmented, haphazardly structured executive branches of both the federal
and state governments.[21] Bureaucratic organization has its "ups and downs" in
modern democracies, in the terms of organizational theorist Johan Olsen, but
its hold remains "tenacious" and its history marked by theoretical and political
arguments over how best to design institutions and rules that might improve
or perfect governmental operations.[22]

These anxieties and arguments about the state originate in two distinct obstructions to the public's ability to view it and to the state's ability to control itself. The first barrier is organizational. Madison may have found it difficult but ultimately possible to draw lines among the various levels and agents of government that wield state authority, but the Anti-Federalists worried that the federal government would prove too "intricate and perplexed, and too mysterious" to be sufficiently monitored from outside and inside.[23] Organizational control and accountability require simplicity, because complexity invites opacity and disorder.

The second barrier is spatial. Hamilton argued that the state could manage its offices and officers across vast distances through the formal and informal relationships among federal, state, and local governments and by the diligent work of an alert press and public. He assumed that a complex organization of governmental institutions and civil society would develop, built in large part on journalists acting as the public's agents and on federal and state capitols that would promote the national and public interest. The Anti-Federalists, by contrast, predicted that the vast post-colonial territory—itself having a small footprint compared to the current United States—would frustrate the development of a functional national government and cohesive civil society.

If transparency abhors the separation between the state and public and requires immediacy, then efforts to make the government's operations fully visible must overcome the organizational and spatial distances that arise naturally from the size and complexity of the American state. The same holds true for secrecy, which requires organizational control to manage the production and flow of information. Writing in the early twentieth century, Max Weber predicted the development of a conflict between an expanding territory and state on the one hand and the populist American desire for an accessible government on the other. "It is obvious," Weber declared, "that technically the large modern state is absolutely dependent upon a bureaucratic basis. The larger the state, and the more it is a great power, the more unconditionally is this the case."[24] He foresaw that the United States, which was then "not fully bureaucratized," would likely become so as the nation faced "greater . . . zones of friction with the outside and . . . more urgent . . . needs for administrative unity at home."[25] The young nation's expanding size—both in population and space—would propel the American state from a relatively small, directly accountable democracy toward an administrative Leviathan that citizens would demand in order to perform the functions they asked of the state.[26]

Thus would the government bureaucracy—a key element of what Weber famously characterized as the anti-democratic, authoritarian, and instrumental rationality of modernity's "iron cage"—enmesh the United States.[27] Its vastly expanded administrative apparatus, which collects and preserves vast quantities of data in its everyday operation, would take advantage of the informational asymmetry that bureaucracies typically enjoy over the public.[28] "Bureaucratic administration," Weber wrote, "means fundamentally domination through knowledge"—domination made possible by the bureaucracy's ability to hoard knowledge and keep its intentions hidden, if not secret.[29]

To the extent that a state's large territory dictates a larger and more powerful administrative apparatus, then, a state the size of the United States, with its necessary bureaucratic rule, will inevitably attempt to protect itself from the public's view. Even with the best of intentions, government efforts to control the state's information production and storage in order to make it more visible must confront the state's vastness. The state's organization would, in sum, make transparency an impossible goal to attain.

Opening and Closing the (Dis)organized State

As a result of the quite conscious intent of its framers, the U.S. Constitution inaugurated a prototypically modern, complex organization that could address the problems of the new post-colonial nation. It set forth in its articles a range of roles (legislator, executive, administrator, judge) and institutions that would shape the behaviors of those who would assume official positions, simply by virtue of the organizational scheme.[30] Contemporary government agencies, many of them subject to additional organizational mandates by their state constitutions, carry on this tradition.[31] Official organizational charts graphically represent how government agencies delegate their institutional authority and tasks, again under the assumption that the correct organization and hierarchy will produce the correct official behavior, which will in turn result in the optimal kind and extent of governance.[32] If linked together, all such governmental charts—those of the co-equal branches of the federal government and their agencies, committees, and respective hierarchies, as well as of state governments and their multitudinous municipal governments and administrative agencies—constitute an atlas representing the American government, a great chain of the state's being that maps the flow of information, as well as authority.[33]

Such maps inscribe a spatial logic that plots the division of labor and allocates authority within units and positions. As the maps expand and proliferate—

down within branches of a particular level of government and across federal, state, and local levels—they form a never-ending, bewildering series of bureaucracies rather than a comprehensible Leviathan. Such complexity constitutes a significant problem for anyone seeking to impose transparency. If the state is to be visible and perceptible, it ought to be visible in its entirety as a whole *and* as constituent parts—from the federal top of the president, the Congress, and the Supreme Court, down to the local government's lowest-level service provider. To implement transparency's inherent promise, public information access laws must thus attempt to bridge or collapse the vast organizational distance the state creates so that the public—as citizens, subjects, and clients—can know the government that ultimately and at least theoretically serves it. Perhaps a Nozickian "nightwatchman state" could be so flat and simple that it proves thoroughly and perfectly visible.[34] But even the relatively simple modern government envisioned by the U.S. Constitution allocates tasks and authorities in a complex system that strains the public's capability to view and comprehend it—especially once the regulatory state, nascent from the colonial period through the early twentieth century, began to grow. And that complex formal organizational chart itself belies the flow of information, and especially of secret information, which can establish its own informational architecture that becomes an informal overlay on top of the formal chart.[35]

Three distinct legal authorities either create or reflect this complexity: the constitutional order, which imposes only minimal and quite variable openness requirements on the various branches and levels of government; statutory transparency obligations placed on the executive branch, whose evolving size and complexity limit those obligations' effectiveness; and the blurred lines between the government and the private entities with which it collaborates and to which it outsources operations that challenge the reach of open government laws.

Constitutional Information Control

The Constitution's initial distribution of authority between the federal and state government and among the federal government's branches blocks the creation of a uniform, comprehensive approach to government information, whether to impose public access or to protect against it. It creates a decentralized agglomeration of government institutions without a uniform standard or set of commands that would make the state as a whole and in its parts fully visible to its public. The constitutional scheme sets forth some limited, variable transparency requirements to individual federal branches while it restrains the ability of any branch to impose further requirements on another. It leaves to individual states the authority to establish their own governmental structure and administrative norms (within constitutional constraints) and limits the federal government from interfering with state governance. The idiosyncratic nature of each branch and level—its different tasks, its distinct history, and the conditions under which each of its bureaucracies works—renders an organizational map that resists transparency as an abstract and absolute norm, especially as each branch and level expands to engage more complex and demanding tasks. The Constitution's organizational plan, then, not only fails to create a transparent state, but it affirmatively stands in the way of creating one.

Consider the informational mandates in the first four constitutional articles. Although the framers engaged in spirited debates about the need for the proposed legislative branch to be open to the public,[36] the Constitution imposes no single openness requirement upon Congress. Instead, it requires certain and limited disclosure practices—Congress must, for example, keep and publish a journal of its proceedings and its members' votes, and it must publish "a regular statement and account of its receipts and expenditures of public money."[37] Even these requirements allow Congress to except from its journal "such parts as may in [its members'] judgment require secrecy" and only requires publication "from time to time."[38] Neither the executive nor the judiciary can impose procedural obligations on Congress.[39] Notably, when Congress saw fit to place disclosure and other procedural requirements on executive branch agencies through the FOIA and the Administrative Procedure Act, it explicitly excluded itself.[40]

The Constitution makes even fewer openness demands of the executive, requiring only that the president "from time to time give to the Congress information of the state of the union."[41] This minimal command has resulted in an annual speech that ritualistically offers self-selected information deemed politically important to the president's agenda and popularity.[42] The only additional transparency requirements made of the presidency and executive branch are those that Congress mandates or that are self-imposed.

Congress has enacted various statutes (including the FOIA) that impose particular openness requirements on a limited universe of entities, most typically those defined by the respective statutes as agencies and advisory committees. But as I have described, both transparency proponents, who lament their limitations, and transparency skeptics, who decry their intrusiveness on the executive branch, have hotly contested these statutory requirements. And as statutory mandates have grown more vigorous and coercive, congressional mandates on the executive branch's openness have approached constitutional common law limits on interbranch interference, most notably through the tangled doctrines of executive privilege and the separation of powers. At the same time, presidential administrations have varied in their commitment to transparency in general and in their willingness to interpret these statutes broadly or narrowly,[43] while cross-agency studies find that compliance with FOIA mandates varies considerably among agencies.[44] Significantly, the Constitution's lack of any general openness requirement encourages such variance among administrations and allows them among agencies.

Some constitutional doctrines force a limited degree of openness on the federal and state judiciary. The Sixth Amendment rights to "a speedy and public trial, by an impartial jury of the State and district where in the crime shall have been committed" require that at least a proportion of the work performed by courts must be "public" and include a degree of public participation,[45] while the First Amendment also requires public access to criminal trials.[46] But there is no constitutional requirement for open judicial deliberation and conferences, and the tradition of published judicial opinions is just that—a tradition rather than a constitutional requirement.[47] Some lower federal courts and some state courts allow cameras in the courtroom, but courts are not bound by a federal constitutional requirement or right, and no systematic approach prevails.[48] At the same time, modern criminal and civil procedural rules place significant emphases on pre-trial procedures and alternative dispute resolutions that undercut the relatively simple and abstract constitutional provisions regarding an open judicial process.[49] The Constitution's lack of a general, expansive right or requirement for judicial transparency allows federal and state courts significant leeway in opening or closing their operations to public view.

Individual state constitutions and governments are free to devise their own open government mandates. Shaped by idiosyncratic institutional designs, states take diverse approaches that mix statutory and constitutional requirements and impose different degrees of openness.[50] Transparency advocates frequently express frustration at this unevenness. A 2015 study by the Center for Public Integrity on state-level transparency—which considered a variety of accountability indexes, including access to government information—found that a majority of states failed to provide sufficient protection against corruption.[51]

Compounding the problem, state officials and judges exhibit varying degrees of commitment to and compliance with their respective open government laws; nongovernmental organizations and media groups that have performed audits of responses to state and municipal government agencies to open record requests often decry and sometimes hesitantly applaud agencies' performances.[52] A decentralized federalist system in an area unregulated by federal constitutional rights and commands thus results in a wide-ranging degree of transparency across states and municipalities.

Branch Versus Branch

The Constitution's construction of separate powers limits by implication the ability of any one branch to impose informational mandates on another. The Supreme Court has found that Article II confers on the president the power to classify and control information regarding national security and foreign policy, especially where Congress has not provided otherwise.[53] Congress can only limit presidential control over executive branch information if it does not prevent the president from accomplishing his or her "constitutionally assigned functions."[54] FOIA may have trimmed presidential and administrative prerogative, but its reach within the executive branch is limited.

Congress has granted certain agencies, most notably the CIA, broad exemptions from disclosure—far broader than would likely be constitutionally required.[55] The NSA too enjoys several specific statutory exemptions; in the "FOIA Handbook" on its website, the NSA cites these provisions as authorities for its limited responses to requests for information that the public might make under the statute.[56] With respect to agencies outside of the intelligence community, FOIA only affirmatively applies to an "agency,"[57] a term that the FOIA defines in an enumerated list.[58] According to the Supreme Court, Congress intended to exclude from that definition the Office of the President, the president's immediate personal staff, and units in the Executive Office of the President whose sole function is to advise and assist the president.[59] The Court has yet to provide an authoritative interpretation of that exclusion,[60] while lower federal courts have developed an indeterminate multifactor test to ascertain whether the FOIA applies to nontraditional and advisory entities that the president or executive branch agencies create within the Executive Office of the President.[61] As a result, FOIA's reach to nontraditional executive branch entities close to the president is vague and uncertain.[62]

It is therefore quite difficult to tame information as it flows through an amorphous and confusing executive branch. When the president or Congress creates a new entity that does not clearly constitute an agency in order to pursue a new executive branch program or oversee existing ones, we will not know its obligations under the FOIA without an extensive, fact-specific survey on the messy organizational map of the federal government, or unless Congress clearly exempts it from or clearly subjects it to the FOIA in an agency-specific statute.[63] And indeed, presidential administrations create such entities regularly, especially to oversee or advise politically significant and controversial programs. Examples include the task force created to oversee deregulatory efforts during the Reagan administration;[64] the Task Force on National Health Care Reform during the Clinton administration, headed by First Lady Hillary Clinton, to which the Federal Advisory Committee Act was held not to apply;[65] and the National Energy Policy Development Group in the George W. Bush administration, headed by Vice President Cheney, to which the Federal Advisory Committee Act was also held not to apply.[66] These entities played key roles in devising and implementing policy for the presidents who created them, and their creators designed and placed them within the executive branch in a way that limited congressionally mandated public access to their proceedings and records.

Congress also cedes to the executive branch significant authority over classifying information as secret. The classification system, largely developed and overseen by the executive branch itself, enables agencies with classification authority to keep information secret almost indefinitely and without interbranch oversight.[67] FOIA explicitly excludes classified documents from disclosure,[68] while the Espionage Act criminalizes the knowing and intentional unauthorized disclosure of classified information.[69]

Congress has long provided deferential, minimal public oversight of the national security state and has done little to curb the well-known problem of overclassification.[70] In the aftermath of the 9/11 attacks, Congress enacted the Critical Infrastructure Information Act of 2002 in order to exempt from FOIA those "systems and assets, whether physical or virtual, so vital to the United States that the incapacity or destruction of such systems and assets would have a debilitating impact on security, national economic security, national public health or safety, or any combination of these matters."[71] The Whistleblower Protection Act specifically excludes personnel in the intelligence community from its protection[72] and more generally excludes civil servant positions of a "confidential, policy-determining, policy-making, or policy-advocating character."[73] It grants the president authority to exempt any positions when the president finds it "necessary and warranted by conditions of good administration."[74] Congress has thereby created or allowed the creation of laws and executive branch authorities that sanction the regular production and protection of secrets.

Like Congress, the judiciary's limited constitutional authority over executive branch information carries over to its review of claims brought under FOIA. Even after the 1974 amendments to the statute that were intended to allow and even encourage more searching judicial consideration of agency decisions to refuse disclosure, courts nearly always affirm agency decisions to deny FOIA requests under the national security exemption.[75] The 9/11 attacks provoked a telling judicial response. In a D.C. Circuit Court decision holding in 2003 that the names of persons detained following the attacks and the details of their detainment fell within FOIA's law enforcement exception,[76] the two-judge majority followed what it described as a long tradition of judicial deference to the Justice Department in FOIA cases that raise national security issues. Because terrorism presents America with an enemy "just as real as its former Cold War foes, with capabilities beyond the capacity of the judiciary to explore," Judge David Sentelle wrote for the majority, a court cannot second-guess executive judgments about the adverse effects that any disclosure would have to ongoing law enforcement proceedings related to the war on terrorism.[77] To do so, the court reasoned, would leave the nation vulnerable to attack. Judicial concerns about terrorism, coupled with judges' concerns about their competence to question government decisions about disclosure's dangers, have largely continued in the years since that decision.[78]

Information from the Hollowed Out State

By contract, regulation, law enforcement, service provision, and other functions, government agencies in the United States constantly interact with private individuals and corporations, gathering information incidentally and by design. U.S. government entities began utilizing private entities to perform seemingly public functions centuries before the NSA contracted with Edward Snowden's employer.[79] The state often explicitly contracts out or privatizes government services.[80] This longstanding tradition of American governance offers, so its proponents say, a more efficient and effective means to deliver services that the government has performed in the past or can perform, and it makes the government leaner and more responsive—a type of reform that enjoys bipartisan support.[81] In an especially poignant example, some parts of the federal government outsource to private firms not only the digital storage of the information they hold,[82] but also the handling of FOIA requests, for the stated reason that private information management companies can provide better, more reliable, and less expensive service than federal civil servants.[83]

For transparency proponents and critics of privatization alike, the public's need to view the state's operations does not disappear merely by virtue of an exciting organizational innovation or a contractual agreement with a private entity.[84] When government contracts out important police-power services, it can limit public oversight of the service provider. Military contracting presents several special dangers: the enormous expense of military operations, the difficulty of monitoring military operations, and the significance of military operations for the nation's security and reputation. And yet the Iraq War and operations that followed relied extensively on contractors, many of whom participated in some of the endeavor's significant scandals—and could not be held accountable in the same manner as military and intelligence personnel.[85]

The government also collaborates or negotiates with private actors in regulatory programs as part of a long tradition of delegating to or working closely with private actors when legislating and regulating.[86] Indeed, these relationships are so longstanding and embedded in public governance that no clear boundary separates the state from the private entities with which it works to regulate and deliver services.[87] Departing from a traditional top-down, command-and-control approach in which an identifiable state agency requires an identifiable private entity to comply with mandatory practices or regulatory targets or face punishment, a state entity adopting a "new governance" approach to achieve a particular outcome works closely with private actors to develop and implement a program or programs that can best achieve its goal.[88] Such "hybridization" of public and private authority promises collaboration among regulators and interested parties, and therefore better regulations based on information that private entities willingly share with regulators, as well as more willing compliance; it also promotes a more "dynamic accountability" than conventional top-down regulatory programs, its proponents argue, by imposing measures like peer review and reporting requirements.[89]

As with contracting out services, however, new governance regulatory efforts raise significant concerns about a resulting program's accountability and visibility to the public.[90] A volume of essays intended to serve as a guide for new governance largely ignores the transparency ideal and includes an essay that concedes that for innovation to occur, "more classical notions of democratic accountability may need to be loosened and more pluralistic conceptions developed."[91]

When the government delegates its regulatory authority to private or hybrid public-private entities, it increases the state's organizational complexity and thereby decreases its visibility to the public by making it more difficult to identify state actors to whom open government laws apply and from whom to request information. According to one critical account, the Canadian federal government's introduction of new public management harmed compliance with FOI laws, as state entities moved functions from state to private entities that were not subject to FOI laws and established new economic barriers to openness, shifting the costs of informational requests to the public.[92] "New" governance can appear like an old, top-down form of governance with greater access to decision making and information for certain elite insiders and less visibility for the general public—all in an effort to create collaboration for some. Its blurring of the public/private boundaries challenges the effort to make the state visible.

At the same time, transparency ideals can threaten to undercut the instrumental and political advantages of privatization and new governance regimes in at least two ways: by restoring the administrative costs and delays that outsourcing and collaboration claim to avoid; and by scaring away potential participants who would prefer to avoid having to comply with intrusive openness regulations. Federal and state laws have taken only halting, uncertain steps to impose transparency norms on private entities with whom the state is contracting or governing.[93] The state must work with private entities in order to meet the public's expectations for regulatory oversight and service provision; but that work may, as a result, either make the state less transparent, or it may provoke an effort to treat private entities as state actors that will in turn undercut the range and quality of services the state can offer. If the state must be visible, its efforts to provide effective regulation and services are likely to suffer, at least to some extent.

Information Control and the Distant State
As the Anti-Federalists predicted, the state's size, political-geographic complexity, and distance from its citizens also impede its visibility. The immense size and intricate overlap of government entities in the United States frustrate any effort to achieve such perfect or even near-perfect visibility. The federal government is sovereign over a significant amount of well-populated and unpopulated territory. Its three branches may all have their headquarters in Washington, but their decisions and administration also occur in agency and congressional offices and federal courthouses scattered throughout Washing-

ton as well as all fifty states. The federal government shares sovereignty over the same territory with state and other territorial governments, and both the federal and state governments overlap municipal governments. Many state and local governments preside over extraordinary amounts of territory from their capitols and city halls—heavily populated Los Angeles County, for example, occupies more than 4,000 square miles of land, while sparsely populated Alaska sits on over 570,000 square miles. Enabling the public to view such diffuse Leviathans proves a difficult challenge, as does enforcing any general edict for openness upon officials in geographically scattered organizations.

The Hamiltonian faith in administration and institutional structure, as well as Weberian warnings of an information-hoarding bureaucracy, foreshadowed ongoing arguments and anxieties about the state's operations in an expansive American territory. Hamiltonian efforts began almost immediately in the Federalist period of the early republic.[94] His general prescription for public and private institutional checks and balances influences the federal and state laws that attempt to provide uniform controls over vast and far-flung bureaucracies. In the present day, federal and state administrative laws impose requirements for public access to information equally on the operations of agencies' headquarters and its offices. At the same time, federal courthouses, enforcing federal law and using uniform federal rules of civil and criminal procedure and providing equal levels of openness, have been dispersed across the nation in an effort both to extend federal authority and federal rights.[95] At least as a structural matter, then, the American state appears to have proven Hamilton correct by successfully addressing the territorial concerns of the Anti-Federalists.

As a matter of practice, however, these formal commands are not self-enforcing. A far larger and more diverse nation than even Hamilton's Anti-Federalist opponents feared, coupled with an administrative apparatus that Weber foresaw but that Hamilton could not have anticipated, has made Hamilton's confident forecast of private collective actions to control the administrative state appear naïve at best. Central authorities have limited control over their dispersed organizations, and not all branches and agencies of the individual units are equally visible to their citizens. Some officials at the center of authority want their inferior officers, the "street-level bureaucrats" on the periphery, to be visible to the public—a desire that appears to vary among agencies and executive administrations, given the variability of their levels of compliance.[96]

Moreover, secrets are endemic to organizational practice, allowing individuals and subunits to amass power or resist it by keeping information from outsiders and others within the organization.[97] Police officers on the beat and public school teachers in the classroom, as well as public information officials and FOIA officers removed from an agency's central command, inevitably have significant discretion to make substantive and administrative decisions in response to what they find in the field.[98] Physical distance, whether counted in miles or by the floors of an office building, limits the extent to which superiors can monitor and exercise authority. If administrative discretion increases across space, and if Weber was correct that bureaucracies prefer to hoard information, then efforts to impose transparency on large, far-flung agencies will be doomed to incomplete success if not failure. The geographic dispersal of authority thus limits both the state's ability to supply bureaucracies that the public can see and the law's ability to command them to be seen.

The state's jurisdictional complexity is an additional obstacle to achieving a populist ideal of transparency. "By its very nature," the political geographer John Short has written, "the nation-state is a spatial phenomenon," one that manifests itself most clearly in the frontiers and borders between nations and in a nation's internal division into such administrative subdivisions as regional, state, and local governments and their sub-agencies.[99] This might suggest that a geographic map, which visualizes a series of logical—if somewhat haphazardly arranged—nested centers and peripheries, would provide a blueprint for political order and behavior.[100] Like an organizational chart that claims to offer a hierarchical rendering of coordinated government entities, a map of the United States implies that political power is dispersed across a territory: the nation, with its federal capitol; the states, with their state capitols; and metropolitan regions, with their city halls, urban cores, and suburban and exurban peripheries.[101] Where authority is dispersed logically, the public can view, comprehend, and hold accountable those officials it can find in the cores of the respective (federal, state, and local) jurisdictional bodies.

As Richard Thompson Ford has noted regarding local governments, however, we cannot assume that territory and the maps that record it accurately reflect an essential, authoritative sovereign power, nor can we assume that a hierarchical relationship among political divisions subordinates the smallest and lowest subunit.[102] A governmental unit's authority, jurisdictional reach, and public accessibility are never as fixed or stable as a map suggests.[103] To the extent that different levels of government might cooperate with, ignore, or contest one another's jurisdiction and policies, the public will struggle to identify the particular government entity or entities from which they need to seek information.[104] This proves equally true at the local level, where municipal governments frequently overlap or have shifting boundaries, requiring regional or cross-jurisdictional coordination and governance and making regulatory responsibility difficult to pinpoint.[105] Moreover, the modern state's sovereignty has long extended beyond its mere territory and been shaped and challenged internally not only by its citizens but by other states, nongovernmental organizations, transnational corporations, supra-national institutions, and the global flows of economic trade and capital.[106]

All of these impediments to transparency also impede the state's ability to keep secrets. The far-flung state is opaque not only to outsiders but also to those within its various bureaucracies. To perform their functions, regional offices and those located outside of the central office must have access to an agency's information, and the weakest links—the contract employee located in Hawaii or the private first class in Iraq—can take advantage of this geographic distance to obtain insecure files. In other words, street-level bureaucrats can leak information just as easily as they can hide it.

Exposing the Built State

Transparency faces an architectural impediment as well. The thoroughly open state must be capable of allowing the public to view where and how government employees work: the physical spaces of the built bureaucratic environment. Most government documents are in fact housed in government offices and can be requested, found, and released (if covered by disclosure laws), while formal meetings regularly occur in official spaces to which the public can have access. Architects can design buildings located in population centers with spaces large enough for public access. But standard architectural elements—like walls, ceilings, doors, and windows—serve naturally to exclude the public and obscure the state. Even if it were physically possible to enable the public to see through the structures that house the state or invite them in, the effort can prove so intrusive and costly as to make the work of public officials difficult if not impossible.

Government buildings and offices enable public employees to perform their tasks by housing the spaces where officials, managers, and civil servants work, converse, officially meet, and where they store and protect official records. By containing state activity within built structures, buildings and offices also enclose that activity within walls and ceilings and control access and visibility to their work via doors and windows. And by allowing officials to work and to sort and protect the records that they collect and produce, government buildings inevitably separate officials from the public that they serve.[107] Accordingly, allowing the public to view and enter government buildings is at once an issue of design and practice: Can the public see and navigate its way into the building, and is the public in fact invited or allowed to enter?[108]

At its best, public architecture aspires to shape the affective relationship between the state and its public, establishing an identity for the national, state, or municipal governmental unit or units that a building hosts.[109] A public building's size, architectural design, and location announce the state's existence and its occupants' relative prominence.[110] In doing so, it may invite members of the public to enter, or it may use distance and physical barriers—fences, gates, and the like—to discourage or exclude their access.[111] The interior design and features of public buildings can also communicate openness or its opposite as they either foster or inhibit interaction among government actors and between the state and the public.[112] Legislative buildings in Germany convey the transparency ideal in a famously intentional way. The successive buildings of the post-war West German Parliament, completed in Bonn in 1949 and 1992, and Berlin's new Reichstag building completed in 1999 to house the newly reunified parliament, have sought to encourage transparency through their use of glass walls and open, accessible spaces, leading one architectural historian to contrast these architectural ideals with the disappointing secrecy of the German state.[113] Public architectural design may consider the public visibility of and access to government officials' work as a significant end, but thoughtful architectural projects are the exception; most U.S. government buildings are designed with only secondary consideration given to inviting public access and observation.[114]

Open government laws attempt to mitigate the enclosure problem for the entire public in several ways. Under the aegis of so-called open meeting or sunshine laws, government officials are required to make certain meetings accessible for public viewing. These laws purport to open doors to the public, allowing anyone to watch government decision making in person. Video recordings and broadcasts of government meetings via C-SPAN and state and local cable television and webcasting channels also make public meetings more widely available, enabling the public to see the state from the comfort of their homes or preferred digital devices, whether live or after the fact. Open records laws (including the FOIA and its state analogues) require that agencies open their files—a dark corner of the state's physical and digital architecture—to members of the public.

None of these efforts provides unlimited physical or visual access to all public buildings, offices, and files at all times, however. As the next section explains, such transparency that they do provide is legally and practically limited to certain pre-planned public events or to files over which the government has initial control. The physical enclosure that walls and ceilings provide almost inevitably offer cover for the state from the public's gaze, and transparency obligations cannot fully overcome or compensate for enclosure's distance.

What Is a Meeting, and Can the Public View It?

Modern, comprehensive open meeting laws emerged in the states largely after World War II, and especially in response to revelations of the Nixon administration's abuses of power (when Congress enacted the Government in the Sunshine Act).[115] These laws extended the openness obligation to federal and state administrative bodies and local governments, unsurprisingly utilizing the visibility and presence metaphors that I previously identified.[116]

The public is not invited to view everything the government does, however. By definition, the only event that these laws make thoroughly visible is the official occasion of a "meeting,"[117] a term whose meaning is not self-evident.[118] How far along in a decision-making body's consideration of a matter does a gathering of its members constitute an official meeting?[119] Does an open meeting mandate apply only to the formal conferences that officials hold in an agency's official meeting space, or does the definition of "meeting" extend outside the official enclosure, to other rooms in government buildings or even to gatherings and encounters held in restaurants and homes? And if the latter, more capacious definition applies, can officials be required to provide notice and public access to *informal* meetings that occur by chance or appointment? If they constitute official meetings—if the government's operations and transparency's reach must extend infinitely across the territories to cover wherever officials travel and communicate about their official duties—then such meetings are much less likely to take place at all.[120]

Consider the following case. Two elected members of a city commission spontaneously decide to dine together with the general manager of a public agency overseen by the commission. The two members alone do not constitute a quorum of the commission, and they do not intend to have their meal circumvent the statutory open meeting requirement in the relevant state.[121] Nevertheless, because they enjoy and are interested in their work, they allow their conversation to turn to matters that are currently before the body or that could conceivably come before the body at a later date. Of course the public cannot monitor the conversation or even know the conversation took place, creating a legal question: Is this a "meeting" that would require the members to give advance notice of their meal and to invite the public to join them?

Most open meeting statutes reach only formal meetings, defined as those that would adopt final actions, or at which a majority or quorum is in attendance; this would allow the dinner meeting to take place without public notice or access because of its small size and the informal nature of the gathering, even if it results in a discussion by the members of an issue before the body.[122] This approach assumes that a meeting occurs at a scheduled time in the normal course of a government entity's operations, most typically though not necessarily in the entity's office or in an official public meeting room.[123] A small number of jurisdictions would bar the meeting, however. Applying their state statute, Florida courts and attorney general opinions would view the case as a violation of Florida's sunshine law unless the public is provided notice and access; to do otherwise, an intermediate appellate court has held, would allow members to "gather with impunity behind closed doors and discuss matters on which foreseeable action may be taken by that board or commission in clear violation of the purpose, intent, and spirit" of the state's open meeting law.[124] An official can transform any space into a government office and meeting room simply by discussing public business with colleagues there.[125]

The latter approach bars officials from avoiding their duty to be visible to the public by escaping into their private lives and identities. Any space that an official occupies must be open to the public when necessary, so the public can view its officials wherever the public's business takes place.[126] Taken to its logical end, this view would allow no space that an official occupies to be securely private—including her home, from which she can make calls and send e-mails.[127]

This is a logical response to actions that seem suspiciously evasive. Secretary of State Hillary Clinton's private e-mail server and account did not transform her State Department e-mail into private documents. The spatial and categorical distinction between public and private is simpler in theory than in practice, however. Secretary Clinton's e-mail server conversely did not make entirely *personal* e-mail she sent via that server and account public documents as a matter of law simply because of the server and account's public usage.[128] Officials must be able to have a private life. At the same time, the blending of official and personal lives—especially in a figure like Clinton, much of whose career has been spent either officially in office or as partner to a government official—can render the distinction almost meaningless. Laws intended to safeguard officials' privacy—an important administrative value for government to pursue as well, especially to recruit and retain competent civil servants and officials—appear to undermine and frustrate transparency and accountability.[129]

Safeguarding officials' privacy also risks allowing officials to disclose information to those outside of the state. Government employees might unintentionally leak secrets by using unsecure phones and digital devices or having their conversations overheard. Or, they might meet with a reporter or enemy spy and purposefully spread information from the state. Proliferating meetings and the complexity of employees' lives thereby demonstrate both the difficulty of making the state more transparent—because officials must communicate with one another, as part of their jobs—and of keeping the state's secrets—because officials have lives outside of work that can lead them or allow them to divulge information.

Where Is a Document?

Government agencies frequently possess in their facilities documents they did not create; conversely, government records end up in the hands of individuals and institutions and are housed in buildings that are not themselves part of the government. The problem becomes acute under two current conditions, both of which have changed the state's operations and structure: the digitization of information and the outsourcing of state functions. Officials can easily copy, store, and transfer digital files, expanding information's access within government bureaucracies while also making such information potentially more vulnerable to unauthorized access and copying, as the Snowden and Manning episodes demonstrate. In the pre-digital era, stealing files required either breaking into a physical file cabinet—as in 1971, when political dissidents raided the FBI's satellite file repository in Media, Pennsylvania—or an insider to borrow or pilfer files—as when Daniel Ellsberg and his co-conspirator's took files from his RAND Corporation office and photocopied them.[130] Ellsberg's earlier relationship with RAND, like Snowden's relationship to the government contractor who employed him, also demonstrates the difficulties of controlling information when it is in the hands of those who are not themselves government employees.

At the same time, open government laws struggle to resolve the issue of whether an agency must disclose a record that it does not possess, and whether it must release a record that it possesses but that originated with another part of the government. Under the FOIA, the issue turns on whether a document is an "agency record," which the statute fails to define, and whether an agency has the duty to obtain and retain records, which the statute fails to specify. The Supreme Court has interpreted the statute to mean that a record must either be *born governmental* in order to be subject to disclosure under the FOIA—it must have, as its provenance, a government pedigree—or the record must be *adopted by* the government—that is, the government must willingly take possession of it.[131] This definition has a spatial dimension: The record must either be produced within the government's domain or later be incorporated within it.

The case of Henry Kissinger's telephone notes illustrates the complexity of this issue.[132] Kissinger served as both national security advisor (from 1969 until 1975) and secretary of state (between 1973 and 1977) under presidents Nixon and Ford. Throughout his service, he regularly recorded his telephone conversations, and the resulting tapes were then transcribed and stored in documentary form in his personal files within the State Department.[133] In October 1976, after obtaining a legal opinion from the legal advisor of the State Department concluding that the transcribed notes constituted personal papers rather than agency records and were therefore his to keep after he left office, Secretary Kissinger arranged to remove the files to the private estate of then-Vice President Nelson Rockefeller.[134] By a later agreement, Kissinger deeded the notes to the Library of Congress with restrictions on public access to the materials prior to the death of the parties to the phone conversations.[135] When journalists and public interest groups subsequently filed requests to view the documents, the State Department claimed that it no longer had possession of the files.[136]

The case reached the Supreme Court in *Kissinger v. Reporters Committee for Freedom of the Press*, and as Justice Brennan highlighted in his dissent, the Court was forced to grapple with the extent to which the FOIA restrains an agency's authority to move documents—especially if a requester claims that the agency intended the documents' removal to make them inaccessible.[137] If the FOIA extends only to documents under the state's physical control and located within the state's facilities, and the law does not require an agency to disclose all of the records it considered in its decision-making process (no matter if the agency ever gained possession of them),[138] then a document's location outside of the state not only matters but determines the dispute's outcome.

Thus, a document outside the state's control is not subject to the FOIA, no matter how it left the government's possession. A majority of the Supreme Court held that a document that an agency does not possess has not been "withheld" under the FOIA, even if it has allowed a public document to leave its possession.[139] To be an agency record, a document must be physically located within the state.[140] Because Secretary Kissinger's telephone records were no longer housed within State Department offices and under the agency's control, the State Department did not violate the FOIA by refusing to release them.[141]

The reverse situation further confounds the transparency ideal. Just as documents created but not retained by an agency are no longer subject to the FOIA when they leave the agency's control, so documents controlled by an agency subject to the FOIA but created by a public or private entity that is not subject to the FOIA might not be subject to the FOIA. Files created while Kissinger was a close advisor to the president (a role that does not fall within the FOIA's ambit under the presidential communications privilege and general separation of power principles[142]) and before he became secretary of state (when documents he created would fall within the FOIA) did not become State Department records when they were moved to his new office.[143]

Similarly, the record of a secret congressional committee hearing did not become an agency record because the CIA came into possession of it; rather, it remained within congressional control and was thus not subject to FOIA, even while it was housed within the CIA's facilities.[144] The D.C. Circuit's current test for these types of cases—a two-part standard to determine whether documents created either by or for Congress but in an agency's possession constitute agency records—inquires into whether Congress has in fact ceded control of the documents and whether the agency has gained full "property" rights, rather than simply has physical possession of them.[145]

Critics have long complained about the underlying logic of these legal rules and their effects.[146] The transparency ideal requires that a document the state created or controls ought to be made available to the public. The state's organizational and physical complexity should not keep it from being visible. But a document located outside the state, *Kissinger* held, is not subject to the FOIA, while a document located within the state is also not necessarily subject to the FOIA. Thus FOIA does not enforce or even follow the transparency ideal, at least in attempting to sort the movement of documents into, out of, and through the state's bureaucracy and buildings.

The law's messy hodgepodge of odd distinctions and classifications appears to allow the government and its officials to move documents around its offices and territory in order to avoid disclosure. At the same time that the mobile document eludes legal disclosure to the public, it becomes vulnerable to intentional and unintentional leaks in spectacular or quotidian fashion. For every Kissinger-like official who hopes to keep his records away from the public, there are others who want to make public all or some of the documents to which they have access.

Not Seeing the State, from Outside or Within

Whether its intent is to force transparency or to allow secrecy, the state's control over its information faces innumerable obstacles in the complex and dispersed American state. These obstacles cannot be easily overcome through institutional and architectural design, legal obligations, or technology. The contemporary state sprawls both within and without, reaching well beyond the strict confines of physical burdens and simple, hierarchical organizational forms. It runs from Henry Kissinger's phone transcripts and Hillary Clinton's e-mails at the highest levels of the National Security Council and State Department down to Chelsea Manning's CD-RW's burned on an army base near Baghdad to the contents of Edward Snowden's laptop hard drive, taken from the NSA via Dell and Booz Allen Hamilton. The organizational charts and maps of nation-states attempt to offer logical, hierarchical, and boundary-focused representations of an ever-changing mess of social institutions that are frequently unwieldy and incoherent, secretive and yet leaky. The contemporary state is an ensemble of institutions and procedures of power—neither a monolithic entity nor a unified set of functions and institutions that administrative theories and laws imagine can be reformed.[147] It cannot be domesticated; its information and communication cannot be controlled. It constitutes a difficult, almost incomprehensible sender of information.

5 The Impossible Archive
of Government Information

Don DeLillo's *Libra*, a preeminent work of fiction about the assassination of John F. Kennedy, tells three stories: of Lee Oswald, from his adolescence through the assassination of John F. Kennedy and his murder by Jack Ruby; of a plot by disaffected and former CIA agents that was initially intended to orchestrate a near-miss assassination in order to drum up support for an invasion of Cuba; and of Nicholas Branch, a retired CIA agent working decades later on an institutional history of the assassination for the agency. The first story is a semi-fictional reconstruction of the life of an accidental agent of history (based in part on available documentary evidence), while the second is a speculative thesis of how a conspiratorial plot comes together through a combination of plan and chance. These two stories feature typical elements of historical novels, with a mix of recognizable and imagined characters and some basis in the facts and timelines of real events. The Nicholas Branch story concerns the effort to make sense of a complex, incomprehensible, and well-known but mysterious historical event through narrative. Most importantly for present purposes, the Nicholas Branch story provocatively imagines the relationship between nearly complete informational access and the ability to understand and narrate state action. In so doing, *Libra* examines and questions the ideal of "government information" as a necessary path to a visible, comprehensible, and responsible state.

Branch's life consists entirely of sorting through the "record" of the assassination. He sits in the safe and controlled environment of his home office day after day, reviewing an endless supply of documents provided to him from the unnamed "Curator" at the CIA:

> The Curator sends transcripts of closed committee hearings. He sends documents released under the Freedom of Information Act, other documents withheld from ordinary investigators or heavily censored. He sends new books all the time, each with a gleaming theory, supportable, assured. This is the room of theories, the room of growing old. Branch wonders if he ought to despair of ever getting to the end.[1]

Living the dream of the most serious historian as well as the most crackpot conspiracy theorist, Branch enjoys uniquely unlimited access to the records of a controversial historical event along with unlimited time to review them. The CIA does not pressure him to reach a particular conclusion, and he appears ready to admit his failure to reach any conclusion at all. He is "objective"—a seeker of truth who is willing and able to allow the full record of government information to speak for itself.

The incompleteness of the JFK assassination record has both inspired and frustrated researchers and conspiracy buffs for more than five decades. The debate surrounding the assassination, especially in the aftermath of Oliver Stone's 1992 film *JFK*, assumes that we know enough to speculate but we do not have enough information to *know*. Congress responded to this concern with legislation that requires "the expeditious public transmission" of records in the government's possession relating to the event. It specifically mandates that "all Government records concerning the assassination of President John F. Kennedy should carry a presumption of immediate disclosure, and all records should be eventually disclosed to enable the public to become fully informed about the history surrounding the assassination."[2] In 2017, when the president's privilege to withhold records whose disclosure would create an "identifiable public harm" ends, we could all be Nicholas Branch.[3]

But what are these records? Branch catalogs his archive, which includes more than the so-called JFK Act will ever kick loose from the CIA:

> Everything is here. Baptismal records, report cards, postcards, divorce petitions, canceled checks, daily timesheets, tax returns, property lists, postoperative x-rays, photos of knotted string, thousands of pages of testimony, of voices droning in hearing rooms in old courthouse buildings, an incredible haul of human utterance. It lies so flat on the page, hangs so still in the lazy air, lost

to syntax and other arrangement, that it resembles a kind of mind-splatter, a poetry of lives muddied and dripping in language.

Documents. There is Jack Ruby's mother's dental chart, dated January 15, 1938. There is a microphotograph of three strands of Lee H. Oswald's pubic hair. Elsewhere (everything in the Warren Report is elsewhere) there is a detailed description of this hair. It is smooth, not knobby. The scales are medium-size. The root area is rather clear of pigment.

Branch doesn't know how to approach this kind of data. He wants to believe the hair belongs in the record. It is vital to his sense of responsible obsession that everything in his room warrants careful study. Everything belongs, everything adheres, the mutter of obscure witnesses, the photos of illegible documents and odd sad personal debris, things gathered up at a dying—old shoes, pajama tops, letters from Russia. It is all one thing, a ruined city of trivia where people feel real pain. This is the Joycean Book of America, remember—the novel in which nothing is left out.[4]

With its uniquely reiterative, contested investigations—as well as the legions of professional historians, amateur investigators, and conspiracy theorists it has inspired—the Kennedy assassination has generated a boundless supply of facts and speculation. In its depiction of Branch and his project, *Libra* chronicles modernity's will to document, collect, and archive this event. It is "all one thing" and everything, all at once.

At the same time, the novel offers an ironic embrace of the resulting mess. DeLillo stages essentially illegible events that Branch struggles to understand. It presents an agent-less conspiracy that succeeds by chance and that stars, in an existential sense, the incoherent figure of Oswald, whose efforts to author a historically significant life only bear fruit when he is stitched into a plot that is not of his own making. The historical narratives DeLillo stages claim little authority besides some plausibility, and he implicitly undercuts whatever plausibility he can claim by having Branch prove unable to find a singular truth despite his full access to the archive.

It is telling that the most mundane, surreal, and seemingly irrelevant artifacts that Branch catalogs—the obscure dental charts and pubic hair photographs—are actual documents that DeLillo found in the Warren Commission Report.[5] The absurd excess of absurd but actual information offers no more or less coherence or relevance than a frame-by-frame analysis of the Zapruder film. The only sense we can make from the information Branch's story provides appears random. We are left with the fiction that DeLillo spins in his conspiracy narrative, one that may be believable but is explicitly concocted—the CIA agents are fictional, and the Mafia don who provides financial assistance to the assassination conspiracy is a compendium of real people with a fictional name.

Branch's story illustrates a key problem with the notion that government information can be made accessible through public disclosure of the kinds of records that Branch reviews and that such accessibility will have direct and certain effects on the public and on the state. The cybernetic conception of government information views the state as driven and defined by what the prominent midcentury political scientist Karl Deutsch characterized as its "streams of information."[6] Viewed that way, Branch works downstream, subject to the Curator's regular addition to his archive of documents that point in no clear direction and toward no authoritative conclusion (except toward more documents and speculation). They might all "belong" to the archive, as he would like them to, because they are documents produced or collected by the government with some connection to the assassination. But Branch cannot bring coherence to that "all one thing" they should constitute, the thing that excites and burdens him. He embraces the torrent of documents that he faces as a sublime vision, though in doing so he must renounce the desire for coherence, causation, and narrative.

Branch's informational sublime has a long history among researchers and librarians, stretching back at least to early modern Europe, when the fear of information overload led archivists to incessant, endless efforts to archive, catalog, and index.[7] The contemporary bureaucratic state continues this tradition by building such archives as a matter of course, producing file rooms, warehouses, computer tapes, hard drives, servers, clouds, and trash heaps with more information than can ever be processed. Perhaps a digital compilation, with an algorithmic search and sorting function, could assist in managing a real archive, but we would all need to be Nicholas Branches working constantly to corral and process this information in order to truly know the state through its documents. Conventional political thrillers feature intrepid reporters, spies, researchers, and the like who find coherence and illumination about corruption and conspiracy in the flood of information they obtain. Nicholas Branch, notably, does not.

The raw numbers of federal recordkeeping offer a sublime vista even greater than the one that DeLillo and the Curator provide for Branch to experience. The National Archives and Records Administration hosts a collection that, as of 2013, included 12 billion sheets of paper, 42 million photographs, miles of video and film, and more than 520 terabytes of electronic records.[8] The recently opened George W. Bush Library includes 70 million pages of textual records, 40,000 artifacts, 4 million photographs, and 80 terabytes of electronic information. The latter includes 200 million e-mails of about five pages each, or 1 billion pages.[9] Federal agencies utilize over 9,260 forms to collect information, receive over 72 billion responses on those forms, and spend over $70 billion annually to collect them.[10]

Not all of those documents hold information of much public interest—indeed, many of them hold no interest for anyone, even the government that collects it. Yet each is a public document, a thing that says something about the bureaucracy that produced or obtained it. The disclosure of a portion of those documents might be contested. Officials can argue that some of them are not subject to disclosure laws, while interested members of the press or public will argue that they must all be disclosed as the failure to do so will keep the state from being visible. This contest proves especially heated when it concerns significant public events, like the JFK assassination. And the contest matters because its players assume both the archive's completeness and its significance. Access to the entirety of the archive could presumably enable the public to know and understand the state—indeed, such access is necessary for the state to be truly seen.

By contrast, Nicholas Branch comes to accept and seems even to revel in his inability to reach a final conclusion; each new document the Curator sends him, from Oswald's pubic hair to Jack Ruby's mother's dental x-rays, suggests that further information awaits him. His research trajectory has become asymptotic to the truth rather than an inexorable movement toward truth as an end point. *Libra* thus captures the *desire* for access to information and the investment in information as essential to democracy, but it rejects the cybernetic ideal of a message's existence in government information by questioning the state's status as an archive made knowable through public access. It challenges the notion that the state can choose or be forced to channel and control its streams of information. *Libra* also challenges the core concept of "government information" itself. The novel envisions a government whose information cannot be comprehensively archived and offers no coherent revelation, while it problematizes archiving itself by presenting it as a process of collection and sorting that itself affects the information it finds. *Libra* suggests that the regulatory apparatus requiring disclosure and allowing secrecy affects the state's development of information and production of information. If the state holds a document, the public must see it precisely because it is part of the state's archive; but the document and the archive as a whole fail to reveal a coherent truth.

This chapter considers how the state's quite complex and contextual process of producing and holding information undermines the notion that the government information that is disclosed or kept secret can serve as a message worthy of transmission or suppression. This thing called "government information" exists, of course, but only as a hypothetical ideal. It makes up a boundless archive that cannot be known. Most importantly, the archive cannot be fully disclosed or kept fully secret. I illustrate this below by discussing the difficulties created by the problem of conceptualizing and therefore controlling the government document, the sheer size of the government's archives, and the effects that the effort to keep information secret and to force its disclosure have on information's production and circulation in the bureaucratic state.

What Is a Document?

Just as legislatures and courts struggle with the state's amorphous, shifting boundaries, they similarly struggle with the amorphous nature of government documents. Defined broadly, documents are everywhere in the state—indeed, in all modern bureaucracies as well as in our personal lives, where the documentary traces we leave as we go through life (from birth certificates and driver's licenses through report cards, diplomas, résumés, work product and evaluations, tax returns and social service forms, to our final document—the death certificate) come to define us. Bureaucracies produce information to document what they observe and do, to record it for memory, and to communicate it both within and outside the entity to which they belong.

The practice of documentation, as the legal anthropologist Annelise Riles has discussed, encompasses a utopian vision of information and transparency in its ability to record all human activity everywhere.[11] Government bureaucracies build upon the presumed authority of documentation as a practice—the paper and electronic files that constitute the communicative abilities and power of the state to classify and track individuals—while they struggle with and cause their subjects to collapse under the errors, red tape, and informational overload that result. Terry Gilliam's film *Brazil* (1985) riotously and frighteningly parodied government bureaucracies that seem to produce documents as if that were their essential purpose, depicting oppressive modern governance as built upon unending reams of paper. The document has come to define state bureaucracy not only from the inside, given its importance for government's functioning, but also from the outside, as the preeminent symbol of bureaucracy's excess. Bureaucracy's official forms are the artifacts and symbols by which ordinary people must relate to the state.[12]

To better view the expansive role the document plays as a symbol in the government's functions, consider the definition of "records" in the Freedom of Information Act, which seeks to establish a broad category including materials of seemingly all sorts:

> "[R]ecords" includes all books, papers, maps, photographs, machine readable materials, or other documentary materials, regardless of physical form or characteristics, made or received by an agency of the United States Government under Federal law or in connection with the transaction of public business and preserved or appropriate for preservation by that agency or its legitimate successor as evidence of the organization, functions, policies, decisions, procedures, operations, or other activities of the Government or because of the informational value of data in them.[13]

Identifying the media that are subject to disclosure under FOIA, the definition broadly defines the information it seeks to free as the product of a rational organization acting logically to produce "evidence" and data with "informational value." As we have already seen in other contexts, however, courts have often narrowed and thereby undercut FOIA's formal breadth. Nicholas Branch might have been able to receive certain objects from the Curator, for example, but the public would not, given a court's ruling in 1971 affirming an agency's denial of a request from a medical pathologist who sought, among other things, Lee Oswald's rifle and the clothing that President Kennedy wore when he was assassinated. Because such items are "objects" rather than "writings," the court decided, they are not "records" subject to FOIA.[14]

That is not the only limit to the statute's broad definition. As the previous chapter discussed, some writings are themselves not "records" subject to FOIA because their provenance or location render them nonofficial. The statute's technical definition assumes that the state's writings contain information that will be freed upon their disclosure—they are "evidence" of the state's functions and operations, as the statutory definition quoted above notes, or they contain data of "informational value."

But a "record" is both more and less than a repository of a quantum of "information," and its disclosure will not mechanically transmit that information to its receiver. It is more than a repository because its meaning exceeds its content—a record's form and context both affect the content's latent meaning and themselves have independent meaning. It is less than a repository because a record's content might not be an accurate representation of an objective truth. The record signifies beyond its "evidence." Moreover, the fact that an object like Oswald's rifle is not subject to FOIA demonstrates the statute's limited understanding of government information. FOIA's technical concept of "record" fails to recognize the full universe of things the government produces and possesses that bear information. Despite its seeming breadth, it ignores the complex meanings of the things that the government holds.

To situate this critique of a "record" as the basis for transparency and secrecy, I want to return instead to the term "document" with which I began this discussion in order to illustrate the entire scope of the government's internal and external communications. In media historian Lisa Gitelman's terms, documents are the "epistemic objects" that serve as "the recognizable sites and subjects of interpretation across the disciplines and beyond, evidential structures in the long human history of clues."[15] Documents claim to reflect and represent knowledge, to know something by communicating it—hence the notion that they are "sites" where interpretation occurs. They show and communicate knowledge, serving as evidence that can constitute something official, especially when produced or held by the state.[16]

This broad understanding of "document" encompasses the entire universe of government files and warehouses and offices and hard drives and computing servers and clouds, as well as the verbal utterances made interpersonally or to colleagues or to the public that are not memorialized (because, as I explain below, such oral communications are important means by which government officials transmit information while avoiding the need to comply with legal disclosure requirements). Understood this way, documents could be anything that evidences something the state has done, even secret whispers—everything that might prove helpful to understand the state's operations, decisions, procedures, and motivations. Secrets, however they are contained (in paper, digital file, personal memory) are documents because, as the cultural theorist Clare Birchall has argued, secrecy is a practice that produces and attempts to hold information that is not reducible to a medium, to communication, or to a physical archive.[17]

By explicitly referring to interpretation in addition to "objects," "sites," and "subjects," Gitelman has expanded the concept of document beyond its apparent content. FOIA assumes, as it must in order to establish a mandate with which officials can comply, that a record's "informational value" is self-evident and that access to it will provide evidence of governmental action. But documents are not simply transparent bearers of meaning and value.[18] To make sense, documents must be interpreted. This is true even of data, which must be processed and contextualized in order to bear and communicate meaning.

Documents are also bureaucratic products and objects whose meaning and interpretation necessarily exist within an institutional context. Officials produce them with the intent that the documents will do something. Literary historian John Guillroy has distinguished the bureaucratic memorandum—the quintessential government document—from literary and journalistic writings as well as from scientific and scholarly writings because of the creators' intent to transmit information to a particular, often quite narrow audience. Literature and journalism, by contrast, purport to offer a notion of truth, while scientific and scholarly writings are oriented to discipline and knowledge.[19] Officials draft government documents to transmit information, inscribing power within an organization in the process. Memoranda may move data, analysis, and recommendations upward in an organizational hierarchy; they may carry directions downward; or they may memorialize some action or information for the files and be intended solely for posterity.[20] The traces of their trajectory through routing slips and the "from" and "to" line bear witness to those who have had access to this information, identifying responsibility and authority within the organization.[21] Other government documents also intend merely to transmit information outside the organization, announce rules, and serve as devices for data collection from applicants who seek services from the state, apply for employment, or bid on a contract.

By stating or following some rule or procedure that the organization has established, documents invoke the structural hierarchy in which they were produced. They serve as a means of bureaucratic control. They enable government entities to coordinate actions and information across organizational space and, in documents intended to flow from or to those outside the bureaucracy, communicate the state's relationship with its subjects, constituents, contractors, and vendors, as well as with other branches of the state and with other states.[22] Documents direct the institution across time as well, serving as a form of organizational memory that allows the future to know how officials have behaved in the past. As objects that speak to, about, and of the organization that holds them, government documents may be the products of a state bureaucracy, but their production and movement through the state help further *produce* that bureaucracy and the social and power relations within it.[23] Each document signifies more than the manifest content it contains. It is not merely self-evident.

Government documents also hew closely to form and genre—specifically, the replicable, formulaic nature of government paperwork and formal internal communication among government employees and officials. Bureaucratic rules, procedures, and routines organize the production and collection of documents. Some are entirely formalized, like pre-printed forms on paper or in a digital format (web forms or pdf documents) that offer empty spaces for a user or applicant to fill in with required information. Other documents follow generic structures, often beginning with an organization-specific template available in a word processing program or a format remembered from repeated use. Many government entities use particular forms for their meeting minutes or memoranda, for example, and employ letterhead for correspondence and for documents that are sent outside the organization or routinely made available to the public.

The degree of documentary standardization varies by organization, situation, and type of document, but very few if any government documents appear wholly new.[24] This standardization extends to a bureaucracy's conventional language, which develops through an agency's and individual's professional identity and the disciplinary conventions required of a profession's education. Government engineers, attorneys, urban planners, and scientists, for example, draft memoranda and other documents not only in the technical language through which they communicate to others with similar training but also according to conventions expected of the department to which they belong.[25] The CIA, for example, has its own style manual to instruct agency officers in "clear, concise writing" that speaks in the expected conventions of intelligence agents and analysts.[26]

Recent scholarship has gleaned two important insights from bureaucratic documents' form and their role as instruments. First, documents are material and social objects that reveal as much about the state and the conditions of their production as they carry and communicate information. The "way of handling files," the German legal historian Cornelia Vismann wrote, "contains its own bureaucracy."[27] At the time of their drafting, documents speak not only through their content but also in their form and their production, circulation, filing, and archiving. In the future, they will be read by different audiences in different contexts, audiences in the future that will know more and less than their authors did, because time has passed—and expected and unexpected events have occurred—while the original context has disappeared.

Second, their formal and instrumental characteristics render them as "inscriptions," in Bruno Latour's term, that claim immutability and mobility—mobile in the sense that they are capable of circulation across geographic and organizational space and immutable in the sense that they purport to remain identical as they circulate.[28] Their instrumental purpose requires these characteristics, and these characteristics in turn help produce their purpose. Documents must move and retain authority across geographic and organizational space. Their form enables this by imposing on them a structure that can communicate and be understood by those working above, below, and to the side of their putative author. As a result, their specific content—the information that they carry—must appear within a formal and institutional framework and will ultimately be subservient to that framework in order to be cognizable to the bureaucracy. Their status as bureaucratic objects matters.

Documents' immutability and instrumental purpose do not, however, mean that they achieve their purpose. Government documents may be intentional, but they cannot control their effects. Nor can they guarantee that they will have any effect at all. Consider the plight of government policy analysts toiling in executive branch agencies.[29] Their work seems highly meaningful and significant because they contribute to the development and evaluation of government decisions. But analysts must offer their descriptions of important issues facing government and policy prescriptions in an uncertain political and institutional environment.[30] They cannot know in advance how any conclusions they draw will be read. At the same time, they must draw such conclusions and offer policy prescriptions despite the ambiguity and uncertainty of the data upon which they must rely. Is their data comprehensive? Is it accurate? Is it current? Is it reflective of the current political climate and controversies? Does it support a particular conclusion or any conclusion? Will policymakers use their analysis—and, if so, will they use it in the way the analysts intended?

Meanwhile, analysts must collaborate with those above and below in their agency or department, and therefore their work requires some political acumen in understanding and deploying language that comports with the institution's and their superiors' expectations. The authors of policy documents—often several, working in an iterative process—write, edit, and rewrite with the hope but not certainty that the documents might be read, used, and transformed to meet future objectives. Accordingly, the government documents that offer policy analysis cannot and do not speak to some static, fundamental truth; rather, they are produced to meet and support certain preferred courses of use—preferences and courses that are subject to context and change after one document draft circulates. Government work occurs within the gaps caused by uncertainty, ambiguity, politics, and personal ambition. Do the resulting documents speak to a particular purpose that a reader can isolate? Does the information that the documents purport to know and show constitute a knowable truth?

Any particular government document, then, is not a singular iteration of information. A given digital file or printed artifact may be a final version of a document that has gone through many drafts, or it may be an early version of a document that has since been superseded. Documents have a "career," one structured by form, organization, and context; they also have a "life cycle," beginning in an early stage in the extraction of information that will go into a draft, through the document's creation and authoring, finalizing, distribution, use, and, ultimately, filing or archiving.[31] An individual document is alterable as it circulates, with each additional change proving traceable. Some degree of authority and authenticity may attach to an original, and each version may be immutable in the sense that any changes to it make it a different document recoverable only by a forensic analysis. Each document has numerous predecessors and successors, and each one is capable of being retained, destroyed, or lost.

The shift from paper to digital as a primary (though not exclusive) medium for document production and circulation only accentuates this process, loosening paper's specifically physical constraints that both enable and limit certain writing actions—what Jacques Derrida described as paper's "force of law."[32] Thus a digital file, unlike paper, might have a hundred or a thousand material versions, each one seemingly wiped with each new save command. That does not make the digital file merely ephemeral or even necessarily less tangible than a paper one.[33] In the midst of the Obama administration scandal over income tax enforcement, for example, the Internal Revenue Service claimed that e-mail sent and received by Lois Lerner, a key official in the IRS unit overseeing the tax-exempt status of nonprofit organizations, had been irrevocably destroyed—as though it had been shredded like a paper file.[34] Critics immediately contested the claim—surely some trace or copy remained, even if the IRS was telling the truth—and, indeed, the IRS's inspector general found copies in disaster backup tapes.[35]

Documents, in sum, float like an infinite number of snowflakes, the memorable nickname used for the memoranda Donald Rumsfeld circulated in the

Department of Defense, occasionally accumulating and constituting a mass but just as likely to disappear unnoticed once they hit ground.[36] Just as each document is not a singular iteration of information, it is many things. It is part of a boundless, hypothetical archive that cannot be collected. It may or may not be locatable or subject to disclosure by law. It contains information and has significance that exceeds its manifest content. It transmits information as well as commands, requests, analysis, and the like, but its ability to achieve its creators' purpose is contingent on the organization, the officials to which it is sent, and the moment of its circulation and recirculation. It may have no effect. It may be created with the intent that it would never be read and was destined from birth to sit in a file cabinet or on a hard drive. It may be read once and shredded, thrown in the (physical or digital) trash, or recycled. Traces of it may exist on a hard drive or a sent mail folder. But each document has the following, embedded within its inscription as an official government document: its latent content, the meaning of that content within a given bureaucratic and professional community at a particular moment, its predecessor and successor documents, the meaning of its form, and its navigation of social and power relations within the organization that produced and circulated it.

Documents Under Law

Legal regimes affect the production of information. Intellectual property rights do so most clearly. By defining and allowing the protection of certain kinds of texts and activities, intellectual property rights create incentives for certain kinds of creativity and disincentives for others. The extent and mechanics of protection structure the kinds of research and creativity that individuals and institutions undertake, and they affect the organization of technological production as well.[37] The rules of open government law similarly lead officials and agencies to behave in particular ways by exempting some documents from disclosure and requiring disclosure for others.

Officials can respond to open government requirements or discovery rules during litigation by deciding whether and how to communicate information in order to avoid the possibility of its unwanted exposure. They can shift the medium, classification, or content of information they produce in order to take advantage of the safe harbors provided by the exceptions to disclosure laws.[38] Thus, for example, members of a legislative or regulatory body subject to open meetings and public records laws may communicate by person-to-person oral communications or by meeting in less than a quorum so that the information

they produce falls outside the ambit of applicable state transparency requirements, or by holding fewer meetings with little substantive discussion.[39]

Laws can also affect the content of discussion among officials, as those who
fear disclosure requirements are less likely to air or memorialize dissenting
views. If they fail to preserve their views, those views will not become part of
government's official record.[40] "[W]hat is not in the records in the first place,"
Cornelia Vismann wrote, "can hardly be remembered. So if one does not want
an action in the real to become significant, it should not be recorded."[41] By
failing to memorialize information and therefore keeping it from becoming a
record, officials can intentionally separate the hypothetical archive of all "documents," understood broadly to include all forms of communication, from the
existing archive of available material records. When officials do so, the government's files cannot provide a full window into government data and operations.
Under a theory of transparency that assumes that the undocumented information is relevant and comprehensible to outsiders, such evasion should not be
allowed to occur.

The most direct and pernicious evasion of transparency norms occurs in
the classification system. As numerous reports from blue ribbon panels and external organizations have documented over the past six decades, officials with
the authority to classify records for national security purposes have used their
authority excessively since the classification system began.[42] Agencies widely
delegate to midlevel managers the authority to classify information within categories that restrict public access.[43] While in 2013 fewer than 59,000 records
were originally classified (that is, deemed by one of the more than 2,000 individuals with original classification authority as including information whose
unauthorized disclosure could reasonably be expected to cause damage to the
national security), more than 80,000,000 documents received derivative classification for incorporating, paraphrasing, or restating information that had previously received original classification designation.[44] Safely classifying a record
requires little more than fitting some of the document's information within
one of the broad and vague categories provided by the executive order establishing the classification system;[45] derivatively classifying the record requires,
at least in theory, little more than incorporating information that had been
originally classified into a new record.[46]

Officials may decide to classify the record for a number of reasons besides
or in addition to reasonably believing that it should properly be classified: to
avoid the risk associated with disclosure, often with a bias towards overestimat-

ing those risks in order to protect the organization and to shield the classifier from any reputational harm that could come from overdisclosure;[47] to seek political gain by keeping secret information that might harm an elected official, political appointee, or political party;[48] to hide an individual official's mistake or departmentwide incompetence;[49] or simply because the classifying official misunderstands classification policy.[50]

Consider, for example, the Bush administration and CIA's infamous use of classified information about Saddam Hussein's weapons of mass destruction (WMD) program in anticipation of the 2003 invasion of Iraq—first via a flawed National Intelligence Estimate (NIE) prepared for the Senate and then in Secretary of State Colin Powell's presentation to the United Nations Security Council.[51] Both warned about Iraq's advanced WMD program in order to build domestic and international support for the coming invasion. The intelligence that formed the NIE's basis represented the ultimate in classified information, much of it gleaned from human and signals sources whose compromise would harm U.S. interests and capabilities to gather future intelligence, and the administration even strictly limited Congress's access to it.[52] Later investigations, however, revealed the NIE's many flawed, unsupported conclusions, its mischaracterizations of the intelligence on which it relied, and its failure to acknowledge the uncertainties of its conclusions or to incorporate dissenting opinions.[53] There was no question, of course, that the flawed intelligence on which it was based could be classified. Rather, the episode demonstrated the pernicious way that government can selectively disclose information in order to shape public policy and public will.

Overclassification and selective declassification are bureaucratic practices—perhaps intentional, perhaps ingrained or reactive—that utilize law to protect information from disclosure. Tellingly, the inadvertent official release of classified documents is far rarer than the inadvertent official classification of information that does not warrant protection. A declassified 2004 Department of Energy study, for example, found that fewer than 1,600 of the 1.36 million pages of data related to nuclear weapons that had been publicly released by military departments between 1995 and 1999 contained information classified as "restricted data" or "formerly restricted data." The report also found that a significant portion of the small number of inadvertently released classified documents should not have been classified in the first place.[54] The tendency to overclassify and underdisclose is more prevalent than overdisclosure by mistake. But as I note in the next section, the mistaken release of classified information occurs nevertheless.

When an agency or an individual government official elects to protect information from disclosure, then, the agency or official is more likely to produce it in a form, circulate it by a method, and/or maintain or destroy it so that the information will either fall outside of disclosure requirements or avoid detection. As a result, no essential thing called government information exists that can be perfectly regulated to achieve transparency. The very fungibility of communication allows officials to gravitate toward or away from technologies and legal rules that will allow them to evade transparency. We might imagine that there is this thing called government information—indeed, we might imagine ourselves or the entire public acting as a Nicholas Branch, studying and deliberating about the meaning of the state's mass of documents. But it is merely a fantasy, based on a model that assumes the state can control and be forced to communicate itself and its inner workings.

The Implausibility of the State's Information Control

Transparency advocates do not hold a monopoly on this fantasy, however. The state may imagine that it can control information by creating and protecting its archive, but information leaks under the same conditions that make transparency difficult. Truly successful bureaucratic secrecy requires powerful group identity and a common cause—and even then, the protected secrets emerge over time.[55] Officials can decide not to reduce information to writing or decide to classify the information in order to keep it from disclosure, but they can also affirmatively decide both to memorialize information in documents that will later enable disclosure and to leak the documents in which the information has been memorialized.

Or they can share the information through spoken communication. High-ranking officials frequently provide information "off the record" or "not for attribution" to a reporter as part of a coordinated plan to communicate with, cajole, or pressure outsiders—including other agencies and branches of government, political parties, private interests, and the general public, for example—or to burnish their personal reputations.[56] Such leaks are pervasive in Washington, ubiquitous elements in a competitive democratic system served by competitive private news organizations.[57] They are only "unauthorized" insofar as they provide information in an informal manner, outside of official channels and formal disclosure processes. These reciprocal relationships between source and press allow officials to trade information in exchange for publicity, information, and status, among other things.[58]

Unlike the high-level leakers or their agents who bear little or no risk of reprisal or prosecution, informal leaks made outside of the bureaucratic or political command chain—or, worse, in specific opposition to the state or administration—bear some risk of prosecution. Government employees enjoy little legal protection from retaliation by their employers when the employees' actions are not subject to statutory whistleblower protection. And when their leaks contain classified information, they may face prosecution under the Espionage Act and the Intelligence Agencies Identity Protection Act.[59] The First Amendment offers leakers only thin protection, if it provides any protection at all,[60] and the reporters to whom they leak enjoy no First Amendment right to shield their sources' identities—although they may have a limited common law federal right to do so, as well as statutory rights in some states.[61] The news organizations that publish leaks enjoy First Amendment protection against prior restraint,[62] although they may still face prosecution under the Espionage Act for leaks of classified information.[63] Prosecutions for illegal disclosures are difficult for the government to win, but the threat of prosecution and the cost of mounting a criminal defense might nevertheless be sufficient to deter many from leaking.[64]

And yet—despite minimal legal protection from retaliation and prosecution, and with all of the punishments and constraints that further increase the risks and costs that government employees face in leaking information—unauthorized disclosures by midlevel government personnel are common.[65] For decades, internal government reports have regularly complained of the prevalence of classified information leaks[66]—the most embarrassing leaks for the government and the ones for which leakers face the greatest risks of punishment and prosecution. Indeed, this phenomenon is as old as the nation itself.[67] It occurred even in the Nixon administration, which sprung numerous unauthorized leaks despite its illegal efforts to stop them.[68]

Leaks do not offer a systemic antidote for defeating the state's excessive protection of its archive—indeed, they are not a system at all. They occur somewhat randomly, and the leaked documents are partial and decontextualized, while the media to whom sources leak are unregulated and largely unaccountable, except by professional norms of conduct and as market actors.[69] The personal and institutional competition that drives journalists and their editors towards the scoop can render their reporting biased, partial, or even factually incorrect.[70] As a system of information control, they under- and overdisclose depending upon individual officials' willingness to risk leaking and the government's ability to stop them. Nevertheless, leaks commonly and regularly move information from the state, undercutting efforts to build and control the state's archive and raising the costs and risks of secrecy.

The CIA aspires to complete control of its information, taking full advantage of relevant FOIA exemptions for properly classified information and for information exempt from disclosure under other statutes that specifically apply to the agency—in the CIA's case, the National Security Act of 1947 and the CIA Information Act of 1984, which allow the agency director to exempt even from searching any "operational files."[71] It produces its own internal histories and its own academic journal (declassified portions of which are made available to the public), while it tightly controls access to its archives and engages in bureaucratic struggles with other agencies (most notably the State Department) to keep documents secret.[72] An actual Office of the Curator at the CIA, quite different from the one that *Libra* imagines, directs the CIA Museum, which "supports the Agency's operational, recruitment and training missions and helps visitors better understand CIA and its contributions to national security."[73] As the CIA website cautions its visitors, however, "because the Museum is located on the CIA compound, it is not open to the public for tours."[74] The curious can enjoy the limited offerings of declassified documents on the agency's website and the videos it has posted to YouTube. The CIA's museum and its treasure chest of documents, in sum, are only available to the CIA and those few with sufficient clearance to access them.

But the CIA's presentation of itself as a hermetically sealed information vault belies the difficulty in holding even the most protected secrets. Its archive might be officially off-limits, but its history is available in broad outline and in great detail, even if not in full, absolute detail. Indeed, as Timothy Melley has explained, the "covert sphere" that the CIA and other intelligence and national security agencies occupy is in fact exceptionally public not only via leaks but through intentional disclosures by intelligence agencies and through popular fiction, which offers covert action and intelligence as a source of "mystery, fascination, speculation, and anxious projection."[75] Consider two examples of these officially and unofficially publicized secrets: the Obama administration's coordinated access to information about the raid on Osama bin Laden's hiding place in Pakistan for the makers of *Zero Dark Thirty* (2012), a film that positively portrayed the action, even as federal agencies refused to disclose the same documents in response to FOIA requests;[76] and a 2015 *New York Times* front-page story entitled "The Secret History of SEAL Team 6," which extensively reported on the Navy's elite, highly secretive counterterrorism unit based on information gleaned from anonymous sources, government documents, and open sources like memoirs and books.[77]

Leaks at least require an affirmative, intentional act; sometimes, however, bureaucracies also allow information to escape by mistake. Lax security, for example, has resulted in unauthorized information disclosure by allowing dissidents to access, remove, and copy secret material. This occasionally results in the equivalent of leaks, though on a massive scale, as in the Ellsberg, Manning, and Snowden cases. In each instance, the state had granted or enabled individual employees to access classified information; the employees grew disillusioned; and they took advantage of their access to copy classified documents, which their superiors and the information security system failed to notice. Although the leaks were intentional, they were the consequence of mistaken trust and insufficient security, especially in Manning's case.[78]

Mistakenly allowing malfeasance is just one bureaucratic failure; sometimes, officials disclose information by simple mistake or inadvertence.[79] As Dana Priest and William Arkin have documented, large quantities of classified and sensitive information are available via simple web searches and peer-to-peer file sharing software, often as a result of government employees' insufficient security measures.[80] In one recent example, the NSA mistakenly posted an unredacted version of a classified internal research article and then hastily declassified it in order to cover up the agency's error.[81] In another, a contractor hired by the Food and Drug Administration mistakenly posted on a public website documents produced in a vast surveillance program that the agency had undertaken to monitor the e-mail traffic of several dissident employees.[82] Mistaken and inadvertent disclosures are not systematic, and many of them are never spotted or exploited, but in the aggregate they undercut government efforts to keep information secret. Whether kept in electronic form and therefore vulnerable to easy transfer by mistake or theft, or stored in someone's memory and capable of being spoken, information is akin to liquid—capable of flowing from the place it is stored in directions and at a speed that make it impossible to fully control.[83]

The universe of information that constitutes the secrets that the state protects also includes information that is available from non-state sources. Indeed, the intelligence community has increasingly relied on what is called "open source intelligence"—information gathered from widely available sources, including mass media, government entities, and academic and professional journals.[84] The fact that it is "open" does not keep it from becoming "secret," at least as a matter of law. The government has argued, with some success in the courts, that the open information that it gathers can become secret when it is classified as a source, on the theory that disclosure of the state's use of that information for national security purposes would allow the state's enemies to learn its sources and piece together its knowledge and methods.[85] No matter how one views the government's claim that it can transform the open into the secret merely by possessing it, the existence of open source intelligence makes plain some salient facts: A great deal of valuable information exists and flows outside of the state's ambit, and many of the state's secrets are themselves based on public information.[86]

Covert operations, for example, are the most secret of a state's actions, and the actions that the state most assiduously attempts to keep secret; yet they are not secret. Covert actions produce an enormous number of internal documents sent by and to management and operations personnel that the state can at least theoretically control. But the state cannot easily control official information that it does not possess.[87] A covert operation will have real world effects that civilian witnesses and the local news media can observe (which may provide the basis for reports and investigations by broader media sources that receive international distribution) and that government officials (whose rule is being challenged) and officials of other states can discover. Put simply, covert actions are not secret to those against whom they are deployed or who witness them. Journalists and then the public first learned about the CIA's post–9/11 "rendition" program, by which suspected terrorists were flown to various locations via private jets, through foreign newspapers, private websites run by aviation enthusiasts, and human rights advocates, all of them relying on public sources of information and eyewitnesses.[88] Any informational sources outside of the state's control that duplicate a secret state document or make available its content, or that allow outsiders to infer some secret, lessen the state's ability to keep secrets.

Finally, the very act of publicly keeping secrets—that is, of controlling information in a manner that allows the public to know of the secrecy process—itself creates information *about* secrecy, as well as speculation about what the secrets contain. To help understand these phenomena, assume the existence of both known and unknown secrets. The first category ("known-unknowns") includes information that the government is known to possess; all that is secret is the precise content of the information. A publicly declared military operation will have numerous operational secrets; the public knows that such operations exist and assumes the existence of secrets regarding those operations. Indeed, controlling such secrecy is a long and widely accepted prerogative of the president—it is as clear an application of the privilege doctrine as exists.[89] Nevertheless, the content of such secrets can be the subject of speculation, as can the steps the military and government take to control information about their operations. In the second category ("unknown-unknowns") is information whose very existence is unknown, such as a covert operation of which the public has not become aware. The secrecy of such a program is complete and deep—the public is not even aware of its own ignorance, and thus cannot speculate about its context.[90]

Now, assume that at some point after a covert operation's completion or after the start of a secret surveillance program, the public learns of its existence, whether from official, authorized disclosures or via leaks or open sources. Many such deep secrets migrate to the known-secrets category over time by the means that this chapter and the previous one identified (legal disclosure mandates, leaks, mistakes, and open sources). In the process, deep secrets are either disclosed or become known-unknowns (i.e., secrets about a known event), and some of them can be inferred from disclosed information. Having learned of this covert operation or secret program, the public has also become aware of the government's willingness to keep information secret and its capability of doing so.

Two consequences flow from this. First, informed members of the public, and especially the press, will infer—from the fact of the past covert operation or secret program and from the knowledge that certain kinds of secrets were kept—that the government might have engaged in or might be developing similar operations. Some investigative reporters and interested individuals will try to uncover any such additional operations. Their efforts might prove easier now that the first operation has become public. Some government officials who are troubled either by another operation or by its secrecy might be more willing to leak information to the press about the additional operation(s), while reporters will now have a better sense not only of what to look for but of where to look and whom to ask. Perhaps the operation's previous success at maintaining control over information proves difficult to repeat, or the circle of individuals included in the covert group widens, increasing the likelihood of leaks and mistakes. The unknown-unknowns will thereby become more difficult to keep secret.

And now that the broader, less-informed public knows that such secret programs exist, some of them, and particularly those opposed to the current government, will begin to speculate about additional secret programs. Their speculation might be wrong, perhaps even wildly wrong, but it can affect the government's broader legitimacy and especially the legitimacy of its secret programs.[91] As the sociologist Georg Simmel wrote, "The natural impulse to idealization, and the natural timidity of men, operate to one and the same end in the presence of secrecy; viz., to heighten it by phantasy, and to distinguish it by a degree of attention that published reality could not command."[92]

Efforts to keep secrets cannot stop the production of information and of meaning about government actions, which in turn constitutes part of the archive of government information, whether it is actual or not. These efforts can control certain types of information about "deep secrets" of which the public is fully ignorant, so long as that information exists in stored media that can be protected. But the state's success in doing so may prove only temporary. Once its extraordinary efforts to retain secrets are revealed—that is, once the government can no longer control information about its own secrecy—the state faces greater resistance against its further efforts to control the flow of government information. The state must now satisfy a more skeptical public that, at least temporarily, is more prone to speculation and investigation.[93] In this regard, the practice of keeping secrets itself constitutes information that both shapes and becomes part of the state's hypothetical, boundless archive.

. . .

The problem that the JFK assassination presents to those who wish to solve its puzzle is not the lack of information but its surplus. This is not just Nicholas Branch's problem; it is also a problem for the public as well as for the state itself. With so many documents (defined, as I have argued in this chapter, as broadly as possible) and so many official and unofficial efforts to synthesize and comment upon these documents, the assassination produces no single meaning. The state's information, as Lawrence Lessig noted in a narrower context about the raw information produced by campaign finance disclosures, is incomplete: It says too much to be fully understood and too little by providing only partial information about complex relationships.[94] This is true of any significant action in which the government plays a role—which is to say, many, many actions. The archive of these actions is potentially infinite. It cannot be assembled; nor, even in its partial collection in government files and hard drives, can it be fully controlled.

6 Disclosure's Effects?

The disclosure of government information must surely make a difference to justify the enormous effort to open the government or to keep parts of it secret. The cybernetic model assumes as much: It views disclosure as a message intentionally released by the sender that will reach the receiver and cause some cognitive and behavioral change. As we have seen, myriad laws and a large international community of transparency advocates also presume such effects, as does most academic commentary on the subject. Government information *must* transform the ignorant public into an informed one; or, alternatively, it *must* reveal something of significance to someone who will use it to harm the state, its operations, or some third party.

Consider WikiLeaks' description of transparency's promise:

> Publishing [leaked material] improves transparency, and this transparency creates a better society for all people. Better scrutiny leads to reduced corruption and stronger democracies in all society's institutions, including government, corporations and other organisations. A healthy, vibrant and inquisitive journalistic media plays a vital role in achieving these goals.[1]

Asserting that it is "part of that media" that spreads transparency, WikiLeaks contends that its publication of authentic documents leaked from governments and powerful private entities will expose "otherwise unaccountable and secretive institutions" that engage in unethical acts and thereby help establish "good government and a healthy society," "alter the course of history in the present, and . . . lead us to a better future."[2] This sequential narrative—in which information disclosure leads to a more engaged public, more democratic politics, and a more efficient state—forms a core tenet of the transparency ideal. Information *transforms* the public and state; therefore, it must be disclosed.

Secrecy advocates hold the opposite view, fearing that the communication of secret information directly affects its receivers and causes them to act in particular, predictably dangerous ways.[3] The classification system is premised upon anticipating risk by sorting documents into the categories of "confidential," "secret," or "top secret," based on the conclusion that the information these documents contain "reasonably could be expected to cause," respectively, "damage," "serious damage," or "exceptionally grave damage" to national security.[4] The Department of Defense manual on classification instructs those with classification authority to ask themselves the following questions as they make their classification decisions:

> What is the level of damage (i.e., damage, serious damage, or exceptionally grave damage) to the national security expected in the event of an unauthorized disclosure of the information? If the answer to this question is damage, classify the information "Confidential." If the answer is serious damage, classify it "Secret." If the answer is exceptionally grave damage, classify the information "Top Secret."[5]

FOIA permits agencies to refuse to disclose classified information, the Espionage Act criminalizes its unauthorized disclosure, and the Constitution's executive privilege and state secret doctrines grant the president authority to withhold information—all under the assumption that disclosure will harm the nation.[6]

Information's transformative power justifies the struggle to control it. Faced with an informational dispute, courts ask whether, in the words of constitutional law scholar Geoffrey Stone, "the value of the disclosure to informed public deliberation outweigh[s] its danger to the national security."[7] Legislatures and courts thus assume, first, that such benefits and costs not only occur but that they can be accounted for and weighted, and second, that such a rough prediction about the future can serve as the basis upon which courts balance and protect the values of an informed public and a secure nation. Faith in information's transformative power sustains efforts both to reveal and to control government information. This faith demands that open government laws recognize a presumption of disclosure while exceptions from disclosure allow for greater state control in certain circumstances.

Disclosure no doubt has some impact. But its effects are neither necessary nor predictable. I ask three questions in this chapter to guide an inquiry into these effects: First, is the public capable of responding rationally and knowledgeably to disclosure? Second, does the public even exist in some discernible form? These two questions pose the core challenge to transparency and secrecy. Critics of the public's ability and willingness to understand the state, as well as humanists and social scientists who study the public's interpretive practices and cognitive limitations, challenge not only the assumption that the public is capable of understanding state information but also the idea that a "public" even exists in some identifiable form. The third question asks whether institutions of various sorts—those state and private organizations that serve on the public's behalf or might undermine the nation's security and well-being—have the capacity to respond to disclosure in rational and predictable ways. To assume that these institutions can do so requires the prior assumption that they too have the capacity to understand and respond rationally to government information—assumptions that rest on a shaky foundation.

Is the Public Ignorant?

Polling seems to reveal an ignorant public, one that misunderstands or pays no attention to uncontested topics for which government information is widely available. Polls regularly find alarming percentages of the public who appear unwilling or unable to incorporate basic, broadly accepted factual information about elementary issues essential to making informed decisions regarding politics and civil society. The public is generally ignorant about the basic structures of government (including the federal government's three branches and the relationships among federal, state, and local governments), ideological distinctions between the two main political parties, and the key policy debates of the day that divide the parties and individual candidates.[8]

Consider also the extent to which U.S. public opinion about the justifications for the 2003 American invasion of Iraq following the September 11 attacks conflicted with information the government has released that the press has discussed extensively. Trusting the claims made by President Bush and his cabinet, a large majority of the public initially believed that Iraq's President Saddam Hussein had developed a viable WMD program.[9] But even in the face of post-invasion, authoritative government reports from a bipartisan commission and

a Pentagon- and CIA-organized mission to Iraq,[10] the public continued to believe the CIA's and Bush administration's misrepresentations of the extent and
significance of the intelligence upon which they had relied.[11]

Wide swaths of the public also continued to believe the Bush administration's pre-war claims that Saddam Hussein had strong ties to al Qaeda, despite
authoritative evidence to the contrary from the best-selling *9/11 Commission
Report*, released in 2004, as well as from well-circulated reports issued by Congress, the Pentagon, and the CIA (many of which were then reported on extensively by the news media).[12] Enactment of the Freedom of Information Act and
other open government laws do not seem to have enabled the development of
better citizens and a more deliberative, rational public.

No doubt these polls are in part finding beliefs anchored in partisan disagreement. Democrats and leftists will tell the story of the Bush administration's decision to go to war and its effort to support that decision (as well as the
war's consequences) quite differently from Republicans. Political disputes often
underlie factual disputes, such as on policy issues like the effects of high corporate taxes and the minimum wage, where different priorities and preferences
might lead individuals to believe or trust particular ways of understanding issues and to gravitate toward studies that reach certain conclusions. But partisanship also affects many people's willingness to acknowledge the existence of
facts that would contradict the presumptions of their beliefs.

Public misperception or ignorance, which is not unique to the United
States,[13] attaches to complex public issues in which a combination of contested
fact and existing moral or political commitments lead individuals to choose an
opinion based on a mix of faith and conjecture. Scientific controversies generate opinions about human health and safety that can prove impervious to
factual challenges; the debates and opinions about genetically modified organ-
isms and childhood vaccines are good examples of issues that not only generate
more heat than light but that also reflect deeply held fears and suspicions about
scientific and governmental authority. The public also has a tendency to believe
in conspiracy theories of various types, from President Obama's forged birth
certificate to President Bush's role in the 9/11 attacks—another tendency that
is more prominent among mainstream members of the Republican Party than
among mainstream Democrats but that is so pervasive that it is neither necessarily left- nor rightwing.[14] Such theories build upon public documents and
government information but interpret them in ways that stray from the documents' intent and meaning, finding plots or malfeasance based on the thinnest

of evidence. The public's willingness to hold opinions that seem at best resistant to refutation and at worst impervious to fact confounds the hopes of transparency advocates and the worries of those who warn of the need for secrecy.

The libertarian scholars Ilya Somin and Bryan Caplan have added important nuance to this notion of a public that is merely stupid.[15] They have argued that individuals are not so much incapable of understanding political information as they are understandably unwilling to invest the time and resources necessary to understand complex political issues. For Somin, the public's ignorance is rational, as it takes an enormous investment of time and effort to be properly informed; for Caplan, the public's ignorance arises from individuals' irrational responses to emotion and ideology. If, as Somin and Caplan claim, the public is unable or structurally unwilling to obtain and process information, then it is incapable of governing a large modern state. As a consequence, there is no functional market for state information; therefore, its disclosure need not serve as a primary administrative norm, since it does no apparent good. Perhaps there has never been a truly knowing public, or at least the public's moment has receded into the far past when a small, well-educated and well-informed polity was fully capable of understanding the state and desirous of gaining information about its actions.

From Ignorance to Interpretation and Cognition

Ignorance is a complex phenomenon, however. Ignorance and knowledge have a fluid relationship; the excess of available information limits the ability to know and understand any part of the state and its operations.[16] Ignorance could be an error of distorted knowledge, in which an individual's confused or inaccurate knowledge is the result of her own mistake or of a strategic ploy. And the absence of knowledge—the epistemological "blank slate" caused either by lack of access to information or an individual decision not to be informed— is merely one state of ignorance. Someone might not know a supposed fact because she has no access to knowledge about it, misinterprets it, has access only to a distorted version of it, or because the fact itself is uncertain or ambiguous.[17]

Viewed this way, ignorance is "something that is made, maintained, and manipulated by means of certain arts and sciences," as the historian of science Robert Proctor has written.[18] Loosely grouped in recent years within the interdisciplinary field of agnotology and inspired by Proctor's work, the study of ignorance leads to two key insights: that ignorance is socially constructed and that it is an essential and pervasive component in social relations, organizations, and culture.[19] Ignorance is made—made by larger social structures, the accessibility of information, individual conscious and unconscious decisions, and a host of other conditions.

Put in the context of the underlying cybernetic model of information and communication, the process by which the public receives government information is filled with "noise," random disturbances introduced by something other than the communicator that inhibit the perfect transmission of information.[20] Noise is not external to the communicative act; context and imperfect human interpretation define the public's interaction with political information and keep the public from perfect knowledge and competence.[21] And if ignorance is social and the result of complex conditions, then information's mere availability might have no necessary effect, or its effects will be contingent on the conditions under which it is released, received, and interpreted. Understanding ignorance too simply, then, misunderstands the role of information in politics and law. People are neither a blank slate waiting to be filled by marginal increases in information, nor are they incapable of adding information to their pool of knowledge.

Humanistic theories of signification and interpretation and social scientific theories of cognition support these insights into ignorance. Literary and cultural theories of "signification"—from the structuralism of semiotics through poststructuralism and postmodernism—have detailed the complexity (and, in some theories, impossibility) of textual meaning production.[22] Texts, language, and symbols are not stable repositories of meaning that move objective data from a sender to a receiver's blank slate. There is no necessary correspondence between a text—whether produced by a novelist or filmmaker or by a government official writing or speaking "government information"—and its reader or audience or the public that may receive it. The intermediary in the transaction—the novel or film, or the document or meeting that contains "government information"—is not a static thing with one stable meaning.[23] Given the complex process of translating data and information between institutional contexts and the different historical and social contexts of the text's production and its interpretation, "government information" has no pure, essential form.[24] Readers bring to the text any number of social and individual characteristics, as well as their own experiences and practices.[25] Disclosure, then, is not a simple process of transmission to a public; instead, different publics, composed of diverse individuals, make sense of and even contest a text's meaning. The communicative and cultural processes by which individuals decode disclosed government information result in multiple interpretations that in turn have multiple, often anticipated effects, or no effect at all.

Cognitive and social psychology support this conclusion from a quite different methodological and disciplinary perspective by reaching a parallel if not identical conclusion regarding the interaction between information and receiver. The field presumes individuals' bounded rationality—the fact that they interpret information and make judgments and decisions under imperfect conditions marked by the uncertainty of the information they have, as well as the limited time and cognitive capacity they bring to their interaction with information.[26] As a result, individuals must rely upon the heuristic devices, or rules of thumb, that shape their judgment processes and lead to reflexive, often inaccurate perceptions.[27]

The most common and benign heuristics are the ready social labels attached to political candidates, party affiliation, endorsements, and ideological markers ("conservative," "liberal") that individuals use to form opinions and cast votes in relatively rational and informed ways.[28] Such shortcuts do not, however, necessarily help individuals to understand and decide on positions regarding complicated matters of national and political importance for which clear heuristic cues are unavailable.[29] In addition, cognitive biases often lead individuals to seek information that is partial and partisan and that will confirm their existing beliefs, without any effort to seek disconfirming and perhaps more authoritative sources.[30] This proves true of less sophisticated voters, who are more likely to misuse or derive incorrect conclusions about the political information to which they are exposed.[31] But it also proves true among those voters who are the most educated about political positions, because their knowledge frequently arises from the very partisan commitments that lead them to become closed-minded ideologues.[32] While more constrained than humanistic approaches, cognitive theories of reception and belief similarly contradict the assumption that the public can interpret government information in a deliberative manner and can make perfect, instrumental uses of seemingly objective information.

Taking these cognitive shortcomings into account, scholars have identified policy innovations that they claim enable the public, in certain circumstances, to overcome the bounded nature of individuals' rationality. After illuminating the public's ignorance about the state and its operations in her book *The Submerged State*, for example, Suzanne Mettler noted that the effective delivery of information can help develop a more knowledgeable public—for instance, when the Social Security Administration informed individuals about the value of their benefits, their knowledge about and confidence in the program rose.[33] Archon Fung and his coauthors have called for "targeted transparency"—efforts to disclose information intended to achieve a specific policy purpose and that require specified disclosers to communicate to the public a limited scope of highly structured information via an identified vehicle.[34] Rather than access, their vision of transparency calls for limited, focused informational regulations that can effectively assist individuals in making better choices in fields like personal finance, workplace safety, and nutrition.[35] Providing information to inform highly motivated, personally consequential decisions is quite distinct from releasing masses of state information to assist citizens in their voting decisions or in holding officials accountable, however. And even targeted disclosure might not be sufficient to overcome individuals' shortcomings. Omri Ben-Shahar and Carl Schneider have argued that regulatory programs focused on mandated disclosure have not proven as effective as their proponents claim, given the relative illiteracy and inattention that individuals bring to the disclosures presented to them, the sheer quantity of such disclosures, and the cognitively complex and unexpected ways people read the information they are given.[36]

By taking into account context, interpretive practices, and cognition, these more complex understandings of public information processing similarly undermine the cybernetic theory of government information. There is no receiver/public awaiting illumination, prepared to be informed and act rationally and predictably in response to a disclosed message. Public ignorance will not disappear if information can finally flow. Although these theories posit that individuals have the capacity to grapple with disclosure, "grapple" is not the same as simply "receive." If ignorance has multiple causes, and if the interpretive and cognitive processes are complex and uncertain, then information disclosure can have effects, but it cannot, by itself, transform.

Does the "Public" Exist?

Public opinion and knowledge is one measure of whether disclosure helps the public engage informatively in democratic governance, but opinion and knowledge will only have such an effect if individuals who are concerned about the state can find each other, ally or at least coordinate, and participate in meaningful political activity. They must act as political subjects who deliberate over and engage with their government in a public sphere composed of accountable state entities, debates in public fora (like public squares and printed and electronic media), and the ballot box. They must act collectively, or at least cooperatively. The *public*'s existence and ability to act is therefore separate from *individual* ignorance—though the former is related to and builds upon the latter. Individuals might understand and respond to disclosed information, but unless they can act through and with a broader public, their illumination will have limited effects.

Of an Illusory or Nascent Public

Throughout the twentieth century, political and social theorists have struggled with identifying, understanding, and trying to improve the performance of a public whose opinions about and connection to politics seem inadequate to the task of a democratic citizenry. A key debate in the early twentieth century between the preeminent public intellectuals Walter Lippmann and John Dewey exemplifies the issues created by the public's apparent ignorance and its weakening as a subject in modern mass politics. Though skeptical of the democratic public's existence as an identifiable, coherent entity, Lippmann and Dewey directed their overlapping critique of the public in distinctive directions, each refusing in his own way to conclude that the public's seeming disappearance renders democracy (and therefore the need for transparency) utterly obsolete.[37] Their two distinct approaches to the public's existence constitute useful positions from which to consider whether the public can in fact act as a political subject and active receiver of government information.

Writing first and for a popular audience that knew him as an early and influential pundit, Lippmann attacked the dominant, ideal vision of the public as a rational, coherent collective that a functional array of political and social institutions helps shape into responsible democratic actors. The citizen ideal of the public is illusory—it is, he wrote, "inexpert in its curiosity, intermittent, . . . it discerns only gross distinctions, is slow to be aroused and quickly diverted; . . . and is interested only when events have been melodramatized as a conflict."[38] Modernity had rendered obsolete the traditional conception of a rational democratic order that can produce functional, popularly accountable political institutions; instead, members of the public interpret the world and government through stereotypes and sentiments that flow from the mental images and fictions they carry.[39] The solution to this distance, Lippmann argued in *Public Opinion* (1922), was to delegate the role of political accountability to experts in "intelligence bureaus" who could gather and process information about the world and the state and who would advise elected officials on policy matters and how best to govern.[40] An embodiment of early twentieth-century progressivism's embrace of expertise, *Public Opinion* called for limiting popular democratic accountability to the review of bureaucratic fact-finding. When informed by voluntary societies and other institutions of civil society including academics and the press, the public could judge expert and political performance by its results and both signal and enforce their preference through the "occasional mobilizations" of popular will in elections.[41] In a time of crisis, public opinion could be mobilized to displace tyrannical rulers in the best circumstances: under sound leadership and with the right amount of education. Lippmann's public was incapable, however, of governing itself directly.[42]

In the immediate post-war period, theorists shared his skepticism and argued that the concept of an attentive and competent public was impossible to attain in a mass-mediated world. Responding to the rise of Cold War politics and the industrial production and consumption of culture, these critics feared the development of an authoritarian state from within an American public that they saw as rendered anxious, isolated, conformist, and alienated by the mass media.[43] Post-war intellectuals who further developed this concept—including the social scientists C. Wright Mills and David Riesman and the cultural critic Dwight MacDonald—feared the combination of new developments in post-war modernity: the political control that an impersonal, mediated mass democracy (enabled by what Mills famously called the "power elite"); the social alienation of the masses within a modern industrial economy, lonely urban environments, and the newly sprawling post-war suburbs; and the consolidation of information control that the industrial production and distribution of the mass media allowed.[44]

Although political centrists described the mass public as part of a Cold War consensus that represented an "end of ideology"[45] and as signaling the triumph of a functional pluralist democracy rather than creeping fascism,[46] they also shared some of the mass society critics' concerns about the relationship between post-war mass politics and the rise of McCarthyism and the "radical right" in the early 1960s.[47] At the same time, a conservative tradition that included the philosopher José Ortega y Gasset, the economist Joseph Schumpeter, and the sociologist Vilfredo Pareto decried the pernicious effects of an excessive democracy controlled by an unfettered, irrational public will.[48]

All of these worried intellectuals—conservatives afraid of the ignorant masses' threat to the social order, centrist liberal pluralists who perceived extremist authoritarianism as threatening the post-war triumph of representative democracy and the capitalist market, and leftist intellectuals fearful of the rise of a corrupt power elite and ignorant, neo-fascist masses—presumed to varying degrees the possibility of a largely passive public that was subject to, or potentially subject to, the vagaries of the market and the madness of mass politics.[49] They shared Lippmann's view that the public, if it existed at all, was ill-prepared to act on political information and incapable of doing so. Even if individuals could respond to political information, their efforts would be stymied by the lack of larger social and political channels through which a broader public could challenge the existing order and reform the state.

The fear of a mass public continued later in the century and into the present. On the left, the critique of propaganda (associated most strongly with Jacques Ellul[50]), the most simplistic and instrumental Marxist understanding of ideology,[51] and Murray Edelman's influential work on the quiescence caused by the symbolic uses of politics[52] all asserted that the public's passivity is caused in large part by false or partial information that leads it to accept the existing ruling order. Leftist critics of the political economy of the media identified the culture industries as key agents in creating this ignorance, whether by instrumental alliance or simply by applying the logic of capitalism. A few small corporate interests whose power the state protects manage the news, concealing the information that the public needs to grasp the full extent of its own ignorance; in exchange, these corporate interests provide audiences with distracting entertainment.[53] Under these conditions, existing exploitative social structures simply reproduce themselves with the masses' consent; unreleased government information is an effect rather than the cause of a mass society, and its release will not automatically change the larger social and political structures that create and maintain that society.

Dewey offered a different way of viewing the public's shortcomings and potential. Reviewing *Public Opinion* and *The Phantom Public* in *The New Republic*, Dewey praised and largely adopted Lippmann's theory of the public—praise that he restated in *The Public and Its Problems* (1927); in this work he described the public as seeming "lost" and "certainly bewildered"; he also declared the idea of the "omni-competent" individual capable of understanding politics an "illusion" and argued that the belief in a public rationally concerned with the state and its policies was merely "superstitious."[54] Like Lippmann, Dewey viewed the present public as being in "eclipse" (p. 126) and too busy seeking amusement to rouse itself from its diffuse, scattered individual and collective activities and interests (pp. 137–139). But unlike Lippmann, Dewey hoped for a "great community" that would summon the public to wakefulness and being, one that could solve the public's eclipse with more rather than less democracy (pp. 146–147). Democracy's educative function could enable the public to recognize its common interests by spurring public discussion and public spirit (p. 207).

Like Lippmann, Dewey recognized the need for experts to improve the quality and information of "debate, discussion and persuasion," but he would have granted experts only the authority to "judge the bearing of the knowledge supplied by others upon common concerns" and to police the quality of information available to the public that would form the basis for its communitarian discussion (pp. 208–209).[55] Unlike the more skeptical Lippmann, Dewey viewed the public as capable of emerging under the right political and social circumstances.

As with later intellectual skeptics of the public who followed Lippmann's concept of an illusory public, a number of prominent intellectuals have carried on Dewey's ideas of an imperfect public that is prepared and ready to progress and improve. Deliberative democrats recognize Dewey's pragmatism and theory of the public as an important predecessor,[56] while Habermas's theory of communicative action as a means for increasing civic competence and enhancing the public sphere and deliberation also follows the centrality of communication in Dewey's theory of the public and community.[57] More explicitly, communications theorist James Carey relied heavily on Dewey's ideas to argue on behalf of the public's potential to engage in and with politics, and to inspire the "public journalism" movement, which attempts to develop an "ethic of citizenship" to broaden public knowledge and democratic engagement.[58]

Lippmann and Dewey's parallel but distinct understandings of the public led them to different, though related, views of government secrecy and publicity. Lippmann asserted that the public had limited interest in and capacity for political information. Under such conditions, secrecy did not cause the public to lose access to a necessary resource; distracted, amused by entertainment and personal concerns rather than politics, the people "cannot really be said to suffer from censorship, or secrecy, the high cost or the difficulty of communication."[59] Nevertheless, Lippmann did not embrace a broad secrecy privilege. His expert bureaus, with their "most extraordinary" focus on information, would serve as the public's agents (albeit unelected and only barely accountable ones) and for that reason should have access to all but "a few diplomatic and military secrets."[60] The public might neither want nor need direct access to government information, but independent experts who can hold the state accountable do.

Dewey's approach to government information considered publicity and therefore access to government information to be essential to the "debate, discussion and persuasion" necessary to the public's reemergence. Because se-crecy is one of the causes of the public's eclipse and information one of the key ingredients to its reemergence, the masses could not transform themselves into a public in publicity's absence.[61] Despite agreeing that no capable, atten-tive public existed in the modern democracy of the early twentieth century, Lippmann and Dewey both saw means to establish functional (albeit quite dif-ferent), unitary democracies in part by lifting the veil of state secrecy. Informa-tion's release would improve the expert efficiency or Great Community that each felt would address the problem caused by the public's absence. Lippmann and Dewey thus represented distinct modern hopes for the nascent public that remain alive in progressive, populist, and even some conservative theories of the public—in which experts (following Lippmann), or a "natural aristocracy" (following Edmund Burke[62]), or Dewey's directly involved public can guide the state because of its ability to rationally process government information.

Of Multiple Publics and the Technological Public Sphere

While these early- and mid–twentieth-century concerns about the relationship between the modern masses and an illusory or nascent public sphere still influ-ence intellectual thought, some more recent social and political theorists have abandoned the concept of a unitary public entirely. Michael Warner's influen-tial work on "publics and counterpublics" explicitly rejects the idea of the lost public and asserts instead that a multiplicity of publics is continually made and remade every time a speaker or writer addresses and thereby invokes the public. The public is not an "it" that lies in wait as an essential, stable constituent of democracy; instead, the public is a "they" that exists as imaginary possibilities, an "indefinite audience" and "virtual social object, enabling a special mode of address."[63] Counterpublics, composed of members of marginalized groups and subcultures who are marked off by their critical relation to power, add to this sense of an unorganized public sphere teeming with potential formation and reformation in a circular discursive process.

Applied to transparency, Warner's multiple publics and counterpublics also appear incapable of responding rationally as a simple, unified public to the supposed communicative act initiated by disclosure. Instead, when a writer or speaker addresses a public that presumably longs to be informed or is likely to be outraged by government information, she calls that public into being, seek-ing its attention and invoking its members' interest and outrage. Neither infor-mation disclosure nor the documents themselves illuminate an existing public;

the act of presenting one or more disclosed documents constitutes an effort to create that public in the process of addressing it as a potential one.[64] Disclosure might create one or more publics—and thereby can have some effect—but it occurs in a nonunitary, unpredictable way, in the process creating a multiplicity of both receivers and messages.[65]

This assumes, of course, that a communicative act in fact occurs via disclosure. In *Publicity's Secret*, the political theorist Jodi Dean offers a poststructuralist return to Lippmann's phantom public, arguing against the public's existence and the communicative ideal that a public exists to receive messages. She critiques claims that new information technologies that privilege "[a]ccess, information, and communication as well as open networks of discussion and opinion formation" have remade democracy in a postmodern age.[66] New technologies do not solve the problems for democratic ideals and practices posed by a mass industrialized society; rather, they create a "technoculture" of instant and omnipresent connectedness that devolve into a "deluge of screens and spectacles" (p. 3). Contemporary technoculture promises that "the truth is out there" and that the "secret," whose availability is presumptively essential to the public's acting in the ways that the classical liberal ideal of the public assumes it must act, will soon be revealed with the next Google search (p. 8). When coupled with liberal democratic theory's ideal political subject who can only meet his potential as a citizen when fully informed, technoculture banishes the secret as an anathema, an antagonist to democratic development with an "irresistible aura" of power and mystery (pp. 11–12). New technologies must unveil that which is hidden. By requiring and promoting an ideally reasoning public under the promise that the public can and should have access to unlimited information, transparency and publicity in a technocultural age unleash the suspicion that the public is not being fully informed (pp. 18–22). In a culture and politics obsessed with information and the secret, the ideal public exists only as a figment in the theoretical imaginary produced by the informational ideal upon which transparency relies. Instead of a public, we are left with a wired audience; instead of democratic process, we have a technological spectacle of gossip, suspicion, and the endless hunt for the latest revelation.

. . .

"The public" is a theoretical construct rather than an actually existing, identifiable group of human beings. This is clearly the case in political theory and social science, where the effort to identify a public—to ascribe intelligence and cognition to the individuals who would compose it or meaning to the collective that embodies it—results in insightful but inconclusive debate. Over the past century, theorists have argued alternatively that individuals are rationally ignorant, cognitively limited, or simply distracted; that the public has disappeared due to modern mass communication or postmodern digital excess; or that it has shattered into a multitude of fragments or is capable of reemerging. There is a widely shared lament, however, for the current state of politics and the public's lack of knowledge about government, as well as its distaste for politics. And yet, the underlying cybernetic theory of transparency assumes the existence of precisely what political theory and social science call into doubt: the existence of individuals and a broader society that will pay attention to the state and respond rationally and predictably to the disclosure of government information. If the final part of the cybernetic transaction fails—if there is no capable receiver at the end of the communicative act—then the transparency ideal is misplaced.

Is the Public Necessary?

Transparency may still survive as an ideal in the face of the public's ignorance, however, if we identify an alternative mechanism by which disclosure necessarily improves the political order. Perhaps the mere fact of disclosure matters more to the public than the disclosures' content. Perhaps the public's agents—other parts of the state or private institutions like the press and NGOs—can use information in order to hold the government accountable without the public's direct intervention. In other words, perhaps government information can still have effects even if the public does not directly participate in the cybernetic transaction. Perhaps the public is not necessary at all.

The Public's Trust

The legitimacy that transparency advocates claim the state gains from disclosure may flow from the very fact that the state is making itself visible. Not only a virtue in and of itself, transparency also signals that the state must be acting in a legitimate and accountable way. If disclosure disciplines official actors and the state—that is, if officials fear exposure and internalize behavioral and political norms as if the public paid attention—then the public's ignorance in the wake of disclosure and its inability to directly hold the state accountable for the substance of its disclosures might not be essential to its effects. This claim assumes at least two things: first, that the state either virtuously self-enforces disclosure requirements or faces sanctions from someone besides the public for failure to disclose fully and honestly; and second, that the public will follow and take interest in the process of disclosure, even if it delegates to others the task of understanding the disclosures' substantive content and holding the state accountable for it. I discuss the other institutions that might hold the state accountable in the next sections; here, I focus solely on the benefits of the public's increased trust because the government has made itself transparent.

A government's regular disclosure of information demonstrates to its political subjects whom it represents and rules, as well as to the world at large, that its officials abide by universal administrative and legal rules; in one international law scholar's terms, "when nations and their agents carry out their assessments [of law and policy] thoughtfully and transparently, against a backdrop of articulated standards, they satisfy the appropriate requirements of rule of law."[67] Mechanically transparent governance—an administrative state that, as a rule, discloses as much as possible of its operations, meeting without question every obligation it has established for itself to be open—is what Max Weber called "value-rational conduct," demonstrating "a conscious faith in the absolute worth of the conduct as such, independent of any aim."[68] Such conduct makes the state legitimate in the eyes of its subjects, increasing their trust in the government's substantive actions regardless of those actions' substance. It creates a virtuous circle: In making itself transparent, the state has internalized norms of behavior that will create good, non-corrupt governance; and in doing so, the public can and will increasingly come to trust the government's actions.

It does not appear, however, that a more transparent state creates a more trusting public. The philosopher Onora O'Neill argues that plentiful disclosure creates uncertainty in the amount of unsorted and unauthoritative information and thus is more likely to breed distrust.[69] In their book *Stealth Democracy*, the political scientists John Hibbing and Elizabeth Theiss-Morse found that exposure to the complicated, messy, and political legislative process erodes public confidence in the resulting substantive legislation and in Congress generally.[70] Several empirical studies have supported these doubts about the relationship between transparency and the public's trust in the state's legitimacy, either finding limited support for the claim or a negative correlation.[71] Researchers have found that the relationship between transparency and trust is contingent upon a variety of factors, including national political cultures and the medium of communication (from government websites to social media), and the extent to which the government allows the public to interact with officials.[72] The results of these studies suggest little support for the strong claim that disclosure as such—as a virtuous act of a democratic government, apart from the content of that disclosure that the public might not notice or understand—creates a more trusting public.[73]

The Public's Agents

Even if the general public does not notice or understand government information, other governmental and private institutions do. The state's so-called checks and balances, redundancies, overlapping jurisdictions, and sheer complexity allow for multiple sources of internal accountability. Congress, the courts, and entities within the executive branch can utilize information gleaned from disclosed documents or other sources to punish official wrongdoers, address government inefficiencies, or change ineffective policies. The CIA's "family jewels," which I discussed in Chapter 1, is a preeminent example of a significant leak that spurred elected representatives to action without necessarily creating popular political mobilization. While it affected public opinion and may have played some role in the 1976 presidential election that saw Jimmy Carter defeat Gerald Ford (who had completed Richard Nixon's second term), the family jewels' disclosure instigated political reforms by spurring the press and Congress to act as the public's agents. The same was true, though in less dramatic fashion (minus major congressional committee investigations in both the Senate and the House), with the Snowden leaks, as I discuss in Chapter 7.

Albert Meijer's helpful taxonomy of transparency's broad effects helps explain this process schematically. He contrasts "horizontal accountability" from outside the state, including the public's participation in the political process, to "vertical accountability" within the state, especially as media and "stakeholder" institutions alert or press state actors about official corruption and ineffectiveness.[74] Vertical accountability takes many forms and, within the U.S. system, comes from different branches and segments within the branches. Congress oversees the executive branch through its lawmaking and appropriation authority, both granting (and limiting) power and funding (or refusing to fund) its exercise. Elected representatives have the capacity to gather and interpret information about the government's performance, and they can receive information directly, through the various committees that the individual houses establish and especially from the congressional staff of civil servants. The president can receive information directly from his or her cabinet officers and executive branch agencies and has several entities upon whom he or she can rely to gather information about agency performance, including especially the Office of Management and Budget (OMB) within the Executive Office of the President and its Office of Information and Regulatory Affairs. Each federal agency has not only reporting requirements it must meet, but also includes quasi-independent inspectors general who can investigate allegations of wrongdoing. These informational checks enable politically accountable officials to gather and act on information without necessarily releasing it and relying directly on the public's knowledge of it and response to it.

But the fact that government institutions *can* successfully serve as active and engaged receivers of government information does not mean that they necessarily do so. The legislative and executive branches are deeply political—not only partisan, but also zealously territorial about protecting the scope of their own authority. The president, his or her cabinet officers and those he or she assigns to gather information, and individual agencies can oversee their own performance, but for political reasons or because of limited resources or simply to further their own interests, they also have incentives either to fail to gather information, turn a blind eye toward that which they gather, or cover it from public view. The executive branch is likely to resent and resist congressional investigations, even when Congress and the president are from the same party.

The problem is institutional and bureaucratic as well as political. The same torrent of documents that makes government information difficult to control also hampers the state's ability to respond to any particular set of documents; the same complex, sprawling governmental structure that hampers the public's ability to understand the state and hold it accountable hinders the state's ability to investigate itself. To handle this problem, congressional oversight committees and presidential efforts to review executive branch performance need expertise—as well as a unified focus and well-established, nonpartisan, and rational procedures in place—to successfully process and respond to the many conflicting, ambiguous signals this mass of information sends. But the ranks of government personnel are too fluid, officials' preferences and the preferences of the interests they serve too divergent, and the processes by which they are required to operate too unwieldy to handle all that information in a controlled, deliberative manner and respond rationally and proportionately.[75]

Indeed, there are good reasons to believe that the state *cannot* rationally process all of the information that it discovers or has submitted to it. Instead, the state operates as an "organized anarchy" engaged in what organizational theorists call the "garbage can model" of decision making, where it acts in response to chance events rather than by rational, ordered deliberation.[76] The state unevenly responds to signals it receives and acts in a pattern of punctuated equilibrium, shifting between long periods of stasis and occasional, relatively brief upheavals.[77] When faced with an external crisis—a terrorist attack, mass internal dissent, a financial crisis—officials finally begin to pay attention and respond quickly and forcefully, if not always effectively or even rationally, to the cascade of informational signals that the crisis creates and prompts.[78] By contrast, during long periods of relative political stability or sclerotic inertia due to partisan deadlock, government officials process the information that floods into the state imperfectly (if at all), often either failing to coordinate sufficiently to establish a response to the ambiguous and contested signals they receive or successfully coordinating in a partisan manner that ignores available information.[79] The state's information processing problem is thus akin to its information control problem. The excess of information it receives and its organizational size and complexity and political orientation, which limit the state's ability to stop leaks and impose transparency, also account for its limited capacity to process and deliberate information in an orderly manner.[80]

If legislatures make for imperfect agencies, perhaps courts—as more deliberative and less partisan institutions than the political branches—can better serve the role. Like the legislature, courts can respond to government information disclosed to them in the course of litigation by holding the state to its legal obligations and limits; indeed, this is the premise upon which most of administrative law rests. Judges are at least nominally independent of political parties, and many of them—including all within the federal judiciary—enjoy extensive job protections against removal for political reasons. Judges have the luxury of deciding only the cases that come before them. This provides two important advantages for their ability to process information. First, they need only draw from a narrower pool of information to settle a dispute, and thus they are less likely to face an information overload problem except in especially complex litigation; and second, they can deliberate over the disclosure of otherwise secret information more carefully and outside of the maelstrom of the public eye, which is itself somewhat ironic insofar as their deliberations about secrecy disputes are themselves entirely private.

But the judiciary often, though not always, shies away from political disputes. This allows courts to avoid directly challenging elected branches and seek the safe harbor of technical legal doctrines and the logic of separate powers. It explains the common law constitutional arguments courts have developed in the field of secret information, including the executive privilege and state secret doctrines. More broadly, the judiciary's independent role in the U.S. system slows courts' decision-making process and circumscribes their authority to serve as a roving independent body. Federal courts only consider the disputes that reach their courtrooms and chambers, restrained by the "cases and controversies" limitation in the Constitution's Article III and the standing doctrine that requires that a petitioner seeking relief face actual injury for which the court can provide relief. They are barred from issuing so-called advisory opinions that would speak to issues besides those presented to them by a live controversy. The judiciary's seeming independence and nonpolitical role thus restrain its authority and agenda.

At the same time, however, judges and courts also play political roles. With its starkly partisan lineup of Supreme Court justices explicitly deciding the result of a presidential election, *Bush v. Gore* stands as the preeminent example of both judicial bias and its political effects. Empirical studies of judicial behavior have found some limited evidence that judges vote in a non-random pattern that is consistent with the political party of the president who appointed them, especially in more political and policy-oriented cases.[81] A recent study of FOIA decisions in the Federal Circuit Court of Appeals for the District of Columbia (the most important lower court for administrative law litigation) found a pronounced political valence in decisions reviewing agency use of the national security exemption, with panels composed of a majority of judges nominated by Republican presidents siding more frequently with the government.[82] If the judiciary wades into political and informational disputes hesitatingly but in a political fashion when it does so, then it cannot serve simply and always as the public's agent in freeing and understanding government information.

The state can create institutions with greater organizational or political independence from the objects of their investigations, a tradition (described briefly in the Conclusion) that includes independent commissions and advisory committees, special counsel, inspectors general, and ombudsmen. In the best of circumstances, these institutions can uncover, process, and release government information, as well as either prosecute lawbreakers or make recommendations to agency officers about punishment of individual employees or institutional reform. But none of these innovations represent perfect solutions for a variety of reasons: Sometimes these institutions prove too independent and face resistance from entrenched institutions, and sometimes they are not independent enough and fail to credibly and fully investigate government actions and disclose the breadth of their findings. They cannot simply replace or represent the public, and they will not fix the problem of identifying effective receivers and users of government information.

Given its historic role in championing FOI laws, the media appear to face none of the institutional restraints that government entities face in paying attention and responding to the information that comes their way. But they are not neutral institutions capable of pursuing, obtaining, and interpreting government information; rather, they operate within the institutional constraints created by the market for their products or the public or private subsidies that they receive. As newspapers and broadcasters have faced declining audiences and advertising revenues, news media budgets have declined as well and have limited their parent companies' willingness to invest in the kinds of long-form reporting and investigative journalism required to obtain and explain documents that reveal government actions and performance.[83] They tend to produce content that will reach the widest possible audience, or they seek narrower but loyal audiences by tailoring their ideological messages to those who hold particular views.[84]

Media companies and their employees seek financial gain, compete with one another, strive to meet professional goals of achievement, and may attempt to further political objectives.[85] More often than serving as a conduit of information that would help create an informed, deliberative public, news organizations cover political scandal, the horseraces of electoral campaigns, and the personalities and personal lives of candidates and high-ranking officials. Contemporary politicians and officials exploit these tendencies by strategically disclosing information through coordinated public relations campaigns that produce pre-packaged, carefully controlled news or attempt to control the coverage of officials, candidates, and issues as tightly as possible.[86] The press's poor performance in accurately reporting the Bush administration's claims prior to the invasion of Iraq or the prevalence of torture in Iraq and throughout the global war on terror follows logically from these developments.[87]

And whether related to that performance or to partisan political trends or general public distrust of professions, the public expresses little confidence in the media and its objectivity.[88] Investigative journalism in particular is the victim of what journalism historian John Nerone has called the shift from "high modern" moment of journalism in the post–World War II era to the "late modern" era that the press now inhabits. The rise of digital media has helped bring about the end of mass communication, with its broad distributive power and its bottlenecks, through vast new technological and institutional competition that has irrevocably shattered the media's prestige and sheen of objectivity.[89]

Perhaps, then, new media technology can produce intermediaries that will replace the twentieth-century institutional press. What Yochai Benkler has called the "networked fourth estate"—composed of a limited number of global media organizations whose news production has become less centralized, as well as nontraditional, web-based news organizations, nonprofit entities, and bloggers—delivers more and more varied news content than the traditional institutions of the mass-mediated fourth estate of the previous century.[90] Distributing the fruits of digital transparency via digital transmission, this emerging and evolving set of institutions could represent a newly networked public and hold the state accountable for its actions while also developing a public that can govern itself, offering the same promise as the digital transparency movement I described in Chapter 2. I consider this possibility in Chapter 8, where I present a study of the effects caused by the WikiLeaks and Snowden leaks.

Accompanying this new media landscape, and often becoming part of it, are nongovernmental, special interest organizations of various sorts that attempt to grab the attention of the media and public with news and opinion. Traditional NGOs like the Sierra Club and the National Rifle Association distribute government information that helps their cause, while NGOs like the ACLU and Judicial Action use FOIA and the discovery phase of litigation to force the government to disclose information that the groups then publicize directly to their donors and supporters as well as to the media. By definition, these organizations have specific agendas. They seek out information and interpret the information they obtain in ways that that will help advance their interests and those of their funders. In an ideally pluralistic political and social order, these interests could, in the aggregate, help represent and advance the public's more general and disparate interests; but they could also misinterpret information—both willfully and negligently—and overrepresent particular interests. They do not epitomize an ideal, objective, and neutral cybernetic receiver.

Enemies of the State
The public does not play the role as direct receiver for most of the dangerous scenarios imagined by secrecy advocates. Instead, various institutional and individual enemies of the state serve that role, including other nations' intelligence services and governments, terrorist organizations, and people engaged in criminal activities, all of whom are keenly interested in the state's secret documents.

Tightly focused on obtaining information valuable to their causes and plans, they can make direct use of any documents to which they gain access and in the process endanger the state and its citizens. The inadvertent or unauthorized disclosure of information about imminent troop movements, ongoing undercover operations and criminal investigations, diplomatic negotiating positions, and the like—nonambiguous, timely information that reveals impending state action—leave the state especially vulnerable. Such information is clearly and for the most part uncontroversially secret, with criminal sanction attaching to unauthorized disclosures and exemptions from open government law.

Those kinds of documents only constitute a portion of what the U.S. government classifies and attempts to keep secret, however. The vast majority of government information does not directly and unambiguously reveal particular actions or plans that rivals or criminals can immediately use. As a result, the state's enemies confront the same information overload problem that the public and state face. Rival intelligence agencies, whose very purpose is to control the state's own information and obtain and analyze information from and about other states and threatening non-state entities, must spend an enormous amount of time and resources attempting to analyze a vast ocean of uncertain, fragmented data.

The U.S. intelligence community, likely the largest and among the best funded on a per capita basis in the world,[91] provides an excellent example of this problem. Composed of a number of huge organizations, the intelligence community and the agencies that compose it operate like other parts of the vast federal government—bureaucratic, territorial, and frequently incapable of making sense of the information they receive. In an influential article published in 1978 that anticipated intelligence failures in foreseeing the fall of the Soviet Union and the 9/11 terrorist attacks, Richard Betts noted the difficulty of intelligence analysis, given the ambiguity of the evidence on which it is based, the ambivalence of the judgment that weighs the evidence, and the impossibility of designing the perfect institution for analysis, policymaking, and implementation.[92] The 9/11 Commission famously criticized the intelligence community's "failure of imagination" in interpreting and acting upon the information to which analysts and agencies had access. Imagination is always essential because it is rare that discovery of a single document will, by itself, create a fully informed and cognizant intelligence service. Terrorist and criminal organizations boast much thinner bureaucracies than the U.S. intelligence community—presumably an advantage over the bloated and sclerotic rival agencies—but they also enjoy significantly fewer resources and personnel to obtain and analyze information, lowering their intelligence capacity. Their much smaller scale and narrow purpose may aid in devising and executing particular attacks, but those conditions do not grant the organizations any greater ability to gather and process intelligence. The 9/11 attacks, for example, were not devised from access to secret state information but from publicly available and observable patterns of security and air travel.

And yet, secrecy proponents view the enemies they identify—from nation-states to terrorist cells—as super-competent. Consider, in this light, the "mosaic theory" supporting the nondisclosure of documents that must otherwise be released in response to a FOIA request. Initially proposed by the government and then adopted by judges, this theory allows government agencies to claim a national security exemption from FOIA for an unclassified document for which no exemption from disclosure is otherwise available, because someone with access to other information can piece together something important from it and develop a more complete, valuable understanding of intelligence that threatens national security. The document, in other words, could be the final or a key piece in a "mosaic" of dangerous information and can only become dangerous when interpreted in a broader context, when "bits and pieces of seemingly innocuous information can be analyzed and fitted into place to reveal with startling clarity how the unseen whole must operate."[93]

Although relatively longstanding, the doctrine took on increased significance in the aftermath of the 9/11 attacks, when federal courts regularly deferred to the government's concerns about "an enemy just as real as [America's] former Cold War foes, with capabilities beyond the capacity of the judiciary to explore."[94] In his trenchant critique of excessive judicial deference to mosaic theory claims, David Pozen argued that taken to its logical limit, assuming both an enemy with enormous capacity to gather and process intelligence and a nation that is unwilling to accept almost any degree of risk, *every* document and *every* piece of information can form part of a dangerous mosaic. But such assumptions are false. As Pozen explains, "[i]nformation poses no intrinsic threat, for to be dangerous, even the recipe for the atomic bomb demands an understanding of what it is, how to interpret it, and access to the ingredients."[95] By ignoring the interpretive and imaginative acts required to perform successful intelligence analysis and instead assuming a perfectly efficient and capable enemy, as well as a stitched-together picture that is continually one piece from completion, the mosaic theory imagines a perfectly competent foe, one who can complete the cybernetic transaction in ways that our own intelligence community cannot.

This is not an argument that U.S. intelligence services are somehow worse than others. All intelligence agencies must perform their important work in extremely difficult circumstances of imperfect information delivered in large quantities. But if the vast, extraordinarily well-funded American intelligence community often fails to correctly interpret the information it obtains, then we cannot assume that disclosure of potentially dangerous information will have anticipated effects. The decision to keep information secret cannot rely on a categorical fear that disclosure will cause particular effects, because disclosure's effects—whether on the imperfect and fractured public, on the public's imperfect agents, or on the state's imperfect enemies—are marginal and unpredictable.

. . .

The cybernetic theory of government transparency, then, does not survive scrutiny of its component parts. As a general phenomenon and in particular cases, secrecy and transparency are contextual; they arise and are imposed in a particular set of contingent historical circumstances, requiring human agents to make sense of the information they attempt to withhold or disclose.[96] Accordingly, information control of whatever sort requires a context-specific definition of transparency and secrecy, viewed in terms of specific policy objectives and system constraints that bureaucratic administration creates.[97] A simple transmission theory cannot describe or explain government information, and laws and policies based upon it cannot help but fail to meet their grandest and broadest goals.

I am not going to propose a substitute for cybernetics as an overriding theory of government information because, as the book's final part demonstrates in a series of case studies and the Conclusion, government information eludes capture by a simplistic explanation or fix. But the linguist Michael Reddy offers a thoughtful alternative in his critique of the powerful sway that cybernetic theory has had over what he called the "conduit metaphor" of language transmission, which presumes that language functions to transfer thoughts bodily from one person to another.[98] Reddy's alternative metaphor makes communication a tool passed from one context to another, which is then used in a different environment and without clear instructions. Like the new tool that might be used as intended but might also be misused or applied in a different manner than intended, "information" communicated is always partially misunderstood and used for different purposes. We cannot assume language's transformative effects. Nor, I have argued, can we evaluate the disclosure or nondisclosure of government information quantitatively—by the sheer amount of signals created, stored, and transferred or protected—on the assumption that information disclosed is information received, and information received is knowledge gained.[99] We would do better to view government information in a much broader context in light of the complex ways that disclosed information fails to have effect, and secret information still escapes.

III THE FAILURES
OF INFORMATION CONTROL

7   The Implausibility
of Information Control

Part II argued that the state sprawls: Its production of information is neither schematic nor uniform; its archiving of that information is incomplete and scattered; the public is unwilling to and incapable of receiving and processing government information in a predictable, rational manner; and therefore the ability to transmit government information cybernetically is impossible. Put more simply, the state is necessarily a mess given what we expect it to do; among the consequences of that messiness are its inability to control information and our inability to understand the information it discloses. The final part of this book, which encompasses the next two chapters and the Conclusion, takes the insights from the previous three chapters and applies them in a series of illustrative case studies that demonstrate the difficulty that the state faces in trying to control government information.

This chapter offers three examples of the ways that information comes out of the state despite official efforts to keep it contained. Chapter 8 describes the subtle and uneven effects of the recent megaleaks by Chelsea Manning and Edward Snowden. These two chapters demonstrate the difficulty of controlling government information in both senses—keeping it secret and forcing it out. But at the same time, each shows how unpredictable, uneven, and often underwhelming disclosure's effects can be. And, finally, the Conclusion reconsiders how the state is imagined and identifies several successful ways of tinkering with it rather than fixing it.

The larger narrative of Chapter 7 is that secrecy is exceedingly difficult to maintain. Information's pathways out of the state's clutches are diverse and multiple. The case studies illustrate the various means by which information seeps out of the state, including deliberate leaks by officials and accidental leaks that occur by bureaucratic mistake, the observation and reporting by people outside the government who witness state action, and the act of keeping secrets itself, which can disclose information about government plans and actions. We first consider a chronicle of the effort by the Bush administration to keep secret the work of Vice President Cheney's National Energy Policy Development Group (NEPDG), a key pre–9/11 episode that foreshadowed later struggles over executive branch secrecy. Cheney, you will recall from Chapter 3, literally wrote the book (or at least the government report) on secrecy's importance and efficacy; my take on the NEPDG episode focuses on both how wrong Cheney's argument was in presuming secrecy's possibility and how right he was in understanding its political risk.

The second case study describes several instances in which redaction—the most open and explicit form of information control, in which black marks on the page physically keep secrets from the public in documents that the public can see—has not kept secret the information it covers; ultimately this discussion reveals that redaction fails to completely stop interpretation and knowledge while it generates imaginative means to gather information and interpret the absent content. The final case study discusses the difficulty that the government faces in controlling even its most prized secrets about covert operations, focusing on one of the most significant such operations in twentieth century U.S. history, the CIA-led 1954 coup in Guatemala.

Dick Cheney's Secrets: The Dark Prince and His Energy Policy, Gradually Illuminated

Although they ultimately hitched their obsession for information control to the fast-moving expansion of military and intelligence operations in response to the 2001 terrorist attacks,[1] George W. Bush's administration and Vice President Cheney had begun to limit public and congressional access to information well before then. During the first months of Bush's first term, Cheney sought to establish tight control over executive branch information in his management of the administration's energy policy.[2] Cheney won this legal battle, as the formal mechanisms intended to limit secrecy could not contain the formal mechanisms that allow it.[3] Although I begin this case study with a narrative telling of the vice president's apparent ability to control information, I then explain how his formal legal victories could not foreclose the seepage of information from the executive branch. A complex set of leaks, along with journalists' and advocates' informed and uninformed inferences about the work Cheney oversaw, undercut the underlying assumptions of the vice president's theory of executive privilege and his desire for information control.

The Dark Prince Rises

George W. Bush established the innocuously titled National Energy Policy Development Group (NEPDG) soon after his inauguration.[4] Intended to organize the incoming administration's development of a comprehensive national energy policy, the task force was chaired by Cheney and run by members of his staff.[5] The project did not begin from a blank slate. One of the Bush campaign's early policy goals was to prioritize energy development over environmental regulation, and a unit of President Bush's post-election transition team had begun to develop an energy policy for the incoming administration.[6] Given the issue's significance, the administration clearly viewed NEPDG's formation as a key moment in the early days of the new presidency. The task force's membership included presidential cabinet members who directed the agencies that would implement many of the group's recommendations, as well as high-ranking appointees in the Executive Office of the President who would oversee and organize presidential oversight of the resulting energy policy.[7] The vice president would ultimately lead a centralized, top-down policy development process in which the chairman's preferences would drive the committee's deliberations and conclusions.[8]

The task force only briefly existed, disbanding when its final report was released four months after its formation. During that period, however, its principals met with hundreds of corporate executives and interest group delegates, the vast majority of whom represented the energy industry and especially the extractive industries.[9] Task force members and staff almost entirely ignored environmental organizations, and any access to NEPDG the latter enjoyed was pro forma.[10] The final report's most significant prescriptions predictably reflected the extractive industries' preferences. It advocated efforts to seek new domestic sources of oil and gas, including on public lands (such as the Arctic National Wildlife Refuge) and offshore, and diplomatic and commercial efforts to forge global trade alliances that would expand U.S. access to foreign oil.[11] It also championed the expansion of nuclear power generation. Although such prescriptions may have proved politically controversial and widely contested as a matter of policy, particularly for environmental groups opposed to many of NEPDG's priorities, the report's substantive conclusions and influence seemed to represent the standard stuff of policy development for a first-term Republican president. They could not have surprised anyone.[12]

The task force's intentional and well-planned commitment to secrecy, however, was both controversial *and* surprising.[13] NEPDG did not open its meetings and deliberations to the public, nor did it provide a list of the private entities and individuals with whom it met to the public, press, or even Congress. Cheney also directed the energy industry executives with whom he and the NEPDG met not to mention their involvement in the group to the press or the public.[14]

The new administration's energy policy, and the process by which it came together, worried and frustrated the political opposition. In April 2001, in response to a request from two Democratic members of Congress, the Government Accountability Office (GAO)—which exists to assist Congress in investigating the government's use of federal funds—began to investigate the membership of NEPDG.[15] Using its broad statutory authority,[16] the GAO formally requested NEPDG's records in early May.[17] Cheney and his legal counsel, David Addington, denied the GAO's request, declaring first to the GAO and then ultimately to Congress that such congressional demands for information "intrude into the heart of Executive deliberations," and that the documents were constitutionally privileged.[18] The denial provoked the comptroller general, who leads the GAO, to take the unprecedented step of filing suit against the vice president to demand the records' disclosure.[19]

The vice president deployed the same strategy he used against Congress and the GAO to defeat claims that the NEPDG owed any duty to reveal information directly to the press and the public. Executive branch control had been intentionally embedded in NEPDG's structure and organizational DNA. Addington had designed NEPDG to avoid falling within the purview of the Federal Advisory Committee Act (FACA),[20] the federal statute that imposes open record and open meeting obligations on advisory committees within the executive branch not entirely composed of federal employees.[21] NEPDG officially included only federal employees as members, although it clearly had close relationships with corporate leaders of the federally regulated extractive industries and their lobbyists. Congress enacted FACA to better control the executive branch's efforts to seek input on regulatory or other matters from organized groups of private citizens.[22] The advisory committees, lawmakers and good government advocates feared, had been captured by the advice of private industry.[23] The statute requires, among other things, that an advisory committee, task force, or similar group established to provide advice to executive branch agencies, and that includes at least one member who is not a federal employee or officer, must hold open meetings and make its records available within a framework similar to that established by FOIA.[24] In mid-2001, Judicial Watch, a conservative governmental watchdog group, and the Sierra Club, an environmental group whose requests for NEPDG documents under FOIA were denied, filed suit after their informational requests were denied.[25]

The vice president ultimately won all of his legal battles to keep NEPDG's internal records secret. The GAO litigation ended in December 2002 after the trial court granted Cheney's motion to dismiss the comptroller general's complaint, ruling that he lacked standing to sue under Article III.[26] Defeated during the post–9/11 period and following a midterm election that saw the administration's political popularity and governmental authority rise to great heights, the GAO decided not to appeal, but it continued to assert that the court's decision was incorrect.[27]

Although more legally and procedurally complicated, the Judicial Watch and Sierra Club suits, which were consolidated and which concerned requests for documents from officials affiliated with NEPDG besides the vice president, met a similar fate as the GAO's suit. After the NGOs had appeared poised to begin receiving documents through civil discovery, Cheney prevailed in the U.S. Supreme Court.[28] The litigation ended when the U.S. Court of Appeals for the D.C. Circuit held that Addington's design of NEPDG, which made government employees the group's only voting members, placed the entity outside of FACA's domain.[29]

Cheney's success seemed to validate his long-term strategy of establishing control over executive branch information. It helped, of course, that the theory that justified his strategy had already gained significant purchase through Republican appointments to the federal bench[30] and its circulation by conservative public law scholars in the legal academy.[31] His victory sent a signal to opponents: The White House would use its vast financial, legal, and political resources to resist the release of any information that it did not want to disclose.[32]

Information Leaks, Even from Dick Cheney

But the administration could not achieve full control over the complex network of executive branch agencies that interacted with the NEPDG merely through the support of a majority of appellate judges in high-profile cases. The Bush administration had in fact lost a number of battles along the way to winning the various lawsuits seeking information. By the time of the dismissal of the public interest groups' lawsuit, several agencies had already complied with the trial court's discovery orders, in the process releasing some documents that the vice president continued to withhold.[33] The National Resources Defense Council was able to obtain documents in early 2002 through a suit against the Department of Energy that showed pervasive industry influence over the resulting administration energy policy.[34] Along with communications between oil and gas lobbyists and NEPDG officials that demonstrated the group's close relationship to industry,[35] Judicial Watch had obtained from the Department of Commerce a series of maps documenting oil fields and prospects for contracts and projects to extract oil in the Middle East, including Iraq.[36]

Meanwhile, information about NEPDG seeped out from nonofficial sources. The press had widely predicted that the administration's favored industry interests would gain from Bush's energy plan[37] and then reported that energy industry representatives had met extensively with task force officials.[38] The *New York Times* revealed that eighteen of the top twenty-five contributors to the Republican Party enjoyed special access to the NEPDG— including, in Enron's case, access to the vice president himself.[39] Less than eighteen months later, the GAO issued its report on the process that NEPDG used in drafting its report, which authoritatively documented the vice president's tightfisted control of the group, as well as contacts among the Office of the Vice President, other principal NEPDG members, and energy industry executives and representatives.[40] The press quickly identified Cheney's obsession with secrecy, and secrecy became an important media story about NEPDG.[41] The *GAO Report* also revealed the vice president's efforts to keep the NEPDG's work secret.

Cheney's failed efforts to control information paralleled the NEPDG's failure as a political entity. Vocal and institutional opposition to what many suspected would emerge as the administration's energy policy coalesced soon after the NEPDG's formation.[42] The *NEPDG Report* did not influence Congress, as a bill that the administration supported and that had passed the Republican-controlled House failed in the Senate (which had a bare majority of Democrats).[43] It was not until 2005, after President Bush's reelection and with larger Republican majorities in both houses of Congress, that Congress finally enacted a new energy bill—one that, notably, did not include some of the most controversial NEPDG proposals, such as opening the Arctic National Wildlife

Refuge to drilling.[44] According to public polling, the report also failed to persuade the public that its prescriptions were objectively wise and worth pursuing, as many Americans thought that Bush was "too closely tied to the energy industry and insufficiently devoted to conservation."[45] The group's substantive prescriptions might never have persuaded the public and political opponents, but secrecy certainly did not help the administration's efforts to sell its policy and might well have hurt them—a hypothesis that even some former members of the Bush administration have espoused.[46]

Environmental NGOs likely agreed, as they used the NEPDG's secrecy, and their legal challenges to it, as evidence of the administration's capture by oil and gas interests. The Sierra Club trumpeted its litigation efforts to its donors as proving its essential role in fighting what it characterized as the vice president's secretive, lawless behavior.[47] As one sympathetic commentator noted about the environmental groups opposed to the Bush administration, the Sierra Club and the National Resources Defense Counsel seemed more agitated about the secretive and exclusionary process by which the energy policy had been developed than about the policy itself.[48]

Administration critics generally viewed the NEPDG episode through such inferences. The authors of *Vice: Dick Cheney and the Hijacking of the American Presidency* characterized the NEPDG as "a government-sanctioned industry cabal" that had drawn up a self-dealing and destructive energy policy and that had worked in secret to cover up the corrupt enterprise.[49] Some critics accused Cheney of trying to hide his efforts to enrich his friends in the energy industry. Some imagined far worse, particularly when viewing the NEPDG retrospectively through the lens of the 2003 invasion of Iraq. The existence of the Iraqi oilfields map that was disclosed during litigation, along with the fact that it had been kept secret, led critics to claim that the war in Iraq and the administration's hawkish, neoconservative foreign policy were products of the administration's energy policy.[50] Worse still, according to those who believe the administration either knew or was involved in the 2001 terrorist attacks, the entire episode unveiled the administration's secret conspiracy to achieve global domination for an imperial America.[51] Such theories no doubt would have developed even in a more open, information-rich environment where authoritative official documents and their provenance were available and widely acknowledged. But they positively blossomed in conditions that were defined by the grand, dramatic struggle to obtain documentary evidence.

The vice president may have thought he could control access to information about the energy policy he was developing for the White House—an assumption that his most vociferous critics share. FOIA and FACA had not provided opponents with the legal authority to challenge Cheney's secrecy. But the vice president could not contain either the circulation of information or the interpretation of that which circulated. The most significant pre–9/11 battle over government secrecy and the executive branch's authority to control information seemed to demonstrate that the laws protecting executive privilege trump open government laws and the apparent ability of a unified White House to manage communication. But it also displayed the role that the complex legal processes, bureaucratic sprawl, focused political pressure, and journalists and political opponents can have in undercutting the effort to keep secrets. It showed too the political price that effort can exact on those who make it. Cheney's secrecy overshadowed any substantive political debate over energy policy. And finally, it revealed how contested information control issues can crowd out substantive political debates over important policy issues.

Redaction Failures: Imperfect Information Control in the Release of Documents

When it releases documents from which text has been "redacted" (that is, obscured with a black mark or erased) for security purposes, the executive branch simultaneously discloses information and quite explicitly and clearly keeps it secret. The public can see the document; it just cannot see every word—or perhaps any word at all, if the entire document or page has been redacted. An agency sometimes redacts a document that it is otherwise required to release under a legal mandate; alternatively, an agency may not have been obliged to release a redacted document but decided to declassify or make it available in an effort to meet public expectations or enhance public understanding of an issue. As a surgical removal of privileged information, redaction constitutes a compromise, a second-best alternative to complete secrecy that is better than no disclosure at all. But by making visible that which is kept secret, redaction reveals secrecy's machinery in ways that the flat refusal to release a document does not. Paradoxically, redactions allow citizens to see precisely what the state has decided they cannot know.

This section demonstrates that understanding redaction as selective but complete censorship proves to be only partially correct, given the myriad ways in which redaction can fail. It begins with a discussion of how laws enable government to use redactions as a strategy to retain control over information, then it illustrates the ways that redaction has failed in recent high-profile cases. It ends by demonstrating how even redaction's textual erasure still produces meaning.

Information Control and Release in Redaction Law
Government agencies redact information most frequently in response to FOIA requests. The Freedom of Information Act requires federal agencies to provide "[a]ny reasonably segregable portion of a record" of documents when they rely upon one of FOIA's exemptions to deny a document request.[52] Agencies must make their redactions explicit and obvious by indicating the amount of deleted information, the exemption that authorized the deletion, and, when possible, where in the document the deletion occurred.[53] Courts occasionally play an active role in the redaction process, and they will sometimes review the precision with which an agency segregates information that cannot be withheld and the reasoning the agency uses when it redacts.[54] Judicial review of agency redaction is notably variable, with different courts reaching different conclusions about similar redactions or about how much they should defer to government decisions to redact.

Intelligence agencies also redact, or demand redaction, in the pre-publication review process that they use for the public writings of their current and former employees.[55] The CIA has long required employees to sign secrecy agreements as a condition of employment.[56] These agreements include provisions that require the employees to submit written manuscripts they plan to publish prior to publication.[57] The CIA delegates manuscript review to its Publications Review Board (PRB), which must respond to the author within thirty days with proposed deletions.[58] Although the PRB's approach has varied over time as different agency directors use their discretion to set their secrecy policy preferences,[59] some authors and critics of the CIA have argued that the PRB over-redacts information, especially when it supports criticism of CIA performance and policy.[60] Frustrated employees have challenged agency efforts to enforce the secrecy agreements on First Amendment grounds,[61] as well as on the grounds that the redacted information is in fact unclassified,[62] or had been officially disclosed previously,[63] or had been improperly classified.[64] Rarely do such challenges prevail.

Redaction's legal authorities thus assume the following. Disclosure is appropriate, within reason, as is secrecy. The two can be reconciled through an agency's precise control of information, down to the page, line, and word whose redaction will keep dangerous content secret. Wielding its black pen, eraser, or software code, the government can limit what it views as disclosure's ill effects.

How Redaction Fails

Redaction can and does fail in a variety of ways, however. The information that it tries to suppress might already be in the public domain. The information can also subsequently leak out or can be inferred from the document or the context in which the redaction appears.[65] The redactions might not successfully suppress information—either due to bureaucratic conflict or due to a technical error.[66] Agencies cannot extend the redaction that they are authorized to make to documents outside their control. Despite its status as an explicit form of information control, then, redaction often reveals secrecy's malfunction.

Consider a couple of examples, beginning with former CIA agent Valerie Plame Wilson's best-selling memoir *Fair Game* (2007).[67] Wilson's career at the agency ended when, in an effort to disparage her husband, members of the Bush administration made unauthorized leaks to news agencies identifying her as a covert agent. Her husband was a former diplomat who had publicly challenged the administration over its evidence of Saddam Hussein's efforts to build weapons of mass destruction.[68] The resulting scandal paradoxically transformed her from secret spy to public celebrity, and she sold the rights to her memoir to a major publishing house for $2.5 million.[69]

Upon reviewing Wilson's manuscript prior to publication, the CIA's PRB required significant redactions, including of factual information about her career that had been already appeared in popular news accounts and in an unclassified letter from a CIA official that was published in the *Congressional Record*.[70] Wilson and her publisher decided to release the book with large portions of the text hidden behind dull gray lines that represented the censored material after she lost her administrative and legal appeals of the redactions.[71] The book's main text has whole pages of redactions, as well as pages that combine visible text and single-word or line-by-line redactions. Two chapter titles are blacked out. Parts of Wilson's life story, including her husband's courtship and parts of her account of the PRB process itself, are so thoroughly edited as to be almost incomprehensible.[72] The book's redactions stand in protest against a secrecy policy to which Wilson objected, forcing the reader to make sense of an explicitly censored text. They make plain that Wilson had lost control of the telling of her own life.

But the book also demonstrates the absurdity and imperfections of the government's censorship efforts. Much of the content that the CIA had forbidden Wilson to publish appears in an afterword written by Laura Rozen, a foreign policy and intelligence reporter who relied for her nearly 100-page contribution on open source materials and personal interviews of Wilson's family, friends, and former colleagues.[73] The CIA could not limit Rozen's access to her sources, and it had no mechanism to censor her use of them in the afterword. One of the most significant redactions from the main text was the country where Wilson had worked undercover, as well as details that would allow a reader to identify the country, and so the chapters that cover her early years in the agency are among the most heavily redacted. As we learn in Rozen's afterword, however, Wilson spent six years undercover in Greece, a fact that was known to Wilson's family (though they did not know she worked for the CIA at that time) and one that had been widely reported in the news.[74] The afterword also describes how she met and ultimately married her husband—information that had appeared in Joseph Wilson's memoir, which had been published three years earlier.[75]

Fair Game also included an appendix that reproduces public documents, including correspondence between the CIA's PRB and her attorneys, court filings, and entries from the *Congressional Record* that included information Wilson could not get past the PRB's censors.[76] The documents provide further details about Wilson's service in the CIA and the PRB review process that were redacted in her portion of the memoir. Readers thereby have access to much of the information that the agency had forced her to redact.[77]

Bureaucratic indifference and conflict rather than absurdly excessive censorship caused another recent redaction failure. *Operation Dark Heart* (2010), Anthony Shaffer's memoir of his experiences as a Defense Intelligence Agency (DIA) officer in the war in Afghanistan, initially went to press without significant censorship after pre-publication review by the army.[78] As the book was set to be released, however, the DIA and other intelligence agencies tried to stop its publication, asserting that it contained classified information whose release could be harmful to national security. The Pentagon purchased and destroyed 10,000 printed copies of the book's original edition, while the book's publisher arranged to publish a second edition with the newly required redactions.[79]

The censorship failed, however, because a few advance copies of the original edition were already in circulation.[80] Those with copies of both versions could identify precisely what the DIA had redacted. An investigative news website posted numerous pages from both editions for a side-by-side comparison, revealing many of the classified "secrets" that the DIA hoped to hide.[81] Once again, the government's ham-fisted efforts to suppress information had nevertheless revealed both the suppressed facts and the process by which that suppression had occurred. By January 2013, the Department of Defense had partially reversed course again, declaring that many of the redactions had subsequently been declassified while retaining classification for many of the others.[82]

Similar episodes occur with some frequency:

- In 2012, the ACLU published a webpage comparing redacted diplomatic cables obtained by FOIA with unredacted documents obtained by WikiLeaks, claiming that the latter show "the government's selective and self-serving decisions to withhold information" via redaction.[83]

- *Guantánamo Diary* (2015), the memoirs of detainee Mohamedou Ould Slahi, fills in the ellipses created by the government's extensive redactions with widely available, unclassified information.[84]

- The CIA redacted significant portions of the report issued by the Senate Select Committee on Intelligence on the use of enhanced interrogation techniques in the war on terror in order to hide information that was already widely available in the public domain. This included the names of nations as well as agency officials who had publicly acknowledged their role in the CIA's program.[85]

- The military's efforts to redact documents that included information about the deaths of Guantánamo detainees similarly failed because of the availability of other sources, while the effort to redact itself appeared to confirm suspicions held by critics of the war on terror that the CIA and Defense Department sought to cover up that the prisoners had died of asphyxiation during torture rather than suicide, as government authorities had alleged.[86]

- State Department FOIA officers may have alerted foreign counterintelligence services about whether certain diplomats were CIA officers by using a particular FOIA exemption to justify redacting their names from released documents.[87]

Examples abound of such redaction failures.

Redaction's Meanings

In addition to failing to keep the actual text hidden from the public, redaction can also fail to stop the public from reading, and reading into, the covering lines themselves. As anthropologist Michael Powell has written, redaction "transforms the way we read these documents, sparking curiosity and often stirring skeptical, critical, and even cynical readings."[88] Few readers will share Valerie Wilson's personal sense of betrayal and outrage at the CIA's PRB process of *Fair Game,* but many will wonder at the CIA's motivations and rationality in its extraordinary efforts to redact information that was readily available. Readers are also likely to speculate about what lies under *all* of the black marks—not just those that are annotated elsewhere in the book—and about the government's motivations in redacting the text. Sometimes informed speculation will prove accurate; sometimes it will lead the public to imagine the worst, perhaps by assuming the existence of a conspiracy or official incompetence where neither existed. Even when redaction successfully censors information, and even when the majority of the public might not pay any attention to the original text and the redaction, black marks cannot fully obstruct the process of producing meaning about the text that it hides.

Redaction can also *create* meaning separate from the hidden content, as contemporary artists have shown by playing with it in their work. In his *FBI Files* series (2000–2002), the painter Arnold Mesches appropriated documents that he obtained from the investigatory files the FBI had produced in their surveillance of his political activities in the 1950s and 1960s.[89] Intermixing the documents into collages with paintings of arresting images from the culture and politics of the era, his works comment on the state that surveilled and infiltrated his life. The collages find beauty in the detritus of official action while they satirize the secret, paranoid world in which J. Edgar Hoover's FBI thrived. Similarly, Jenny Holzer's recent series *Redaction Paintings* uses oil paint on linen to reproduce, in larger size, declassified, redacted documents about detainee abuse obtained through FOIA requests filed by the ACLU.[90] In a 2004 exhibition, Holzer projected redacted documents from the Bush administration—documents explaining and authorizing the global war of terror—onto the faces of buildings in the Austrian city of Bregenz.[91] These works demonstrate how redactions perform a literal but partial censorship alongside disclosure, while they allow the redactions' black marks and blots to reveal the invisible but programmatic physical violence that the documents record.[92]

Mesches has described the inspiration provided by "the sheer aesthetic beauty of the [redacted] pages themselves—the bold, black, slashing, eradicating strokes" that look like artistic renderings made by the menacing bureaucratic police apparatus.[93] In reproducing redacted documents as art, he and Holzer reveal redactions' fruitful censorship, which in their work comes to represent the enormity of the security state that the Cold War and post–9/11 reaction produced, as well as the tremendous efforts the security state takes to keep itself secret.

The same proves true in published texts that reproduce or create redactions. Former CIA agent Joseph Weisberg's 2007 novel *An Ordinary Spy*, which narrates the story of an incompetent, conscience-wracked American agent, includes almost as many redactions as Wilson's *Fair Game*. But unlike Wilson, Weisberg redacted his own text to heighten the book's authenticity.[94] According to one account, the book's black bars "concealed the names of countries, the particulars of tradecraft and other details that might be classified information, *if the story were true*."[95] But the novel was fabricated; Weisberg himself removed most of the material to which the PRB would have objected, and the board redacted only a little more than Weisberg had. Moreover, as a novelist, Weisberg could have simply created unobjectionable material to replace that which the PRB redacted. Instead, he probably believed that redaction would increase the reader's pleasure and sense of the novel's accurate portrayal of the spy's daily life, even as it blacked out the details of that life. Weisberg sought realism through redaction—as though (attempted) secrecy is so much part of the CIA that a spy novel must include it in order to gain credibility.

The secret, in short, is aesthetically rich. Mesches and Holzer make use of blots and black lines that signify as well as censor; Weisberg uses them to enrich a narrative. This is true well beyond redaction. Trevor Paglen's photography of "blank spots"—most prominently the U.S. Air Force's infamous Area 51, where it tests new aircraft and where, as conspiracy lore tells us, the government stores its captured alien spacecraft—offers blurry, distanced representations of what might be viewed as spatial redactions. These are "black sites" that we know exist or can learn about but are removed from view by security perimeters and fences. Exhibited in galleries, profiled in *The New Yorker*, and recounted in his writings, Paglen's artistic practice demonstrates both what is available for view and what we do not know.[96] These artists reveal how the attempt to keep things hidden inspires further interpretation and creates new meaning.

"Secret History": The Struggle to Control Information About Covert Operations

By definition, covert state actions are secret. They are designed and executed in order to be the most unknown of the unknowns. At least in theory, they are a means by which the president and intelligence community attempt to change the course of history without leaving any historical traces. The issue of whether the state should make later disclosures of their existence and details generates fierce debate between the press, historians, and transparency advocates on the one hand and members of the intelligence community on the other.[97] The U.S. government has committed itself, or at least parts of itself, to disclose some of its past covert activities.[98] But these efforts to make historical documents available have faced formal and informal resistance through law and bureaucratic recalcitrance that protect some degree of secrecy about the official past.

Public Secrets and Public History Law

The State Department has published the *Foreign Relations of the United States* (*FRUS*) series, an official documentary record of foreign policy decisions and diplomatic activity,[99] more or less continuously since 1861. The *FRUS* carries on a longstanding tradition of State Department documentary reports to Congress that dates back to the early republic.[100] As America's geopolitical position changed after World War II and its State and Defense departments and intelligence services grew exponentially, political and bureaucratic conflict have repeatedly delayed the *FRUS* publication process.[101] To address these concerns, the State Department formed a permanent advisory committee composed of academic historians in 1957,[102] and, more recently, Congress enacted legislation requiring the State Department to engage more thoroughly with academic historians and to declassify documents on a scheduled basis.[103] Congress's interest in *FRUS* was itself part of broader legislative efforts to advance the declassification of documents concerning particularly controversial historical events, like the legislation enacted in 1992 to open records relating to the JFK assassination.[104]

Another statute, the Presidential Records Act (PRA),[105] clarified an uneven and informal practice of making the papers of a departing president publicly available.[106] Enacted at the tail end of the post-Watergate period of open government statutes, the PRA addressed the issue that arose out of former President Nixon's efforts to control the documents from his presidency, when it became clear that former presidents could not be trusted to allow public access to their historical papers.[107] The statute allows for public access to presidential records through the FOIA beginning five years after the end of the administration, but it allows the president to invoke as many as six specific restrictions to public access for up to twelve years.[108]

These efforts to open the historical record have faced significant resistance. Every struggle over the receding past takes place in the shadow both of an underlying constitutional conflict over presidential privilege—as when George Herbert Walker Bush explicitly noted the president's ongoing constitutional prerogative over diplomatic information in his statement upon signing the bill that finally gave the *FRUS* explicit congressional authorization[109]—and of the bureaucratic barriers that the classification system creates, as the State Department and other agencies remind the world when they delay publication of each *FRUS* volume.[110] The *FRUS* volumes have come more slowly and sporadically as a result of such battles, especially due to long delays in declassifying documents.[111]

At the same time, the PRA does not provide unfettered access to the historical record. Presidential records continue to fall within FOIA's exceptions even after the twelve-year period that allows former presidents to place additional restrictions on public access.[112] Presidential administrations also vary in the extent of their willingness to comply with the statute's spirit and letter, thereby illustrating once again that the existence of disclosure laws and policies does not ensure disclosure.[113] The legal and bureaucratic machinery of secrecy can, at least in theory, continue to hide the state's covert actions.

Documenting Guatemala's Secret History

As with Dick Cheney's energy policy and redaction, however, the executive branch's ability to exercise control over the flow of information is itself frequently undercut by informal means. In the case of information about past American covert operations, informal disclosure occurs because the operations inevitably have real world effects that leave a public record and create a public memory. The struggle over information about American involvement in Guatemalan history perfectly illustrates this dynamic.

The CIA's covert operation resulting in the 1954 coup that deposed the popularly elected Guatemalan President Jacobo Arbenz became the model for many similar secret interventions that followed, including the failed Bay of Pigs invasion in Cuba in 1961, and the operation had long-term devastating effects on Guatemala's political and social stability.[114] Although direct and extensive American involvement in the coup was widely recognized throughout Latin America and Europe at the time and subsequently,[115] the Eisenhower administration portrayed the coup as a popular domestic uprising and, with the complicity of U.S. news editors and publishers, kept the CIA's role relatively secret from the American public.[116] The coup continues to float in a kind of historical twilight, at once well known in Latin American and among historians and Americans well versed in Central American history, but shrouded in the impenetrable mystery that clings to controversial CIA Cold War covert operations. Numerous monographs on Guatemalan history, memoirs from coup participants, and books that more broadly treat covert American interventions in the post-war era have brought to light some of the American role in sponsoring and assisting the coup.[117] Nevertheless, several historians have complained that the event's details have been lost or remain locked inside government archives.[118]

Historians' work has been made more difficult because the CIA's files remained off-limits to researchers into the 1990s.[119] A 1983 *FRUS* volume, putatively concerning Guatemala, included no documents suggesting CIA involvement in the coup.[120] In 1992, however, as part of an "openness" initiative following the Soviet Union's collapse,[121] the CIA commissioned Nick Cullather, a recently minted history Ph.D. and new member of the agency's history staff, to write an insider history of the CIA's role in the 1954 coup, using full access to the agency's classified files. The agency intended the resulting history to serve as a training manual for future covert operatives rather than as a full or official account of the operation; nevertheless, the agency planned ultimately to release Cullather's text to the public, along with some of the documents on which Cullather relied.[122] The openness proved temporary, however, and Cullather's report, completed in 1993, remained classified until it was declassified and deposited in the National Archives in 1997.[123] Stanford University Press subsequently published it in 1999 with the title *Secret History: The CIA's Classified Account of Its Operations in Guatemala, 1952–1954.*[124]

In theory, *Secret History* could constitute a milestone text in the disclosure of American Cold War secrets as an institutional CIA history of a key covert operation. Through no fault of Cullather, however, it did not. The declassified version of his manuscript was extensively redacted, with not only names but also parts of the operation removed—including, ironically, a passage on how the Eisenhower administration kept news of the CIA's involvement in the coup secret from Americans.[125] The scope of Cullather's assigned project did not lend itself to serving as a comprehensive history anyway, and the documentary release that the CIA originally stated would accompany Cullather's report ultimately included a limited amount of materials.[126] *Secret History* only serves as a partial disclosure, then, because the bureaucratic apparatus of the clandestine service appears to have proven capable of retaining history's secrets long after the coup it engineered.

Indeed, the historic record remains contested regarding details, personal identities, and especially the larger historiographical questions about American motives.[127] Was U.S. involvement motivated by the desire to protect the United Fruit Company, a powerful American corporation, from nationalization and land reform?[128] Or to save Guatemala from communist and especially Soviet influence?[129] Or simply to protect national, and perhaps neocolonial, American interests?[130] These questions remain "secret" in the sense that answers may lie buried in some file cabinet in CIA headquarters or in a secret archive of Eisenhower administration secrets. Having incrementally increased the historical record, Cullather's account provided confirmation about some aspects of existing historical hypotheses but could not rule out competing ones or lay bare the full truth.[131] Viewed this way, the secrecy apparatus won—some of the operational specifics and the larger motivations of the Guatemala coup remain as obscure today as they were in the coup's immediate aftermath.[132]

But this view of *Secret History* and the Guatemala coup is incomplete for two reasons, each of which should be familiar by this point. Despite the CIA's broad use of its classification authority, general and specific information about American involvement was immediately available and in fact known within Guatemala[133] and throughout Western Europe,[134] and it became more widely known in the United States through incidental disclosures and responses to FOIA requests beginning in the 1970s.[135] The intervening decades have seen the disclosure of more information. In 2003, nearly fifty years after the coup, the State Department issued a *FRUS* volume with a more expansive collection of documents about the coup, and the CIA has made thousands of documents (many of them redacted) available via its website.[136] Additional documents had previously come to light during Guatemala's truth and reconciliation process, in aid of which the Clinton administration declassified thousands of documents. The National Security Archive, a private entity based at George Washington University, produced a documentary history tracing American involvement in Guatemala from the coup through the 1990s.[137] Formal and informal mechanisms of information disclosure and circulation have curtailed the secrecy that elements of the state continue to try to impose.

Secret History thus has become part of the broader unveiling of the secret history of the U.S. role in Guatemala's 1954 coup, only some of which has been the consequence of official state action. This is not to defend the CIA's effort to keep secrets, nor is it to deny the value of disclosure and the more complete picture that further access to documents can bring. The CIA's resistance to making the historical record of its operations available to the public within a reasonable period of time is inexcusable. But the CIA could only exert its full control over its own secret history, not the history to which the public gained access through other sources and authorities. At the same time, its secrecy merely increased the CIA's mythological status—in the United States as a preeminent tool of American foreign policy and elsewhere as a representative of American imperialism.[138] If most Americans remain ignorant of their nation's sordid history in Guatemala, the cause is as much ideological and willful or negligent public ignorance as it is the public's difficulty in obtaining information about it.[139]

In the second edition of *Secret History*, published in 2006, Cullather suggests a second way that secrecy has proven implausible. He explained his decision to keep the original redactions imposed by the CIA untouched, even though he could have inserted them with information gleaned from open sources:

> I have received more compliments on the eloquence of the gaps than on any of the legible passages. Readers have found they can check their speculations for fit, and search the blank spaces for clues on the aspects of the operation that the agency, even after 50 years, prefers to cloak in "plausible deniability."[140]

Redactions might impose secrecy, Cullather's readers told him, but they do not foreclose the effort—informed by other sources—to find the hidden meaning that the state has tried to conceal. "Eloquence" suggests that the empty spaces speak both of the missing content and of what those empty spaces say about the state that has removed their content.[141]

Secrecy law and practice can render history "secret," but it cannot fully control historical information, practice, and knowledge.[142] The state can attempt to cover the open secret—the information that is widely known yet cannot be publicly acknowledged—but it cannot stop discussion and speculation about it.[143] It may keep parts of the state veiled, but in doing so it reveals the state's efforts to veil itself—and in the process reveals the powerfully antidemocratic tendencies of the United States.

What Can We Learn from the Implausibility of Information Control?

Deep, long-lasting secrecy proves quite difficult to accomplish in practice. The legal limits on secrecy, as well as the informal means by which information flows out of the state, perform the crucial service of making the state more visible. We should not, however, mistake this movement of information for transparency, or even for a step toward a gloriously transparent state. As I argued in Part II, we can never achieve a perfectly visible government. The concept of transparency, like the concept of secrecy, assumes the ability of the law and bureaucracy to control information—an assumption belied by decades of frustrating experience with open government laws. Both concepts are implausible.

This is no reason to despair, however. Secrecy is, paradoxically, a very public issue, and one for which excessively secretive officials can be held politically accountable. As Vice President Cheney himself noted, secrecy can not only fail, revealing the information it sought to hide, but it can also be exposed and criticized as an undemocratic practice. In the "leaky city" of the nation's capitol, Cheney wrote in an essay published three years after completion of the congressional investigation of Iran–Contra, no secret stays buried too long, and no president's failed coverups go unpunished.[144] The more secrets, and the deeper they are kept, the greater the risk that the president takes in keeping them—a risk that can prove effective as an alternative to formal laws and legal proceedings in disciplining the executive branch. Such political costs cannot replace the legal limitations on secrecy that open government laws (not to mention, for criminal conspiracies and perjury, criminal laws) provide, but they serve as a mechanism by which the informal limits on secrecy can punish wrongdoers.

This understanding of secrecy as a tool whose use has potential political costs suggests a more foundational informal check on information control. If "the cover-up is worse than the crime,"[145] as the conventional wisdom teaches about Watergate, then secrecy appears to have an ethical dimension based upon a widely shared, intuitive distinction between legitimate and illegitimate secrecy. Partisans might disagree about whether any individual instance of secrecy is excessive and illegitimate, but in doing so they must frame their arguments in widely acknowledged and widely used terms.

The NEPDG episode illustrates this well: NEPDG's policy development process appeared absurdly secretive, as opponents and even members of the administration noted, and its secrecy provided the administration no political benefit and likely exacted political costs. The more significant and pervasive secrecy that followed in the Bush administration's post-9/11 anti-terrorism campaign, which the NEPDG episode rehearsed, proved more effective at temporarily controlling information. But information about many of the administration's programs, from the torture of prisoners and detainees to the warrantless wiretaps of domestic communications, ultimately leaked to the public over the course of the administration's second term.[146] By the end of the Bush presidency, the administration (and especially Cheney) had become quite politically unpopular, at least partially because of its seemingly unethical, excessive secrecy.

Barack Obama explicitly included open government as a platform in his 2008 campaign, in part to contrast himself with the Bush–Cheney White House.[147] The political price that Hillary Clinton paid during her presidential campaign for using a private e-mail address and server while she served as secretary of state, and her slow response to the controversy, illustrates this same dynamic. Political opponents can use an official act's secrecy as a weapon against the official who keeps it secret.

The first implication of secrecy's implausibility, then, is that it reveals the *political* nature of information control, and it demonstrates how politics serves both as a key motivation to use secrecy and as a crucial check on its overuse. It also shows the necessity of these informal means of disclosure, and the importance of avoiding draconian leak laws[148] and excessive prosecution of those who do leak.[149]

A second implication of information control's implausibility is the shift it suggests away from understanding secrecy and transparency as part of a binary, black-and-white conception of the state as either open and transparent or closed and opaque. We live in what Seth Kreimer has called an "ecology of transparency" that includes more than the struggle over legal disclosure mechanisms.[150] As my description of historic covert operations illustrated, events that are kept in deep secrecy become known as their details leak out over time, whether through formal or informal channels. Most events exist in a gray world of partial secrecy and partial disclosure, where even information about events whose existence the government denies is available from open sources, and where even events about which the government has made broad disclosures remain somewhat secret and mysterious.[151] Government information is not subject to control via an on–off switch; instead, it appears incrementally over time, both around and in spite of the literal and figurative black marks of government efforts to control its spread.

8   The Disappointments of Megaleaks

"Megaleaks," the unauthorized release of massive numbers of classified or se-cret government documents, offer an opportunity to test disclosure's effects. If transparency matters, then the unauthorized revelation of huge caches of documents revealing unknown government actions and programs should en-able the public to learn more and engage in more knowledgeable ways with the issues the documents raise, increasing public accountability with more en-lightened political debate and participatory democracy. But if disclosure proves harmful and secrecy is essential, then the leak of these materials should wreak havoc or at least significantly increase the nation's vulnerability in discernible ways and harm its relationships with the international community. Megaleaks therefore allow us to see what actually happens when disclosure occurs in cases where a statute and regulations would support the government's decision to withhold the leaked information, and when a court, balancing the anticipated beneficial and negative effects of the records' release, would most likely have denied disclosure.

Released in 1971, the Pentagon Papers constituted the first such megaleak in the modern era. It was composed of classified documents—indeed, the Pen-tagon did not fully declassify them until 2011, forty years after Ellsberg and his cohorts released them. Ellsberg and his supporters confidently predicted that the documents' release would transform the public's opinions about the Viet-nam War; government officials authoritatively asserted they would endanger the America military's war effort. It is entirely unclear whether these expected consequences in fact occurred. Key military and diplomatic witnesses who had testified about the likely dangerous effects of disclosure conceded a decade later that the release of the Pentagon Papers did not have the calamitous effects they had predicted.[1] A 2007 *Air Force Magazine* article similarly concluded that the Pentagon Papers appears to have had little or no effect on the remaining course of the war despite what they revealed to the North Vietnamese military.[2]

On the other side, several commentators (including some of Ellsberg's supporters) have acknowledged that the Pentagon Papers had little direct effect on public opinion or civilian and military policy regarding the Vietnam War.[3] Even those who claim that the Pentagon Papers caused or hastened the end of the war concede the contested nature of such a claim, and Daniel Ellsberg himself was reportedly disappointed by his leak's impact.[4] A large majority of the public had already favored pulling American troops out of Vietnam before the papers' publication as part of a dip in support for the war that had begun in 1967.[5] And despite their publication, Richard Nixon won the 1972 presidential election in a landslide, defeating a candidate who pledged to pull troops out immediately—the course of action that Ellsberg had hoped his leak would lead the public to support.[6]

With the mixed and murky record of The Pentagon Papers' release in mind, this chapter considers the extent to which WikiLeaks' distribution of documents stolen by Chelsea Manning and Edward Snowden's well-organized release of documents he took from the NSA affected national security, public knowledge and engagement, and existing policy. It is not a scientific undertaking and must rely on available open source information. I have neither access to classified information that might reveal some significant negative (or positive) effect, nor can I precisely calculate the influence of the leaked documents on wider historical events. The presence or absence of impacts now does not preclude the later manifestation of long-term effects, the disappearance of earlier impacts, or the possibility that effects have been classified for some strategic or military purpose—and thus, ironically, the secret effects of disclosed secrets. Moreover, it is difficult to trace the disclosures' causal effects as a natural experiment, given both the improbability of identifying a control group against which to compare and the complex set of conditions at play in the world before, during, and after the disclosure.[7] Nevertheless, given both the rhetoric of transparency and secrecy advocates and the theory on which they build their parallel assumptions of disclosure's effects, one would expect some discernible impact.

It is difficult, however, to trace any clear or meaningful pattern of effects that these disclosures caused.[8] The leaks clearly had some effects—at minimum, they upended how the Pentagon, NSA, and other intelligence agencies handle classified information in order to prevent the next megaleak from occurring. But besides that predictable behavioral impact on the government to seek better control of its information, I argue that other effects are uneven and unclear, and their murkiness does not support the strongest claims that advocates make about disclosure's necessity or danger. Nor does it augur well for any legal standard that asks judges or officials to balance the benefits and risks of disclosure. The chapter ultimately questions whether we can draw *any* clear conclusion about disclosure's effects, good or bad, strong or weak.

WikiLeaks

The most influential of the recent megaleaks began in April 2010 with WikiLeaks' uploading of a video (titled *Collateral Murder*) showing a lethal 2007 U.S. Army Apache helicopter attack on a group of men in Baghdad.[9] Part of the huge cache of digital files that Private First Class Chelsea Manning purloined, the video showed a brutal attack on a crowd that included reporters and other civilians with audio of the soldiers as they observed and then fired their weapons on the gathering.[10] More traditional documentary releases followed: in July 2010, tens of thousands of classified documents from the war in Afghanistan; in late October 2010, hundreds of thousands of documents about the Iraq War; from late November 2010 through early 2011, diplomatic cables between the U.S. State Department and its diplomatic missions around the world; and in April 2011, files concerning detainees held as suspected terrorists at the Guantánamo Bay military prison.[11] In September 2011, all of the State Department cables were made publicly available in unredacted form after reporters for the *Guardian* newspaper inadvertently disclosed the encryption key for the files, copies of which were accessible on the Internet.[12] As I noted in Chapter 2, none of the documents Manning leaked was classified above "secret," but they were all classified and unavailable to the public and likely would have remained so.[13]

After granting preview access to major Western newspapers that independently reviewed and reported on the documents, WikiLeaks posted the raw documentary sources on its site with minimal redactions to protect the anonymity of sources and other individuals who might face reprisal if their identities were revealed.[14] The so-called War Logs from Iraq and Afghanistan generally revealed unflattering and at times damning information about the conduct of the

American military during two wars. They presented evidence of civilian deaths, abuse, and torture by local militias friendly to the United States; the U.S. military's reliance on private contractors to perform difficult, controversial operations; and the problems that American forces faced both on the ground and in managing complex internal and international political alliances (for example, with Pakistan in Afghanistan). The diplomatic cables revealed a broad range of information about how U.S. diplomats viewed foreign leaders and the political and economic conditions in countries and regions around the world.[15] The Guantánamo files revealed that many of the detainees held as terrorists were low risk and that some of the intelligence relied on in capturing and holding them was flawed.[16]

I briefly identify and evaluate five potential effects that were discussed extensively by government officials and commentators and reported on by the press and in other open sources in anticipation of the WikiLeaks releases or in their immediate aftermath. Three concern the state's interest in limiting the potential adverse effects of disclosure: (1) The disclosures cost the lives of American military personnel and of their allies in Iraq and Afghanistan; (2) the disclosures would affect diplomatic relations between the United States and other nations; and (3) the disclosures would harm the flow of information among units of the American military, intelligence agencies, and State Department. The other two potential effects concern the public interest in disclosure: (4) The disclosures would enlighten and enliven the American public; and (5) the disclosures would have beneficial external effects outside the United States.

WikiLeaks' Direct and Indirect Effects on Military Operations

Military officials made numerous allegations in the aftermath of the Afghanistan releases about the immediate and likely future effects of the disclosures on American military operations.[17] The allegations seemed reasonable after a Taliban spokesman quickly announced that the organization would use WikiLeaks documents to identify collaborators.[18]

Then, in a joint statement e-mailed to WikiLeaks, five human rights groups, including Amnesty International and the International Crisis Group, complained that the release of uncensored Afghanistan documents would endanger their operations by disclosing the names of those with whom they worked.[19] Many of the cables released included the names of sources in ongoing conflict areas.[20] For example, the cables disclosed the names of leaders in the UN's development program, workers in several provincial reconstruction teams, and informants and collaborators who offered military intelligence.[21] The cables also disclosed the names of local military leaders who operated independently of the U.S. military but who also offered insight about local opinions regarding the U.S. occupation.[22] Some of the key leaders who engaged with U.S. forces were targeted by local insurgencies and sometimes killed after their identities were disclosed.[23] Such claims seem to demonstrate that the disclosures created grave danger to innocent human life and to the nation's military operations.[24]

In the aftermath of the disclosures, U.S. military officials concluded that they had both a legal and moral duty to reach out to the informants who had been outed. As a result, the military conducted operations to notify the informants that their covers had been compromised.[25] These operations often raised suspicion about the informant and compelled substantial alteration or termination of the informant's mission.[26] Additionally, the disclosures caused backlash against U.S. anti-proliferation efforts in Pakistan.[27] Pakistani officials had previously cooperated with U.S. officers to reclaim enriched uranium from Pakistan, but they were less willing to do so after Pakistani citizens and groups criticized their government for collaborating with the United States.[28]

But these damages were limited. No corroborated incident has come to light demonstrating that a document that WikiLeaks released caused significant physical damage to the U.S. military or directly and significantly damaged the diplomatic efforts of the United States.[29] The prosecution did not present evidence at Manning's court martial that anyone had died in reprisal following the disclosures.[30] Defense Secretary Robert Gates, who had complained in July 2010 that WikiLeaks would have "potentially dramatic and grievously harmful consequences,"[31] concluded less than three months later that the disclosures did not reveal any sensitive intelligence methods or sources.[32] Although Gates continued to warn about attacks against individuals named in the documents, a NATO official interviewed at the same time denied that any such attacks happened.[33]

Doubts that WikiLeaks' disclosures would directly affect military operations and individual lives cannot alleviate the fear that such effects occurred later or could occur in the future; but they do suggest that the *assumption* that such effects would necessarily follow—an assumption made by military officials and conservative political figures—was unwarranted. Although it is difficult to assess the significance of such threats without access to intelligence stating otherwise, WikiLeaks' disclosures and their aftermath at least suggest that the risk of disclosure is just that—a *risk* that does not constitute a necessary and essential effect of disclosure.[34]

However, the indirect effects of the WikiLeaks' disclosures on military operations are more certain. The leaks required the Pentagon and intelligence analysts to assess the potential harm of the documents WikiLeaks released and to mitigate them as much as possible. At Chelsea Manning's court martial, a military analyst testifying for the prosecution stated that her unit was forced to spend nearly 1,000 man-hours, at a cost of $200,000, to assess and analyze the impact of the released documents, diverting resources from other activities in Afghanistan.[35] Other military and intelligence bureaucracies undoubtedly also expended resources to review the disclosures, as the enormous organizational machinery of which Manning was a part reacted to the release of the information it had produced.[36] The disclosure's adverse effects on the U.S. military's reputation abroad likely also had material effects on the security of troops stationed in Iraq and elsewhere, raising the costs of those military engagements.

WikiLeaks' Direct and Indirect Effects on Diplomatic Relations

The claim that disclosures would affect the State Department and U.S. diplomatic relations exhibits a similar dynamic. On the eve of the release of the diplomatic cables, Harold Koh, the State Department's legal advisor, warned Assange in a letter made public that WikiLeaks' planned disclosure violated U.S. law; Koh complained of the certain increased danger that the disclosure of diplomatic cables would create for innocent civilians named in the documents, for ongoing military operations, and for cooperation and relations between the United States and other nations.[37] The State Department also warned hundreds of human rights activists, officials of foreign governments, and businesspeople who were identified in the diplomatic cables of the threats their identification might create for them.[38]

Again, however, no clear evidence has come to light of any direct ill effects the disclosures have caused, and while it may have, in Koh's words, "endanger[ed] the lives of countless individuals," it seems not to have caused any deaths. Administration officials did not publicly identify any additional harassment that its sources experienced as a result of the WikiLeaks' disclosures.[39] The U.S. ambassador to Mexico was forced to resign after the release of cables in which he criticized the Mexican government's efforts to fight drug trafficking,[40] and the ambassador to Ecuador was expelled after the release of her cable complaining of widespread corruption among that country's police force.[41] The ambassadors were punished for accurately reporting to Washington open secrets about the nations where they were stationed—that is, for being exposed doing their jobs. But no direct harm was traced to the cables. The disclosures did not seem to permanently damage U.S.–Mexico relations, and the cable's disclosure did not permanently damage the already-strained relationship between the United States and Ecuador, as the countries reestablished diplomatic relations within five months of the initial explusion.[42]

Koh's letter to Assange also warned of the indirect effects that the disclosures would have on diplomatic confidences, as did Secretary of State Hillary Clinton in a news conference immediately after the cable release began.[43] The warning assumed that internal communications between U.S. diplomats and the State Department would be less forthright for fear of later exposure, and foreign sources would be less likely to disclose information or share opinions with American diplomats for fear that the United States could not protect their statements and identities from disclosure.[44] This claim concerns marginal, though perhaps significant, effects on diplomatic discourse and deliberation as engaged in by participants; as such, it is not one for which evidence can easily be marshaled except through the statements of those who are current or former State Department employees.[45] Courts tend to defer to such claims made by the executive branch regarding information about national security and diplomatic efforts,[46] but this deference to claims of anticipated effects made by the executive branch is not the same as concluding that such effects in fact occur.

Later statements by cabinet secretaries have suggested that these damaging effects may not have occurred and may not be expected to occur in the future. In a news conference soon after the start of the diplomatic cable disclosures, Secretary Gates confidently declared that the releases would have little effect on diplomatic relations;[47] a few days later, Secretary Clinton also significantly downplayed her concerns after she attended an Organization for Security and Cooperation in Europe meeting where she spoke with foreign leaders who assured her that diplomatic relations would continue as before.[48] An anonymous State Department official told Reuters in 2011 that the revelations were more embarrassing than destructive and that "[l]ong-term damage to US intelligence and defense operations [] is unlikely to be serious."[49] Several commentators even hypothesized that the cables' release might in fact *improve* diplomatic relations, insofar as they revealed the similarity between the U.S.'s public and private statements, increasing American diplomats' credibility[50]—a sentiment echoed in part by Defense Secretary Gates.[51] By the time of Snowden's leaks a few years later, commentators and diplomatic sources looked back on the State Department cables as relatively innocuous.[52]

WikiLeaks' Effects on Intra-Governmental Information Sharing
Chelsea Manning had apparently downloaded the video and document caches that she passed along to WikiLeaks from the Department of Defense's SIPRNet network, to which she had authorized access.[53] After the WikiLeaks disclosures, government agencies reviewed their use of classified databases and began to implement various security measures to prevent future leaks.[54] The measures that drew the most attention were those involving information sharing among federal agencies.[55] The 9/11 Commission had denounced organizational "stovepipes" that had developed within units of agencies and across agencies for having contributed to the failure of counterterrorism agencies to prevent the 9/11 attacks.[56] These bureaucratic and technological impediments to the flow of information going out of and coming into agencies left units without current intelligence or even sufficient information to perform their tasks. Without access to documents obtained or developed by one agency, employees and units working on similar or related projects were uninformed about the development of the terrorist threat.[57] In a post–9/11 response, agencies took concerted steps to make information relevant to counterterrorism efforts available throughout the federal government.[58] This informational reorganization provided Manning with access to documents she would not have been able to steal prior to the reforms.

In the wake of the WikiLeaks' disclosures, many both within and outside the government charged that the effort to share information had made data networks insecure and left classified information vulnerable to theft and leaking.[59] The State Department disconnected itself from Defense's SIPRNet, thereby securing its information from potential leaks by non–State Department employees and removing the agency from at least part of its information-sharing commitment with Defense, and thereby inhibiting information sharing.[60] At the same time, however, numerous commentators have criticized the lax data-security and security-clearance measures that allegedly allowed Manning to copy the data she ultimately released to WikiLeaks,[61] and Secretary Gates and State Department representatives announced necessary security upgrades to military and diplomatic information networks.[62] Manning's leak was therefore at least preferable to a hack by a foreign intelligence service that could have secretly exploited the same lax security without the U.S. security forces' knowledge.

WikiLeaks' Effects on the American Public
Arguments about the beneficial effects of transparency begin with the assumption that the public will pay attention to, understand, and act or threaten

to act on the government information they receive. When the public's actions and the connection between those actions and disclosed information are clear, these effects are easy to identify. In the case of the WikiLeaks' disclosures, however, even the precise nature of the disclosed information—and especially whether the disclosed documents reveal new, significant information—is deeply contested.

To some American commentators, especially those on the left who were critical of the Bush administration and had grown increasingly wary of the Obama administration, the WikiLeaks' disclosures proved exceptionally reve-latory. In order to support their claim, a number of WikiLeaks' advocates in late 2010 and early 2011 developed lists of the most important events and is-sues that the disclosures illuminated—lists too long and varied to recount in any detail but that, according to one commentator, demonstrated "the breadth of the corruption, deceit, brutality and criminality on the part of the world's most powerful factions."[63] Because these commentators generally assume that increased transparency causes or should cause increased public knowledge, popular political engagement, and better government, they concluded that the public would learn, act, and respond to the disclosed information.[64]

For WikiLeaks' skeptics and critics, however, the disclosures had limited in-formational value. The information WikiLeaks revealed may have provided ad-ditional details to general information widely known by engaged elites,[65] such commentators argued, but it did not provide evidence of any significant gov-ernment misconduct or abuses of power.[66] Because of the likelihood that the disclosures had already, or would certainly, harm foreign policy and American interests, WikiLeaks failed the rough, intuitive balancing test those critics ap-plied. The disclosures offered only a minimal gain in public knowledge, but they posed a significant risk to the state, diplomacy, and national security.[67] According to First Amendment attorney Floyd Abrams, who helped defend the *New York Times* in the Pentagon Papers case,

> [WikiLeaks] revels in the revelation of "secrets" simply because they are secret. It assaults the very notion of diplomacy that is not presented live on C-SPAN. It has sometimes served the public by its revelations but it also offers, at con-siderable potential price, a vast amount of material that discloses no abuses of power at all.[68]

The general public's response to WikiLeaks is in fact difficult to gauge, but polls found that the public was not especially interested in WikiLeaks and that a strong majority of the American public disliked the site and its disclosures.[69] At least one poll conducted in late July and early August 2010 (after the leak of documents from the Afghanistan conflict) showed a nearly even split in public opinion about the site and about the extent of the public's interest in its disclosure,[70] but WikiLeaks' popularity and public interest in the site dropped considerably by the end of the year, following the diplomatic cable releases. Multiple polls taken in December 2010 showed strong majorities that both disapproved of the site and thought it did more harm than good to the public interest.[71] One poll that broke down its results by party and ideological affiliation found that Democrats and Republicans disapproved of the site in roughly equal numbers, and that even 64 percent of self-identified liberals expressed disapproval.[72] To explain the disinterest its polling had found, the Pew Center noted that coverage of the wars in Afghanistan and Iraq had decreased, and public interest in them had diminished as well.[73]

Even conceding the limits of public opinion polling, it is difficult to conclude based on this data that WikiLeaks made a significant positive impact on the general public's engagement with and knowledge about the state and politics.[74] If we assume, with WikiLeaks' proponents, that the site disclosed important and unknown information about outrageous American governmental policy and misconduct, and if we assume, with transparency proponents and according to WikiLeaks' theory of information's effects, that information disclosures increase public knowledge and political engagement, then one would expect to find widespread discontent organized around popular political movements in the United States as a result of WikiLeaks' disclosures. But the only insurgent movement in the November 2010 election cycle was the Tea Party faction of the Republican Party, which was focused far more on the size and cost of government than on the wars in Iraq and Afghanistan or American foreign policy.[75]

No popular political movement of any significant size formed or was energized in the United States as a consequence of the disclosures.[76] Nor was there significant or even discernible movement to change existing military engagements or foreign policy in the period following the WikiLeaks' disclosures, except in terms of tightening controls on classified information. The end of the Iraq War in late 2011 appeared unrelated to WikiLeaks' disclosures about American conduct during the war;[77] indeed, President Obama's troop withdrawal was consistent with a pledge he had made in February 2009, before the WikiLeaks' disclosures began.[78] Obama seemed not to have changed his policy in either country in response to the WikiLeaks' disclosures; it was not until June 2011, nearly a year after the Afghanistan War Logs were released, that he announced a withdrawal of troops in response to the occupation's costs and a weakened al Qaeda leadership.[79] The reformist claims that WikiLeaks had affected public opinion or inspired popular political activism thus seem unpersuasive.

WikiLeaks' International Effects

The diplomatic cables that WikiLeaks released concerned U.S. relations with other nations and with the leading political figures abroad, and the information that they revealed was well covered by the international press and domestic journalists in those other nations. One can only guess at the effect of this information on popular elections. Commentators on Peru's 2011 presidential election posited that the diplomatic cables that discussed one candidate, Keiko Fujimori, daughter of a former Peruvian president, might have assisted Ollanta Humala's winning campaign.[80] More significantly, several autocratic regimes in the Middle East and North Africa faced major popular uprisings that were grouped together as part of an Arab Spring during the period of the cables' release. Regional, national, and local media within the region also gained significant credibility with their readership by partnering with WikiLeaks and were able to provide important information about their governments' relations with the United States.[81]

Some observers and commentators have asserted that WikiLeaks' disclosures directly affected Tunisia, whose president, Zine al-Abidine Ben Ali, fled the country in the face of widespread and increasingly violent protests against his corrupt, repressive regime.[82] The WikiLeaks' cables concerning Tunisia revealed American diplomats' contempt for Ben Ali's "system without checks" in a government whose kleptomania began with the first family.[83] The Tunisia-related cables were translated and made available to Tunisians via locally produced websites.[84] According to various reports, the cables' distribution further radicalized an already angry and alienated citizenry, helped spur them to increasingly vehement dissent, and suggested that the United States would not intervene on Ben Ali's behalf.[85]

This purported effect is a complex one, as the cables themselves revealed nothing new to protesters about their government's corruption, while their influence would be difficult to isolate—indeed, their influence is contested by both Tunisians and Americans.[86] Rather, the impact of the cables may have come from informing Tunisians of others' perceptions and knowledge about

their corrupt government—information that enlightened and further energized protesters about the righteousness and likely success of their cause.[87] If,
as has been widely reported, the Tunisian revolt in turn inspired other popular
uprisings in the region,[88] including especially the overthrow of Hosni Mubarak
in Egypt,[89] and WikiLeaks in fact played some role in inspiring the Tunisian
protesters, then the disclosures had significant direct and indirect effects (to
whatever small degree) in setting potentially democratic change in motion.[90]
Of course the claim that these uprisings constitute a positive development that
is traceable in some material way to WikiLeaks must in turn rely on a second
claim about the Arab Spring's positive longitudinal effects.

If we assume that both claims are true, what can we learn about transparency, secrecy, and open government law and policy from the external, international effects of disclosures from one nation's classified documents? American
information-access law seems to take no consideration of spillover effects that
take place outside American borders and affect only foreign governments. Instead, the public interest, as understood and accounted for in the prevailing
balancing test, implicitly refers to an *American* public interest. The idea that
such beneficial effects can occur outside the nation's borders, however, is inherent in the operations and ideals of data networks that recognize no national
boundaries and can be used to actively resist them, as well as in international
human rights law, which recognizes a right to receive information "regardless
of frontiers."[91]

It therefore seems only fair to consider these effects in calculating the value
of WikiLeaks' disclosures. But it is also exceedingly unlikely that they would
be considered sufficiently important to include in national laws within a geopolitical world governed by Westphalian states with sovereignty over their
territory and domestic political order. At least in the United States, open government laws are territorial, governing only the units within their borders—
state and local borders for sub-federal governments and for units operating
within national borders (and territories) or part of its organizational chain for
the federal government. The laws' principal concerns are with open government's costs and benefits within those territories. A legislature and court might
be willing to balance external, extraterritorial benefits of disclosure, but it is
unlikely that those benefits would outweigh a government entity's concerns
for disclosure's threat to domestic national security or law enforcement. Thus,
WikiLeaks' arguably most discernible effect would have little impact on the
debates surrounding the expansion of national open government laws.

Snowden

In the first part of a humorous and insightful segment that ran on his HBO series *Last Week Tonight*, the comedian John Oliver attempted to gauge the public's reaction to Edward Snowden's disclosure of the NSA's surveillance of U.S. citizens, non-U.S. citizens, and foreign leaders.[92] Snowden had declared the intent of his leaks in his initial interview with *The Guardian*:

> I really want the focus to be on these documents and the debate which I hope this will trigger among citizens around the globe about what kind of world we want to live in. My sole motive is to inform the public as to that which is done in their name and that which is done against them.[93]

Oliver's segment offered two observations to demonstrate that the disclosures were not meeting Snowden's goals: First, the average person—as represented by a series of individuals interviewed outside Manhattan's Times Square—either knew little of Snowden or confused him with Julian Assange. The ignorance of these random passersby, who struggled to recall the fragments of international news stories from more than a year before, greatly amused Oliver and his studio audience. Second, he conceded that even he could not fully grasp the technological and legal complexity of Snowden's disclosures—which helped explain both the public's ignorance about the leaks and the limited impact the leaks appeared to have had to that point.

But Oliver suggested a solution. Americans could prove capable of outrage and anger at the surveillance programs that Snowden revealed once they understood the programs' effects on their everyday lives. Oliver provided the plainest, most personal means to explain the NSA's surveillance: The government could intercept "dick pics," photos of a man's penis sent to his lover. The same people-on-the-street who plainly did not understand what Snowden had disclosed quickly grasped and opposed the program once it was reduced to that absurd level of intimacy.

Oliver's report illustrated how Snowden's leaks differed from the Manning/WikiLeaks' disclosures in important ways. The latter illuminated diffuse, distant issues—the fog and violence of war, the missteps and hypocrisy of U.S. foreign policy—that were not susceptible to specific policy or political prescription. The *Collateral Murder* video would disgust those already convinced of American brutality and the foolishness of the U.S. occupation of Iraq, but the video did not cause a significant change in American public opinion.[94] "Cablegate" revealed specific aspects of American foreign policy for those who lived in those countries that the cables concerned, but it appeared to be of minimal interest to American voters. Snowden's leaks, by contrast, narrowly focused on a particular government practice, and he emphasized in interviews and writings that he hoped to spur a "conversation" and debate on NSA surveillance, an issue that he has consistently framed as affecting everyone.[95]

However, the Snowden leaks did not by themselves appear to have the kind of direct effect on public opinion that he and his collaborators likely expected. It clearly had some impact, of course, if only by the press's attention to it. His initial and later disclosures focused attention on government surveillance of American citizens and pressured the NSA and Obama administration to admit the existence of previously secret surveillance programs. Press critic and academic Jay Rosen claimed to have found a "Snowden effect"—the "[d]irect and indirect gains in public knowledge from the cascade of events and further reporting" that followed the leaks.[96] But the leak and the government's admission by themselves might not have changed the programs nor led to any significant impact on public attention to and knowledge of them.

Part of the disclosures' uncertain impact no doubt arose from the *ad hominen* attacks on Snowden himself, as well as the story of his exile ultimately in Russia in order to avoid extradition to the United States. Like Assange, Snowden quickly became a polarizing figure, and heated discussion of his whistleblower status, rather than of the substance of those leaks, dominated much of the coverage.[97] Perhaps, as the legal academic Orin Kerr argued in a blog post, the sheer volume and diversity of the information Snowden disclosed and the somewhat scattered way that the press reported on the myriad surveillance programs did not inspire a single, focused debate about one galvanizing issue.[98] Polls taken before, immediately after, and more than a year after the leaks began to be reported upon reveal virtually unchanged public opinion of government surveillance.[99] The leaks may have led to some change in short-term private behavior, as some individuals and businesses elevated their encryption capabilities to circumvent government collection of data.[100] But they seem not to have transformed public opinion or led to widespread popular political protest in the United States.

Individual opinion and concerted popular political action are not the only sources of accountability in response to disclosure, however, and Snowden's leaks had some impact even without widespread public interest in them. By documenting the role that foreign governments, wireless telephone companies, and e-mail and cloud storage providers played in the NSA's surveillance programs, the disclosures angered powerful institutional agents with reason to distance themselves from and even oppose the programs once they became public knowledge.[101] U.S.-based technology companies were concerned not merely with alienating their American customers but also with the outcry in Europe, where much stronger privacy protections prevail and where customers plausibly threatened to abandon American-based e-mail and cloud storage providers.[102] U.S. companies began to offer customers the use of servers located outside of the United States to avoid NSA surveillance, while the disclosures proved a boon to European cloud storage and e-mail companies.[103]

The disclosures harmed diplomatic relations with foreign governments as well. European and Latin American governments not only expressed outrage at the surveillance of their citizens but at Snowden's revelation that the NSA had spied on German, Brazilian, and Mexican leaders.[104] The leaks revealed shared surveillance operations and intelligence among the "Five Eyes" consortium of nations (the United States, the United Kingdom, Canada, Australia, and New Zealand), which included spying on other countries and even on one another. Snowden thus shamed the United States not only for its surveillance programs but also for its poor information security. In response to the evolving story and disclosures, President Obama softened his rhetoric between August 2013 and January 2014 and began to offer Snowden grudging respect and to concede the need to reform the NSA's various programs.[105]

The disclosures also led to real, if marginal, changes in U.S. law. Oliver's April 2015 coverage of Snowden's disclosures and his interview of Snowden in Russia (where the leaker confirmed the government's "dick pic" capability) came almost two years after those disclosures began, but his show knowingly presented the segment at a propitious time. Key parts of what the NSA viewed as its legal authority to conduct its formerly secret surveillance programs would have ended on June 1, 2015, less than two months after the segment aired, unless Congress reauthorized the program by statute. Section 215 of the Patriot Act authorized the collection of business records for the ongoing investigation of terrorist and counterintelligence operations and was the basis for the NSA's obtaining telecommunications records from U.S. service providers. Congress was therefore forced to reconsider the legislative status quo while public attention and interest groups, especially those concerned with protecting privacy, were attentive to and knowledgeable about the NSA's programs to an extent that they had not been in the thirteen years between the Patriot Act's initial enactment and Snowden's disclosures.[106]

The Obama administration declined to seek reauthorization of Section 215 after the Snowden disclosures and instead endorsed the USA Freedom Act, which Obama signed into law on June 2, 2015.[107] The statute made several reforms to existing surveillance law that increased oversight and privacy protections.[108] Civil liberties groups were not satisfied with the more limited surveillance authorization that the new law provides—and were frustrated that it went no further than to address the programs that Section 215 established—but they considered it an improvement over the Patriot Act.[109] Snowden himself declared victory in the *New York Times*, even though he did not specify exactly what had been won.[110]

If the case for a positive "Snowden effect" therefore is stronger than the one for Chelsea Manning and WikiLeaks, critics claim that it also created significant dangers in the fight against terror. The NSA and White House warned about the Snowden leaks immediately after they began. Senator Dianne Feinstein, a Democrat from the reliably liberal and tech-friendly state of California, even called Snowden's actions treasonous.[111] In a February 2015 news conference, NSA Director Admiral Mike Rodgers claimed that the leak "has had a material impact on our ability to generate insights as to what terrorist groups around the world are doing. . . . Anyone [who] thinks this has not had an impact . . . doesn't know what they are talking about."[112] Stewart Baker, formerly a high-ranking Homeland Security official and General Counsel of the NSA, was one of Snowden's most publicly vocal critics, alleging that Snowden might have been in the employ of a foreign intelligence service and that his disclosures significantly impaired the country's ability to defend itself, especially given the specific details about the NSA's programs that Snowden disclosed.[113]

As with Cablegate and the Iraq War Logs disclosures, critics offered little in the way of specific proof of the costs of the disclosures, besides the direct costs of the time that personnel had to spend to assess and mitigate the damage and the costs of changing the disclosed programs, if possible or necessary. As time passed, the warnings appeared to dissipate. Director of National Intelligence James Clapper conceded in a June 2014 interview that "it doesn't look like [Snowden] took as much" as initially feared. The same article quoted an anonymous senior intelligence official who conceded that the disclosures' greatest impact would be the "damage in foreign relations" they caused as well as the extent to which the leaks had "poisoned" the NSA's relations with commercial providers.[114]

But Snowden's disclosures continue to offer a ready excuse for intelligence failures, as CIA Director John Brennan appeared to blame Snowden for the difficulty in stopping the terrorist attacks in Paris in November 2015, complaining that the leaks had made "our ability collectively, internationally, to find these terrorists much more challenging."[115] Clapper's vague claim only illustrates the difficult of assigning causation to complex events. Even if the Paris terrorists used encryption to keep their plans secure from surveillance, it is still nearly impossible to prove, or even conclude with any confidence, that French intelligence, military, and police authorities would have thwarted the attack but for Snowden's disclosures.[116] Indeed, prior to the attacks, private security firms and media outlets had offered conflicting accounts of how much and how well terrorist groups in the Middle East have responded to the leaks.[117] It is likely that the NSA has found it more difficult to gather intelligence on future terrorist threats due to the leaks and the political response to them. It is possible that some future attack will occur that might have been preventable but for the relinquished intelligence sources. But the public cannot and likely will not learn of the relationship between the disclosures and any past or future terrorist action—and it is also quite possible that the intelligence community would not be able to prove a connection between the two.

Notably, Snowden leaked a top-secret internal study by the NSA of the immediate effects of the *New York Times*'s 2005 revelation of the warrantless wiretapping program.[118] The memo, whose authorship was attributed to the NSA's general counsel, offered vague though considerable concern about the story's short- and long-term impact on the NSA's ability to monitor terrorists' communications.[119] The report predicted that "three events" would take place as a consequence of the story's publication:

> (1) The U.S. Government will lose valuable intelligence, (2) the U.S. Government will need to seek alternative intelligence sources and methods at additional costs, and (3) the people of the United States and our allies will be even more vulnerable to surprise attacks because the ability to identify, track and disrupt terrorist related individuals, plans and activities is degraded.[120]

The report was issued three days after the wireless wiretapping story appeared and stated that no mention of the story or NSA program had been heard in "adversary communications" to that point. The risk, of course, was real, but the report offered no evidence that the threats had harmed intelligence gathering or that the disclosure revealed a program that the terrorists did not already know or suspect existed.

The NSA no doubt continued to study the impact of the story, and perhaps it found that terrorist groups and others that would otherwise have been subject to its surveillance programs had developed means to circumvent eavesdropping; perhaps, too, the NSA itself was forced to improve its technology and analysis. The agency did not, however, prevent Snowden from purloining its own immediate analysis of the story's impact several years later, despite the analysis's top-secret classification. And of course in the endlessly recursive nature of the relationship between secrecy and disclosure, we cannot precisely evaluate the impact of Snowden's leak of the study of an earlier leak's impact. The participants in this relationship continue to maintain that all such disclosures will have or are likely to have some real world effect. It is no wonder that an ironist like John Oliver finds this endless dance so fertile for his comedy.

The Consequences of Disclosure's Uncertain Effects

A world with regular megaleaks is different from one without. Whether it is a drastically more dangerous one is impossible to assess, as is the extent of the marginally greater danger the leaks might have created. At the same time, it is equally difficult to conclude that the disclosures even approach the beneficial effects typically claimed by transparency advocates to the nation whose information is disclosed. Disclosure will not necessarily transform the United States or any Western democracy into a model of popular deliberation, participatory decision making, and perfect governance. Western governments and societies are too complex and decentralized, their publics too dispersed, and their information environments too saturated for transparency, by itself, to have significant transformative potential.

The ability of WikiLeaks and Snowden to steal and distribute massive quantities of secret information challenges the underlying assumptions of the cybernetic theory of the informational state in three ways. First, WikiLeaks' ability to receive and distribute leaked information cheaply, quickly, and seemingly unstoppably allows it to bypass the legal framework that allows secrecy while it requires transparency. Snowden's leaks similarly demonstrate the fragility of the state's information security and the difficulties of information control. For this reason, the WikiLeaks/Manning and Snowden model threaten to make laws attempting to impose secrecy and transparency irrelevant.[121]

Second, megaleaks should force us to reconsider and test the assumption that disclosure produces effects that can serve as the basis for judicial and administrative prediction, calculation, and balancing. Courts can continue to rely upon the idea that they are "balancing" various "interests," but all they do in such instances is make intuitive guesses as to what might happen in the wake of disclosure or its absence. If courts continue to balance interests, they should require more than a worried, unsubstantiated prediction—an administrative version of an *ipse dixit* (the Latin term lawyers and legal scholars use for a dogmatic and unproven claim)—before granting a request for secrecy. Megaleaks thereby threaten not only the law's effects but the very assumption that courts and legislatures can balance measurable consequences that can be estimated before and after the fact. "Balancing" requires more than estimates of disclosure's effects—it requires one to decide how best to prioritize the normative ends of democratic debate and national security.

Finally, the implications of this conclusion are conceptually profound for the study and theory of government information.[122] If we cannot assume or predict the existence of effects from a massive disclosure of classified documents, then some core theoretical concepts and assumptions about secrecy and transparency are incoherent if not conceptually bankrupt. Just as we must remain committed to keeping ourselves secure without allowing the government to successfully assert that every potential piece of information must remain secret indefinitely, so should we remain committed to creating the conditions of a democratic state without simply assuming and asserting transparency's utopian effects.

Conclusion

The West Wing, *the West Wing, and*
Abandoning the Informational Fix

Especially in its first seasons, *The West Wing* (1999–2006) offered its weekly
network television viewers an authentic-seeming White House. The show's
elaborate sets, its famously long tracking shots that led and followed characters
down the corridors of executive power, and its dialogue-heavy debates engaged
in by a devoted and ambitious staff offered a documentary-like take on what
power looks and feels like. We may be barred from seeing the actual version
of elected officials' private debates and personal crises, just as we are barred
from the physical corridors of the West Wing except in tours booked months
in advance through our congressional representative or diplomatic embassy.
But Josiah Bartlet's presidency was fully available. The president and his advisors tried their best to rationally and deliberately solve problems the nation
faced—problems recognizable to its audience, like health care, terrorism, and
taxes—while making the political compromises necessary to implement those
solutions as best they could. *The West Wing* provided its audience complete
transparency, albeit of an imaginary White House.

At the same time, the series presented a transparently fictional account. In
addition to recasting known actors as political officials (most notably Martin
Sheen and Rob Lowe), the show's effort to portray the presidency also seam-
lessly blended narrative film and television genres with its seemingly realistic
political storylines. Individual episodes alternately invoked the political thriller,
the melodramatic soap opera, and the romantic comedy, shifting tone from
scene to scene. The series also looked beautiful, employing the very highest of

Hollywood production values in its fantastic, almost mythical vision of what the highest level of power looks and feels like. The imaginary White House looked much better than the real one.

The show complemented its visual depiction of the White House's inner sanctums with an idealized depiction of U.S. politics. Critics on the left and right understandably derided the show as liberal fantasy, a fanciful vision of what a Clinton presidency *should* have looked like if you found it ideologically attractive.[1] The show might have successfully recreated the White House's architectural features (although some commentators suggested otherwise), but its bureaucracy was strangely thin, its president absurdly deliberative and contemplative, and its depiction of officialdom notably devoid of the quotidian acts and compromises required of governing a complex federal administrative state. The seeming authenticity of its politics and physical setting served more as scaffolding to its presentation of politics as a fictional, character-driven melodrama than as the perfectly reconstructed backdrop of a true-to-life documentary.

As cultural critics and theorists have long argued, however, narrative texts can project, manipulate, and in turn affect viewers' opinions and common sense. *The West Wing*'s success suggests that it met a popular desire, held especially strongly by the political and demographic elites attracted to the show, for viewing the interior workings of politics and government—and for wishing or imagining it to be a world populated with brilliant, articulate, idealistic, and physically attractive officials who act with reason, honor, and competence. The show provided a window into "good government" for those who long for it. Its realistic gloss offered a normative vision of how the state should operate, making the desired appear possible as well as necessary: We should know our elected officials, and they should be good. By allowing viewers to "see" into the White House, *The West Wing* gave *its* "public"—the virtual, presumptively cosmopolitan and liberal citizens of a Bartlet presidency—the kind of access it sought to the kind of government it wanted. The show provided the vision of a transparent state to a community of viewers likely composed of those who would most loudly claim to want a real one.[2]

Tinkering, Rather Than Fixing

As I have argued through this book, neither the ideal of a transparent government nor the hope of an informationally secure one can meet their collective promise to deliver a truly democratic, administratively efficient, and secure state. We can see *The West Wing*, but we cannot see the state in a meaningful way—to view its workings and documents, to have access to the information that officials produce and obtain. I cannot confidently propose a solution that opens the state enough to the public's view and improves bureaucratic efficiency without interfering with the state's functions, including especially its efforts to keep the nation secure and protect the public's health, safety, and welfare. I too wish the West Wing—and Congress, and the Supreme Court, and state governors' mansions and legislatures, and local governments—could become *The West Wing* and produce and then reveal visible, honorable governing institutions in a manner that does not adversely affect those institutions' performance. But I can offer no single programmatic answer to a problem with so many moving parts.

Indeed, as I argued in Part I, the desire for a fix is symptomatic of the democratic wish for a fully visible administrative state, one that cannot be fulfilled given the tasks we demand of it. I have explained the implausibility of fixing state information in two ways. First, I have described the obstructions that impede political and legal efforts to regulate the state's control of information. But second, I have questioned the very idea of seeing the state by critiquing the central role that information plays in our misunderstanding of the state and its governance. Our frustration with an opaque state, in other words, comes not only from *how* we attempt to impose transparency and maintain secrecy but also *why* we do so.

Notwithstanding the improbability of fixing the state's information problems, government *can* improve how and when it releases information, and, with the insistence or assistance of private actors, has attempted to do so. Each of the various reform movements I described in Part I has helped produce marginally more information to the public than would be available in their absence. This assumes, of course, that these reforms have not had the unanticipated consequence of creating conditions that have encouraged greater government secrecy. (For example, one could argue that the FOIA has encouraged *more* government secrecy by leading officials to classify excessively, avoid reducing communications to writing, and so on. While an interesting thought experiment, it is also an unprovable counterfactual claim. For simplicity's sake, I will assume the truth of the more intuitive, equally unprovable claim that transparency reforms have marginally improved the availability of government information.) I want to briefly mention several less heralded and non-sexy reforms that also improve the flow of government information: small, innovative institutions within the executive branch and temporal requirements for disclosure. My purpose is not to suggest that these changes can fix the state's information problems, but that, like all of the reforms I have noted in the book, the state can be tinkered with. But not without unintended consequences, as I will also note below.

I have written elsewhere about the surprising success of the 9/11 Commission and the potential for the advisory investigative commission as a transparency-forcing institution;[3] I have also described the ombudsman offices that numerous states and, more recently, the federal government have created to assist the public in seeking information and to help government entities comply with the legal transparency obligations.[4] Other scholars and observers have identified additional institutional mechanisms that have shown promise as models for increasing government accountability and disclosure. Expert and advocate Steven Aftergood of the Federation of American Scholars has praised the work of the Interagency Security Classification Appeals Panel (ISCAP), which is staffed by high-level officials from across the intelligence community; this group has discretionary authority to review secrecy decisions, including an agency's refusal to declassify old documents or to require an agency that refuses a public request to disclose a document to provide additional, satisfactory reasons for doing so.[5] And as legal scholar Shirin Sinnar and others have explained, inspectors general offer mechanisms from within agencies to investigate allegations of wrongdoing, most notably in their disclosures to Congress and the public about post-9/11 human rights abuses by intelligence and law enforcement agencies.[6]

These institutional innovations share one important attribute: They enjoy relative independence from the entity or entities whose performance they are reviewing, independence that can give their efforts credibility for state actors as well as for the public. At the same time, the institutions' location within the executive branch and their independence from a competing branch makes their position less adversarial and therefore a useful supplement to an adversarial process overseen ultimately by courts and the electoral process. They provide what legal scholars have championed as an "internal separation of powers" that can check and balance executive branch institutions, especially in the areas of foreign policy and national security where other branches have only limited constitutional authority and tend to defer to presidential actions.[7] Some of them can also offer something that the mere release of documents cannot: a comprehensible report that provides context and explanation for the information they disclose.

Of course these institutions and institutional mechanisms can also disrupt the operations of the government's existing institutions in counterproductive and dangerous ways, and they can potentially harm the state by becoming too independent or by seeming independent while in fact acting as the captured agent of an entrenched interest. The 9/11 Commission's success at projecting independence and authority, for example, enabled it to propose influential reforms to the intelligence community that might not have helped and may have harmed national security agencies.[8] Powerless or feckless inspectors general and ombudsmen can give the appearance of fighting secrecy while merely burying information or allowing agencies to skirt compliance with their legal mandates. Even tinkering, in other words, has its risks.

The timing of disclosure also matters. The value of government information to the state and the public shifts over time.[9] The shift in value occurs in two directions. First, the costs of disclosure can diminish as time passes, whether because a threat to national security or law enforcement dissipates or because disclosure might no longer affect officials' deliberation on a sensitive issue. Laws and regulations have increasingly focused on this issue, albeit with quite long delays in disclosure. The FOIA Improvement Act of 2016 limits agencies' ability to use the deliberative process privilege to exempt documents from disclosure, removing the exemption for internal government memoranda after twenty-five years.[10] The Obama administration's executive order reestablishing the classification system similarly revived a mandate begun under the Clinton administration that requires the declassification after twenty-five years of documents that are determined to have "permanent historical value."[11] And for an agency to avoid mandatory disclosure for a series of files, its director must submit a notification to ISCAP that the document still requires classification, allowing high-level representatives from within the executive branch to provide some external check on the agency's attempt to avoid disclosure.[12] The Presidential Records Act similarly subjects presidential documents to staged release over time.[13]

Unsurprisingly, such commitments have not proven entirely successful. Not all of the time limits are mechanical in application, and insufficient resources and institutional commitments can slow down the declassification and disclosure process, making some time limits less than fully mandatory in practice.[14] Twenty-five years is also an awfully long time; even the twelve-year period before restricted presidential records begin to be released under the Presidential Records Act seems excessively protracted. Perhaps subsequent administrations or a later Congress will shorten these time limits; perhaps too Congress can revisit the deliberative process exemption expiration, and agencies can release documents that would otherwise be eligible for the exemption prior to the quarter-century mark. While Congress may never do so, an imperfect program and time limit are better than no program nor time limit at all.

The second shift in information's value over time occurs because the public can find disclosure especially relevant at particular moments, especially *before* the government makes key decisions. Having access to information after the decision is better than having no information at all; but having access prior to the decision can enable the nation to avoid errors that prove costly over an extended period of time. For example, had a 9/11 Commission-like entity reviewed the available intelligence on Iraq's WMD program and alleged ties to al Qaeda before the 2003 invasion of Iraq, the public's support for the invasion might not have proved sufficient to support the Bush administration's plans. The public and its representatives within civil society and the state might prove better able to focus on and understand complex information at a key decisional moment.

Because each such decision is likely to arise in a fraught, contingent moment, as in the aftermath of the 9/11 attacks, it is unlikely that Congress would be willing or able to create a formal institutional structure that could anticipate and pre-commit to effective disclosure. One model to consider is the German ad hoc parliamentary Committees of Inquiry, in which a minority of legislators can call for the creation of a committee to investigate a particular issue—often national security—that is granted extraordinary powers for its investigation. The model could prove more useful for the pre-war review of available intelligence than the institutional congressional committee structure, which has proven incapable of conducting sufficient oversight of the intelligence and national security agencies.[15]

But this book has been a critical project rather than a normative one. Notwithstanding the marginal success of these reforms in tinkering with and chipping away at the problem of controlling government information, none can make the state sufficiently open to meet the theoretical model of a visible state while keeping it sufficiently closed to meet the theoretical model of a secure one. They do not constitute a cure-all for the insoluble problem of information control in a contemporary administrative state upon which we depend for a dizzying array of services and legal and regulatory enforcement.[16] Nor can they make the administrative state plainly visible to a public that often seems disinterested in its operations. At their best, their tinkering with existing structures and practices can disrupt bureaucracies that attempt and fail to control information—whether that failure is due to their refusal to disclose information that should, within a democracy, be disclosed or to their inability to protect information that should be better protected.

The West Wing and the Complexity of Government Information

Let's return, then, to Daniel Ellsberg in his Pentagon office at night. He sees documents; those documents contain secret truths to which only a few have access. Truth must be set free. He can use his access to set those documents, and the truth they contain, free; and once freed, the truth will change the course of history. As I have argued, this chain of logic—important though it may be to pervasive understandings of politics and administration—simply does not hold up as stated. Government information is far more complex and contingent than the logic assumes.

The West Wing is no better, of course. Even as it forced its viewers to consider why state secrets are not necessarily anathema to a democratic state and "good government," its romantically simplified presentation of the executive branch and anxious insider's view of presidential prerogative still assumed, with Dick Cheney, that disclosure would have predictable effects. One of the storylines in a third-season episode forced the White House to deliberate over how to handle news that a test of a dead cow in Nebraska returned a positive result for Mad Cow disease. Should the administration release this information to the public, even though the test results were preliminary and a final determination would not come for three days? Most of the president's advisors argued that they should keep the initial test results secret until the conclusive determination; the public would panic at the news, they asserted, irrevocably harming the cattle industry (as well as the administration's relationship with ranching interests) if the test proved to be a false positive. Arguing the other side, the press secretary—C.J. Cregg (played by Alison Janney), the one woman in the president's closest circle of official advisors—exclaimed, "I don't know how many more times we can get caught keeping a secret." She then rattled off the following three-point argument supporting her position that the administration should announce the preliminary test results:

> What I meant was that the public will not forgive a president who withheld information that could have helped them or saved lives. Second, in a crisis, people need to feel like soldiers, not victims. Third, information breeds confidence. Silence breeds fear.

The administration ultimately decided upon a middle course: release the information, but quietly and through officials far removed from the White House. C.J., the press secretary, won the intellectual debate—notably, her one victory in an episode in which she strongly argued that selling arms to an Arab nation that systematically oppresses women violated the administration's commitment to women and human rights. But the information was managed, released only in a technical sense, with minimal effort to bring the potential crisis to the public's attention. The episode unsettles: Its resolution satisfied neither the Bartlet White House nor viewers, perhaps because of the information's high stakes. (Indeed, the series never revealed if the final test returned a positive result.) It provided no easy answer to the issue it raised and even suggested that no clear answer exists.

The West Wing thus presented a fairly sophisticated debate about the policy and political implications of fully disclosing information that a presidential administration would prefer to keep secret. In doing so, the show advanced an ironic commentary on transparency and the public's desire to see the government that represents it. With the full trappings of quality network television, *The West Wing* presented an idealized, fully available White House that met the public's desire to see the state. At the same time, the series convincingly portrayed why the real White House cannot be entirely visible. Only by making a fictional but realistic state transparent, the show implicitly argued, can the public understand why the actually existing state cannot in fact be truly transparent.

But despite its seeming sophistication, the show nevertheless offered the fantasy that the Bartlet administration could not only deliberate about information control but could implement it successfully. It could "take out the trash" of bad information in a quiet manner to avoid detection, as another early episode explained—as if that information was manageable, capable of being bagged, put in a receptacle, and incinerated. This ideal—like its mirror image of the information that can be posted, fully and openly, in the public square for all to see, understand, and incorporate in their political participation—does not hold. My hope is that this book has helped dispel the myth of government information. My purpose has been to refocus our political and administrative concerns on the substantive matters of governance—its policymaking, policy implementation, and service-provision operations—and to loosen our political and administrative obsession with how to fix the state by opening and closing it to view, as if one or the other is possible.

Epilogue

Donald Trump's surprising defeat of Hillary Clinton in 2016, and the effects of Trump's authoritarian populism on the presidency, could signify or bring about a break from the conflict between transparency and secrecy, leading one of these concepts to dominate the other. At the risk of making a doomed prediction in order to save the relevance of the conflict at the heart of this book, however, I want to very briefly explain why I don't think that will occur.

First and foremost, both presidential campaigns focused on their opponents' proclivity for secrecy in highly predictable ways that I discuss throughout the book. Hillary Clinton's use of a personal e-mail server while serving as secretary of state (as well as her well-compensated and secret speeches to bankers) came to define her public service and apparent penchant for controlling information. Indeed, they may have cost her the presidency. At the same time, Donald Trump stubbornly refused to release his tax returns (unprecedented in recent presidential campaigns), obfuscating his tangled finances and business interests.

Missing documents were thus a focal point of the election. But they concerned information that everyone seemed to know. Clinton's "missing" e-mails did not in fact seem to be missing by the time of the campaign; FBI Director James Comey's last-minute re-opening and re-closing of his agency's investigation confirmed this in the most dramatic way possible. The anonymous leaking of a small portion of one of Trump's tax returns appeared to vindicate the widely held belief that Trump's business success has been defined as much by his strategic manipulation of complex tax laws and bankruptcy protections as it has been by his acumen.

In other words, voters did not lack access to information that was essential to their decision, despite allegations that they were being denied it. I am not claiming that voters were fully informed and knowledgeable about the candidates' respective campaign platforms or that the two campaigns engaged in equal measures of information control. While the press had carefully investigated Clinton's long history of government service, Trump frequently threatened reprisal and litigation against anyone who critically covered his business practices. But I maintain that any voter could have learned the broad outlines of the candidates' apparently secret issues. Lack of information was less important than distaste for one or both candidates—whether or not that distaste was based on confirmed reporting, objective criteria, or a more pernicious animus.

Meanwhile, it is impossible to imagine that Trump will strictly comply with the spirit, much less the letter, of open government laws and norms in a manner consistent with his criticism of "Crooked Hillary." President-elect Trump dropped his concern about what he had earlier considered Clinton's egregious lawbreaking immediately after his victory, demonstrating that his commitment to fighting secrecy was strategic and temporary. His hostility to criticism and apparent distaste for the First Amendment, his penchant for controlling information about himself, and his never having been subject to public transparency laws in his business career suggest that his administration will not be more open than those that came before and may well be less so. Moreover, Republican dominance of both legislative houses will likely dampen efforts to strengthen existing open government and administrative laws and to initiate congressional investigations of the executive branch, unless the new administration is caught up in scandals from information leaked to the press or outside groups. Whether the resulting political price for these scandals will prove significant to President Trump and his party will have less to do with his departure from informational norms than with his success in maintaining his leadership of the GOP and his slim electoral majority in Midwestern swing states.

Similar to his predecessor, Trump rode into office claiming that he would save the nation from secretive, establishment politicians and lobbyists; his opposition will soon paint him, no doubt correctly, as being inattentive to transparency laws and norms—even scornful of them. Transparency advocates might look nostalgically at the Obama administration and its imperfect record of informational reform. Its efforts to curb overclassification, for example, showed some modest but real signs of success during the latter years of President Obama's second term. But these efforts did not meet the nation's desire to fix its informational state. And so we begin again.

Notes

Introduction

1. Daniel Ellsberg, *Secrets* (New York: Viking, 2002), 81.

2. Daniel Ellsberg, "Secrecy and National Security Whistleblowing," *Social Research* 77, no. 3 (2010): 773–804, 778.

3. Jana Costas and Christopher Grey, *Secrecy at Work: The Hidden Architecture of Organizational Life* (Stanford, Calif.: Stanford University Press, 2016), 138–140; see also Brian Rappert, *How to Look Good in a War: Justifying and Challenging State Violence* (London: Pluto Press, 2012), 6.

4. Michael Herman, *Intelligence Power in Peace and War* (Cambridge, U.K.: Cambridge University Press, 1996), 328–330.

5. Georg Simmel, *The Sociology of Georg Simmel*, trans. and ed. Kurt H. Wolff (New York: Free Press, 1950), 314, 332–333.

6. David Halberstam, *The Best and the Brightest* (New York: Random House, 1972), 652.

7. Ellsberg, *Secrets*, x.

8. The *Oxford English Dictionary* definition is "the property of transmitting light, so as to render bodies lying beyond completely visible; that can be seen through" (*OED*, 2nd ed., 1989), 419.

9. Max Weber, *Economy and Society*, volume 2, eds. Guenther Roth and Claus Wittich (Berkeley: University of California Press, 1992), 992.

10. Recent examples of books that argue this point include Jason Ross Arnold, *Secrecy in the Sunshine Era* (Lawrence: University of Kansas Press, 2014); Ronald Goldfarb, *In Confidence: When to Protect Secrecy and When to Require Disclosure* (New Haven, Conn.: Yale University Press, 2009), 37–58; and Heidi Kitrosser, *Reclaiming Accountability: Transparency, Executive Power, and the U.S. Constitution* (Chicago: University of Chicago Press, 2015).

11. See, e.g., Freedom of Information Act, Public Law 89-554, 80 Stat. 383 (1966) (codified as amended at 5 U.S.C. § 552) (establishing disclosure requirements for federal administrative agencies); Government in the Sunshine Act, Public Law 94-409, 90 Stat. 1241 (1976) (codified as amended at 5 U.S.C. § 552(b)) (establishing open meeting requirements for federal administrative agencies); Cal. Gov't Code § 11120 et seq. (establishing open meeting requirements for California public agencies).

12. Louis D. Brandeis, *Other People's Money and How the Bankers Use It*, reprint ed. (New York: A. M. Kelley 1914, 1986), 92 ("Sunlight is said to be the best of disinfectants; electric light the most efficient policeman").

13. Detroit Free Press v. Ashcroft, 303 F.3d 681, 683 (6th Cir. 2002).

14. Congress did not use the FOIA title in originally enacting the statute as an amendment to

the Administrative Procedure Act, but the statutory provisions were referred to by that title soon afterward.

15. For a summary of previous government commissions criticizing overclassification, see *Secrecy: Report of the Commission on Protecting and Reducing Government Secrecy*, 103rd Cong., Report Pursuant to Public Law, S. Doc. 105-2, xxi (Comm. Print 1997), G-1–G-2. This report, known as the Moynihan Commission in honor of its chairman Senator Daniel Patrick Moynihan, itself became part of this long, blue ribbon trail.

16. Jonathan Easley, "Obama Says His Is 'Most Transparent Administration' Ever," *The Hill's Blog Briefing Room*, February 14, 2013. http://thehill.com/blogs/blog-briefing-room/news/283335 -obama-this-is-the-most-transparent-administration-in-history

17. Greg Munno, "FOIA Suits Jump in 2014," *The FOIA Project*, December 22, 2014. http://foia project.org/2014/12/22/foia-suits-jump-in-2014/

18. "The White House Beat, Uncovered: What the Hacks of 1600 Penn Really Think," *Politico*, May/June 2014. http://www.politico.com/magazine/story/2014/04/whca-survey-the-white-house -beat-uncovered-106071

19. See, for example, Arnold, *Secrecy in the Sunshine Era*, 6; Kathleen Clark, "'A New Era of Openness?' Disclosing Intelligence to Congress Under Obama," *Constitutional Commentary* 26, no. 3 (2010): 313–337; Ronald J. Krotoszynski Jr., "Transparency, Accountability, and Competency: An Essay on the Obama Administration, Google Government, and the Difficulties of Securing Effective Governance," *University of Miami Law Review* 65, no. 2 (2011): 449–482, 467–475.

20. Trevor Timm, "2011 in Review: The Year Secrecy Jumped the Shark," *Deep Links* (Blog), December 23, 2011. https://www.eff.org/deeplinks/2011/12/2011-review-year-secrecy-jumped-shark

21. McBurney v. Young, 133 S.Ct. 1709, 1718–1719 (2013).

22. For accounts of the federal government's resistance to disclosure, see Thomas Blanton, "Beyond the Balancing Test," in *National Security and Open Government: Striking the Right Balance* (Syracuse, N.Y.: Campbell Public Affairs Institute, Maxwell School of Citizenship and Public Affairs, Syracuse University, 2003), 34–54; Christina E. Wells, "'National Security' Information and the Freedom of Information Act," *Administrative Law Review* 56, no. 4 (2004): 1195–1221, 1201.

23. Nancy Chang, "How Democracy Dies: The War on Our Civil Liberties," in *Lost Liberties: Ashcroft and the Assault on Personal Freedom*, ed. Cynthia Brown (New York: New Press, 2003), 33–51, 36–39; Wells, "'National Security' Information," 1197; Kristen Elizabeth Uhl, "The Freedom of Information Act Post–9/11: Balancing the Public's Right to Know, Critical Infrastructure Protection, and Homeland Security," *American University Law Review* 53, no. 1 (2003): 261–311; Patrice McDermott, "Withhold and Control: Information in the Bush Administration," *Kansas Journal of Law and Public Policy* 12, no. 3 (2003): 671–691, 672–674.

24. Indeed, commentators made similar complaints about the Clinton administration. Blanton, "Beyond the Balancing Test," 51–54 (describing secrecy during the current Bush administration and arguing that it began during Clinton's second term); Jonathan Turley, "Paradise Lost: The Clinton Administration and the Erosion of Executive Privilege," *Maryland Law Review* 60, no. 1 (2001): 205–257 (condemning the Clinton administration's reliance on sweeping executive privilege claims to keep information about White House activities secret).

25. See, e.g., John Ashcroft, "Memorandum for Heads of All Federal Departments and Agencies on the Freedom of Information Act," October 12, 2001. http://nsarchive.gwu.edu/NSAEBB/ NSAEBB84/Ashcroft%20Memorandum.pdf (declaring that, "[i]t is only through a well-informed citizenry that the leaders of our nation remain accountable to the governed and the American people can be assured that neither fraud nor government waste is concealed," while also advising

agencies that DOJ will defend decisions to deny FOIA requests "unless they lack a sound legal basis or present an unwarranted risk of adverse impact on the ability of other agencies to protect other important records").

26. See, e.g., NLRB v. Robbins Tire & Rubber Co., 437 U.S. 214, 242 (1978) (noting that "[t]he basic purpose of FOIA is to ensure an informed citizenry, vital to the functioning of a democratic society, needed to check against corruption and to hold the governors accountable to the governed," before proceeding to affirm denial of the FOIA request on the grounds that the witness statements in an unfair labor practices hearing before the National Labor Relations Board fell within a FOIA exception because its release would interfere with enforcement proceedings); Environmental Protection Agency v. Mink, 410 U.S. 73, 80 (1973) (characterizing FOIA as "broadly conceived" and intended "to permit access to official information long shielded unnecessarily from public view and . . . to create a judicially enforceable public right to secure such information from possibly unwilling official hands," before proceeding to hold that an agency's classification of documents may not be reviewed by court in camera).

27. With respect to matters of national security and foreign policy, for example, most challenges to agency denials to disclose documents end at the summary judgment stage, when courts typically defer to agency affidavits stating the applicability of FOIA exemption (b)(1). James T. O'Reilly, *Federal Information Disclosure* § 11:11, 524 (3rd ed., 2000) (discussing 5 U.S.C. § 552(b)(1)). And as a political matter, disappointment among disclosure advocates about the disjunction between the public statements of presidents in favor of openness and their actual efforts to keep information secret dates back to the earliest years of FOIA. Elias Clark, "Holding Government Accountable: The Amended Freedom of Information Act," *Yale Law Journal* 84, no. 4 (1975): 741–769, 746.

28. This distinction between transparency as a primary, intrinsic value and as a tool to meet other values has been well-developed elsewhere. David Heald, "Transparency as an Instrumental Value," in *Transparency: The Key to Better Governance?*, eds. Christopher Hood and David Heald (Oxford, U.K.: Oxford University Press, 2006), 59–74, 68; Lawrence Lessig, "Against Transparency," *New Republic*, October 9, 2009, 37–41 (questioning the likely consequences of what he describes as the "naked transparency" movement); Michael Schudson, *The Rise of the Right to Know: Politics and the Culture of Transparency, 1945–1975* (Cambridge, Mass.: Harvard University Press, 2015); William J. Stuntz, "Secret Service: Against Privacy and Transparency," *New Republic*, April 17, 2006, 12–15 ("Transparency makes politics a running argument about decision-making, not about decisions").

29. Gilbert Schoenfeld, *Necessary Secrets* (New York: Norton, 2010), 22, 267.

30. The most vocal proponents of transparency in its strongest form are journalists and open government advocates. See, e.g., National Freedom of Information Coalition, "About NFOIC—History, Board, Staff, Bylaws," last updated 2016. http://www.nfoic.org/about-nfoic (describing the group as "a nonpartisan alliance of citizen-driven nonprofit freedom of information organizations, academic and First Amendment centers, journalistic societies and attorneys"); Reporters Committee for Freedom of the Press, "RCFP Freedom of Information Resources," last updated October 2016. https://www.rcfp.org/ (describing organization as "the nation's leading advocate for open government issues on behalf of journalists").

31. For a parallel project in the field of communications and organizational theory, see Lars Thøger Christensen and George Cheney, "Peering into Transparency: Challenging Ideals, Proxies, and Organizational Practices," *Communication Theory* 25, no. 1 (2015): 70–90.

32. Donald F. Kettl, "Public Bureaucracies," in *The Oxford Handbook of Political Institutions*, eds. R. A. W. Rhodes et al. (New York: Oxford University Press, 2006), 366–384, 373; see also Kenneth J. Meier and Gregory C. Hill, "Bureaucracy in the Twenty-First Century," in *The Oxford*

Handbook of Public Management, eds. Ewan Ferlie et al. (New York: Oxford University Press, 2005), 51–66, 51 ("[L]arge-scale tasks that government must perform . . . will remain key functions of governments in the twenty-first century and . . . bureaucracies, likely public but possibly private, will continue to be the most effective way to do these tasks").

33. David Beetham, *Bureaucracy,* 2nd ed. (Minneapolis: University of Minnesota Press, 1996), 101–102.

Chapter 1

1. The term, which originated with Alfred Hitchcock, refers to a storytelling device intended to move a plot forward—one whose status as a mere device is made plain both by its seeming complexity and the fact that the story ignores it in order to focus on developing the drama's characters and placing them in conflict with one another.

2. Morton Halperin and Daniel N. Hoffman, *Top Secret: National Security and the Right to Know* (Washington, D.C.: New Republic Books, 1977), 14–17.

3. On Hersh's story and the Family Jewels, see Harold P. Ford, *William E. Colby as Director of Central Intelligence* (Washington, D.C.: Central Intelligence Agency History Staff, 1993), 97–107.

4. Senate Select Committee to Study Governmental Operations with Respect to Intelligence Activities and the Rights of Americans (Book II), S. Rep. 94-755 (1976), 292.

5. Robert H. Wiebe, *The Search for Order: 1877–1920* (New York: Hill and Wang, 1967), 164–185.

6. Louis D. Brandeis, *Other People's Money and How the Bankers Use It,* reprint ed. (New York: A. M. Kelley, 1986 [1914]), 92.

7. Juha Manninen, "Anders Chydenius and the Origins of World's First Freedom of Information Act," in *The World's First Freedom of Information Act: Anders Chydenius' Legacy Today*, ed. Juha Mustonen (Kokkokla, Finland: Anders Chydenius Foundation, 2006), 18–53, 52–53.

8. Terhi Rantanen, "The Struggle for Control of Domestic News Markets (1)," in *The Globalization of News*, eds. Oliver Boyd-Barrett and Terhi Rantanen (Thousand Oaks, Calif.: Sage, 1998), 35–48, 36–37.

9. Margaret Blanchard, *Exporting the First Amendment* (New York: Longman, 1986), 6–7; Terhi Rantanen, "Foreign Dependence and Domestic Monopoly: The European News Cartel and U.S. Associated Presses, 1861–1932," *Media History* 12, no. 1 (2006): 19–30; Terhi Rantanen, "Mr. Howard Goes to South America: The United Press Associations and Foreign Expansion," *Roy W. Howard Monographs in Journalism and Mass Communication Research* 2 (1992): 22–24.

10. Blanchard, *Exporting the First Amendment*, 7; Kent Cooper, *Barriers Down* (New York: Farrar & Rinehart, 1942), 43.

11. On the relationship between ideals of the "free flow of information" and the Cold War, see Hanno Hardt, "Comparative Media Research: The World According to America," *Critical Studies in Mass Communication* 5, no. 2 (1988): 129–146, 132–133.

12. Graham Storey, *Reuters' Century, 1851–1951* (New York: Crown, 1951), 186–194; Herbert Brucker, *Freedom of Information* (New York: Macmillan, 1949), 214–215. The U.S. campaign also sought to export its ideals of press freedoms abroad; it would later be resurrected in the 1990s, after the collapse of the Soviet Union. Craig L. LaMay, *Exporting Press Freedom: Economic and Editorial Dilemmas in International Media Assistance* (New Brunswick, N.J.: Transaction, 2007), 76–84.

13. Significantly, AP's general manager Kent Cooper gave his memoir of AP's fight against the cartel, published in the midst of World War II, the martial title *Barriers Down*. For a more accurate account of AP's complicated history, see Terhi Rantanen, "After Five O'Clock Friends: Kent Cooper and Roy W. Howard," *Roy W. Howard Monographs in Journalism and Mass Communication Research* 4 (1998): 25–27.

14. Daniel R. Headrick, *The Invisible Weapon: Telecommunications and International Politics 1851–1945* (New York: Oxford University Press, 1991), 189–190; Emily S. Rosenberg, *World War I and the Growth of United States Predominance in Latin America* (New York: Garland, 1987), 187.

15. See, e.g., Kent Cooper, "Newspaper Statesmanship for Peace," in *Journalism in Wartime*, ed. Frank Luther Mott (Washington, D.C.: American Council on Public Affairs, 1943), 215–216 (noting, in a short article exhorting the press to exert itself in peace negotiations because of the importance of a free press and informed public to ending wars, the relationship between wars and the prosperity of the international news industry).

16. "The Press: Storm Warning," *Time*, December 11, 1944. http://content.time.com/time/mag azine/article/0,9171,883902,00.html (quoting *The Economist*).

17. Ibid.

18. Brucker, *Freedom of Information*, 215.

19. For a general description of the incident and of the ongoing tensions between American and European diplomats and press representatives in the post-war negotiations about United Nations freedom of information agreements, see Blanchard, *Exporting the First Amendment*, 23–25.

20. George Kennedy, "Advocates of Openness: The Freedom of Information Movement" (Ph.D. dissertation, University of Missouri at Columbia, 1978). Cooper himself called for such a campaign that same year in the pages of *Life*. Kent Cooper, "Freedom of Information: Head of Associated Press Calls for Unhampered Flow of World News," *Life*, November 13, 1944, 55.

21. Blanchard, *Exporting the First Amendment*, 2.

22. Alice Fox Pitts, *Read All About It! 50 Years of ASNE* (Easton, Pa.: American Society of Newspaper Editors, 1974), 174–181. The tour was led by Ralph McGill, an editor for the *Atlanta Journal-Constitution* and chairman of the ASNE's Freedom of Information Committee. Leonard Ray Teel, "The Shaping of a Southern Opinion Leader: Ralph McGill and Freedom of Information," *American Journalism* 5, no. 1 (1988): 14–27.

23. Blanchard, *Exporting the First Amendment*, 52–89; Pitts, *Read All About It!*, 182–185.

24. Blanchard, *Exporting the First Amendment*, 155–163, 174–197.

25. Ibid., 174–175.

26. Erwin D. Canham, "International Freedom of Information," *Law and Contemporary Problems* 14, no. 4 (1949): 584–598.

27. See generally Fred S. Siebert, Theodore Peterson, and Wilbur Schramm, *Four Theories of the Press* (Urbana: University of Illinois Press, 1956); see also William E. Berry et al., *Last Rights: Revisiting Four Theories of the Press*, ed. John C. Nerone (Urbana: University of Illinois Press, 1995), 7–16 (historicizing and updating the "four theories" model).

28. Cooper, *Right to Know*, 163–165.

29. Blanchard, *Exporting the First Amendment*, 2. AP general manager Kent Cooper would later warn that a passive "American layman," allowing the state to "do[] his thinking for him," will allow the government to infringe his "Right to Know" (Cooper, *Right to Know*, 308). State influence on the press and the public was not the press's only concern about government interference. During the New Deal, the Roosevelt administration had fought to impose against news organizations federal laws and regulations that applied to employers, including the Social Security Act, the National Industrial Recovery Act, federal labor laws and the Wagner Labor Relations Act, as well as federal laws and regulations intended to regulate advertising. Claiming that these laws would infringe constitutional free speech rights if applied to the press, newspapers and their owners, whose relative conservatism made them skeptical if not hostile to the New Deal anyway, resisted the state's intrusion into their business. Margaret A. Blanchard, "The Hutchins Commission, the Press, and the Responsibility Concept," *Journalism Monographs* no. 49 (May 1977): 4–8. The press ultimately

lost these arguments. Associated Press v. NLRB, 301 U.S. 103, 132 (1937) ("The publisher of a newspaper has no special immunity from the application of general laws").

30. E. Pendleton Herring, *Public Administration and the Public Interest* (New York: McGraw-Hill, 1936), 362–367, 373–376; John Dewey, *Individualism Old and New* (New York: Minton, Balch & Co., 1930), 43. See generally Michael Schudson, *Discovering the News* (New York: Basic Books, 1978), 134–144.

31. On the history of journalism's understanding of itself as a profession with a distinct and crucial social and political position and a self-developed and enforced code of conduct, see Howard Tumber and Marina Prentoulis, "Journalism and the Making of a Profession," in *Making Journalists*, ed. Hugo de Burgh (London: Routledge, 2005), 60–68.

32. Commission on Freedom of the Press, *A Free and Responsible Press* (Chicago: University of Chicago Press, 1947), 21–28. On the Hutchins Commission generally, see Blanchard, "Hutchins Commission," 88–89.

33. Michael Schudson, "The Objectivity Norm in American Journalism," *Journalism* 2, no. 2 (2001): 149–170; Wolfgang Donsbach, "Lapdogs, Watchdogs and Junkyard Dogs," *Media Studies Journal* 9, no. 4 (1995): 17–30; Gaye Tuchman, "Objectivity as Strategic Ritual: An Examination of Newsmen's Notions of Objectivity," *American Journal of Sociology* 77, no. 4 (1972): 660–678. Freedom of information advocates employed the labor press supported by unions as a foil when they sought to define the true objectivity practiced by privately owned news organizations. Leonard Ray Teel, *The Public Press, 1900–1945* (Westport, Conn.: Praeger, 2006), 172–174; Brucker, *Freedom of Information*, 248–251.

34. Cass Sunstein, *The Second Bill of Rights: FDR's Unfinished Revolution and Why We Need It More Than Ever* (New York: Basic Books, 2004), 78–79. The phrase did not appear in FDR's "four freedoms" speech he made to Congress in 1941, which instead only referred to the "freedom of speech and expression—everywhere in the world."

35. Sanford J. Ungar, "The Role of a Free Press Strengthening Democracy," in *Democracy and the Mass Media*, ed. Judith Lichtenberg (New York: Cambridge University Press, 1990), 368–398, 393.

36. Teel, *The Public Press, 1900–1945*, 17–18; Kiyul Uhm, "The Cold War Communication Crisis: The Right to Know Movement," *Journalism and Mass Communication Quarterly* 82, no. 1 (2005): 131–147, 139.

37. Brucker, *Freedom of Information*, 276.

38. UN General Assembly, Resolution 59, "U.N. Document A/RES/59(I)," December 14, 1946. Two years later, a draft convention on Freedom of Information that failed to garner sufficient support defined the term as "the free interchange of information and opinions, both in the national and in the international sphere" (Blanchard, *Exporting the First Amendment*, 410–414). Although Article 19 of the Universal Declaration of Human Rights adopted the general language of free expression and the right to receive and impart information, the more specific provisions considered in the 1948 Convention on Freedom of Information, which both protected individuals from the state and allowed states to support and protect their domestic press (for example, "in the interest of national safety" and to "develop its national news enterprises"), faced significant opposition, not least from the U.S. delegation. On the influence of the press on the U.S. delegation, see Blanchard, *Exporting the First Amendment*, 174–175.

39. Kent Cooper, *The Right to Know* (New York: Farrar, Straus & Cudahy, 1956); "The Right to Know," *New York Times*, January 23, 1945, 18; Kent Cooper, "The Right to Know: Toward World Press Freedom," *Free World* 10, no. 3 (1945): 53–55.

40. Cooper, *The Right to Know*, 16.

41. Cooper, "The Right to Know: World Press Freedom."

42. Ibid.

43. James W. Carey, "Journalism and Criticism: The Case of an Undeveloped Profession," *Review of Politics* 36, no. 2 (April 1974): 227–249, 231–233.

44. Cooper, *The Right to Know*, 69.

45. For an alternative to a rights-based conception of government information, see Cornelia Vismann's account of the West German, and then federal German, notion of these terms in her book *Files: Law and Media Technology*, trans. Geoffrey Winthrop-Young (Stanford, Calif.: Stanford University Press, 2008), 147–158.

46. David R. Davies, *The Postwar Decline of American Newspapers, 1945–1965* (Westport, Conn.: Praeger, 2006), 31–38; Herbert N. Foerstel, *Freedom of Information and the Right to Know* (Westport, Conn.: Praeger, 1999), 14–18; Kennedy, "Advocates of Openness," 24–28; Pitts, *Read All About It!*, 172–173; Erwin D. Canham, "The Battle for News," in *Journalism in Wartime*, ed. Frank Luther Mott (Washington, D.C.: Council of Public Affairs, 1943), 44–47.

47. Uhm, "The Cold War Communication Crisis," 136–137.

48. Ibid., 134–138.

49. Harold Cross, *The People's Right to Know* (New York: Columbia University Press, 1953).

50. Pope, foreword to Cross, *The People's Right to Know*, vii, ix, xi.

51. James Russell Wiggins, *Freedom or Secrecy* (New York: Oxford University Press, 1956), 3–4.

52. Cross, *The People's Right to Know*, xiii.

53. Ibid., 4, 6, 10.

54. Ibid., 129–132. He borrowed the phrase "neglected constitutional right" from an earlier student-written essay: "Access to Official Information: A Neglected Constitutional Right," *Indiana Law Journal* 27, no. 2 (1952): 209–230. Cross was the most prominent early advocate. Zechariah Chafee's 1947 treatise *Government and Mass Communications* pointed out the problem of expanded secrecy in the post-war era but did not develop the First Amendment argument that Cross would later pursue. Zechariah Chafee Jr., *Government and Mass Communication*, volume 1 (Chicago: University of Chicago Press, 1947), 12–13. Alexander Meiklejohn claimed that the democratic values inherent in the First Amendment must allow the public access to information, but he never specifically considered the relevance and problem of state information: *Free Speech and Its Relations to Self-Government* (New York: Harper Brothers, 1948), 26, 66, 89.

55. Sam Lebovic, *Free Speech and Unfree News* (Cambridge, Mass.: Harvard University Press, 2016), 183–184.

56. On the history of the APA, especially as a political solution to the response to the administrative state's growth in the New Deal, see Ronen Shamir, *Managing Legal Uncertainty: Elite Lawyers in the New Deal* (Durham, N.C.: Duke University Press, 1995); George B. Shepherd, "Fierce Compromise: The Administrative Procedure Act Emerges from New Deal Politics," *Northwestern University Law Review* 90, no. 4 (1996): 1557–1683; McNollgast, "The Political Origins of the Administrative Procedure Act," *Journal of Law, Economics, and Organization* 15, no. 1 (1999): 180–217.

57. Cross, *The People's Right to Know*, 223–225. The APA's original government information provision included exceptions for information involved in "any function of the United States requiring secrecy in the public interest," and allowed information not otherwise barred from disclosure by statute to be made available by published rule "to persons properly and directly concerned except information held confidential for good cause found" (ibid., 226) (quoting 5 U.S.C.A. § 1002(1), 1002(c) (1946)). In addition to analyzing the APA's weaknesses, Cross's book also listed all of the existing statutory exceptions from disclosure (ibid., 231–234).

58. Ibid., 246.

59. For historical accounts of the FOIA's development that begins at this point and focuses

on the political and especially interparty nature of the statute's enactment, see Michael Schudson, *The Rise of the Right to Know: Politics and the Culture of Transparency* (Cambridge, Mass.: Harvard University Press, 2015), 37–62; Daniel J. Metcalfe, "The History of Government Transparency," in *Research Handbook on Transparency*, eds. Padideh Ala'i and Robert G. Vaughn (Northampton, Mass.: Edward Elgar, 2014), 247–262, 252–253. My focus on the preeminent role that the press played privileges the conceptual underpinnings for that political struggle, which long predated the Moss Committee's work.

60. On the political nature of the Moss hearings (at least in their early years), see Sam Archibald, "The Early Years of the Freedom of Information Act—1955 to 1974," *PS: Political Science and Politics* 26, no. 4 (December 1993): 726–731; Robert Okie Blanchard, "The Moss Committee and a Federal Public Records Law, 1955–1965" (Ph.D. dissertation, Syracuse University, 1966); Richard G. Gray, "Freedom of Access to Government Information: A Study of the Federal Executive" (Ph.D. dissertation, University of Minnesota, 1964). On Dawson's appointment as chair of Government Operations in 1948, see Christopher Manning, *William L. Dawson and the Limits of Black Electoral Leadership* (Dekalb: Northern Illinois University Press, 2009), 119–121.

61. Archibald, "The Early Years of the Freedom of Information Act," 726–727.

62. Ibid., 727; Blanchard, "The Moss Committee," 108–125; Kennedy, "Advocates of Openness," 64–73.

63. Kennedy, "Advocates of Openness," 68–70, 94–96.

64. Robert O. Blanchard, "Present at the Creation: The Media and the Moss Committee," *Journalism and Mass Communication Quarterly* 49, no. 2 (June 1972): 271–279.

65. Uhm, "The Cold War Communication Crisis," 140; Kennedy, "Advocates of Openness," 96.

66. Gerald Wetlaufer, "Justifying Secrecy: An Objection to the General Deliberative Privilege," *Indiana Law Journal* 65, no. 4 (1990): 845–926, 868–869. On the subcommittee's frustrations with the inadequate results of its successful amendment to the 1789 Housekeeping Statute under which executive agencies refused to disclose documents, see Foerstel, *Freedom of Information*, 33–35.

67. Archibald, "The Early Years of the Freedom of Information Act," 728.

68. Archibald, "The Early Years of the Freedom of Information Act," 729–730; Blanchard, "The Moss Committee," 167–210. After Cross's death, Jacob Scher, another media lawyer and journalism professor, took his place as the Moss Committee's legal advisor and continued to follow Cross's approach. Blanchard, "The Moss Committee," 89–91, 138–139.

69. Bill Moyers, "Bill Moyers on the Freedom of Information Act," *PBS*, April 5, 2002. http://www.pbs.org/now/commentary/moyers4.html

70. H.R. 1497, 89th Cong. (1966), 12 (reprinted in 1966 U.S.C.C.A.N. 2418, 2429).

71. See, e.g., NLRB v. Robbins Tire & Rubber Co., 437 U.S. 214, 242 (1978) ("[T]he basic purpose of FOIA is to ensure an informed citizenry, vital to the functioning of a democratic society, needed to check against corruption and to hold the governors accountable to the governed"); EPA v. Mink, 410 U.S. 73, 80 (1973) ("[FOIA was] broadly conceived. . . . [T]o permit access to official information long shielded unnecessarily from public view and . . . to create a judicially enforceable public right to secure such information from possibly unwilling official hands"), superseded by statute, 5 U.S.C. § 552(b)(1), as recognized in C.I.A. v. Sims, 471 U.S. 159 (1985).

72. 5 U.S.C. § 552(a)(3)(A).

73. 5 U.S.C. § 552(a)(4)(B). On FOIA's fairly radical departure as to issues like the standard of judicial review and standing, see Robert G. Vaughn, "The Associations of Judicial Transparency with Administrative Transparency," in *Research Handbook on Transparency*, eds. Padideh Ala'i and Robert G. Vaughn (Northampton, Mass.: Edward Elgar, 2014), 80–112, 99.

74. Public Law 93-502, 88 Stat. 1561 (codified as amended at 5 U.S.C. § 552 (1994)).

75. Electronic Freedom of Information Act Amendments of 1996, Public Law 104-231, 110 Stat. 3048 (codified at 5 U.S.C. § 552 (Supp. II 1996)). For a description of how these amendments changed agency obligations to make information available electronically and reduce delays in responding to FOIA requests, see Mark H. Grunewald, "E-FOIA and the 'Mother of All Complaints': Information Delivery and Delay Reduction," *Administrative Law Review* 50, no. 2 (1998): 345–370.

76. Government in the Sunshine Act, Public Law 94-409, 90 Stat. 1241 (1976) (codified as amended at 5 U.S.C. § 552(b)).

77. Federal Advisory Committee Act of 1972, Public Law 92-463, 86 Stat. 770 (codified as amended at 5 U.S.C. App. 2 §§ 1–16).

78. Presidential Records Act of 1978, Public Law 95-591, 92 Stat. 2523 (codified as amended at 44 U.S.C. §§ 2201–2207 (2006)).

79. On the APA's rulemaking provisions as open government laws, see Jeffrey S. Lubbers, "Transparency in Policymaking: The (Mostly) Laudable Example of the U.S. Rulemaking System," in *Research Handbook on Transparency*, eds. Padideh Ala'i and Robert G. Vaughn (Northampton, Mass.: Edward Elgar, 2014), 284–311.

80. Some states have adopted constitutional provisions granting a right to access, while all have statutes that perform analogous functions as the federal FOIA and Government in the Sunshine Acts. See, e.g., Cal. Const. Art. I, § 3(b)(1) (granting "the right of access to information concerning the conduct of the people's business"); Fla. Const. Art. I, § 24 (granting "the right to inspect or copy any public record made or received in connection with the official business of any public body, officer, or employee of the state, or persons acting on their behalf"). The Reporters Committee for Freedom of the Press produces a comprehensive guide of states' open government laws (including the District of Columbia's). Reporters Committee for Freedom of the Press, *Open Government Guide*, 6th ed., 2011. http://rcfp.org/open-government-guide. San Francisco's sunshine ordinance is a good example of the local open government phenomenon: *San Francisco Sunshine Ordinance*, § 67 of San Francisco's Municipal Code: http://sfgov.org/sunshine/provisions-sunshine -ordinance-section-67#67

81. The general concern with democratic values and effective representation focuses on the republican separation of the state from the public via elected representatives. In contrast, the ideals of populist self-rule minimize both the separation and the emphasis on representation. Most discussions of transparency's meaning present a duality rather than the three categories I elaborate below. David Heald has made a similar, influential distinction between what he calls the "intrinsic" and "instrumental" values that transparency furthers. With this distinction, he separates viewing transparency as a "core concern" and end in itself from viewing it as a "building block for other valued objects sought by public policy." David Heald, "Transparency as an Instrumental Value," in *Transparency: The Key to Better Governance?*, eds. Christopher Hood and David Heald (Oxford, U.K.: Oxford University Press, 2006), 59–73. More recently, Stephen Kosack and Archon Fung have distinguished public transparency from private transparency by arguing that freedom of state information focuses on improving a self-governing citizenry and enabling accountability for the state's performance and service provision. Stephen Kosack and Archon Fung, "Does Transparency Improve Governance?" *Annual Review of Political Science* 17 (2014): 65–87.

82. Ajume H. Wingo, *Veil Politics in Liberal Democratic States* (Cambridge, U.K.: Cambridge University Press, 2003), 16–18 (discussing the importance of transparency in Locke's *First Treatise of Government*).

83. John Stuart Mill, "Considerations of Representative Democracy," in *Utilitarianism, On Liberty and Considerations on Representative Government*, ed. H. B. Action (London: J. W. Dent and Sons, 1972 [1861]), 262.

84. Jean-Jacques Rousseau, "Dedication to the Republic of Geneva," in *Discourse on the Origin of Inequality*, trans. G. D. H. Cole (New York: Dutton, 1950), 32–33.

85. Jeremy Bentham, *Political Tactics*, ed. Michael James et al. (New York: Oxford University Press, 1999), 29–44.

86. Immanuel Kant, "Eternal Peace," in *The Philosophy of Kant*, ed. Carl J. Friedrich (New York: Modern Library, 1949), 470.

87. Mill, "Considerations of Representative Democracy."

88. Bentham, *Political Tactics*, 29–34.

89. Ibid.

90. Edward Shils, *The Torment of Secrecy* (Glencoe, Ill.: Free Press, 1956), 23.

91. Jürgen Habermas, *The Structural Transformation of the Public Sphere*, trans. Thomas Berger (Cambridge, Mass.: MIT Press, 1989), 53–54.

92. Michael Schudson persuasively argues that the founders' conception of an informed public is quite different from the contemporary understanding of transparency. Schudson, *The Rise of the Right to Know*, 28–29.

93. John Adams, "A Dissertation on the Canon and Feudal Law," *Boston Gazette*, September 30, 1765, republished in *Papers of John Adams*, volume 1, ed. Robert J. Taylor et al. (Cambridge, Mass.: Belknap Press of Harvard University Press, 1977), 120–121.

94. Letter from James Madison to W. T. Barry, August 4, 1822, *The Complete Madison*, ed. Saul Padover (New York: Harper, 1953), 337.

95. Michael Doyle, "Misquoting Madison," *Legal Affairs*, July/August 2002. https://www.legal affairs.org/issues/July-August-2002/scene_doyle_julaug2002.msp

96. Richard D. Brown, *The Strength of a People: The Idea of an Informed Citizenry in America, 1650–1870* (Chapel Hill: University of North Carolina Press, 1996).

97. Ibid., 120–123.

98. John Rawls, *A Theory of Justice* (Cambridge, Mass.: Belknap Press of Harvard University Press, 1971), 16, 454.

99. Friedrich A. Hayek, *The Road to Serfdom* (Chicago: University of Chicago Press, 1944), 74–75; Rawls, *Theory of Justice*, 238. William Sage has connected transparency as a concept with libertarian politics, arguing that transparency rhetoric operates as part of a "resurgent rhetoric of individualism and self-reliance in American politics, reflecting diminished expectations of government and heightened skepticism regarding public programs and public institutions," despite widespread public distrust of the market and of concentrations of corporate power. William M. Sage, "Regulating Through Information: Disclosure and American Health Care," *Columbia Law Review* 99, no. 7 (1999): 1701–1829, 1707.

100. See generally Robert G. Vaughn, "Introduction," in *Freedom of Information*, ed. Robert G. Vaughn (Burlington, Vt.: Ashgate, 2000), xv–xvi, xv (discussing how approaches to administrative law that privilege the formal rule of law understand the need for open government).

101. John Dewey, *The Public and Its Problems* (New York: Henry Holt and Co., 1927), 167 ("There can be no public without full publicity in respect to all consequences which concern it. Whatever obstructs and restricts publicity, limits and distorts thinking on social affairs").

102. Amy Gutmann and Dennis Thompson, *Democracy and Disagreement* (Cambridge, Mass.: Belknap Press of Harvard University Press, 1996), 100–101; Joshua Cohen, "Democracy and Liberty," in *Deliberative Democracy*, ed. Jon Elster, (New York: Cambridge University Press, 1998), 185–231, 193–194.

103. Habermas, *The Structural Transformation of the Public Sphere*, 208–209.

104. See, e.g., Joseph F. Zimmerman, *Participatory Democracy: Populism Revived* (New York:

Praeger, 1986), 178–179. On populism as a mobilizing force, see Ernesto Laclau, *On Populist Reason* (London: Verso, 2005), 18; Margaret Canovan, "Trust the People! Populism and the Two Faces of Democracy." *Political Studies* 47, no. 1 (1999): 2–16, 4–5.

105. Michael Kazin describes populism as a flexible, rhetorical mode of persuasion in politics and offers a historical survey of populist movements in *The Populist Persuasion* (New York: Basic Books, 1995). It can also appear as a challenge to institutional parties either from activists within their ranks (e.g., in the reformist insurgency in the Democratic Party in 1968 and 1972 and the conservative insurgency in the Republican Party in 1960 and 1964), or from third parties, as in the Populist campaigns of the late nineteenth century. Each movement deployed the ideals of the "people" and popular sovereignty to identify secret corruption and excessive concentration of state and/or private power that together threaten the nation and its moral and democratic order (ibid., 192–193). I have described the populist logic in American political culture in an earlier work: Mark Fenster, *Conspiracy Theories: Secrecy and Power in American Culture*, revised ed. (Minneapolis: University of Minnesota Press, 2008), 84–89.

106. James A. Morone, *The Democratic Wish*, revised ed. (New Haven, Conn.: Yale University Press, 1998), 5–9. On the relationship between populism and progressivism, see Francisco Panizza, "Introduction: Populism and the Mirror of Democracy," in *Populism and the Mirror of Democracy*, ed. Francisco Panizza (London: Verso, 2005), 1–31, 14; J. M. Balkin, "Populism and Progressivism as Constitutional Categories," *Yale Law Journal* 104, no. 7 (1995): 1935–1990, 1945. An edited collection includes several examples of "good government" populism: *The New Populist Reader*, ed. Karl G. Trautman (Westport, Conn.: Praeger, 1997), 164–206.

107. These concerns differ from the substantive concerns of many populist movements, which are sometimes moral (e.g., William Jennings Bryan's political career and populist elements in Prohibition) and sometimes economic (e.g., its producerist ethic and concerns about trusts and monopolies).

108. WikiLeaks, "About WikiLeaks: Principled Leaking." https://wikileaks.org/wiki/WikiLeaks :About#Principled_leaking

109. Frederick Schauer, "Transparency in Three Dimensions," *University of Illinois Law Review* 2011, no. 4 (2011): 1339–1357, 1350–1351. The distinction between the more theoretical and normative prior categories of democratic and populist ideals and the seemingly more practical and technocratic consequentialism is a matter of emphasis rather than of categorical distinction. Consequentialism is clearly normative, in the sense that it privileges certain kinds of specified outcomes, and it is equally theoretical in the assumptions it makes about institutional and individual behaviors. One could therefore distinguish them in terms of layers of abstraction, but that too suggests some epistemological distinction. Democracy and self-rule have consequences; consequential analysis assumes certain notions of democracy and self-rule as well. Their emphases are sufficiently distinct to warrant viewing them separately, however.

110. See, e.g., Common Cause v. Nuclear Regulatory Commission, 674 F.2d 921, 928 (D.C. Cir. 1982) (Skelley Wright, J.) (explaining that Congress's intent in enacting the Sunshine Act requiring open agency meetings was to "enhance citizen confidence in government, encourage higher quality work by government officials, stimulate well-informed public debate about government programs and polices, and promote cooperation between citizens and government. In short, it sought to make government more fully accountable to the people").

111. See, e.g., Mill, "Considerations on Representative Government."

112. *Secrecy: Report of the Commission on Protecting and Reducing Government Secrecy*, 103rd Cong., Report Pursuant to Public Law, S. Doc. 105-2, xxi (Comm. Print 1997); *The 9/11 Commission Report: Final Report of the National Commission on Terrorist Attacks Upon the United States*, autho-

rized ed. (New York: Norton, 2004). Several scholars have insightfully complicated the relationship between transparency and accountability, arguing that institutional misalignments may prevent information from having internal effects on the state; shameless officials might openly continue to act against the public's wishes even if their acts are publicized, and reformers may attach different meanings to the contested concepts and employ different approaches to reach the same theoretical end. Jonathan Fox, "The Uncertain Relationship Between Transparency and Accountability," *Development in Practice* 17, no. 4/5 (2007): 663–671; Christopher Hood, "Accountability and Transparency: Siamese Twins, Matching Parts, Awkward Couple?" *West European Politics* 33, no. 5 (2010): 989–1009.

113. Ann Florini, "The End of Secrecy," *Foreign Policy* no. 111 (1998); Benjamin S. DuVal Jr., "The Occasions of Secrecy," *University of Pittsburgh Law Review* 47, no. 3 (1996): 579–674, 606 (1986). Articulating this principle in the first of the "Fourteen Points" he presented to Congress in 1918 as an ideal means to resolve the international disputes that had led to World War I, Woodrow Wilson called for "[o]pen covenants of peace, openly arrived at, after which there shall be no private international understandings of any kind, but diplomacy shall proceed always frankly and in the public view." George A. Finch, "The Peace Conference of Paris, 1919," *American Journal of International Law* 13, no. 2 (1919): 159–186, 161.

114. Cass R. Sunstein, "Informing America: Risk, Disclosure, and the First Amendment," *Florida State University Law Review* 20, no. 3 (1993): 653–678, 662–665.

115. Yale M. Braunstein, "Economic Considerations of Federal Information Policies," in *United States Government Information Policies: Views and Perspectives*, eds. Charles R. McClure, Peter Hernon, and Harold C. Relyea (Norwood, N.J.: Ablex, 1989), 190–204, 191–193.

116. Secretary of State Hillary Rodham Clinton, "Remarks at the Open Government Partnership High-Level Meeting," U.S. Department of State. July 12, 2011. http://www.state.gov/secretary/20092013clinton/rm/2011/07/168049.htm

117. Jon Elster, "Deliberation and Constitution Making," in *Deliberative Democracy*, ed. Jon Elster (Cambridge, U.K.: Cambridge University Press, 1998), 97–122; Jon Elster, "The Market and the Forum: Three Varieties of Political Theory," in *Deliberative Democracy: Essays on Reasons and Politics*, eds. James Bohman and William Rehg (Cambridge, Mass.: MIT Press, 1986), 3–34; Daniel Naurin, "Transparency and Legitimacy," in *Political Theory and the European Constitution*, eds. Lynn Dobson and Andreas Follesdal (London: Routledge, 2004), 139–150, 140–142.

118. See, e.g., Joseph E. Stiglitz, "On Liberty, the Right to Know, and Public Discourse: The Role of Transparency in Public Life," Oxford Amnesty Lecture, Oxford, U.K., January 27, 1999, 26–27 (associating the instrumental and intrinsic benefits of transparent democracy).

119. Some organizations, such as the Reporters Committee for Freedom of the Press (established in 1970) and the National Freedom of Information Coalition (established in 1989), have had longstanding and institutional commitments to supporting the press and are led by executives and board members from the institutional press and their legal representatives.

120. The Sunshine Week website annually describes and links to such stories. "Participants," http://sunshineweek.rcfp.org/sw-participants/. Other organizations that campaign on behalf of legislative freedom of information laws in the United States include the coalition of transparency-focused organizations that utilize the OpenTheGovernment.org portal, as well as the Center for Effective Government (formerly OMB Watch).

121. Thomas I. Emerson, "Legal Foundations of the Right to Know," *Washington University Law Quarterly* no. 1 (1976): 1–24. For more wide-ranging summaries of the human rights–based arguments in favor of a right to information, see John M. Ackerman and Irma E. Sandoval-Ballesteros, "The Global Explosion of Freedom of Information Laws," *Administrative Law Review*

58, no. 1 (2006): 85–130, 88–93; Roy Peled and Yoram Rabin, "The Constitutional Right to Information," *Columbia Human Rights Law Review* 42, no. 2 (2011): 357–402, 359–373.

122. On the international FOI movement, see Lawrence Repeta, "Mr. Madison in the Twenty-First Century: Global Diffusion of the People's 'Right to Know,'" in *Soft Power Superpowers: Cultural and National Assets of Japan and the United States*, eds. Watanabe Yasushi and David L. McConnell (Armonk, N.Y.: M. E. Sharpe, 2008), 245–261, 250–255; Thomas Blanton, "The World's Right to Know," *Foreign Policy* 131 (2002): 50–58.

123. For a history and account of this success, see Maeve McDonagh, "The Right to Information in International Human Rights Law," *Human Rights Law Review* 13, no. 1 (2013): 25–55.

124. Colin Darch and Peter G. Underwood, *Freedom of Information and the Developing World: The Citizen, the State and Models of Openness* (Oxford, U.K.: Chandos Publishing, 2010), 51–52, 103. For general descriptions of the international FOI advocacy movement, see Alasdair Roberts, *Blacked Out: Government Secrecy in the Information Age* (New York: Cambridge University Press, 2006), 107–111; Ackerman and Sandoval-Ballesteros, "The Global Explosion of Freedom of Information Laws," 121–123; Greg Michener, "FOI Laws Around the World," *Journal of Democracy* 22, no. 2 (2011): 145–159.

125. Article 19,"Mission," https://www.article19.org/pages/en/mission.html

126. *Open Society Foundations*, "Freedom of Information," https://www.opensocietyfoundations.org/topics/freedom-information ("The Open Society Foundations work to uphold the right to speak and to know—in order to support public involvement in government and accountability, and to challenge corruption and human rights abuses").

127. Colin Darch and Peter Underwood insightfully apply diffusion theory to FOI laws in *Freedom of Information and the Developing World*, 7, 54. For an excellent account of India's Right to Information Act, see Prashant Sharma, *Democracy and Transparency in the Indian State* (London: Routledge, 2015). Sharma reveals how the legislation was the product of various active interest groups, including academic and government elites and international NGOs, who harnessed not only the ideal of a free press and active public but also an increasingly prevailing market ideology that viewed the state as inherently corrupt and excessively bureaucratic, requiring the kind of discipline that information disclosure can impose.

Chapter 2

1. Christopher Hood has noted the "quasi-religious significance" of transparency and its ongoing conceptual evolution in "Transparency in Historical Perspective," in *Transparency: The Key to Better Governance?*, eds. Christopher Hood and David Heald (2006), 3–23, 3–5.

2. Fredrik Galtung and Jeremy Pope, "The Global Coalition Against Corruption: Evaluating Transparency International," in *The Self-Restraining State: Power and Accountability in New Democracies*, eds. Andreas Schedler, Larry Diamond, and Marc F. Plattner (Boulder, Colo., and London: Lynne Rienner Publishers, 1999), 257–292, 258.

3. Ibid., 260; Luís de Sousa and Peter Larmour, "Transparency International: Global Franchising and the War of Information Against Corruption," in *Research Companion to Corruption in Organizations*, eds. Ronald J. Burke and Cary L. Cooper (Cheltenham, U.K., and Northampton, Mass.: Edward Elgar, 2009), 269–294, 270–277; Luís de Sousa, "TI in Search of a Constituency: The Institutionalization and Franchising of the Global Anti-Corruption Doctrine," in *Governments, NGOs, and Anti-Corruption: The New Integrity Warriors*, eds. Luís de Sousa, Peter Larmour, and Barry Hindess (Birmingham, U.K.: Routledge, 2009), 186–208, 194–196.

4. Transparency International, "What Is Transparency International," http://www.transparency.org/about/

5. De Sousa and Larmour, "Transparency International," 270, 272.

6. Steven Sampson, "The Anti-Corruption Industry: From Movement to Institution," *Global Crime* 11, no. 2 (2010): 261–278, 276–277. On the then-nascent role of NGOs in the anti-corruption field, see Susan Rose-Ackerman's influential book, *Corruption and Government* (Cambridge, U.K.: Cambridge University Press, 1999) 168–171. On the development of transnational advocacy networks generally, see Margaret E. Keck and Kathryn Sikkink, *Activists Beyond Borders: Advocacy Networks in International Politics* (Ithaca, N.Y.: Cornell University Press, 1998), 2; Sidney Tarrow, *The New Transnational Activism* (Cambridge, U.K.: Cambridge University Press, 2005), 28–29.

7. James Thuo Gathii, "Defining the Relationship Between Human Rights and Corruption," *University of Pennsylvania Journal of International Law* 31, no. 1 (2009): 125–202, 144–145.

8. Beginning in 1998, the International Monetary Fund began to evangelize on behalf of public "fiscal transparency" and in some places to impose transparency requirements on governments receiving IMF support. "IMF Manual on Fiscal Transparency: Introduction," International Monetary Fund. http://www.imf.org/external/np/fad/trans/manual/intro.htm. In 2010, the World Bank implemented a similar public access to information policy: Rebecca Harris, "Knowledge Is Power: Transparency and Participation Will Be the Drivers of Effective Development," *Huffington Post*, updated June 19, 2011. http://www.huffingtonpost.com/rebecca-harris/knowledge-is-power -transp_b_851020.html; Stephanie Strom, "Cracking Open the World Bank," *New York Times*, July 3, 2011, BU1.

9. Staffan Andersson and Paul M. Heywood, "The Politics of Perception: Use and Abuse of Transparency International's Approach to Measuring Corruption," *Policy Studies Journal* 57, no. 4 (2009): 746–767, 747; "Evaluation of Transparency International," Department of Evaluation, Norwegian Agency for Development Cooperation. http://www.development-today.com/magazine /2010/DT_3/Market_Update/5339

10. Transparency International, "Corruption Perceptions Index 2015," http://www.transpar ency.org/cpi2015

11. There are two prominent extractive industry NGOs: the Extractive Industries Transparency Initiative (http://eiti.org), founded in 2002 and funded by the private sector, and Publish What You Pay (http://www.publishwhatyoupay.org/), also founded in 2002 and formed and initially funded by NGOs and foundations.

12. Global Integrity (GI), begun in 1999 within the Center for Public Integrity (a U.S. domestic investigative journalism NGO) before spinning off independently in 2005, seeks to "play a catalytic role in promoting accountability and transparency reforms by developing tools that address the needs of the public, private, and civil sectors equally": Global Integrity, "Global Integrity: What We Do," http://www.globalintegrity.org/what-we-do/

13. Margaret Hanson, "The Global Promotion of Transparency in Emerging Markets," *Global Governance: A Review of Multilateralism and International Organizations* 9, no. 1 (2003): 63–79, 66–68. To its great credit, TI also has also attempted aggressively to disclose the sources of their own funding—a practice that other transparency-focused NGOs have adopted. "FAQs on Transparency International," Transparency International. https://www.transparency.org/whoweare/organisation/ faqs_on_transparency_international/9/ (explaining how TI is funded and how its national chapters are financed independently).

14. Transparency International, "FAQs on Corruption," http://www.transparency.org/whowe are/organisation/faqs_on_corruption

15. Keck and Sikkink, *Activists Beyond Borders*, 12–13; Tarrow, *The New Transactional Activism*, 145–146; Steve Charnovitz, "Nongovernmental Organizations and International Law," *American Journal of International Law* 100, no. 2 (2006): 348–372, 361–363.

16. The CPI's seeming precision in reducing a complex phenomenon to an ordinal rating is a key feature that helps win it media attention when TI releases it annually. De Sousa and Larmour, "Transparency International," 277–278. For criticisms of the CPI, see Andersson and Heywood, "The Politics of Perception," 752–754; Christiane Arndt and Charles Oman, *Uses and Abuses of Governance Indicators* (Paris: Development Centre of the Organisation for Economic Co-operation and Development, 2006), 91–92.

17. For a broader critique of NGOs' role in promoting a neoliberal globalization, see Jean-François Bayart, *Global Subjects: A Political Critique of Globalization* (Cambridge, U.K.: Cambridge University Press, 2007), 58–67. Similarly, the turn toward transparency in international environmental regulation linked democratization to the expansion of global and domestic neoliberal market reforms, especially in the manner in which transparency has been imposed via international agreement and norm—for example, by excluding private businesses from disclosure requirements. Michael Mason and Aarti Gupta, "Transparency Revisited," in *Transparency in Global Environmental Governance,* eds. Aarti Gupta and Michael Mason (Cambridge, Mass.: MIT Press, 2014), 321–339, 323–326.

18. TI's rise has run concurrently with the rise of New Public Management (also known as New Governance), whose emphasis on accountability has proven attractive to the diverse political interests that advocate for public fiscal restraint, particularly in the provision of public services. Michael Power, *The Audit Society: Rituals of Verification* (Oxford, U.K.: Oxford University Press, 1997), 43–44.

19. Ed Brown and Jonathan Cloke, "Neoliberal Reform, Governance and Corruption in the South: Assessing the International Anti-Corruption Crusade," *Antipode* 36, no. 2 (2004): 275–287.

20. Hanson, "Global Promotion of Transparency," 63; Barry Hindess, "International Anti-Corruption as a Programme of Normalization," in *Governments, NGOs and Anti-Corruption*, 19–32, 23. On the more general relationship between the transparency ideal and global neoliberalism, see Zygmunt Bauman, *Globalization: The Human Consequences* (New York: Columbia University Press, 1998), 29–33 (characterizing the expert imposition of transparency as a means to ease administration over differentiated, local cultures); Christina Garsten and Monica Lindh de Montoya, "The Naked Corporation: Visualization, Veiling and the Ethico-Politics of Organizational Transparency," in *Transparency in a New Global Order* (Cheltenham, U.K.: Edward Elgar, 2008), 79, 90–91 (describing transparency as a seemingly moral, apolitical means to "mak[e] the globalizing world hospitable for trans-organizational, transnational and sometimes super-national interventions and administrative procedures").

21. Brown and Cloke, "Neoliberal Reform, Governance, and Corruption in the South," 285; Barry Hindess, "Good Government and Corruption," in *Corruption and Anti-Corruption*, eds. Peter Larmour and Nick Wolanin (Canberra: Australian National University E Press, 2001), 1, 5–7; Hindess, "International Anti-Corruption as a Programme of Normalization." For a classic study of the unintended negative consequences of imposing anti-corruption reforms, see Frank Anechiarico and James B. Jacobs, *The Pursuit of Absolute Integrity: How Corruption Control Makes Government Ineffective* (Chicago: University of Chicago Press, 1996).

22. Andersson and Heywood, "The Politics of Perception"; Brown and Cloke, "Neoliberal Reform, Governance, and Corruption in the South." See also Jon Beasley-Murray, *Posthegemony: Political Theory and Latin America* (Minneapolis: University of Minnesota Press, 2011), 107–108 (critiquing transparency's transformative power on the state and society, and its relationship to neoliberalism).

23. The Sunlight Foundation, for example, has established a wide range of online programs that overlap with traditional freedom of information and campaign finance disclosure laws; it

is focused especially on making Congress's work more visible via the Internet. "Policy," Sunlight Foundation. http://sunlightfoundation.com/policy/ (listing the projects it is pursuing, which include disclosing congressional earmarks, participating in the FOI campaign's Sunshine Week and Freedom of Information Day, and attempting to increase the transparency of lobbyists' influence).

24. See, generally, Patrice Flichy, *The Internet Imaginaire* (Cambridge, Mass.: MIT Press, 2007) (documenting the utopian claims made on the Internet's behalf, especially in the early 1990s); Fred Turner, *From Counterculture to Cyberculture* (Chicago: University of Chicago Press, 2005), 249–262 (providing an intellectual history of the utopian claims about cyberspace and the Internet); Philip Agre, "The Market Logic of Information," *Knowledge, Technology, and Policy* 13, no. 3 (2000): 67–77; Richard Barbrook and Andy Cameron, "The Californian Ideology," *Science as Culture* 6, no. 1 (1996): 44–72; Julie E. Cohen, "Cyberspace As/And Space," *Columbia Law Review* 107, no. 1 (2007): 210–256.

25. John Perry Barlow, "The Economy of Ideas," *Wired*, March 1994, 84, 89, 129.

26. Don Tapscott, "Foreword," in *Open Government: Collaboration, Transparency, and Participation in Practice*, eds. Daniel Lathrop and Laurel Ruma (Sebastopol, Calif.: O'Reilly Media, 2010), xv–xviii (hereinafter *Open Government*).

27. Tim O'Reilly, "Government as Platform," in *Open Government*, 11–39, 15–24, 32–34; Danielle Keats Citron, "Open Code Governance," *University of Chicago Legal Forum* no. 1 (2008): 371–387; compare to Lawrence Lessig, *Code: Version 2.0* (New York: Basic Books, 2006), 153 ("[Open code] functions as a kind of Freedom of Information Act for network regulation. As with ordinary law, open code requires that lawmaking be public, and thus that lawmaking be transparent").

28. Douglas Rushkoff, "Open Source Democracy: How Online Communication Is Changing Offline Politics," *Demos*, 2003. http://www.demos.co.uk/files/OpenSourceDemocracy.pdf

29. Micah L. Sifry, "The Rise of Open-Source Politics," *Nation*, November 4, 2004. https://www.thenation.com/article/rise-open-source-politics/

30. Jared Duval, *Next Generation Democracy: What the Open-Source Revolution Means for Power, Politics, and Change* (New York: Bloomsbury, 2010).

31. Gavin Newsom, *Citizenville: How to Take the Town Square Digital and Reinvent Government* (New York: Penguin, 2013), 94.

32. See, e.g., Beth Simone Noveck, *Wiki Government: How Technology Can Make Government Better, Democracy Stronger, and Citizens More Powerful* (Washington, D.C.: Brookings Institute Press, 2009), xii–xiii (characterizing the ideal of "open government" as concerning both data access and collaboration with the public).

33. Micah L. Sifry, *WikiLeaks and the Age of Transparency* (Berkeley: Counterpoint, 2011), 15–17, 49; "Sunlight Agenda 2016," Sunlight Foundation. http://sunlightfoundation.com/policy/agenda/

34. Barack Obama, "Memorandum on Transparency and Open Government to the Heads of Executive Departments and Agencies," 74 Fed. Reg. 4685, January 26, 2009. https://www.white house.gov/the_press_office/TransparencyandOpenGovernment; Wendy R. Ginsberg, *The Obama Administration's Open Government Initiative: Issues for Congress*, Congressional Research Service Report No. R41361, January 28, 2011. https://www.fas.org/sgp/crs/secrecy/R41361.pdf; Paul T. Jaeger and John Carlo Bertot, "Transparency and Technological Change: Ensuring Equal and Sustained Public Access to Government Information," *Government Information Quarterly* 27, no. 4 (2010): 371–376, 373. The OGI's implementation, announced in December 2009 by Office of Management and Budget Director Peter Orszag, declared that the administration would promote "[t]he three principles of transparency, participation, and collaboration [which] form the cornerstone of an open government" through specific policies that each federal agency would implement. Executive Office of the President, Office of Management and Budget, "Memorandum for the Heads of Ex-

ecutive Departments and Agencies: Open Government Directive, Washington, DC," December 8, 2009, 1. https://www.whitehouse.gov/sites/default/files/omb/assets/memoranda_2010/m10-06.pdf

35. See, e.g., Noveck, *Wiki Government,* 18–20, 38–44. On Noveck's role in the administration, see Daniel Terdiman, "Obama's Open-Government Director Opens Up," *Cnet News,* December 8, 2009. https://www.cnet.com/news/obamas-open-government-director-opens-up/#ixzz1LsYZuLmt

36. Jennifer Shkabatur, "Cities @ Crossroads: Digital Technology and Local Democracy in America," *Brooklyn Law Review* 76, no. 4 (2011): 1413–1486, 1443–1464; Mark Fenster, "The Transparency Fix: Advocating Legal Rights and Their Alternatives in the Pursuit of a Visible State," *University of Pittsburgh Law Review* 73, no. 2 (2012): 443–503, 484–485.

37. Yochai Benkler, "Participation as Sustainable Cooperation in Pursuit of Public Goals," in *Rebooting America: Ideas for Redesigning American Democracy for the Internet Age,* eds. Allison H. Fine et al. (New York: Personal Democracy Press, 2008), 48–60, 52–53. The blogger and journalist Jeff Jarvis similarly imagines a world in which everyone creates "personal political pages" where they discuss their own beliefs and commitments, "manage" their "relationship" with politicians and government officials, and have their pages aggregated by Google ("the polling place that never closes"). Jeff Jarvis, "The Ethics of Openness," in *Rebooting America,* 215–224, 218–220.

38. See, e.g., Kevin Kelly, *What Technology Wants* (New York: Viking, 2010), 317. This ideal is not new among Internet futurists and advocates. Flichy, *The Internet Imaginaire,* 155–177 (describing the libertarian vision of a limited state among early cyberspace proponents). The conflict between the collective and individualist strains of digital transparency is akin to the similar conflict in the romantic ideals of the open source movement. Thomas Streeter, *The Net Effect: Romanticism, Capitalism, and the Internet* (New York: New York University Press, 2011), 154–167.

39. John Geraci, "The Four Pillars of an Open Civic System," *O'Reilly Radar,* June 15, 2009. http://radar.oreilly.com/2009/06/the-four-pillars-of-an-open-ci.html

40. O'Reilly, "Government as Platform," 12–13. Jeff Jarvis, too, views government as a "platform" that its citizens collaboratively use. Jeff Jarvis, *Public Parts: How Sharing in the Digital Age Improves the Way We Work and Live* (New York: Simon & Schuster, 2011), 201–202.

41. O'Reilly, "Government as Platform," 12–15.

42. See, e.g., Nancy Scola, "Washington's I.T. Guy," *American Prospect,* July/August 2010, 21, 21–24 (describing the decades-long efforts of Carl Malamud to get government information online).

43. Sifry, *WikiLeaks,* 77–82.

44. Ellen S. Miller, "Using the Web for Greater Government Openness and Transparency," *Business of Government,* Fall/Winter 2009, 50, 51–52; Douglas McGray, "iGov: How Geeks Are Opening Up Government on the Web," *The Atlantic,* January/February 2009, 36.

45. On the notion of information as a public good, see Cass Sunstein, *Republic.com 2.0* (Princeton, N.J.: Princeton University Press, 2007), 107–109.

46. For a skeptical account of digital transparency's effects, see Jennifer Shkabatur, "Transparency With(out) Accountability: Open Government in the United States," *Yale Law and Policy Review* 31, no. 1 (2012): 79–140, 91–117.

47. Julie Cohen, *Configuring the Networked Self: Law, Code, and the Play of Everyday Practice* (New Haven, Conn.: Yale University Press, 2012), 117; Evgeny Morozov, *To Save Everything, Click Here* (New York: PublicAffairs, 2013), 93–97.

48. Sifry, *WikiLeaks,* 102 ("In this understanding, the relationship between governments and their constituents is a two-way street, and data is the road that connects them"). For a critique of the distinction between "data" and "information," see Jonathan Fox, "The Uncertain Relationship Between Transparency and Accountability," *Development in Practice* 17, no. 4–5 (2007): 663–671.

49. On the relationship between the romantic self-conception of digital technologists and

neoliberal ideals about the state's withering away as an agent of regulation and redistribution, see Thomas Streeter, "'That Deep Romantic Chasm': Libertarianism, Neoliberalism, and the Computer Culture," in *Communication, Citizenship, and Social Policy*, eds. Andrew Calabrese and Jean-Claude Burgelman (Lanham, Md.: Rowman & Littlefield, 1999), 49–64.

50. For an effective critique of app-developer-driven politics, see Catherine Tumber, "Unreal Cities?," *The Nation*, February 3, 2014, 35–37.

51. Harlan Yu and David G. Robinson, "The New Ambiguity of 'Open Government,'" *UCLA Law Review Discussion* 59, no. 1 (2012): 178–209.

52. Dave Eggers, *The Circle* (New York: Knopf, 2013).

53. For thorough and more fully sourced accounts of WikiLeaks' history, see Yochai Benkler, "A Free Irresponsible Press: WikiLeaks and the Battle Over the Soul of the Networked Fourth Estate," *Harvard Civil Rights–Civil Liberties Law Review* 46, no. 2 (2011): 311–397, 341–343; Mark Fenster, "Disclosure's Effects: WikiLeaks and Transparency," *Iowa Law Review* 97, no. 3 (2012), 753–807; for additional background information, see generally David Leigh and Luke Harding, *WikiLeaks: Inside Julian Assange's War on Secrecy* (New York: PublicAffairs, 2011); Greg Mitchell, *The Age of WikiLeaks* (New York: Sinclair Books, 2011); Molly Sauter, "WikiLeaks FAQ," *The Future of the Internet—and How to Stop It* (Blog), December 7, 2010. http://blogs.harvard.edu/futureoftheinternet/2010/12/07/wikileaks-cable-faq/. In addition to government documents, WikiLeaks also receives and distributes documents purloined from private corporations, but I will focus here only on the government documents it has released.

54. Leigh and Harding, *WikiLeaks*, 57–64; Manfred Goetzke, "WikiLeaks Website Offers Promising Outlet for Fighting Corruption," *Deutsche Welle*, November 26, 2009. http://www.dw.com/en/wikileaks-website-offers-promising-outlet-for-fighting-corruption/a-4930880

55. WikiLeaks, "About: What Is WikiLeaks," May 7, 2011. http://wikileaks.org/About.html

56. Mitchell, *The Age of WikiLeaks*, 38–50; Alex Altman, "Afghan Leaks: Is the U.S. Keeping Too Many Secrets?," *Time*, July 30, 2010. http://content.time.com/time/nation/article/0,8599,2007224,00.html; Ginger Thompson, "Early Struggles of Soldier Charged in Leak Case," *New York Times*, August 9, 2010, A1.

57. Daniel W. Drezner, "Why WikiLeaks Is Bad for Scholars," *Chronicle of Higher Education*, December 5, 2010. http://chronicle.com/article/Why-WikiLeaks-Is-Bad-for/125628/ (characterizing diplomatic cables as documents that would have been unavailable to academics for decades); Dan Murphy, "WikiLeaks Releases Video Depicting U.S. Forces Killing of Two Reuters Journalists in Iraq," *Global News* (Blog), April 5, 2010. http://www.csmonitor.com/World/Global-News/2010/0405/Wikileaks-releases-video-depicting-US-forces-killing-of-two-Reuters-journalists-in-Iraq (noting that the *Collateral Murder* video showed an attack about which Reuters had unsuccessfully sought information through the Freedom of Information Act).

58. Most of the documents that composed the Afghanistan and Iraq "War Logs" were classified "secret." Of the more than 250,000 diplomatic cables WikiLeaks obtained, approximately 11,000 were classified "secret," 4,000 were classified "secret" and "noforn" (that is, not to be shared with a foreign government), and 9,000 were classified "noforn." "Piecing Together the Reports, and Deciding What to Publish," *New York Times*, July 25, 2010. http://www.nytimes.com/2010/07/26/world/26editors-note.html; Scott Shane and Andrew Lehren, "Leaked Cables Offer Raw Look at U.S. Diplomacy," *New York Times*, November 28, 2010. http://www.nytimes.com/2010/11/29/world/29cables.html

59. Fenster, "Disclosure's Effects," 38–55 (summarizing arguments made by WikiLeaks' critics and proponents on the relative significance of the site's disclosures, and attempting to discern their wider impact on the general public).

60. Hans Ulrich Obrist, "In Conversation with Julian Assange, Part II," *E-Flux Journal* 26, June 2011, 7. http://worker01.e-flux.com/pdf/article_238.pdf (claiming that WikiLeaks can enforce the human right to know, the right to speak, and, above all, the right to communicate information).

61. "About: What Is WikiLeaks."

62. Julian Assange, "Don't Shoot Messenger for Revealing Uncomfortable Truths," *The Australian*, December 8, 2010. http://www.theaustralian.com.au/in-depth/wikileaks/dont-shoot-messenger-for-revealing-uncomfortable-truths/story-fn775xjq-1225967241332

63. At the height of WikiLeaks' visibility, a disgruntled former member named Daniel Domscheit-Berg launched another rival site, while the *New York Times*, WikiLeaks' U.S. journalistic collaborator (with whom it has had a stormy relationship), considered establishing a competing site that would allow whistleblowers to anonymously pass documents to the newspaper. Michael Calderone, "*NY Times* Considers Creating an 'EZ Pass Lane for Leakers,'" *Yahoo! News* (Blog). January 25, 2011. https://www.yahoo.com/news/blogs/cutline/ny-times-considers-creating-ez-pass-lane-leakers-20110125-053811-988.html; "A Swarm of Leaks," *The Economist*, December 11, 2010. http://www.economist.com/node/17674089?story_id=17674089

64. Decrypted Matrix, "Leak Site Directory," http://decryptedmatrix.tumblr.com/post/23900366553/leak-site-directory

65. See, e.g., "About: What Is WikiLeaks."

66. Bivol, "Julian Assange: I Believe in the Right to Privacy of Communication and History," May 1, 2011. https://wlcentral.org/node/1727

67. Fenster, "Disclosure's Effects," 27.

68. Julian Assange, "The Hidden Curse of Thomas Paine," *Guernica: A Magazine of Art & Politics*, April 29, 2008. https://www.guernicamag.com/daily/the_hidden_curse_of_thomas_pai/; Aaron Bady, "Julian Assange in Berkeley," *Zunguzungu*, December 12, 2010. https://zunguzungu .wordpress.com/2010/12/12/julian-assange-in-berkeley/ (transcript of an Assange talk in which he complained that bloggers and the like "don't give a fuck about the material" and write in order to speak to and gain status with peers, not because of their inherent interest in the material or willingness to investigate it further).

69. "WikiLeaks: Big Picture," WikiLeaks. https://wikileaks.org/wiki/WikiLeaks:Big_picture

70. See, generally, Leigh and Harding, *WikiLeaks*, 110–115 (describing the negotiated agreements between WikiLeaks and its newspaper partners to redact documents); Benkler, "A Free Irresponsible Press," 323–324 (summarizing the WikiLeaks' releases and describing the site's relationship with the established print news media).

71. The best resource for information about Assange's early career as a hacker and cypherpunk and the development of WikiLeaks is Robert Manne, "The Cypherpunk Revolutionary," *The Monthly* (Australian), March 2011. http://cryptome.org/0003/assange-manne.htm

72. Julian Assange, "Conspiracy as Governance," November 10, 2006. http://cryptome.org /0002/ja-conspiracies.pdf (hereinafter Assange, "Conspiracy"). For fuller descriptions of the radical strain in Assange's writings, see Aaron Bady, "Julian Assange and the Computer Conspiracy; 'To Destroy This Invisible Government,'" *Zunguzungu*, November 29, 2010. https://zunguzungu.word press.com/2010/11/29/julian-assange-and-the-computer-conspiracy-%E2%80%9Cto-destroy-this -invisible-government%E2%80%9D/; Fenster, "Disclosure's Effects," 20–29.

73. Assange, "Conspiracy," 1 (calling for a "course of ennobling and effective action to replace the structures that lead to bad governance with something better").

74. Ibid., 4–5; Slavoj Žižek, *Living in the End Times*, revised ed. (London: Verso, 2011), 408–409; Bady, "Julian Assange." In an essay intended to dismiss WikiLeaks' importance, Umberto Eco concedes this point, noting that even an "empty secret" whose content is widely known can cause

"irreparable damage" to those who thought they controlled access to the secret. Umberto Eco, "Not Such Wicked Leaks," *VoxEurop*, trans. Eric Rosencrantz, December 2, 2010. http://www.voxeurop.eu /en/content/article/414871-not-such-wicked-leaks

75. Finn Brunton, "Keyspace: WikiLeaks and the Assange Papers," *Radical Philosophy,* March/ April 2011, 8–20, 13. http://www.radicalphilosophy.com/commentary/keyspace-wikileaks-and-the -assange-papers

76. Benedetta Brevini and Graham Murdock, "Following the Money: WikiLeaks and the Political Economy of Disclosure," in *Beyond WikiLeaks: Implications for the Future of Communications, Journalism, and Society,* eds. Benedetta Brevini, Arne Hintz, and Patrick McCurdy (London: Palgrave Macmillan, 2013), 35–55.

77. Benkler, "A Free Irresponsible Press."

78. Emma Grey Ellis, "WikiLeaks Has Officially Lost the Moral High Ground," *Wired,* July 27, 2016. https://www.wired.com/2016/07/wikileaks-officially-lost-moral-high-ground/

79. As Jack Balkin has characterized it, the U.S. efforts to punish WikiLeaks and Chelsea Manning were a combination of "new-school" mechanisms of informal censorship that effectively target third-party intermediaries and "old-school" efforts to punish leakers. Jack M. Balkin, "Old-School/New-School Speech Regulation," *Harvard Law Review* 127, no. 8 (2014): 2296–2342.

Chapter 3

1. Ann E. Marimow, "A Rare Peek into a Justice Department Leak Probe," *Washington Post,* May 19, 2013. https://www.washingtonpost.com/local/a-rare-peek-into-a-justice-department-leak -probe/2013/05/19/0bc473de-be5e-11e2-97d4-a479289a31f9_story.html

2. Timothy Melley, *The Covert Sphere: Secrecy, Fiction, and the National Security State* (Ithaca, N.Y.: Cornell University Press, 2012).

3. "Policy Basics: Where Do Our Federal Tax Dollars Go?" Center on Budget and Policy Priorities, last updated March 4, 2016. http://www.cbpp.org/research/policy-basics-where-do-our -federal-tax-dollars-go

4. Sisella Bok, *Secrets* (New York: Pantheon, 1983), 175–176; Robert L. Saloschin, "The Department of Justice and the Explosion of Freedom of Information Act Litigation," *Administrative Law Review* 52, no. 4 (2000): 1401–1408.

5. Jeremy Bentham, *Political Tactics,* ed. Michael James et al. (New York: Oxford University Press, 1999), 39.

6. See, e.g., Joseph E. Stiglitz, "On Liberty, the Right to Know, and Public Discourse: The Role of Transparency in Public Life," Oxford Amnesty Lecture, Oxford, U.K., January 27, 1999, 18–25 (discussing legitimate, limited exceptions to transparency).

7. Bok, *Secrets,* 171–190.

8. Ibid., 191–194.

9. See, e.g., Amy Gutmann and Dennis Thompson, *Democracy and Disagreement* (Cambridge, Mass.: Belknap Press of Harvard University Press, 1996), 103–126 (evaluating various possible exceptions to the norm of publicity).

10. Dennis F. Thompson, "Democratic Secrecy," *Political Science Quarterly* 114, no. 2 (Summer 1999): 181–193.

11. Ibid., 182.

12. Alexander Hamilton, *The Federalist No. 70,* in *The Federalist Papers,* ed. Clinton Rossiter (New York: Penguin, 1961), 423–431, 424.

13. James Madison, *The Federalist No. 48,* in *The Federalist Papers,* ed. Clinton Rossiter (New York: Penguin, 1961), 308–313, 309.

14. Rahul Sagar, *Secrets and Leaks: The Dilemma of State Secrecy* (Princeton, N.J.: Princeton University Press, 2013), 18–21.

15. Ibid., 21–30.

16. Antonin Scalia, "The Freedom of Information Act Has No Clothes," *Regulation*, March/April 1982, 14–19, 15.

17. Ibid., 15.

18. On Cheney's penchant and reputation for secrecy, see Michael Isikoff and David Corn, *Hubris: The Inside Story of Spin, Scandal, and the Selling of the Iraq War* (New York: Crown, 2006), 423; Robert M. Pallitto and William G. Weaver, *Presidential Secrecy and the Law* (Baltimore: Johns Hopkins University Press, 2007), 46; Alasdair Roberts, *The Collapse of Fortress Bush* (New York: New York University Press, 2008), 135–136.

19. "Minority Report, Report of the Congressional Committees Investigating the Iran–Contra Affair," H.R. Rep. 100-433, S. Rep. 100-216 (1987) (hereinafter "Minority Report"). On the significance of the "Minority Report," see Jack Goldsmith, *The Terror Presidency* (New York: Norton, 2007), 86–88; Frederick A. O. Schwarz Jr. and Aziz Z. Huq, *Unchecked and Unbalanced: Presidential Power in a Time of Terror* (New York: New Press, 2007), 154–155, 159–160, 200.

20. Jane Mayer, "The Hidden Power: The Legal Mind Behind the White House's War on Terror," *The New Yorker*, July 3, 2006, 44; Seymour M. Hersh, "The Redirection: Is the Administration's New Policy Benefitting Our Enemies in the War on Terrorism?," *The New Yorker*, March 5, 2007, 65.

21. "Minority Report," 469 (see n.18) (noting the president's "primary role in conducting the foreign policy of the United States"); ibid., 457 (arguing that the Constitution grants the president substantive, independent powers in foreign affairs).

22. Ibid., 459–460.

23. Ibid., 460 (quoting Hamilton, *The Federalist No. 70*).

24. Ibid., 463–469.

25. "Report of the Congressional Committees Investigating the Iran–Contra Affair, H.R. Rep. 100-433, S. Rep. 100-216 (1987), 387–392 (hereinafter "Iran–Contra Report").

26. "Minority Report," 457–458 (citing Madison, *The Federalist No. 48*).

27. Ibid., 463–469.

28. Ibid., 458–459 (discussing the foreign affairs powers given to the Congress during the Constitutional Convention), 471–473 (citing Youngstown Sheet and Tube Co. v. Sawyer, 343 U.S. 579 (1952); Dames & Moore v. Regan, 453 U.S. 654 (1981); and U.S. v. Curtiss-Wright Export Corp., 299 U.S. 304 (1936)).

29. Ibid., 475–476.

30. Ibid., 452.

31. Scalia, "Freedom of Information Act," 19.

32. Ibid., 15.

33. Ibid., 19.

34. Kathryn S. Olmsted, *Challenging the Secret Government: The Post-Watergate Investigations of the CIA and FBI* (Chapel Hill: University of North Carolina Press, 1996), 11–39.

35. United States v. Nixon, 418 U.S. 683, 705–706 (1974).

36. New York Times v. United States, 403 U.S. 713, 714 (1971) (*per curiam*).

37. *New York Times*, 403 U.S. at 728–729 (Stewart, J., concurring).

38. David J. Barron and Martin S. Lederman, "The Commander in Chief at the Lowest Ebb—A Constitutional History," *Harvard Law Review* 121, no. 4 (2008): 941–1113, 1094–1097.

39. Brief for Petitioners, 34, Cheney v. U.S. Dist. Ct., 124 S. Ct. 2576 (2004) (No. 03–475) (citing Art. II, § 1, Art. II, § 2, cl. 1, Art. II § 3, cl. 1); see also Steven G. Calabresi and Christopher S. Yoo, *The*

Unitary Executive (New Haven, Conn.: Yale University Press, 2008), 407 (identifying the government's argument in its brief in *Cheney* as a key example of how the Bush administration "staunchly protected the autonomy of the executive branch in the courts").

40. Heidi Kitrosser, "Secrecy and Separated Powers: Executive Privilege Revisited," *Iowa Law Review* 92, no. 2 (2007): 417–488, 501–502.

41. Joel D. Bush, "Congressional-Executive Access Disputes: Legal Standards and Political Settlements," *Journal of Law and Politics* 9, no. 4 (1993): 735–746.

42. William Van Alstyne, "A Political and Constitutional Review of United States v. Nixon," *UCLA Law Review* 22, no. 1 (1974): 116–140, 123.

43. Louis Fisher, "Congressional Access to National Security Information," *Harvard Journal on Legislation* 45, no. 1 (2008): 219–236, 219–220; Mark J. Rozell, "Executive Privilege Revived?: Secrecy and Conflict During the Bush Presidency," *Duke Law Journal* 52, no. 2 (2002): 403–422, 404.

44. Scalia, "Freedom of Information Act," 15 (calling FOIA "the Taj Mahal of the Doctrine of Unanticipated Consequences, the Sistine Chapel of Cost-Benefit Analysis Ignored").

45. "Minority Report," 437–438.

46. Ibid., 576–578.

47. Ibid., 579.

48. This data is from the Department of Justice's "Summary of Annual FOIA Reports for Fiscal Year 2015," Department of Justice, which agglomerates all of the data submitted by individual agencies. https://www.justice.gov/oip/reports/fy_2015_annual_foia_report_summary/download

49. On the history of FOIA's fee-shifting provision and its enforcement through the late-1990s, see Charles J. Wichmann III, "Ridding FOIA of Those 'Unanticipated Consequences': Repaving a Necessary Road to Freedom," *Duke Law Journal* 47, no. 6 (1998): 1213–1256, 1221–1223.

50. Margaret Kwoka, "FOIA, Inc.," *Duke Law Journal* 65 no. 7 (2016): 1361–1437, which provides a quantitative study of requests at several agencies; Kwoka also discusses the 2006 study, which is summarized at "Frequent Filers: Businesses Make FOIA Their Business," Society for Professional Journalists, last updated July 3, 2006. http://www.spj.org/rrr.asp?ref=31&t=foia

51. Wichmann, "Ridding FOIA of Those 'Unanticipated Consequences,'" 1219–1221.

52. Frederick Schauer conducted a conceptual cost-benefit analysis of transparency in "Transparency in Three Dimensions," *University of Illinois Law Review* 2011, no. 4 (2011): 1339–1357, 1353–1354.

53. Savage v. CIA, 826 F.2d 561 (7th Cir. 1987) (complaining that judicial consideration of "petty" FOIA requests is a monumental waste of judicial resources); Abner Mikva, "Knowing You, Knowing Me," *Legal Times*, January 6, 1997, 23 (describing administrative burden of FOIA enforcement on federal district courts).

54. Kenneth F. Bunting, "Is Brown (Act) Out in California? Time May Tell," *Huffington Post*, July 31, 2012. http://www.huffingtonpost.com/kenneth-f.../jerry-brown-act_b_1707724.html; John King, "Open Government at Heart of Budget Cut," *S.F. Gate*, July 14, 2012. http://www.sfgate.com/bayarea/place/article/Open-government-at-heart-of-budget-cut-3707501.php

55. Legislative Analyst's Office, "Analysis of Proposition 42," last updated June 3, 2014. http://www.lao.ca.gov/ballot/2014/prop-42-062014.aspx

56. Alisha Green and Laurenellen McCann, "California Crying Wolf About Cost of Public Records?" *Sunshine Foundation* (Blog), June 26, 2013. http://sunlightfoundation.com/blog/2013/06/26/california-crying-wolf-about-cost-of-public-records/

57. Wendy Fry, "Assembly Walks Back Changes to Public Records Act," *NBC 7 San Diego*, June 19, 2013. http://www.nbcsandiego.com/news/local/Assembly-Walks-Back-Changes-To-Public-Records-Act-212244671.html; Sharon McNary, "What Is Prop 42 and Why Should It Matter to Voters?"

Represent! (Blog), *89.3 KPCC*, May 28, 2014. http://www.scpr.org/blogs/politics/2014/05/28/16709/what-is-prop-42-and-why-should-it-matter-to-voters/

58. 5 U.S.C. § 552(a)(3)(A) (1996).

59. Eight states have such provisions, which were upheld against constitutional challenge in the Supreme Court in McBurney v. Young, 133 S. Ct. 1709 (2013).

60. Amy E. Rees, "Recent Developments Regarding the Freedom of Information Act: A 'Prologue to a Farce or a Tragedy; or, Perhaps Both,'" *Duke Law Journal* 44, no. 6 (1995): 1183–1224, 1184.

61. The most thorough recent treatment of this issue is David Brin's book *The Transparent Society* (Reading, Mass.: Perseus Books, 1998), whose prescience about the relationship between information technology and privacy has kept the book relevant despite its publication during an earlier era of the Internet.

62. The Privacy Act of 1974 appears at 5 U.S.C. § 552a et seq. The Department of Justice's valuable and extensive "Overview of the Privacy Act" is available from "Overview of the Privacy Act," Department of Justice, updated July 17, 2015. http://www.justice.gov/opcl/privacy-act-1974

63. 5 U.S.C. §§ 552(b)(6), (b)(7)(C). Patrice McDermott, *Who Needs to Know? The State of Public Access to Federal Government Information* (Lanham, Md.: Bernan Press, 2007), 73–74.

64. Critical Mass Energy Project v. NRC, 975 F.2d 871, 874 (D.C. Cir. 1992); William L. Casey et al., *Entrepreneurship, Productivity and the Freedom of Information Act* (Lexington, Mass.: Lexington Books, 1983). An exemption from FOIA requirements covers "matters that are trade secrets . . . obtained from a person and privileged or confidential" (5 U.S.C. § 552(b)(4)).

65. Benjamin S. DuVal Jr., "The Occasions of Secrecy," *University of Pittsburgh Law Review* 47, no. 3 (1986): 579–674, 621–625.

66. In recent years, rightwing think tanks and groups have sought records from a scientist at the University of Virginia working on climate change, from an outspoken leftist historian at the University of Wisconsin, and from a law professor at the University of North Carolina who runs a think tank working on poverty issues. Doug Lederman, "Court Shields Scholar's Emails," *Inside Higher Ed*, April 18, 2014. http://www.insidehighered.com/news/2014/04/18/virginias-high-court-protects-privacy-researchers-emails; Jane Stancill, "Gene Nichol Speaks Loudly, Just Not for UNC," *Raleigh News-Observer*, April 12, 2014. http://blog.ecu.edu/sites/dailyclips/blog/2014/04/14/gene-nichol-speaks-loudly-just-not-for-unc-the-news-observer/; Susan Stroller, "Chalkboard: UW History Prof Targeted for Records Request by Republican Party," *The Capitol Times*, March 25, 2011. http://host.madison.com/ct/news/local/education/blog/chalkboard-uw-history-prof-targeted-for-records-request-by-republican/article_54c271b2-56e6-11e0-b524-001cc4c002e0.html. Gay and lesbian activists have sought records from a University of Virginia law professor whose position on a case before the Supreme Court they opposed, while a student group in Kansas has sued to obtain e-mails concerning a libertarian economist hired as a lecturer by the University of Kansas's Center for Applied Economics, which was established in 2004 by a donation from a foundation endowed by one of the conservative Koch brothers. Kaitlin Mulhere, "Scrutiny of Scholar's Emails," *Inside Higher Ed*, January 14, 2015. https://www.thefire.org/scrutiny-scholars-emails/; Derek Quizon, "LGBT Activists Take UVA Professor to Task for His Stance on Cases," *(Charlottesville) Daily Progress*, May 23, 2014. http://www.dailyprogress.com/news/local/lgbt-activists-take-uva-professor-to-task-for-his-stance/article_f15797b4-e2cf-11e3-aeo2-001a4bcf6878.html. For a general discussion of the legal issues in these instances, see Amy Gajda, "Academic Freedom, the Presumption of Openness, and Privacy," *International Journal of Open Governments/Revue Internationale des Governments Ouverts* 1 (March 2015): 151–162.

67. Bok, *Secrets*, 175–176; Sarah A. Binder and Frances E. Lee, "Making Deals in Congress," in *Negotiating Agreement in Politics*, eds. Jane Mansbridge and Cathie Jo Martin (Washington, D.C.:

American Political Science Association, 2013), 54–72; David Stasavage, "Does Transparency Make a Difference? The Example of the European Council of Ministers," in *Transparency: The Key to Better Governance?*, eds. Christopher Hood and David Heald (Oxford, U.K.: Oxford University Press, 2006), 160–179; Jennifer Lerner and Philip Tetlock, "Accounting for the Effects of Accountability," *Psychological Bulletin* 125, no. 2 (1999): 255–275. Courts often affirm this belief, perhaps based on their own practice of closed deliberations and conferences. See, e.g., United States v. Nixon, 418 U.S. 683, 705 (1974) ("Human experience teaches that those who expect public dissemination of their remarks may well temper candor with a concern for appearances and for their own interests to the detriment of the decisionmaking process"); In re Sealed Case, 121 F.3d 729, 750 (D.C. Cir. 1997) ("If presidential advisers must assume they will be held to account publicly for all approaches that were advanced, considered but ultimately rejected, they will almost inevitably be inclined to avoid serious consideration of novel or controversial approaches to presidential problems").

68. Nicholas Johnson, "Open Meetings and Closed Minds: Another Road to the Mountaintop," *Drake Law Review* 53, no. 1 (2004): 11–54, 22–24; Randolph J. May, "Taking the Sunshine Act: Too Much Exposure Inhibits Collegial Decision Making," *Legal Times*, February 5, 1996, 24; Kathy Bradley, "Do You Feel the Sunshine? Government in the Sunshine Act: Its Objectives, Goals, and Effect on the FCC and You," *Federal Communications Law Journal* 49, no. 2 (1997): 473–490, 481–485.

69. Stephen Hansen, Michael McMahon, and Andrea Prat, "Transparency and Deliberation Within the FOMC: A Computational Linguistics Approach," CFM discussion paper series, CFM-DP2014-11 (London: Centre for Macroeconomics, 2014).

70. Russell Hardin, "Citizens' Knowledge, Politicians' Duplicity," in *The Economics of Transparency in Politics*, eds. Albert Breton, Gianluigi Galeotti, Pierre Salmon, and Ronald Wintrobe (Burlington, Vt.: Ashgate, 2007), 37–54, 45–47.

71. Kristin M. Lord, *The Perils and Promise of Global Transparency* (Albany: State University of New York Press, 2006), 204.

72. Francis Fukuyama, *Political Order and Political Delay: From the Industrial Revolution to the Globalization of Democracy* (New York: Farrar, Straus and Giroux, 2014), 504. Jonathan Rauch made a similar argument in his 2016 cover story in *The Atlantic* that was critical of contemporary governance and the unintended consequences of good-government reforms. Jonathan Rauch, "How American Politics Went Insane," *The Atlantic*, July/August 2016. http://www.theatlantic.com/magazine/archive/2016/07/how-american-politics-went-insane/485570/

73. Such competing, apparently oppositional approaches arise throughout theories of government, and administrative law must inevitably operate within and resolve these contradictory claims. Thomas O. Sargentich, "The Reform of the American Administrative Process: The Contemporary Debate," *Wisconsin Law Review* no. 2 (1984): 385–442, 392–397 (identifying the "rule of law," "public purposes," and "democratic process" as core conflicting ideals of administrative process).

74. United States v. Nixon, 418 U.S. 683, 711–712 (1974).

75. Nixon v. Administrator of General Services, 433 U.S. 425, 452–453 (1977).

76. EPA v. Mink, 410 U.S. 73, 80 n.6 (1973) (quoting S. Rep. 813, 89th Cong., 1st Sess., 5 (1965)).

77. Ibid.

78. 5 U.S.C. (b)(1)–(7).

79. See, e.g., Fla. Const. Art. I, § 24(c) (authorizing legislature to construct narrow restrictions to open records requirement that are "no broader than necessary to accomplish the stated purpose of the law"); Fink v. Lefkowitz, 393 N.E.2d 463, 466 n.* (N.Y. 1979) (characterizing New York's Freedom of Information Law as "patterned after the federal analogue"); Times Mirror Co. v. Superior Court, 813 P.2d 240, 247 (Cal. 1991) (characterizing California's Public Records Act as "modeled on" the federal FOIA, with general disclosure requirements and specific exceptions).

80. Louis Harris and Associates, *Harris Survey*, July, 1971 (survey question), USHARRIS.71JUL. Cornell University, Roper Center for Public Opinion Research, Ithaca, N.Y.: iPOLL (distributor); Emily Ekins, "57 Percent Say the Obama Administration Is Not the Most Transparent Ever," *Reason.com*, December 11, 2013. http://reason.com/blog/2013/12/11/poll-57-percent-of-americans-say-the-ob2

81. This is precisely what happened following the 2000 election, when the kinds of allegations of rampant secrecy that plagued the Clinton administration were visited upon the Bush administration. On the Clinton era, see Gary Ferguson and David Bowermaster, "Whatever It Is, Bill Clinton Likely Did It," *U.S. News & World Report*, August 8, 1994, 29; Philip Weiss, "Clinton Crazy," *New York Times Magazine*, February 23, 1997, 36.

82. "Majority Says CIA Harsh Interrogations Justified," *Washington Post–ABC News Poll*, January 4, 2015. https://www.washingtonpost.com/politics/polling/majority-says-cia-harsh-interro gations-justified/2015/01/04/b6f9d79e-8518-11e4-abcf-5a3d7b3b20b8_page.html; "Americans Find Some Tortures More Acceptable Than Others," *YouGov US*, December 12, 2014. https://today.you gov.com/news/2014/12/12/torture-report/

83. Louis Harris and Associates, "CBS News Poll, February 2006."

84. Gallup Organization, Gallup/Newsweek Poll, June, 1971 (survey question). USGALNEW.71PENT. Cornell University, Roper Center for Public Opinion Research, Ithaca, N.Y.: iPOLL (distributor).

85. Polls taken in late 2013 and 2014 found varying results. The most supportive findings came from YouGov.com, in polls taken in January and March 2014, which found an even split among respondents approving and disapproving of Snowden and his actions as well as supporting and opposing his prosecution. Peter Moore, "Poll Results: Snowden," *YouGov.com*, March 28, 2014. https://today.yougov.com/news/2014/03/28/poll-results-snowden/; Katie Jagel, "Poll Results: Snowden," *YouGov.com*, January 22, 2014. https://today.yougov.com/news/2014/01/22/poll-results-snowden/. Other polls found less support for Snowden, although they also found less support for the NSA's surveillance program than distaste for the person who leaked information about it. Sarah Dutton et al., "Poll: Most Think Edward Snowden Should Stand Trial in U.S.," *CBS News*, January 22, 2014. http://www.cbsnews.com/news/poll-most-think-edward-snowden-should-stand-trial-in-us/; "Snowden and the NSA—November 2013," *Washington Post*, November 21, 2013. https://www.wash ingtonpost.com/politics/polling/snowden-nsa-november-2013/2013/11/21/efac2a02-5269-11e3-9ee6 -2580086d8254_page.html

Chapter 4

1. Wilbur Schramm, "Information Theory and Mass Communication," *Journalism Quarterly* 32, no. 2 (1955): 131–146.

2. Claude E. Shannon and Warren Weaver, *The Mathematical Theory of Communication* (Urbana: University of Illinois Press, 1949), 33–34.

3. Gary Genosko, *Remodelling Communication: From WWII to the WWW* (Toronto: University of Toronto Press, 2012), 115; James Gleick, *The Information: A History, a Theory, a Flood* (New York: Vintage, 2011), 221, 262–268.

4. Denis McQuail and Swen Windahl, *Communication Models for the Study of Mass Communications* (London: Longman, 1993), 16–17; Hanno Hardt, *Critical Communication Studies: Communication, History and Theory in America* (London: Routledge, 1992), 77–90.

5. John T. Dorsey Jr., "A Communication Model for Administration," *Administrative Science Quarterly* 2, no. 3 (1957): 307–324, 308–310.

6. John Durham Peters, *Speaking into the Air* (Chicago: University of Chicago Press, 1999), 23–25.

7. Shannon and Weaver, *Mathematical Theory of Communication*, 31.

8. Ibid., 4.

9. Hans Krause Hansen and Mykkel Flyverbom, "The Politics of Transparency and the Calibration of Knowledge in the Digital Age," *Organization* 22, no. 6 (2015): 872–889.

10. Armand Mattelart and Michèle Mattelart, *Rethinking Media Theory*, trans. James A. Cohen and Marina Urquidi (Minneapolis: University of Minnesota Press, 1992), 43–47.

11. Walter J. Ong, *Orality and Literacy* (London: Routledge, 2002 [1982]), 171–172.

12. Summaries of Snowden's life appear in Glenn Greenwald, *No Place to Hide* (New York: Metropolitan Books, 2014), 41–44; Christopher Drew and Scott Shane, "Résumé Shows Snowden Honed Hacking Skills," *New York Times*, July 4, 2013. http://www.nytimes.com/2013/07/05/us/resume-shows-snowden-honed-hacking-skills.html

13. Greenwald, *No Place to Hide*, 36.

14. Edward Jay Epstein, "Was Snowden's Heist a Foreign Espionage Operation?" *Wall Street Journal*, May 9, 2014. http://online.wsj.com/news/articles/SB10001424052702304831304579542402390653932?mg=ren064-wsj

15. Alex Johnson, "Edward Snowden 'Probably' Not a Russian Spy, New NSA Chief Says," *NBC News*, June 3, 2014. http://www.nbcnews.com/storyline/nsa-snooping/edward-snowden-probably-not-russian-spy-new-nsa-chief-says-n121926; Jane Mayer, "Snowden Calls Russian-Spy Story 'Absurd' in Exclusive Interview," *The New Yorker*, January 21, 2014. http://www.newyorker.com/online/blogs/newsdesk/2014/01/snowden-calls-russian-spy-story-absurd.html

16. Kurt Eichenwald, "How Edward Snowden Escalated Cyber War," *Newsweek*, October 31, 2013. http://www.newsweek.com/2013/11/01/how-edward-snowden-escalated-cyber-war-243886.html

17. David Pozen, "The Leaky Leviathan: Why the Government Condemns and Condones Unlawful Disclosures of Information," *Harvard Law Review* 127, no. 2 (2013): 512–635.

18. James Madison, *The Federalist No. 37*, in *The Federalist Papers*, ed. Clinton Rossiter (New York: New American Library, 1961), 227–232.

19. George Clinton, *Anti-Federalist No. 14*, in *The Anti-Federalist Papers*, ed. Morton Borden (East Lansing: Michigan State Press, 1965), 36–38.

20. Alexander Hamilton, *The Federalist No. 84*, in *The Federalist Papers*, ed. Clinton Rossiter (New York: New American Library, 1961), 510–520, 516–517; Madison too saw territory as a problem that could be overcome, arguing that a republic encompassing a larger territory, and therefore a larger population, would have salutary effects by including more distinct parties and interests and therefore more factions that would check one another's tendency to dominate. Madison, *The Federalist No. 10*, in *The Federalist Papers*, ed. Clinton Rossiter (New York: New American Library, 1961), 77–84, 83.

21. On the cyclical, endless efforts to reorganize the federal government, see Paul C. Light, *The Tides of Reform: Making Government Work, 1945–1995* (New Haven, Conn.: Yale University Press, 1998); James L. Sundquist, *The Decline and Resurgence of Congress* (Washington, D.C.: Brookings Institution, 1981), 52–55; Jerry L. Mashaw, "Reinventing Government and Regulatory Reform: Studies in the Neglect and Abuse of Administrative Law," *University of Pittsburgh Law Review* 57, no. 2 (1996): 405–442, 406–408; on the long history of state government reform, see James L. Garnett, *Reorganizing State Government: The Executive Branch* (Boulder, Colo.: Westview Press, 1980); Jeffrey L. Brudney et al., "Reinventing Government in the American States: Measuring and Explaining Administrative Reform," *Public Administration Review* 59, no. 1 (1999): 19–30.

22. Johan P. Olsen, "The Ups and Downs of Bureaucratic Organization," *Annual Review of Political Science* 11 (2008): 13–37, 27.

23. Clinton, *Anti-Federalist No. 14*, 37.

24. Max Weber, *Economy and Society*, volume 2, eds. Guenther Roth and Claus Wittich (Berkeley: University of California Press, 1968), 971.

25. Ibid.

26. Ibid., 949–952 (discussing the limits of direct democracy).

27. Max Weber, *The Protestant Ethic and the Spirit of Capitalism*, trans. Talcott Parsons (New York: Scribner, 1958), 178–181; Duncan Kennedy, "The Disenchantment of Logically Formal Legal Rationality, Or Max Weber's Sociology in the Genealogy of the Contemporary Mode of Western Legal Thought," *Hastings Law Journal* 55, no. 4 (2004): 1031–1076, 1056–1058; Edward Rubin, "Let's Make the Administrative Procedure Act Administrative," *Cornell Law Review* 89, no. 1 (2003): 95–190, 149–150.

28. Weber, *Economy and Society*, volume 1, 218–223.

29. Ibid., 225; Weber, *Economy and Society*, volume 2, 992.

30. Sheldon S. Wolin, *Politics and Vision*, expanded ed. (Princeton, N.J.: Princeton University Press, 2004), 348–352; on the significance of roles for modern bureaucracies, see Weber, *Economy and Society*, volume 2, 956.

31. Jim Rossi, "Overcoming Parochialism: State Administrative Procedure and Institutional Design," *Administrative Law Review* 53, no. 2 (2001): 551–574.

32. Wolin, *Politics and Vision*, 351–352.

33. Doris A. Graber, *The Power of Communication: Managing Information in Public Organizations* (Washington, D.C.: CQ Press, 2003), 64–89.

34. Robert Nozick, *Anarchy State Utopia* (New York: Basic Books, 1974). A proponent of a minimal state would view transparency as merely a practical problem of institutional design and would rely more heavily on markets than on the regulation of governmental behavior. Malcolm Thorburn, "Rethinking the Night-watchman State?," *University of Toronto Law Journal* 60, no. 2 (2010): 425–443.

35. Jana Costas and Christopher Grey, *Secrecy at Work: The Hidden Architecture of Organizational Life* (Stanford, Calif.: Stanford University Press, 2016), 11.

36. Adrian Vermeule, "The Constitutional Law of Congressional Procedure," *University of Chicago Law Review* 71, no. 2 (2004): 361–438, 410–422.

37. U.S. Constitution Art. I, § 5, cl. 3; Art. I, § 9, cl. 7; Art. I, § 7, cl. 2.

38. U.S. Constitution Art. I, § 5, cl. 3.

39. U.S. Constitution Art. I, § 5, cl. 2 ("Each House may determine the Rules of its Proceedings"). Congress opens itself to view through rules established either by each house or by statute. Elizabeth Garrett, "Conditions for Framework Legislation," in *The Least Examined Branch: The Role of Legislatures in the Constitutional State*, eds. Richard W. Bauman and Tsvi Kahana (Cambridge, U.K.: Cambridge University Press, 2006), 294–319; Aaron-Andrew P. Bruhl, "Using Statutes to Set Legislative Rules: Entrenchment, Separation of Powers, and the Rules of Proceedings Clause," *Journal of Law and Politics* 19, no. 4 (2003): 345–416, 346.

40. Administrative Procedure Act, 5 U.S.C. § 551(1)(a) (2006). The APA's definition is in turn incorporated in many open government statutes, such as the Privacy Act, 5 U.S.C. § 552a(a)(1) (2006), the FOIA, 5 U.S.C. § 552(f) (2006), the Government in the Sunshine Act, 5 U.S.C. § 552b(a)(1) (2006), and the Federal Advisory Committee Act, § 3(3), 5 U.S.C. app. at 1176.

41. U.S. Constitution Art. II, § 3, cl. 1.

42. Richard Primus, "Limits of Interpretivism," *Harvard Journal of Law and Policy* 32, no. 1 (2009): 159–178, 173–174 (describing current understanding and interpretive tradition of the State of the Union Clause).

43. The attorneys general typically issue a memorandum to the federal branch agencies

declaring their interpretation of the FOIA and how their Department of Justice plans to litigate contested cases. The memos tend to vary with each change of party control in the White House—with a Democratic president, the memo tends to favor disclosure, and with a Republican president, it tends to favor nondisclosure. See, e.g., Eric Holder, "Memorandum on the Freedom of Information Act, to Heads of Executive Departments and Agencies," March 19, 2009. https://www.justice .gov/sites/default/files/ag/legacy/2009/06/24/foia-memo-march2009.pdf (withdrawing memorandum from Attorney General Ashcroft and announcing "a clear presumption: In the face of doubt, openness prevails"); John Ashcroft, "Memorandum for Heads of All Federal Departments and Agencies on the Freedom of Information Act," October 12, 2001. https://epic.org/open_gov/foia gallery/memorandum.html ("When you carefully consider FOIA requests and decide to withhold records, in whole or in part, you can be assured that the Department of Justice will defend your decisions unless they lack a sound legal basis").

44. Coalition of Journalists for Open Government, "The Waiting Game: FOIA Performance Hits New Lows." http://cdm16064.contentdm.oclc.org/cdm/ref/collection/p266901coll4/id/1004 (comparing agency request backlog across 1998, 2002, 2005, 2006 and finding variability over time and among agencies). Reports in 2015 and 2012 similarly found poor compliance with FOIA's mandates. Nate Jones and Lauren Harper, "Most Agencies Falling Short on Mandate for Online Records," National Security Archive, March 13, 2015. http://nsarchive.gwu.edu/NSAEBB/NSAEBB505/; Jim Snyder and Danielle Ivory, "Obama Cabinet Flunks Disclosure Test with 19 in 20 Ignoring Law," *Bloomberg Business*, September 29, 2012. http://www.bloomberg.com/news/articles/2012-09-28/ obama-cabinet-flunks-disclosure-test-with-19-in-20-ignoring-law?version=meter+at+null&mod ule=meter-Links&pgtype=Blogs&contentId=&mediaId=&referrer=&priority=true&action=click &contentCollection=meter-links-click

45. U.S. Constitution, Amend. VI.

46. Richmond Newspapers, Inc. v. Virginia, 448 U.S. 555, 575–576, 581 (1980) (plurality opinion); Heidi Kitrosser, "Secrecy in the Immigration Courts and Beyond: Considering the Right to Know in the Administrative State," *Harvard Civil Rights–Civil Liberties Law Review* 39, no. 1 (2004): 95–168, 106–111.

47. Marci A. Hamilton and Clemens G. Kohnen, "The Jurisprudence of Information Flow: How the Constitution Constructs the Pathways of Information," *Cardozo Law Review* 25, no. 1 (2003): 267–330, 289–293. Moreover, despite their status as government documents free from the restraints of copyright protection, many judicial documents in the federal system are difficult for the public to view without paying expensive electronic access fees. Stephen Schultze, "Electronic Public Access Fees and the United States Federal Courts' Budget: An Overview." http://www.open pacer.org/hogan/Schultze_Judiciary_Budgeting.pdf

48. Courtroom Television Network, LLC v. State, 769 N.Y.S.2d 70, 96–97 (N.Y. Sup. Ct. 2003) (giving overview of federal and state approaches to cameras in the courtroom).

49. Stephanos Bibas, "Transparency and Participation in Criminal Procedure," *New York University Law Review* 81, no. 3 (2006): 911–966; Kenneth Feinberg, "Transparency and Civil Justice: The Internal and External Value of Sunlight," *DePaul Law Review* 58, no. 2 (2009): 473–478; Judith Resnik, "Uncovering, Disclosing, and Discovering How the Public Dimensions of Court-Based Processes Are at Risk," *Chicago-Kent Law Review* 81, no. 2 (2006): 521–570, 542–560.

50. Teresa Dale Pupillo, "The Changing Weather Forecast: Government in the Sunshine in the 1990's—An Analysis of State Sunshine Laws," *Washington University Law Quarterly* 71, no. 4 (1993): 1165–1188; Rossi, "Overcoming Parochialism," 554–555.

51. Nicholas Kusnetz, "Only Three States Score Higher than D+ in State Integrity Inves-

tigation; 11 Flunk," Center for Public Integrity, November 9, 2015. https://www.publicintegrity. org/2015/11/09/18693/only-three-states-score-higher-d-state-integrity-investigation-11-flunk

52. National Freedom of Information Coalition, "FOI Audits." http://www.nfoic.org/foi-audits (collecting and linking to audits performed in different states)

53. Department of Navy v. Egan, 484 U.S. 518, 527, 530 (1988); Haig v. Agee, 453 U.S. 280, 291 (1981).

54. Nixon v. Administrator of General Services, 433 U.S. 425, 443 (1977) (upholding the Presidential Recordings and Materials Preservation Act against constitutional challenge for violating the separation of powers).

55. See, e.g., 50 U.S.C. § 403-3(1)(5) (directing the CIA to protect "intelligence sources and methods from unauthorized disclosure"); § 403g (exempting the CIA from any law requiring "disclosure of the organization, functions, names official titles, salaries, or numbers of personnel employed by the agency"); CIA v. Sims, 471 U.S. 159, 167–168 (1985) (applying statutory exemption to the CIA). Exemption 3 of the FOIA, 5 U.S.C. § 552(b)(3), provides that the FOIA does not apply to matters that are "specifically exempted from disclosure by statute," so long as the statute meets certain requirements.

56. National Security Agency, "Freedom of Information Handbook," last updated September 12, 2016. https://www.nsa.gov/resources/everyone/foia/foia-handbook/; 50 U.S.C. § 3605 (exempting NSA from disclosure requirements under any other law); 50 U.S.C. 3024(i) (protecting all intelligence sources and methods from disclosure); 18 U.S.C. § 1798 (prohibiting the release of classified information concerning communications intelligence and communications security information to unauthorized persons)

57. 5 U.S.C. § 552(a).

58. 5 U.S.C. § 552(f)(1) (defining "agency" as "any executive department, military department, Government corporation, Government controlled corporation, or other establishment in the executive branch of the Government (including the Executive Office of the President), or any independent regulatory agency").

59. Kissinger v. Reporters Committee for Freedom of the Press, 445 U.S. 136, 156 (1980) (quoting H.R. Conference Report 93-1380, 15 (1974)). More recent congressional enactments that incorporate the FOIA's definition of "agency" similarly make plain the distinction between "Executive Office" and "Office of the President." Wilson v. Libby, 535 U.S. 697, 708 (D.C. Cir. 2008) (explaining that the Privacy Act, 5 U.S.C. § 552(a), which followed and incorporates the FOIA's definition of agency, similarly excludes the president, vice president, and their close advisors from liability).

60. The Court considered this issue briefly in *Kissinger* but did no more than resolve the issue that Kissinger was acting in his capacity as national security advisor when the documents in the controversy were created and therefore were not the records of an agency under the FOIA. *Kissinger*, 445 U.S. at 156. The Court made no effort to develop a test for lower courts to apply in more difficult cases.

61. Citizens for Responsibility and Ethics in Washington, 566 F.3d 219, 222–223 (D.C. Cir. 2009). On the complexity of the EOP, and the fact that presidential decision making exempt from FOIA is in fact decisions made by executive branch bureaucrats, not by the president him- or herself, see Peter L. Strauss, "Overseer, or 'The Decider'? The President in Administrative Law," *George Washington Law Review* 75, no. 4 (2007): 696–760, 753.

62. I discuss the hodgepodge that courts have made of this doctrine in Mark Fenster, "Seeing the State," *Administrative Law Review* 63, no. 2 (2010): 617–672, 644–647.

63. Congress occasionally exempts new, innovative agency-like entities from FOIA obliga-

tions. See, e.g., 15 U.S.C. § 7215(b)(5)(A) (2006) (exempting the Public Company Accounting Oversight Board, created as part of the Sarbanes-Oxley Act, from the FOIA).

64. *Meyer*, 981 F.2d at 1293–1296.

65. Association of American Physicians and Surgeons v. Clinton, 997 F.2d 898 (D.C. Cir. 1993).

66. In re Cheney, 406 F.3d 723 (D.C. Cir. 2005) (*en banc*). See also Judicial Watch, Inc. v. Department of Energy, 412 F.3d 125, 131–132 (D.C. Cir. 2005) (holding that employees of the Department of Energy, whose work for that agency would be subject to the FOIA, produced work that was not "agency records" subject to FOIA when they were detailed to the National Energy Policy Development Group, which was not subject to FOIA). I discuss this case and the politics surrounding it in detail in Chapter 7.

67. Executive Order 13526, 3 C.F.R. 298, § 1.2(a)(1)–(3) (2010). https://www.gpo.gov/fdsys/pkg/CFR-2010-title3-vol1/pdf/CFR-2010-title3-vol1-eo13526.pdf (Obama administration's executive order authorizing classification system). In dicta, the Supreme Court has found classification authority in the Constitution's Commander in Chief Clause. *Egan*, 484 U.S. at 527–528.

68. 5 U.S.C. § 552(b)(1).

69. 18 U.S.C. § 793(d)–(e).

70. On the poor congressional oversight of the intelligence agencies, and the reasons for its shortcomings, see Amy B. Zegart, *Eyes on Spies* (Stanford, Calif.: Hoover Institution Press, 2011).

71. The definition is from 42 U.S.C. 5195(e), part of the Critical Information Infrastructure Act of 2002, codified at 6 U.S.C. § 131 et seq., which was enacted as part of the Homeland Security Act of 2002, Public Law 107-296. On the CIIA generally, see Harold C. Relyea, "Security Classified and Controlled Information: History, Status, and Emerging Management Issues," Congressional Research Service, Report RL33494 (2008).

72. 5 U.S.C. § 2302(a))(2)(C)(ii).

73. Ibid., § 2302(a)(2)(B)(i).

74. Ibid., § 2303(a)(2)(B)(ii). The Whistleblower Protection Act also explicitly precludes from protection disclosures of information "specifically prohibited by law . . . and specifically required by Executive order to be kept secret in the interest of national defense or the conduct of foreign affairs." 5 U.S.C. § 1213(a); Stephen I. Vladeck, "The Espionage Act and National Security Whistleblowing After Garcetti," *American University Law Review* 57, no. 5 (2008): 1531–1546, 1537.

75. Susan Nevelow Mart and Tom Ginsburg, "[Dis-]Informing the People's Discretion: Judicial Deference Under the National Security Exemption of the Freedom of Information Act," *Administrative Law Review* 66, no. 5 (2014): 725–784. This was the case for the first decades after the 1974 amendments and continued through the 1990s. Robert P. Deyling, "Judicial Deference and De Novo Review in Litigation over National Security Information Under the Freedom of Information Act," *Villanova Law Review* 37, no. 1 (1992): 67–112; Paul R. Verkuil, "An Outcomes Analysis of Scope of Review Standards," *William and Mary Law Review* 44, no. 2 (2002): 679–736, 713–714.

76. Center for National Security Studies v. DOJ, 331 F.3d 918 (D.C. Cir. 2003), *cert. denied* 540 U.S. 1104 (2004).

77. Ibid., 928, 932.

78. Margaret B. Kwoka, "Deferring to Secrecy," *Boston College Law Review* 54, no. 1 (2013): 185–242; Meredith Fuchs, "Judging Secrets: The Role Courts Should Play in Preventing Unnecessary Secrecy," *Administrative Law Review* 58, no. 1 (2006); 131–176, 133–134.

79. Donald F. Kettl, *Sharing Power: Public Governance and Private Markets* (Washington, D.C.: Brookings Institution, 1993); Dan Guttman, "Governance by Contract: Constitutional Visions; Time for Reflection and Choice," *Public Contract Law Journal* 33, no. 2 (2004): 321–360, 322–323.

80. Gillian E. Metzger, "Privatization as Delegation," *Columbia Law Review* 106, no. 6 (2003):

1367–1502, 1369–1371. The academic literature on the privatization of public services is vast; a useful discussion of it is in Chris Sagers, "The Myth of 'Privatization,'" *Administrative Law Review* 59, no. 1 (2007): 37–78, 43–48.

81. David G. Frederickson and H. George Frederickson, *Measuring the Performance of the Hollow State* (Washington, D.C.: Georgetown University Press, 2006), 21; Paul C. Light, *The True Size of Government* (Washington, D.C.: Brookings Institution, 1999), 6. This claim is widely contested, particularly in terms of the actual size of government and the limits placed on government control and management of contractors' work. Frederickson and Frederickson, *Measuring the Performance*, 20–21; Light, *True Size*, 176–179.

82. U.S. Department of Justice Office of Information and Privacy, "FOIA Post—Treatment of Agency Records Maintained for an Agency by a Government Contractor for Purposes of Records Management, OIP Holds Silver Anniversary Celebration," September 9, 2008. http://www.justice .gov/oip/foiapost/agencyrecords.htm

83. Christopher Lee, "On FOIA Front, More Agencies Contract Out," *Washington Post*, June 8, 2001, A21.

84. Paul Verkuil, *Outsourcing Sovereignty* (New York: Cambridge University Press, 2007), 90, 105–106.

85. P. W. Singer, *Corporate Warriors* (Ithaca, N.Y.: Cornell University Press, 2003), 152–168.

86. Louis L. Jaffe, "Law Making by Private Groups," *Harvard Law Review* 51, no. 2 (1937): 201–253. For a summary of new governance, see Jason M. Solomon, "Law and New Governance in the 21st Century Regulatory State," *Texas Law Review* 86, no. 4 (2008): 819–856, 823–837.

87. Light, *True Size*, 5.

88. Lester M. Salamon, "The New Governance and the Tools of Public Action: An Introduction," in *The Tools of Government: A Guide to the New Governance*, ed. Lester M. Salamon (New York: Oxford University Press, 2002), 1–47, 9–22 (defining new governance "paradigm" and listing various tools that fall within it).

89. Charles F. Sabel and William H. Simon, "Epilogue: Accountability Without Sovereignty," in *Law and New Governance in the EU and the US*, eds. Gráinne de Búrca and Joanne Scott (Oxford, U.K.: Hart, 2006), 395–412, 400–401; see also Archon Fung, Mary Graham, and David Weil, *Full Disclosure: The Perils and Promise of Transparency* (Cambridge, U.K.: Cambridge University Press, 2007), 1–7; Janet A. Weiss, "Public Information," in *The Tools of Government: A Guide to the New Governance*, ed. Lester M. Salamon (New York: Oxford University Press, 2002), 217–254, 227–233.

90. Jody Freeman, "The Private Role in Public Governance," *New York University Law Review* 75, no. 3 (2000): 543–675, 586–587; Orly Lobel, "The Renew Deal: The Fall of Regulation and the Rise of Governance in Contemporary Legal Thought," *Minnesota Law Review* 89, no. 2 (2004): 342–470, 455–457; Paul L. Posner, "Accountability Challenges of Third-Party Government," in *The Tools of Government: A Guide to the New Governance*, ed. Lester M. Salamon (New York: Oxford University Press, 2002), 523–551, 524–28.

91. The book is Lester M. Salamon, ed., *The Tools of Government: A Guide to the New Governance* (New York: Oxford University Press, 2002). Its only essay that mentions and appears to embrace open-ended public transparency appears as the twentieth of twenty-three chapters and includes the topic as one among many "policy tools" that further democratic ends. Steven Rathgeb Smith and Helen Ingram, "Policy Tools and Democracy," in ibid., 579. The collection's introduction fails to include transparency as one of its criteria for evaluating particular new governance tools. Salamon, "The New Governance and the Tools of Public Action," 23–24.

92. Alasdair S. Roberts, "Less Government, More Secrecy: Reinvention and the Weakening of Freedom of Information Law," *Public Administration Review* 60, no. 4 (2000): 308–320.

93. Alasdair Roberts, *Blacked Out: Government Secrecy in the Information Age* (Cambridge, U.K.: Cambridge University Press, 2006), 160–161; Martin D. Bunker and Charles N. Davis, "When Government "Contracts out": Privatization, Accountability, and Constitutional Doctrine," in *Access Denied: Freedom of Information in the Information Age*, eds. Charles N. Davis and Sigman L. Spichal (Ames: Iowa State University Press, 2000), 85–102, 90–93; Craig D. Feiser, "Privatization and the Freedom of Information Act: An Analysis of Public Access to Private Entities Under Federal Law," *Federal Communications Law Journal* 52, no. 1 (1999): 21–62.

94. Leonard D. White, *The Federalists: A Study in Administrative History, 1789–1801* (Westport, Conn.: Greenwood Press, 1948), 199–209; Jerry L. Mashaw, "Recovering American Administrative Law: Federalist Foundations, 1787–1801," *Yale Law Journal* 115, no. 6 (2006): 1256–1345, 1305–1307.

95. Judith Resnik, "Whither and Whether Adjudication?," *Boston University Law Review* 86, no. 5 (2006): 1101–1154, 1106–1108.

96. Michael Lipsky, *Street-Level Bureaucracy* (New York: Russell Sage Foundation, 1980), 16–18. Economists have come to a similar conclusion. Albert Breton, "Transparency and Efficiency," in *The Economics of Transparency in Politics*, eds. Albert Breton, Gianluigi Galeotti, Pierre Salmon, and Ronald Wintrobe (Burlington, Vt.: Ashgate, 2007), 55–69, 56–59.

97. Weber, *Economy and Society*, volume 2, 992; Costas and Grey, *Secrecy at Work*, 90–103.

98. James Q. Wilson, *Bureaucracy* (New York: Basic Books, 1989), 327–329.

99. John R. Short, *An Introduction to Political Geography* (London: Routledge, 1982), 123.

100. On maps' representational ideal, see Michael R. Curry, "Shelf Length Zero: The Disappearance of the Geographical Text," in *Space and Social Theory*, eds. Georges Benko and Ulf Strohmayer (Oxford, U.K.: Blackwell, 1997), 288–312.

101. John Agnew, "Maps and Models in Political Studies: A Reply to Comments," *Political Geography* 15, no. 2 (1996): 165–168.

102. Richard Thompson Ford, "The Boundaries of Race: Political Geography in Legal Analysis," *Harvard Law Review* 107, no. 8 (1994): 1841–1928, 1860–1861; compare to Nicholas K. Blomley, *Law, Space, and the Geographies of Power* (New York: Guilford, 1994), 90–91.

103. I am relying here on Henri Lefebvre's conceptions of the state's abstract political space and of its complex and unfolding relationship with its territory. Henri Lefebvre, *State, Space, World*, eds. Neil Brenner and Stuart Elden; trans. Gerald Moore, Neil Brenner, and Stuart Elden (Minneapolis: University of Minnesota Press, 2009), 224–225; Henri Lefebvre, *The Production of Space*, trans. Donald Nicholson-Smith (Oxford, U.K.: Blackwell, 1991), 278–285.

104. This issue concerns the overlapping itself, not whether multiagency and multigovernment cooperation, their opposites, or some point along a continuum of cooperation and conflict will provide an optimal level of transparency. On the concept of cooperative federalism, see Susan Rose-Ackerman, "Cooperative Federalism and Co-Optation," *Yale Law Journal* 92, no. 7 (1983): 1344–1348; for an account that seeks to complicate the cooperative concept, see Jessica Bulman-Pozen and Heather K. Gerken, "Uncooperative Federalism," *Yale Law Journal* 118, no. 7 (2009): 1256–1311; and on the role of thoroughgoing conflict between federal and state governments, see Ernest A. Young, "Welcome to the Dark Side: Liberals Rediscover Federalism in the Wake of the War on Terror," *Brooklyn Law Review* 69, no. 4 (2003): 1277–1312, 1295–1300.

105. Jon C. Teaford, *The Metropolitan Revolution* (New York: Columbia University Press, 2006), 5 (describing growth of major metropolitan service areas); compare to Peter Calthorpe and William Fulton, *The Regional City* (Washington, D.C.: Island Press, 2001), 61–63 (describing the patchwork of local governments in an increasingly "regional city").

106. John A. Agnew, *Globalization and Sovereignty* (Lanham, Md.: Rowan & Littlefield, 2009), 6–7; Saskia Sassen, "Bordering Capabilities Versus Borders: Implications for National Borders,"

Michigan Journal of International Law 30, no. 3 (2009): 567–597; see generally Kal Raustiala, *Does the Constitution Follow the Flag?* (New York: Oxford University Press, 2009), 5–9 (discussing the long history of, and controversy over, the relationship between American territory and the reach of American law).

107. Costas and Grey, *Secrecy at Work*, 116–118.

108. Harold D. Lasswell, with Merritt B. Fox, *The Signature of Power: Buildings, Communication, and Policy* (New Brunswick, N.J.: Transaction, 1979), 18; Mary R. Domahidy and James F. Gilsinan, "The Back Stage Is Not the Back Room: How Spatial Arrangements Affect the Administration of Public Affairs," *Public Administration Review* 52, no. 6 (1992): 67–80.

109. Charles T. Goodsell, *The American Statehouse: Interpreting Democracy's Temples* (Lawrence: University of Kansas Press, 2001), 3–4, 15–34; Amos Rapoport, *The Meaning of the Built Environment* (Beverly Hills, Calif.: Sage, 1982), 55–56.

110. Freeman, "Private Role in Public Governance," 572; Ed Gibson, "Tales of Two Cities: The Administrative Facade of Social Security," *Administration and Society* 35, no. 4 (2003): 408–437.

111. Lasswell, *Signature of Power*, 16–17; Arthur Goldberg, "An Inside Perspective on the 1962 Guiding Principles for Federal Architecture," *Design Quarterly* no. 94/95 (1975): 16–18; Richard Briffault, "Facing the Urban Future After September 11, 2001," *Urban Lawyer* 34, no. 3 (2003): 563–582, 568–569.

112. Dvora Yanow, "Built Space as Story: The Policy Stories That Buildings Tell," *Policy Studies Journal* 23, no. 3 (1995): 407–422, 417–419.

113. Deborah Ascher Barnstone, *The Transparent State: Architecture and Politics in Postwar Germany* (London: Routledge, 2005).

114. Dieter Zinnbauer, "Architecting Transparency Back to the Roots—and Forward to the Future?" Working paper, June 10, 2015. https://papers.ssrn.com/sol3/papers.cfm?abstract_id=2616655 See also Elizabeth Fisher, "Exploring the Legal Architecture of Transparency," in *Research Handbook on Transparency*, eds. Padideh Ala'i and Robert G. Vaughn (Northampton, Mass.: Edward Elgar, 2014), 59–79, 60–62. The Americans with Disabilities Act, which requires that public buildings be "readily accessible to and usable by individuals with disabilities," imposes access requirements, although it does not expand the amount of access that the entire public has to government. 42 U.S.C. § 12183(a)(1) (2000).

115. Ann Taylor Schwing, *Open Meeting Laws,* 3rd ed. (Anchorage, Alaska: Fathom, 2011), § 1.1.

116. The federal open meeting statute is called the "Government in the Sunshine Act," Public Law 94-409, 90 Stat. 1241 (1976), codified at 5 U.S.C. § 552(b). Analogous state laws are referred to similarly, and state court decisions frequently wax metaphorically. Attorney General, State of Florida, "Open Government—The 'Sunshine' Law." http://myfloridalegal.com/pages.nsf/Main/DC0B20B7DC22B7418525791B006A54E4 (summarizing Florida's open government laws); Regents of University of California v. Superior Court, 976 P.2d 808, 826 (Cal. 1999) ("There is rarely any purpose to a nonpublic premeeting conference except to conduct some part of the decisional process behind closed doors").

117. See, e.g., 5 U.S.C. § 552b(a)(2) (federal Government in the Sunshine Act, defining "meetings" as "the deliberations of at least the number of individual agency members required to take action on behalf of the agency where such deliberations determine or result in the joint conduct or disposition of official agency business").

118. Schwing, *Open Meetings Laws*, § 6.6 (discussing various definitions of "meeting" in open meeting law and describing it as the "most telling single element to determine whether an open meeting act is strong and encompassing or weak and limited in scope").

119. David A. Barrett, "Facilitating Government Decision Making: Distinguishing Between

Meetings and Non-meetings Under the Federal Sunshine Act," *Texas Law Review* 66, no. 6 (1988): 1195–1228.

120. State open meetings laws take a variety of approaches to the issue of what constitutes a "meeting" to which sunshine laws apply. Schwing, *Open Meeting Laws*, § 6.6.

121. This hypothetical case is based on two actual cases that did not result in reported decisions. Peter H. Seed, "Florida's Sunshine Law: The Undecided Legal Issue," *University of Florida Journal of Law and Public Policy* 13, no. 2 (2002): 209–267, 212–213; Joseph W. Little and Thomas Tompkins, "Open Government Laws: An Insider's View," *North Carolina Law Review* 53, no. 3 (1975): 451–490.

122. Elizabeth Johnson Wallmeyer, "Open Meeting Laws: A Comparison of the Fifty States and the District of Columbia" (Ph.D. dissertation, University of Florida, 2000), 60–62 (noting that thirty of forty-two states whose open meeting laws define "meeting" require either a quorum or majority of members).

123. See, e.g., Georgia Code Annotated § 50–14–1(a)(2) (defining meeting as a gathering of a quorum of members at a designated time and place to discuss or take action on official business); North Carolina General Statutes § 143–318.10(d) (defining meeting as "a meeting, assembly, or gathering together at any time or place . . . of a majority of the members of a public body for the purpose of conducting hearings, participating in deliberations, or voting upon or otherwise transacting the public business within the jurisdiction, real or apparent, of the public body").

124. Hough v. Stembridge, 278 So.2d 288, 289 (Fla. Dist. Ct. App. 1973). Other states take a similar approach. See, e.g., Virginia Code Annotated (Michie Supp. 2008), § 2.2-3701 (defining meeting to include the "informal assemblage of (i) as many as three members or (ii) a quorum, if fewer than three, of the constituent membership"); Mayor and City Council of El Dorado v. El Dorado Broadcasting Co., 544 S.W.2d 206, 207–208 (Ark. 1976) (holding that the state Freedom of Information Act applies to informal meetings of less than a quorum of members).

125. Schwing, *Open Meetings Laws*, § 5.74 (discussing how state open meeting laws consider the public or private character of the government's meeting place).

126. Sacramento Newspaper Guild v. Sacramento County Board of Supervisors, 263 Cal. App.2d 41, 55 (1968) ("An informal conference or caucus permits crystallization of secret decisions to a point just short of ceremonial acceptance").

127. Goodson Todman Enterprises, Ltd. v. City of Kingston Common Council, 550 N.Y.S.2d 157, 159 (N.Y. A.D. 1990) (holding that a meeting in a council member's home can be subject to open meeting law if it is planned and discusses government business); Stephen Schaeffer, "Sunshine in Cyberspace? Electronic Deliberation and the Reach of Open Meeting Laws," *St. Louis University Law Journal* 48, no. 2 (2004): 755–789, 761–764 (discussing the application of open meetings laws to telephone and videoconferences).

128. United States Department of Justice v. Tax Analysts, 492 U.S. 136, 145 (1989) ("[T]he term 'agency records' is not so broad as to include personal materials in an employee's possession, even though the materials may be physically located at the agency"); Gallant v. National Labor Relations Board, 26 F.3d 168, 172 (D.C. Cir. 1994) (rejecting argument that FOIA applies to personal correspondence of NLRB member seeking reappointment).

129. Lawrence Cappello, "Can Government Function Without Privacy," *The Atlantic*, November 1, 2015. http://www.theatlantic.com/politics/archive/2015/11/can-government-function-without-privacy/413419/

130. Betty Medsger, *The Burglary: The Discovery of J. Edgar Hoover's FBI Files* (New York: Knopf, 2014); David Rudenstine, *The Day the Presses Stopped: A History of the Pentagon Papers Case* (Berkeley: University of California Press, 1998), 33–47.

131. *Tax Analysts*, 492 U.S. at 144–146. Note that this only goes to the question of whether a record was improperly "withheld," not to the question of whether it is an "agency record" subject to FOIA. The latter issue is complicated by the organizational question of which entities are in fact subject to FOIA, an issued discussed in Chapter 5.

132. *Kissinger*, 445 U.S. at 136.

133. Ibid., 140.

134. Ibid.

135. Ibid., 141–142.

136. Ibid., 142–143. Some of the requests were filed prior to the files' removal; ibid.

137. Ibid., 159 (Brennan, J., concurring and dissenting).

138. Forsham v. Harris, 445 U.S. 169, 188 (1980) (Brennan, J., dissenting).

139. *Kissinger*, 445 U.S. at 150–151.

140. A companion case to *Kissinger*, decided by the Court on the same day, came to a similar conclusion, holding that medical records that were produced by a private research organization under the aegis and with the funding of a federal agency are not subject to FOIA because they were neither made nor received by a federal agency. *Forsham*, 445 U.S. at 186.

141. Ibid., 155.

142. Ibid., 156.

143. Ibid., 157.

144. Goland v. CIA, 607 F.2d 339 (D.C. Cir. 1978), *vacated in part on other grounds*, 607 F.2d 367 (D.C. Cir. 1979) (*per curiam*).

145. Ibid., 347; see, e.g., United We Stand America, Inc. v. Internal Revenue Service, 359 F.3d 595 (D.C. Cir. 2004) (records created by IRS for congressional Joint Committee on Taxation were agency records because, other than in its initial request, Congress failed to show sufficient intent to retain control over them); Paisley v. CIA, 712 F.2d 686, 695–696 (D.C. Cir. 1983), *vacated in part on other grounds*, 724 F.2d 201 (D.C. Cir. 1984) (*per curiam*) (records created by CIA to aid a congressional investigation were agency records subject to the FOIA because Congress did not manifest sufficient intent to retain control over them); Holy Spirit Ass'n for the Unification of World Christianity v. CIA, 636 F.2d 838, 842–843 (D.C. Cir. 1980), *vacated in part on other grounds*, 445 U.S. 997 (1982) (documents created by CIA for Congress, then sent to Congress and then returned to CIA, constituted agency records subject to the FOIA because Congress failed to retain control over them).

146. See, e.g., Feiser, "Privatization and the Freedom of Information Act," 58 (criticizing *Kissinger*'s approach as "cramped" and arguing that, "this approach would keep its records out of the public eye unless the FOIA agency actually possesses and uses the documents"); Adam M. Samaha, "Government Secrets, Constitutional Law, and Platforms for Judicial Intervention," *UCLA Law Review* 53, no. 4 (2006) 909–976, 971–972 (criticizing *Kissinger* as exemplifying one of the FOIA's main weaknesses: the ability of the government to avoid accountability to the public by moving or destroying documents).

147. Michel Foucault, *Security, Territory, Population: Lectures at the Collège de France* (Basingstoke, U.K.: Palgrave Macmillan, 2007), 108–110.

Chapter 5

1. Don DeLillo, *Libra* (New York: Viking, 1988), 59.

2. President John F. Kennedy Assassination Records Collection Act of 1992, §§ 2(a)(2), 2(b)(2), Public Law 102-526, 106 Stat. 3443 (October 26, 1992), codified as a note to 44 U.S.C. § 2107.

3. Ibid., § 5(g)(2)(D).

4. DeLillo, *Libra*, 181–182.

5. Ibid., 458 ("Author's Note"); Adam Begley, "Interview: Don DeLillo, The Art of Fiction No. 135," *Paris Review,* no. 128 (Fall 1993).

6. Karl W. Deutsch, *The Nerves of Government: Models of Political Communication and Control* (Glencoe, Ill.: Free Press, 1963), 76–84, 129.

7. Ann M. Blair, *Too Much to Know: Managing Scholarly Information Before the Modern Age* (New Haven, Conn.: Yale University Press, 2010).

8. National Archives and Records Administration, "Preserving the Past to Protect the Future: 2013 Performance and Accountability Report," 2013, 7. https://www.archives.gov/files/about/plans -reports/performance-accountability/2013/par-summary.pdf

9. Ibid., 3.

10. Office of Information and Regulatory Affairs, "Inventory of Currently Approved Informa- tion Collections." http://www.reginfo.gov/public/do/PRAReport?operation=11

11. Annelise Riles, "Introduction: In Response," in *Documents: Artifacts of Modern Knowledge,* ed. Annelise Riles (Ann Arbor: University of Michigan Press, 2006), 1–38, 5–6.

12. Michael Herzfeld, *The Social Production of Indifference* (Chicago: University of Chicago Press, 1992), 8.

13. 44 U.S.C.A. § 3301 (2009). Because FOIA itself fails to define "records," courts have im- ported to FOIA the statutory definition that Congress enacted for the management of federal re- cords. Forsham v. Harris, 445 U.S. 169, 178 n.8 (1980).

14. Nichols v. United States, 325 F.Supp. 130, 135–136 (D. Kan. 1971).

15. Lisa Gitelman, *Paper Knowledge: Toward a Media History of Documents* (Durham, N.C.: Duke University Press, 2014), 1.

16. Ibid., 2–3.

17. Clare Birchall, "Transparency, Interrupted: Secrets of the Left," *Theory, Culture & Society* 28, no. 1 (2011): 60–84, 71.

18. Ben Kafka, "Paperwork: The State of the Discipline," *Book History* 12 (2009): 340–353, 341.

19. John Guillroy, "The Memo and Modernity," *Critical Inquiry* 31, no. 1 (Autumn 2004): 108– 132, 111–112.

20. Ibid., 112–116.

21. Especially relevant here is Bruno Latour's description of and emphasis upon the routing of a file through the French administrative courts: "Even though it is not attributed any place in legal theories, it is by moving through this palace while following this little animal [the file] that we are going to become acquainted with all the various functions of the Palais-Royal." Bruno Latour, *The Making of Law,* trans. Marina Brilman and Alain Pottage (Cambridge, U.K.: Polity Press, 2010), 71.

22. JoAnne Yates, *Control Through Communication: The Rise of System in American Manage- ment* (Baltimore: Johns Hopkins University Press, 1989), xvii–xviii.

23. Matthew S. Hull, *Government of Paper* (Berkeley: University of California Press, 2012), 19.

24. Carol A. Heimer, "Conceiving Children: How Documents Support Case Versus Biological Analyses," in Riles, ed., *Documents: Artifacts of Modern Knowledge,* 95–125, 98–99.

25. Guillroy, "Memo and Modernity," 129–132.

26. Directorate of Intelligence, *Style Manual and Writers Guide for Intelligence Publications,* 8th ed., 2011, 3. https://www.scribd.com/doc/233259974/Directorate-of-Intelligence-Style-Manual -Writers-Guide-for-Intelligence-Publications-Eighth-Edition-2011

27. Cornelia Vismann, *Files: Law and Media Technology,* trans. Geoffrey Winthrop-Young (Stanford, Calif.: Stanford University Press, 2008), 122.

28. Bruno Latour, "Visualisation and Cognition: Drawing Things Together," *Knowledge and Society: Studies in the Sociology of Culture Past and Present,* 6 (1986): 1–40.

29. What follows is based on Martha G. Feldman, *Order Without Design: Information Production and Policy Making* (Stanford, Calif.: Stanford University Press, 1989).

30. J. Garry Clifford, "Bureaucratic Politics," *Journal of American History* 77, no. 1 (1990), 161–168.

31. Richard H. R. Harper, *Inside the IMF: An Ethnography of Documents, Technology, and Organisational Action* (San Diego: Academic Press, 2009), 44–45; Abigail J. Sellen and Richard H. R. Harper, *The Myth of the Paperless Office* (Cambridge, Mass.: MIT Press, 2001), 202–209.

32. Jacques Derrida, *Paper Machine*, trans. Rachel Bowlby (Stanford, Calif.: Stanford University Press, 2005), 46–47.

33. Matthew G. Kirschenbaum, *Mechanisms: New Media and the Forensic Imagination* (Cambridge, Mass.: MIT Press, 2008), 50–59.

34. Rachael Bade, "IRS Accounts for Lost Lerner Emails," *Politico*, July 18, 2014. http://www.politico.com/story/2014/07/irs-full-account-of-lost-lerner-emails-109122; Philip Bump, "Here's How the IRS Lost Emails from Key Witness Lois Lerner," *Washington Post, The Fix* (Blog), June 16, 2014. https://www.washingtonpost.com/news/the-fix/wp/2014/06/16/heres-how-the-irs-lost-emails-from-key-witness-lois-lerner/

35. Josh Hicks, "IRS Inspector General Finds Up to 30,000 of Lois Lerner's E-Mails," *Washington Post*, November 21, 2014. https://www.washingtonpost.com/news/federal-eye/wp/2014/11/21/irs-inspector-general-finds-up-to-30000-of-lois-lerners-e-mails/

36. "Snowflakes" was the name used in the Pentagon for Defense Secretary Donald Rumsfeld's memoranda, which he issued by the dozen on a daily basis; circulating through the Defense Department, they numbered in the tens of thousands by the time he resigned. Robin Wright, "From the Desk of Donald Rumsfeld . . . ," *Washington Post*, November 1, 2007. http://www.washingtonpost.com/wp-dyn/content/article/2007/10/31/AR2007103103095.html. He has adopted the term himself, apparently with some pride. Donald Rumsfeld, "About the 2001–06 Snowflakes," The Rumsfeld Papers. http://papers.rumsfeld.com/library/page/200106-snowflakes

37. James Boyle, *Shamans, Software, and Spleens* (Cambridge, Mass.: Harvard University Press, 1996), 13, 205.

38. Jonathan Turley, "Paradise Lost: The Clinton Administration and the Erosion of Executive Privilege," *Maryland Law Review* 60, no. 1 (2001): 205–248, 209.

39. Peter Strauss, "The President and the Constitution," *Case Western Law Review* 65, no. 4 (2015): 1151–1173, 1170–1171.

40. William P. Marshall, "The Limits on Congress's Authority to Investigate the President," *University of Illinois Law Review* 2004, no. 4 (2004): 781–828, 814.

41. Cornelia Vismann, "Out of File, Out of Mind," in *New Media, Old Media: A History and Theory Reader*, eds. Wendy Hui Kyong Chun and Thomas Keenan (New York: Routledge, 2006), 97–104, 98.

42. Commission on Protecting and Reducing Government Secrecy, *Secrecy: Report of the Commission on Protecting and Reducing Government Secrecy*, 103rd Cong., Report Pursuant to Public Law, S. Doc. 105-2 (Comm. Print 1997), 7–8 (hereinafter *Moynihan Commission Report*); Christina E. Wells, "'National Security' Information and the Freedom of Information Act," *Administrative Law Review* 56, no. 4 (2004): 1195–1223, 1201–1202. Classification decisions are governed by executive order: Exec. Order 13292, 3 C.F.R. 196 (2003) (providing the current standards, authority, categories, and duration by which information may classified); see generally Wells, "'National Security' Information and the Freedom of Information Act," 1198–1199.

43. Nearly 4,000 federal officials have the delegated authority to stamp a document "top secret," "secret," or "confidential" under multiple sets of complex rules. Michael J. Sniffen, "'Secrets'

Perplex Panel; Classified Data Growing to Include 'Comically Irrelevant,'" *Washington Post*, September 3, 2004, A17. Agencies as diverse as the Department of Transportation and the Department of Agriculture delegate such authority widely among administrators.

44. *Moynihan Commission Report*, 31. Those with so-called derivative classification authority perform the vast majority of classification actions; ibid. (citing figure of 94 percent of classification actions over six-year period prior to the report).

45. *Ibid.*, 21–22.

46. For a more extensive discussion and critique of derivative classification, see Elizabeth Goitein and David M. Shapiro, "Reducing Overclassification Through Accountability," *Brennan Center for Justice*, October 5, 2011, 14–15. http://www.brennancenter.org/publication/reducing-over-classification-through-accountability

47. *Moynihan Commission Report*, 19; Robert L. Saloschin, "The Department of Justice and the Explosion of Freedom of Information Act Litigation," *Administrative Law Review* 52, no. 4 (2000): 1401–1408, 1406.

48. Robert Corn-Revere, "New Technology and the First Amendment: Breaking the Cycle of Repression," *Hastings Communications and Entertainment Law Journal* 17, no. 1 (1994): 247–346, 336.

49. Erwin N. Griswold, "Secrets Not Worth Keeping," *Washington Post*, February 15, 1989, A25.

50. Sniffen, "'Secrets' Perplex Panel," A17.

51. An excellent analytical account of this episode is Leslie Gielow Jacobs, "Bush, Obama, and Beyond: Observations on the Prospect of Fact Checking Executive Department Threat Claims Before the Use of Force," *Constitutional Commentary* 26, no. 2 (2010): 433–482. There are also numerous efforts to consider the episode as a telling failure of intelligence, whether due to the repeated failures of the CIA itself (see John Diamond, *The CIA and the Culture of Failure* (Stanford; Calif.: Stanford University Press, 2008), 374–417) or as a more generalizable example of when intelligence fails (see Richard Betts, *Enemies of Intelligence: Knowledge and Power in American National Security* (New York: Columbia University Press, 2007), 114–123; and David C. Gompert, Hans Binnendijk, and Bonny Lin, *Blinders, Blunders, and Wars: What America and China Can Learn* (Santa Monica, Calif.: RAND Corporation, 2014), 161–174).

52. Dana Priest, "Congressional Oversight of Intelligence Criticized," *Washington Post*, April 27, 2004, A1.

53. Senate Select Committee on Intelligence, *Prewar Intelligence Assessments on Iraq*, S. Rep. 108-301 (2004), 14–29, 253–257. http://nsarchive.gwu.edu/NSAEBB/NSAEBB129/part7-powell.pdf

54. U.S. Department of Energy Office of Classification and Information Control, *Fifteenth Report on Inadvertent Releases of Restricted Data and Formerly Restricted Data under Executive Order 12958*, DOE/SO-10-0015 (Deleted Version). https://www.osti.gov/opennet/reports/fifteenthrpt.pdf

55. See, e.g., Christopher Grey, *Decoding Organization* (Cambridge, U.K.: Cambridge University Press, 2012), 121–32 (describing the role of secrecy in Bletchley Park, Britain's highly successful World War II cryptographic unit, as well as its ultimate disclosure).

56. Jack Goldsmith, *Power and Constraint* (New York: Norton, 2012), 70–71; Keith Erickson, "Presidential Leaks: Rhetoric and Mediated Political Knowledge," *Communication Monographs* 56, no. 3 (1989): 199–214, 201; Adrienne M. Jamieson, "The Messenger as Policy Maker: Thinking About the Press and Policy Networks in the Washington Community," *Democratization* 3, no. 1 (1996): 114–132, 118–119; Leon V. Sigal, "Official Secrecy and Informal Communication in Congressional-Bureaucratic Relations," *Political Science Quarterly* 90, no. 1 (1975): 71–92, 72–74. David Pozen persuasively argues that the institutional dynamics within the executive branch, which create incentives not only for individuals to leak but excellent reasons for the Department of Justice to under-enforce anti-leaking laws, lead to few formal criminal prosecutions of leakers and, as best

as he could learn, few formal administration sanctions. David Pozen, "The Leaky Leviathan: Why the Government Criminalizes, and Condones, Unauthorized Disclosures of Information," *Harvard Law Review* 127, no. 2 (2013): 512–635.

57. Max Frankel, "Affidavit submitted to U.S. District Court for the Southern District of New York, June 17, 1971," in *The Pentagon Papers in the Federal Courts*, ed. Jake Kobrick (Washington, D.C.: Federal Judicial Center, 2014), 15–16 (noting that extensive government secrecy is "unraveled by that same Government, by Congress and by the press in one continuing round of professional and social contacts and cooperative and competitive exchanges of information"). Frankel more recently wrote that the phenomenon continues to exist more than three decades later. Max Frankel, "The Washington Back Channel," *New York Times Magazine*, March 25, 2007, 40, 43.

58. Itzhak Galnoor, "Government Secrecy: Exchanges, Intermediaries, and Middlemen," *Public Administration Review* 35, no. 1 (1975): 32–42, 40–41.

59. 18 U.S.C. § 792 (1948) et seq.; 50 U.S.C. § 421 et seq.

60. Garcetti v. Ceballos, 547 U.S. 410, 422 (2006). Scholars vigorously disagree over this proposition. See, for example, Stephen I. Vladeck, "The Espionage Act and National Security Whistleblowing After *Garcetti*," *American University Law Review* 57, no. 5 (2008): 1531, 1537–1542 (asserting that recent Supreme Court precedent provides no First Amendment protection outside of statutory whistleblower protection); Mary-Rose Papandrea, "The Free Speech Rights of Off-Duty Government Employees," *Brigham Young University Law Review* 2010, no. 6 (2010): 2117–2174, 2119 (characterizing current doctrine as distinguishing between government employee speech when on duty, when First Amendment protections do not apply, and when off duty, when they do); Heidi Kitrosser, "Free Speech Aboard the Leaky Ship of State: Calibrating First Amendment Protections for Leakers of Classified Information," *Journal of National Security Law and Policy* 6, no. 2 (2012): 409–446 (arguing in favor of First Amendment protection based on "constitutional text, structure, and principle").

61. It is unlikely that reporters enjoy a First Amendment right to protect the identity of their leaks against criminal prosecution, and it is unclear if they enjoy a federal common law right to do so. Branzburg v. Hayes, 408 U.S. 665, 697 (1972) (no First Amendment right to protect identity of sources from a criminal investigation); In re Grand Jury Subpoena, Judith Miller, 438 F.3d 1141, 1145–1149 (D.C. Cir. 2006) (holding that *Branzburg* foreclosed a First Amendment right for reporters to shield sources against a grand jury investigation); ibid., 1149–1150 (noting split opinion among three-judge panel on question of common law privilege, but deciding that it would not apply in this case).

62. New York Times Co. v. United States, 403 U.S. 713 (1971) (*per curiam*).

63. *New York Times Co.*, 403 U.S. at 743–748 (Marshall, J., concurring) (stating that the government can criminally prosecute newspapers after publication); ibid., 733, 737 (White, J., concurring) (stating he would have "no difficulty" sustaining a conviction under the Espionage Act after publication).

64. Scott Shane and Charlie Savage, "Administration Took Accidental Path to Setting Record for Leak Cases," *New York Times*, June 19, 2012. http://www.nytimes.com/2012/06/20/us/politics/accidental-path-to-record-leak-cases-under-obama.html. On the difficulty of prosecuting leaks generally and especially the megaleaks of WikiLeaks, see Patricia L. Bella, "WikiLeaks and the Institutional Framework for National Security Disclosures," *Yale Law Journal* 121, no. 6 (2012): 1448–1527.

65. Richard B. Kielbowicz, "The Role of News Leaks in Governance and the Law of Journalists' Confidentiality, 1795–2005," *San Diego Law Review* 43, no. 3 (2006) 425–494, 432–441, 478–480; compare to Pozen, "Leaky Leviathan" (arguing that the minimal formal legal protections for leaking belies the DOJ's practice of under-enforcing criminal sanctions).

66. See, e.g., Deputy Inspector General for Intelligence and Special Program Assessments,

Report on Sensitive Compartmented Information Leaks in the Department of Defense, Report 2012-056, February 27, 2012. http://www.dodig.mil/sar/SAR_MAR_2012_Reduced.pdf; *Commission on the Intelligence Capabilities of the United States Regarding Weapons of Mass Destruction, Report to the President of the United States*, March 31, 2005. https://fas.org/irp/offdocs/wmd_report.pdf

67. Kielbowicz, "The Role of News Leaks," 433.

68. Stanley I. Kutler, *The Wars of Watergate* (New York: Knopf, 1990), 108–125.

69. Jack Goldsmith, "Secrecy and Safety," *New Republic*, August 13, 2008, 31, 34; Gilbert Schoenfeld, *Necessary Secrets* (New York: Norton, 2010), 263–265.

70. Elie Abel, *Leaking* (Newewe w York: Priority Press, 1987), 68; "Media Incentives and National Security Secrets," *Harvard Law Review* 122, no. 8 (2009): 2228–2249, 2236–2244.

71. 50 U.S.C. § 3141(b) (1947).

72. The CIA's Center for the Study of Intelligence publishes an academic journal, *Studies in Intelligence*, and the agency makes unclassified extracts of the journal available on its website. I discuss the CIA's and State Department's internal historical publications in Chapter 8.

73. Central Intelligence Agency, "About CIA: CIA Museum," last updated September 30, 2014. https://www.cia.gov/about-cia/cia-museum

74. Ibid.

75. Timothy Melley, *The Covert Sphere: Secrecy, Fiction, and the National Security State* (Ithaca, N.Y.: Cornell University Press, 2012), 8–10, 28.

76. Glenn Greenwald, "WH Leaks for Propaganda Film," *Salon*, May 23, 2012. http://www .salon.com/2012/05/23/wh_leaks_for_propaganda_film/; Andrea Stone, "Obama Officials Gave Hollywood Filmmaker Access to Team That Killed Bin Laden, Records Show," *Huffington Post*, May 23, 2012. http://www.huffingtonpost.com/2012/05/23/white-house-kathryn-bigelow-bin-laden _n_ 1538847.html

77. Mark Mazzetti et al., "The Secret History of SEAL Team 6," *New York Times*, June 7, 2015, 1.

78. Dana Priest and William M. Arkin, *Top Secret America: The Rise of the New American Security State* (New York: Little, Brown, 2011), 267 (noting the series of security errors that allowed Manning to take and leak data).

79. Steven Aftergood, "National Security Secrecy: How the Limits Change," *Social Research* 77, no. 3 (2010): 839–852, 845–846.

80. Priest and Arkin, *Top Secret America*, 263–266.

81. Steven Aftergood, "NSA Declassifies Secret Document After Publishing It," *Secrecy News*, May 14, 2012. https://fas.org/blogs/secrecy/2012/05/nsa_secret/

82. Eric Lichtblau and Scott Shane, "Vast FDA Effort Tracked E-mails of Its Scientists," *New York Times*, July 15, 2012, A1, A15.

83. Joel Brenner, *America the Vulnerable* (New York: Penguin, 2011), 207–209.

84. Richard A. Best Jr. and Alfred Cumming, *Open Source Intelligence (OSINT): Issues for Congress*, Congressional Research Service, Report No. RL34270, 2007, 6; Stephen C. Mercado, "Sailing the Sea of OSINT in the Information Age," *Studies in Intelligence* 48, no. 3 (2004). https://www .cia.gov/library/center-for-the-study-of-intelligence/csi-publications/csi-studies/studies/vol48no3/ article05.html

85. For a full discussion of the legal implications of the government's efforts to claw back information from the public domain, see Jonathan Abel, "Do You Have to Keep the Government's Secrets? Retroactively Classified Documents, the First Amendment, and the Power to Make Secrets Out of the Public Record," *University of Pennsylvania Law Review* 163, no. 4 (2015): 1037–1097.

86. Alasdair Roberts, *Blacked Out* (Cambridge, U.K.: Cambridge University Press, 2006), 38–39. For example, environmental and geospatial information that the federal government sought to

remove from the Internet after the September 11 attacks was nevertheless available from "industry and commercial businesses, academic institutions, NGOs, state and local governments, international suppliers, and even private citizens who publish their own relevant materials on the Internet." John C. Baker et al., *Mapping the Risks: Assessing the Homeland Security Implications of Publicly Available Geospatial Information* (Santa Monica, Calif.: RAND Corporation, 2004), 124.

87. Galnoor, "Government Secrecy: Exchanges, Intermediaries, and Middlemen," 34–35.

88. Brenner, *America the Vulnerable*, 168–169.

89. Near v. Minnesota, 283 U.S. 697 (1931) ("No one would question but that [at time of war] a government might prevent . . . the publication of the sailing dates of transports or the number and location of troops"); N.Y. Times Co. v. United States, 403 U.S. 713, 726 (1971) (Brennan, J., concurring) (quoting *Near*).

90. This secrecy does not preclude the president's required reporting of his finding that the action "is necessary to support identifiable foreign policy objectives of the United States and is important to the national security of the United States" to congressional intelligence committees in at least a "timely fashion." 50 U.S.C. § 413b(a)–(c). Congressional access to the information is strictly limited by statute. 50 U.S.C. § 413b(c).

91. Kathryn S. Olmsted, *Real Enemies* (New York: Oxford University Press, 2009), 238–240; Kermit L. Hall, "The Virulence of the National Appetite for Bogus Revelation," *Maryland Law Review* 56, no. 1 (1997): 1–56, 36–38.

92. Georg Simmel, "The Sociology of Secrecy and of Secret Societies," *American Journal of Sociology* 11, no. 4 (1906): 441–498, 465.

93. In one recent episode, the Obama administration continued to claim that its use of drone aircraft to attack terrorists in foreign countries was classified and therefore exempt from the Freedom of Information Act long after members of the administration had bragged of the program's successes. Conor Friedersdorf, "The Increasingly Absurd Conceit That Drone Strikes Are Secret," *The Atlantic*, June 22, 2012. http://www.theatlantic.com/politics/archive/2012/06/the-increasingly-absurd-conceit-that-drone-strikes-are-secret/258842/. It did so despite the fact that the program's existence was extensively documented in a largely flattering portrayal in a prominent national newspaper. Jo Becker and Scott Shane, "Secret 'Kill List' Proves a Test of Obama's Principles and Will," *New York Times*, May 29, 2012. http://www.nytimes.com/2012/05/29/world/obamas-leader ship-in-war-on-al-qaeda.html

94. Lawrence Lessig, *Republic, Lost* (New York: Twelve, 2011), 250–260.

Chapter 6

1. WikiLeaks, "What Is WikiLeaks?," *About WikiLeaks*, May 7, 2011. https://wikileaks.org/About.html

2. Ibid.

3. Gabriel Schoenfeld, *Necessary Secrets: National Security, the Media, and the Rule of Law* (New York: Norton, 2010), 21.

4. Office of the Press Secretary, the White House, "Executive Order 13526—Classified National Security Information," December 29, 2009. https://www.whitehouse.gov/the-press-office/execu tive-order-classified-national-security-information

5. Department of Defense, "Instructions for Developing Security Classification Guides," DOD Manual 5200.45, April 2, 2013, 11. http://www.dtic.mil/whs/directives/corres/pdf/520045m.pdf; see also Peter Galison, "Removing Knowledge: The Logic of Modern Censorship," in *Agnotology: The Making and Unmaking of Ignorance*, eds. Robert N. Proctor and Londa L. Schiebinger (Stanford, Calif.: Stanford University Press, 2008), 37–54, 43–44.

6. FOIA's exemption from disclosure of classified information appears at 5 U.S.C. § 552(b)(1), while the Espionage Act defines classified national security very broadly at 18 U.S.C. § 793(d)–(e). For the constitutional protections, see, for example, United States v. Nixon, 418 U.S. 683, 705 (1974) (recognizing the executive privilege doctrine for internal communications on the grounds that "[h]uman experience teaches that those who expect public dissemination of their remarks may well temper candor with a concern for appearances and for their own interests to the detriment of the decisionmaking process"); United States v. Reynolds, 345 U.S. 1, 10 (1953) (establishing the state secrets doctrine for cases in which the government can show "there is a reasonable danger that compulsion of the evidence will expose military matters which, in the interest of national security, should not be divulged").

7. Geoffrey R. Stone, *Top Secret: When Our Government Keeps Us in the Dark* (Lanham, Md.: Rowman & Littlefield, 2007), 2.

8. The most recent collection of evidence on this point is in Ilya Somin's *Democracy and Political Ignorance* (Stanford, Calif.: Stanford University Press, 2013), chapters 1 and 2, which surveys the polling data and academic literature on the subject. Other important books that share this general finding are Christopher H. Achen and Larry M. Bartels, *Democracy for Realists* (Princeton, N.J.: Princeton University Press, 2016); Bryan Caplan, *The Myth of the Rational Voter* (Princeton, N.J.: Princeton University Press, 2008); and Michael X. Delli Carpini and Scott Keeter, *What Americans Know About Politics and Why It Matters* (New Haven, Conn.: Yale University Press, 1996).

9. For a thoroughgoing discussion of the public confusion (or ignorance) of the stated reasons for the Iraq War, see W. Lance Bennett et al., *When the Press Fails: Political Power and the News Media from Iraq to Katrina* (Chicago: University of Chicago Press, 2008), 22–24.

10. *Commission on the Intelligence Capabilities of the United States Regarding Weapons of Mass Destruction, Report to the President of the United States,* March 31, 2005, 8–9. http://www.gpo.gov/fdsys/pkg/GPO-WMD/pdf/GPO-WMD.pdf; *Comprehensive Report of the Special Advisor to the DCI on Iraq's WMD,* September 30, 2004. https://www.cia.gov/library/reports/general-reports-1/iraq_wmd_2004; Frank Newport, "Americans Still Think Iraq Had Weapons of Mass Destruction Before War," Gallup, June 16, 2003. http://www.gallup.com/poll/8623/americans-still-think-iraq-had-weapons-mass-destruction-before-war.aspx

11. Harris Interactive, "Significant Minority Still Believe That Iraq Had Weapons of Mass Destruction When U.S. Invaded," *Business Wire,* November 10, 2008. http://www.businesswire.com/news/home/20081110005136/en/Significant-Minority-Iraq-Weapons-Mass-Destruction-U.S. (finding in polls taken every year between 2004–2008 that the percentage of those who believed in an advanced Iraq's WMD program was as high as 50 percent and never dipped below 36 percent); Dan Froomkin, "Yes, Iraq Definitely Had WMD, Vast Majority of Polled Republicans Insist," *Huffington Post,* June 21, 2012. http://www.huffingtonpost.com/2012/06/21/iraq-wmd-poll-clueless-vast-majority-republicans_n_1616012.html (reporting a 2012 YouGov poll that found that 62.9 percent of Republican respondents still thought that Iraq possessed WMDs when the United States invaded); Kendall Breitman, "Poll: Half of Republicans Still Believe WMDs Found in Iraq," *Politico,* January 7, 2015. http://www.politico.com/story/2015/01/poll-republicans-wmds-iraq-114016; Don Cassino, "Ignorance, Partisanship Drive False Beliefs About Obama, Iraq," Fairleigh Dickinson University's *PublicMind Poll,* January 7, 2015. http://publicmind.fdu.edu/2015/false/ (finding in 2014 that 50 percent of Republicans continued to believe in the existence of Iraq's WMD program and that nearly a third of Democrats believed it was probably or definitely true as well).

12. *The 9/11 Commission Report: Final Report of the National Commission on Terrorist Attacks Upon the United States,* authorized ed. (New York: Norton, 2004), 66; Walter Pincus and Dana Milbank, "Al-Qaeda-Hussein Link Is Dismissed," *Washington Post,* June 17, 2004. http://www.wash

ingtonpost.com/wp-dyn/articles/A47812-2004Jun16.html; for a list of these reports and links to them, see "Saddam Hussein and al-Qaeda Link Allegations," *Wikipedia*, last updated September 8, 2106. http://en.wikipedia.org/wiki/Saddam_Hussein_and_al-Qaeda_link_allegations#9.2F11_ Commission_conclusions. For polling on the issue, see, e.g., Brian Kraiker, "Poll: What Americans (Don't) Know," *Newsweek*, September 4, 2007. http://www.newsweek.com/poll-what-americans -dont-know-100099 (finding that 41 percent of those polled by *Newsweek* in 2007 believed that Iraq played a key role in the terrorist attacks); Harris Interactive, "Significant Minority Still Believe That Iraq Had Weapons of Mass Destruction When U.S. Invaded," Defense-Aerospace, September 10, 2008. http://www.defense-aerospace.com/articles-view/release/3/99556/one_third-of-us-adults -still-believe-iraq-had-wmds.html (finding that the percentage believing in an Iraq–al Qaeda alliance ranged from 62 percent in 2004 to 52 percent in 2008).

13. A fourteen-nation survey of public knowledge of a range of social and political issues that public policy currently addresses (including voting, teen pregnancy, and immigration) showed widespread ignorance. Ipsos-MORI, "Perceptions Are Not Reality: Things the World Gets Wrong," October 29, 2014. https://www.ipsos-mori.com/researchpublications/researcharchive/3466/percep tions-are-not-reality-10-things-the-world-gets-wrong.aspx

14. The most telling evidence of this fact is the Republican Party's nomination of Donald Trump, one of the most vocal challengers to President Obama's birth certificate, for president in 2016.

15. Somin, *Democracy and Political Ignorance*; Caplan, *The Myth of the Rational Voter*. See also Pierre Salmon and Alain Wolfelsperfer, "Acquiescence to Opacity," in *The Economics of Transparency in Politics*, eds. Albert Breton, Gianluigi Galeotti, Pierre Salmon, and Ronald Wintrobe (Burlington, Vt.: Ashgate, 2007), 11–36, 14–16 (arguing that the public does not have the capacity to develop the specialization required to "consume" information about government performance, leading it to acquiesce to opacity).

16. Brian Rappert, *How to Look Good in a War: Justifying and Challenging State Violence* (London: Pluto Press, 2012), 4.

17. Michael Smithson, *Ignorance and Uncertainty: Emerging Paradigms* (New York: Springer Verlag, 1989), 5–10; Robert N. Proctor, "Agnotology: A Missing Term to Describe the Cultural Production of Ignorance (and Its Study)," in *Agnotology: The Making and Unmaking of Ignorance*, eds. Robert N. Proctor and Londa L. Schiebinger (Stanford, Calif.: Stanford University Press, 2008), 1–33, 3–11. The philosopher Nicholas Resecher provides a further typology of ignorance in his monograph *Ignorance* (Pittsburgh: University of Pittsburgh Press, 2009), 140–141. Settling which typology or account is more accurate is not my purpose; rather, the effort to unpack "ignorance" complicates the idea that mere lack of access to information is the sole reason for ignorance.

18. The typology that follows comes from Smithson, *Ignorance and Uncertainty*, 9.

19. Smithson, *Ignorance and Uncertainty*, 216–239.

20. Claude Shannon and Warren Weaver, *The Mathematical Theory of Communication* (Urbana: University of Illinois Press 1949); Wilbur Schramm, "Information Theory and Mass Communication," *Journalism Quarterly* 32, no. 2 (1955): 131–146, 135–136.

21. Graeme Patterson, *History and Communications* (Toronto: University of Toronto Press, 1990), 100–101. Michel Serres's writings on noise's generative qualities are especially insightful. Michel Serres, *The Parasite* (Minneapolis: University of Minnesota Press), 14; Michel Serres, *Hermes: Literature, Science, Philosophy* (Baltimore: Johns Hopkins University Press, 1982), 66–67.

22. By "signification," I refer not only to the term's initial use within semiotics as a process of meaning creation (see Paul Perron, "Semiotics," in *The Johns Hopkins Guide to Literary Theory and Criticism*, eds. Michael Groden and Martin Kreisworth (Baltimore: Johns Hopkins University

Press, 1994), 658–665), but also to the concept of meaning production that has since been taken up by virtually all structuralist and poststructuralist literary and cultural theories. Richard Johnson, "What Is Cultural Studies Anyway?," in *What Is Cultural Studies? A Reader*, ed. John Storey (New York: St. Martins, 1996), 75–114, 96–98.

23. Stuart Hall, "Encoding/Decoding," in *Culture, Media and Language*, eds. Stuart Hall et al. (London: Routledge, 1980), 129–139.

24. Steven Mailloux, "Interpretation," in *Critical Terms for Literary Study*, 2nd ed., eds. Frank Lentricchia and Thomas McLaughlin (Chicago: University of Chicago Press, 1995), 121–134.

25. To avoid an exceedingly long footnote, I offer Terry Eagleton, *Literary Theory: An Introduction*, anniversary ed. (Minneapolis: University of Minnesota Press, 2008), chapters 2–4.

26. The concept is most closely associated with Herbert Simon. Herbert A. Simon, *Models of Bounded Rationality* (Cambridge, Mass.: MIT Press, 1982).

27. Reid Hastie and Robyn M. Dawes, *Rational Choice in an Uncertain World*, 2nd ed. (Thousand Oaks, Calif.: Sage, 2010); Thomas Gilovich and Dale Griffin, "Introduction—Heurists and Biases, Then and Now," in *Heuristics and Biases: The Psychology of Intuitive Judgment*, eds. Thomas Gilovich et al. (Cambridge, U.K.: Cambridge University Press, 2002), 1–17.

28. Anthony Downs, *An Economic Theory of Democracy* (New York: Harper & Row, 1957), 100, 210; Richard R. Lau and David P. Redlawsk, "Voting Correctly," *American Political Science Review* 91, no. 3 (1997): 585–598.

29. Michael S. Kang, "Democratizing Direct Democracy: Restoring Voter Competence Through Heuristic Cues and 'Disclosure Plus,'" *UCLA Law Review* 50, no. 5 (2003): 1141–1188, 1160–1161.

30. R. S. Nickerson, "Confirmation Bias: A Ubiquitous Phenomenon in Many Guises," *Review of General Psychology* 2, no. 2 (1998): 175–220.

31. Richard R. Lau and David P. Redlawsk, "Advantages and Disadvantages of Cognitive Heuristics in Political Decision Making," *American Journal of Political Science* 45, no. 4 (2011): 951–971; Larry M. Bartels, "Uninformed Votes: Information Effects in Presidential Elections," *American Journal of Political Science* 40, no. 1 (1996): 194–230.

32. This point was made first by Philip Converse in "The Nature of Belief Systems in Mass Publics," in *Ideology and Discontent*, ed. David Apter (New York: Free Press, 1964), 206–264. Jeffrey Friedman, the most articulate champion of Converse's work on public ignorance, provides a current context for this work in "Public Competence in Normative and Positive Theory: Neglected Implications of 'The Nature of Belief Systems in Mass Publics,'" *Critical Review* 18, no. 1–3 (2006): i–xliii, v–ix.

33. Suzanne Mettler, *The Submerged State* (Chicago: University of Chicago Press, 2011), 119–121.

34. Archon Fung, Mary Graham, and David Weil, *Full Disclosure: The Perils and Promise of Transparency* (Cambridge, U.K.: Cambridge University Press, 2007), 39–46.

35. Ibid., 96–101.

36. Omri Ben-Shahar and Carl E. Schneider, *More Than You Wanted to Know: The Failure of Mandated Disclosure* (Princeton, N.J.: Princeton University Press, 2014).

37. For opposing accounts on the relationship between Lippmann and Dewey's views of the public during this period, see James W. Carey, *Communication as Culture* (Winchester, Mass.: Unwin Hyman, 1989), 75–82, emphasizing their differences, and Michael Schudson, "The 'Lippmann–Dewey Debate' and the Invention of Walter Lippmann as an Anti-Democrat 1986–1996," *International Journal of Communication* 2 (2008): 1031–1042, criticizing Carey's account and emphasizing Lippmann and Dewey's similarities.

38. Walter Lippmann, *Phantom Public* (New Brunswick, N.J.: Transaction, 1993 [1925]), 54–55.

39. Water Lippmann, *Public Opinion* (New York: Harcourt Brace and Co., 1922), 9–13.

40. Lippmann, *Public Opinion*, 379–394. Edward Purcell placed Lippmann's skepticism about democracy in the context of the political theory and social sciences of the era. Edward A. Purcell, *The Crisis of Democratic Theory* (Lexington: University of Kentucky Press, 1973), 104–107.

41. Lippmann, *Public Opinion*, 399–402; Lippmann, *Phantom Public*, 52–59.

42. Lippmann, *Phantom Public*, 58–61, 116, 188–189. On the evolution of Lippmann's pessimism during this period, see Ronald Steel, *Walter Lippmann and the American Century* (New York: Little, Brown, 1980), 211–214.

43. Thomas Hill Schaub, *American Fiction in the Cold War* (Madison: University of Wisconsin Press, 1991), 15–19.

44. Dwight Macdonald, *Against the American Grain* (New York: Random House, 1962); C. Wright Mills, *The Power Elite* (New York: Oxford University Press, 1956), 298–324; David Riesman, with Nathan Glaser and Reuel Denney, *The Lonely Crowd* (New Haven, Conn.: Yale University Press, 1950).

45. Daniel Bell, *The End of Ideology* (New York: Free Press, 1960).

46. William Kornhauser, *Politics of Mass Society* (Glencoe: Free Press, 1959).

47. Bell, *End of Ideology*, 103–123; Richard Hofstadter, *The Paranoid Style in American Politics* (New York: Knopf, 1966).

48. Gustave Le Bon, *The Crowd: A Study of the Popular Mind* (London: T. Fisher Unwin, 1920 [1896]); Vilfredo Pareto, *The Mind and Society*, trans. Andrew Bongiorno and Arthur Livingston; ed. Arthur Livingston (New York: Harcourt Brace and Co., 1935); José Ortega y Gasset, *The Revolt of the Masses* (New York: Norton, 1994 [1930]); Joseph A. Schumpeter, *Capitalism, Socialism and Democracy*, 3rd ed. (New York: Harper & Row, 1950), chapter 22.

49. Andrew Ross, *No Respect: Intellectuals and Popular Culture* (New York: Routledge, 1989), 50–55.

50. Jacques Ellul, *Propaganda: The Formation of Men's Attitudes* (New York: Vintage, 1973). For a history of propaganda studies, see J. Michael Sproule, *Propaganda and Democracy: The American Experience of Media and Mass Persuasion* (New York: Cambridge University Press, 1997).

51. On the history of Marxist theories of ideology, see John B. Thompson, *Ideology and Modern Culture* (Stanford, Calif.: Stanford University Press, 1990).

52. Murray Edelman, *The Symbolic Uses of Politics* (Urbana: University of Illinois Press, 1964). For a critique of Edelman's work, see Mark Fenster, "Murray Edelman: Polemicist of Public Ignorance," *Critical Review* 17, no. 3–4 (2005): 367–391.

53. The most famous critique of the media industries is Edward S. Herman and Noam Chomsky, *Manufacturing Consent: The Political Economy of the Mass Media* (New York: Pantheon, 2002).

54. John Dewey, *The Public and Its Problems* (New York: Henry Holt and Co., 1927), 124, 158. Textual page numbers that follow refer to this book.

55. On Dewey's departure from Lippmann, see Robert B. Westbrook, *John Dewey and American Democracy* (Ithaca, N.Y.: Cornell University Press, 1991), 309–318.

56. See, for example, Amy Gutmann and Dennis Thompson, *Why Deliberative Democracy?* (Princeton, N.J., and Oxford, U.K.: Princeton University Press, 2004), 9; see generally Shane J. Ralston, "Dewey and Goodin on the Value of Monological Deliberation," *Ethics and Politics* 12, no. 1 (2010): 235–255; R. B. Westbrook, "Pragmatism and Democracy: Reconstructing the Logic of John Dewey's Faith," in *The Revival of Pragmatism: New Essays on Social Thought, Law, and Culture*, ed. Morris Dickstein (Durham, N.C.: Duke University Press, 1998), 128–140.

57. Robert J. Antonio and Douglas Kellner, "Communication, Modernity, and Democracy in Habermas and Dewey," *Symbolic Interaction* 15, No. 3 (1992): 277–297.

58. James W. Carey, "In Defense of Public Journalism," in *The Idea of Public Journalism*, ed. Theodore Lewis Glasser (New York: Guilford, 1999), 49–66.

59. Lippmann, *Public Opinion*, 50.

60. Ibid., 392.

61. Dewey, *The Public and Its Problems*, 167, 208–209.

62. Edmund Burke, *An Appeal from the New to the Old Whigs* (1791), in *The Works of the Right Honourable Edmund Burke*, volume 1 (London: Harry G. Bohn, 1841), 525. On Burke's belief in aristocratic rule and his differences from the more conservative wing of the founders (including Madison), see Ernest Young, "Rediscovering Conservatism: Burkean Political Theory and Constitutional Interpretation," *North Carolina Law Review* 72, no. 3 (1994): 619–723, 656–658.

63. Michael Warner, *Publics and Counterpublics* (New York: Zone Books, 2002), 55–67.

64. Ibid., 73.

65. Ibid., 143.

66. Jodi Dean, *Publicity's Secret* (Ithaca, N.Y.: Cornell University Press, 2002), 3. Textual page numbers that follow refer to this book.

67. Eleanor M. Fox, "Rule of Law, Standards of Law, Discretion and Transparency," *SMU Law Review* 67, no. 4 (2014): 795–800.

68. Max Weber, *Max Weber on Law in Economy and Society*, trans. Max Rheinstein and Edward Shils; ed. Max Rheinstein (Cambridge, Mass.: Harvard University Press, 1954). Duncan Kennedy offers a full discussion of Weber's sociology of law and theory of legal rationality in "The Disenchantment of Logically Formal Legal Rationality, or Max Weber's Sociology in the Genealogy of the Contemporary Mode of Western Legal Thought," *Hastings Law Journal* 55, no. 5 (2004): 1031–1076.

69. Onora O'Neill, *A Question of Trust* (Cambridge, U.K.: Cambridge University Press, 2002), 72–73.

70. John Hibbing and Elizabeth Theiss-Morse, *Stealth Democracy: Americans' Beliefs About How Government Should Work* (Cambridge, U.K.: Cambridge University Press, 2002), 212–213.

71. See, generally, Frank Bannister and Regina Connolly, "The Trouble with Transparency: A Critical Review of Openness in e-Government," *Policy and Internet* 3, no. 1 (2011): article 8; Deirdre Curtin and Albert Jacob Meijer, "Does Transparency Strengthen Legitimacy?," *Information Polity* 11, no. 2 (2006): 109–122.

72. Stephan Grimmelikhuijsen et al., "The Effect of Transparency on Trust in Government: A Cross-National Comparative Experiment," *Public Administration Review* 73, no. 4 (2013): 575–586; Gregory Porumbescu, "Linking Transparency to Trust in Government and Voice," *American Review of Public Administration*, October 5, 2015. doi: 10.1177/0275074015607301

73. Stephan G. Grimmelikhuijsen and Albert J. Meijer, "The Effects of Transparency on the Perceived Trustworthiness of a Government Organization: Evidence from an Online Experiment," *Journal of Public Administration Theory and Research* 24, no. 1 (2014): 137–157.

74. Albert Meijer, "Transparency," in *The Oxford Handbook of Public Accountability*, eds. Mark Bovens, Robert E. Goodin, and Thomas Schillemans (New York: Oxford University Press, 2014), 507–524.

75. Doris A. Graber, *The Power of Communication: Managing Information in Public Organizations* (Washington, D.C.: CQ Press, 2003), 30–36; Bryan D. Jones and Frank R. Baumgartner, *The Politics of Attention: How Government Prioritizes Problems* (Chicago: University of Chicago Press, 2005), 3, 7–17; Peter H. Schuck, *Why Government Fails So Often* (Princeton, N.J.: Princeton University Press, 2014), 165–172.

76. The classic statement of the garbage can model is Michael Cohen, James March, and Johan

Olsen, "A Garbage Can Model of Organizational Choice," *Administrative Science Quarterly* 17, no. 1 (1972): 1–25. It was explicitly adapted for politics and legislative agenda setting by John W. Kingdon, *Agendas, Alternatives, and Public Policies* (Boston: Little, Brown, 1984).

77. Bryan D. Jones and Frank R. Baumgartner, *Agendas and Instability in American Politics* (Chicago: University of Chicago Press, 1993).

78. Jones and Baumgartner, *The Politics of Attention,* 17–21.

79. James G. March and Johan P. Olsen, *Democratic Governance* (New York: Free Press, 1995), 157–158.

80. For a broader theoretical discussion of the cognitive limitations of how organizations process information, see Elinor Ostrom, *Understanding Institutional Diversity* (Princeton, N.J.: Princeton University Press, 2005), 104–109.

81. For a review of this literature emphasizing the role of politics in appellate judicial decisions, see Thomas J. Miles and Cass R. Sunstein, "The Real World of Arbitrariness Review," *University of Chicago Law Review* 75, no. 2 (2008): 761–814. More skeptical analyses appear in Frank B. Cross, *Decision Making in the U.S. Courts of Appeal* (Stanford, Calif.: Stanford University Press, 2007); Brian Z. Tamanaha, *Beyond the Formalist–Realist Divide* (Princeton, N.J.: Princeton University Press, 2010), 132–155.

82. Susan Nevelow Mart and Tom Ginsburg, "[Dis-]Informing the People's Discretion: Judicial Deference Under the National Security Exemption of the Freedom of Information Act," *Administrative Law Review* 66, no. 5 (2014): 725–784.

83. James T. Hamilton, *Democracy's Detectives: The Economics of Investigative Journalism* (Cambridge, Mass.: Harvard University Press, 2016).

84. Cass R. Sunstein, *Democracy and the Problem of Free Speech* (New York: Free Press, 1993), 58–62; Robert W. McChesney, *The Political Economy of Global Communication,* in *Capitalism and the Information Age,* eds. Robert W. McChesney et al. (New York: Monthly Review Press, 1998), 15–20; John B. Thompson, *Political Scandal: Power and Visibility in the Media Age* (Malden, Mass.: Blackwell, 2000), 75–84.

85. Denis McQuail, *McQuail's Mass Communication Theory,* 6th ed. (Thousand Oaks, Calif.: Sage, 2010), 191–305; Herbert I. Schiller, *Information Inequality* (New York: Routledge, 1996), 43–47.

86. Kevin R. Kosar, *Public Relations and Propaganda: Restrictions on Executive Agency Activities,* Congressional Research Service, Report No. RL3275, updated February 8, 2005, 1–4 (listing recent controversies surrounding administrative agencies' use of public relations campaigns); David Barstow and Robin Stein, "Under Bush, a New Age of Prepackaged News," *New York Times,* March 13, 2005, A1 (reporting that at least 20 federal agencies have produced news segments that were subsequently incorporated, without attribution, into local television broadcasts).

87. Bennett et al., *When the Press Fails.*

88. Public opinion polling over the past decade has revealed the extent of the traditional press's reputational slide. Pew Research Center, "Public Esteem for the Military Still High," July 11, 2013. http://www.pewforum.org/2013/07/11/public-esteem-for-military-still-high/

89. John Nerone, *The Media and Public Life: A History* (Cambridge, U.K.: Polity Press, 2015); see also Pew Research Center, "The Media: More Voices, Less Credibility," January 25, 2005. http://www.people-press.org/2005/01/25/the-media-more-voices-less-credibility/

90. Yochai Benkler, "A Free Irresponsible Press: Wikileaks and the Battle over the Soul of the Networked Fourth Estate," *Harvard Civil Rights–Civil Liberties Law Review* 46, no. 2 (2011): 311–398.

91. Because intelligence budgets are generally closely held information, the relative size of the U.S. intelligence community is not easy to estimate, but one analysis, comparing documents leaked

by Edward Snowden to estimates of military budgets around the world, concluded that the U.S. intelligence budget, standing alone, is better funded than all but three militaries (the United States, China, and Russia). Zachary Keck, "US Intelligence Community: The World's 4th Largest Military?," *The Diplomat,* August 30, 2013. http://thediplomat.com/2013/08/us-intelligence-community-the-worlds-4th-largest-military/

92. Richard K. Betts, "Analysis, War, and Decision: Why Intelligence Failures Are Inevitable," *World Politics* 31, no. 1 (1978): 61–89. For accounts that emphasize the CIA's failures, see John Diamond, *The CIA and the Culture of Failure* (Stanford; Calif.: Stanford University Press, 2008), and Tim Weiner, *Legacy of Ashes: The History of the CIA* (New York: Doubleday, 2007). For books that discuss the Soviet Union's own mixed record of intelligence gathering and analysis, see Raymond L. Garthoff, *Soviet Leaders and Intelligence: Assessing the American Adversary During the Cold War* (Washington, D.C.: Georgetown University Press, 2015), and Jonathan Haslam, *Near and Distant Neighbors: A New History of Soviet Intelligence* (New York: Oxford University Press, 2015). For a comparative study of intelligence failures, see David C. Gompert, Hans Binnendijk, and Bonny Lin, *Blinders, Blunders, and Wars: What America and China Can Learn* (Santa Monica, Calif.: RAND Corporation, 2014).

93. Halkin v. Helms, 598 F.2d 1, 8 (D.C. Cir. 1978).

94. Center for National Security Studies v. U.S. Department of Justice, 331 F.3d 918, 928 (D.C. Cir. 2003).

95. David E. Pozen, "The Mosaic Theory, National Security, and the Freedom of Information Act," *Yale Law Journal* 115, no. 3 (2005): 628–679, 664–665.

96. Kim Lane Scheppe, *Legal Secrets: Equality and Efficiency in the Common Law* (Chicago: University of Chicago Press, 1988), 15–16.

97. Neal D. Finkelstein, "Introduction: Transparency in Public Policy," in *Transparency in Public Policy,* ed. Neal D. Finkelstein (New York: St. Martin's Press, 2000), 1–9.

98. Michael J. Reddy, "The Conduit Metaphor: A Case of Frame Conflict in Our Language About Language," in *Metaphor and Thought,* 2nd ed., ed. Andrew Ortony (Cambridge, U.K.: Cambridge University Press, 1993), 164–201.

99. Frederick Schauer, "Transparency in Three Dimensions," *University of Illinois Law Review* no. 4 (2011): 1339–1357, 1344–1345.

Chapter 7

1. Nancy V. Baker, *General Ashcroft: Attorney at War* (Lawrence: University of Kansas Press, 2006), 176–196.

2. Biographical studies of Cheney offer a general introduction to the episode, as well as an inside glimpse of Cheney and the Office of the Vice President's work on the energy policy task force. Barton Gellman, *Angler: The Cheney Vice Presidency* (New York: Penguin, 2008), 81–82, 90–94, 104–107; Stephen F. Hayes, *Cheney: The Untold Story of America's Most Powerful and Controversial Vice President* (New York: HarperCollins, 2007), 310–318, 323–327.

3. Expansive treatments of the legal and political issues in this episode, which are uniformly critical of the administration and especially of the vice president, include Louis Fisher, *The Politics of Executive Privilege* (Durham, N.C.: Carolina Academic Press, 2004), 183–196; Eric R. Dannenmaier, "Executive Exclusion and the Cloistering of the Cheney Energy Task Force," *NYU Environmental Law Journal* 16, no. 2 (2008): 329–379; Mark J. Rozell and Mitchel A. Sollenberger, "Executive Privilege and the Bush Administration," *Journal of Law and Politics* 24, no. 1 (2008): 1–48, 12–27.

4. National Energy Policy Development Group, *National Energy Policy: Reliable, Affordable, and Environmentally Sound Energy for America's Future,* 2001, viii. https://www.netl.doe.gov/publications/press/2001/nep/nep.html (hereinafter *NEPDG Report*).

5. Hayes, *Cheney*, 311–313; Mike Allen and Dana Milbank, "Cheney's Role Offers Strengths and Liabilities," *Washington Post*, May 17, 2001, A1.

6. Gary C. Bryner, "The National Energy Policy: Assessing Energy Policy Choices," *University of Colorado Law Review* 73, no. 1 (2002): 341–412, 343; Susan Milligan, "Energy Bill a Special-Interests Triumph," *Boston Globe*, October 4, 2004, A1.

7. *NEPDG Report*, v.

8. U.S. General Accounting Office, *Report to Congressional Requesters, Energy Task Force: Process Used to Develop the National Energy Policy*, August 2003, 6–8. http://www.gao.gov/new.items/ d03894.pdf (hereinafter *GAO Report*); Gellman, *Angler*, 88–91; Ron Suskind, *The Price of Loyalty* (New York: Simon & Schuster, 2004), 146–149.

9. Michael Abramowitz and Steven Mufson, "Papers Detail Industry's Role in Cheney's Energy Report," *Washington Post*, July 18, 2007, A1.

10. Ibid.

11. *NEPDG Report*, 5-20–5-22 (summarizing recommendations for increasing domestic energy supply); ibid., 8-1–8-3 (on "Strengthening Global Alliances"). For a summary of the policy, see Michael T. Klare, "The Bush/Cheney Energy Strategy: Implications for U.S. Foreign and Military Policy," *NYU Journal of International Law and Politics* 36, no. 2 (2004): 395–424, 397–403; for the immediate political reaction to it, see Joseph Curl, "Bush Sees Dual Goals of Energy, Environment," *Washington Times*, May 18, 2001, A1; Carolyn Lochhead, "Bush Faces Tough Fight on Energy Strategy," *San Francisco Chronicle*, May 18, 2001, A1.

12. Lou Dubose and Jake Bernstein, *Vice: Dick Cheney and the Hijacking of the American Presidency* (New York: Random House, 2006), 6.

13. Suskind, *Price of Loyalty*, 143–144.

14. Gellman, *Angler*, 92.

15. Walker v. Cheney, 230 F. Supp. 2d 51, 55 (D.D.C. 2002); Jerry Seper, "Justice Asks Court to Dismiss GAO Suit Against Cheney," *Washington Times*, May 23, 2002, A3.

16. 31 U.S.C.A. § 712 (2006) (requiring the comptroller general to investigate federal government expenditures of public money).

17. Jeff Gerth, "Accounting Office Demands Energy Task Force Records," *New York Times*, July 18, 2001, A20; Seper, "Justice Asks Court to Dismiss GAO Suit Against Cheney," A3.

18. Walker v. Cheney, 230 F. Supp. 2d, 57; Gellman, *Angler*, 104.

19. Walker v. Cheney, 230 F. Supp. 2d, 54.

20. Public Law 92-463, 86 Stat. 770 (1972) (codified as amended at 5 U.S.C. App. II SS 1–15).

21. Gellman, *Angler*, 91; Hayes, *Cheney*, 313–314.

22. Steven P. Croley and William F. Funk, "The Federal Advisory Committee Act and Good Government," *Yale Journal on Regulation* 14, no. 2 (1997): 451–557, 458–465. For a detailed account of FACA's shortcomings, see Jason Ross Arnold, *Secrecy in the Sunshine Era* (Lawrence: University of Kansas Press, 2014), 97–133.

23. Croley and Funk, "The Federal Advisory Committee Act," 464–465.

24. 5 U.S.C. app. §§ 3, 9, 10.

25. Judicial Watch v. Nat'l Energy Policy Dev. Grp., 219 F. Supp. 2d 20, 25–26 (D.D.C. 2002).

26. Walker v. Cheney, 230 F. Supp. 2d, 74–75.

27. *GAO Report*, 3; Peter M. Shane, *Madison's Nightmare: How Executive Power Threatens American Democracy* (Chicago: University of Chicago Press, 2009), 125–126; Louis Fisher, "Congressional Access to Information: Using Legislative Will and Leverage," *Duke Law Journal* 52, no. 2 (2002): 323–402, 391–392; Peter Brand and Alexander Bolton, "GOP Threats Halted GAO Cheney Suit," *The Hill*, February 19, 2003, 51.

28. Cheney v. United States Dist. Court, 542 U.S. 367, 378 (2004), *reversing* In re Cheney, 334 F.3d 1096, 1108 (D.C. Cir. 2003) (ordering limited discovery on the question of NEPDG membership).

29. In re Cheney, 406 F.3d 723 (D.C. Cir. 2005) (*en banc*).

30. The separate Supreme Court opinions in *Cheney* lined up to some degree along a continuum, with Justices Ginsburg and Souter in dissent, Justice Stevens offering a much more limited concurrence, a four-justice plurality (with, to be sure, Justice Breyer joining), and Justices Thomas and Scalia providing a partial concurrence that emphasized the serious constitutional concerns for the separation of powers and the relative autonomy of the executive branch if the public interest groups could proceed with discovery. More strikingly, Republican appointees decided the key lower court decisions in the administration's favor. Judicial Watch, Inc. v. Department of Energy, 412 F.3d 125, 130–132 (D.C. Cir. 2005) (Ginsburg, J., Reagan appointee); In re Cheney, 406 F.3d 723 (D.C. Cir. 2005) (*en banc*) (Randolph, J., George H. W. Bush appointee); Walker v. Cheney, 230 F.Supp.2d 51, 55 (D.D.C. 2002) (Bates, J., George W. Bush appointee).

31. Steven M. Teles, *The Rise of the Conservative Legal Movement* (Princeton, N.J.: Princeton University Press, 2008), 147–169. The unitary executive theory has also made inroads into center-left jurisprudence, where a version holds sway among proponents of a strong presidency to manage the administrative state. Lawrence Lessig and Cass R. Sunstein, "The President and the Administration," *Columbia Law Review* 94, no. 1 (1994): 1–123, 105–106; Elena Kagan, "Presidential Administration," *Harvard Law Review* 114, no. 8 (2001): 2245–2386, 2252.

32. Gellman, *Angler*, 93–94.

33. In re Cheney, 406 F.3d 723, 727 n.1 (D.C. Cir. 2005) (*en banc*).

34. Nat'l Res. Def. Council v. Dep't of Energy, No. 01-2545 (D.D.C. filed February 21, 2002) (granting plaintiff's motion for release of responsive records). https://www.nrdc.org/resources/cheney-energy-task-force; National Resources Defense Council, "Cheney Energy Task Force Records," March 10, 2016. https://www.nrdc.org/resources/cheney-energy-task-force. This litigation endured until 2005, when the D.C. Circuit ruled in the Department of Energy's favor. Judicial Watch, Inc. v. Dep't of Energy, 412 F.3d 125, 130–132 (D.C. Cir. 2005).

35. Charlie Savage, *Takeover: The Return of the Imperial Presidency and the Subversion of American Democracy* (New York: Little, Brown, 2007), 34–38.

36. Judicial Watch, "Maps and Charts of Iraqi Oil Fields," February 14, 2012. http://www.judicial watch.org/bulletins/maps-and-charts-of-iraqi-oil-fields/

37. Joseph Kahn and David E. Sanger, "President Offers Plan to Promote Oil Exploration," *New York Times*, January 30, 2001, A1; Jim VandeHei, "Democrats Take Aim at Bush Weak Spot: Administration's Ties to Energy Industry," *Wall Street Journal*, May 16, 2001, A24; Dan Morgan, "Coal Scores with Wager on Bush," *Washington Post*, March 25, 2001, A5; Tom Hamburger, Laurie McGinley, and David Cloud, "Influence Market: Industries That Backed Bush Are Now Seeking Return on Investment," *Wall Street Journal*, March 6, 2001, A1.

38. These reports came in waves, first in March 2001 and then two months later. Dana Milbank, "Bush Energy Order Wording Mirrors Oil Lobby's Proposal," *Washington Post*, March 28, 2002, A27; Dana Milbank and Mike Allen, "Energy Task Force Belatedly Consulted Environmentalists," *Washington Post*, March 27, 2002, A2; Mike Allen, "Cheney, Aides Met with Enron 6 Times in 2001," *Washington Post*, January 9, 2002, A3; Don Van Natta Jr. and Neela Banerjee, "Bush Energy Paper Followed Industry Push," *New York Times*, March 27, 2002, 20; Bob Davis and Rebecca Smith, "Power Politics: In Era of Deregulation, Enron Woos Regulators More Avidly Than Ever," *Wall Street Journal*, May 18, 2001; Mike Allen and Dana Milbank, "Cheney's Role Offers Strengths and Liabilities," *Washington Post*, May 17, 2001, A1.

39. Don Van Natta Jr. and Neela Banerjee, "Top G.O.P. Donors in Energy Industry Met Cheney Panel," *New York Times*, March 1, 2002, A1.

40. *GAO Report*, 6–8, 15–18.

41. Dana Milbank and Eric Pianin, "Energy Task Force Works in Secret," *Washington Post*, April 16, 2001, A1.

42. Jeanne Cummings, "Power Politics: Energy Crisis Offers Clues to the Workings of Bush Administration," *Wall Street Journal*, February 16, 2001, A1; John J. Fialka and Jeanne Cummings, "White House Sets Cabinet-Level Study to Develop a National Energy Policy," *Wall Street Journal*, January 30, 2001, A6.

43. Mike Allen, "Bush's Energy Plan Stalled," *Washington Post*, August 23, 2003, A6; Eric Pianin, "A Stinging Repudiation, Engineered by 3 Democrats," *Washington Post*, April 19, 2002, A9.

44. Energy Policy Act of 2005, Public Law 109-58; Charles Babington and Justin Blum, "On Capitol Hill, a Flurry of GOP Victories," *Washington Post*, July 30, 2005, A1.

45. Greg Hitt, Shailagh Murray, and Jeffrey Ball, "Increasingly Skeptical Congress Takes up Bush Energy Plan," *Wall Street Journal*, July 31, 2001, A20.

46. Gellman, *Angler*, 93; Hayes, *Cheney*, 324.

47. See, e.g., Sierra Club, *Success Highlights: Celebrating Sierra Club's 2010 Charitable Victories*, 2010. https://www.yumpu.com/en/document/view/30940302/2010-accomplishments-the-sierra -club-foundation (identifying its role in litigation as evidence of its chairman's "leadership"); Sierra Club, *2004 Annual Report*, 2004, 6–7 (identifying its role in litigation as one of the year's "highlights").

48. Dannenmeier, "Executive Exclusion," 375–376.

49. Dubose and Bernstein, *Vice*, 21. See also Robert Bryce, *Cronies: Oil, the Bushes, and the Rise of Texas, America's Superstate* (New York: PublicAffairs, 2004); John W. Dean, *Worse Than Watergate* (New York: Little, Brown, 2004), 42–53; John Nichols, *Dick: The Man Who Is President* (New York: New Press, 2004).

50. Dubose and Bernstein, *Vice*, 15–16; Jane Meyer, "Contract Sport: What Did the Vice-President Do for Halliburton?" *The New Yorker*, February 16, 2004, 80.

51. Jon Gold, "The Facts Speak for Themselves," *9/11Truth.org*, September 25, 2008. http://www.911truth.org/the-facts-speak-for-themselves/; Michael Kane, "Crossing the Rubicon: Simplifying the Case Against Dick Cheney," *FromTheWilderness.com*, January 18, 2005. http://www.fromthe wilderness.com/free/ww3/011805_simplify_case.shtml

52. 5 U.S.C. § 552(b); Center for Auto Safety v. E.P.A., 731 F.2d 16, 21 (D.C. Cir. 1984) ("The 'segregability' requirement applies to all documents and all exemptions in the FOIA").

53. 5 U.S.C. § 552(b).

54. See, e.g., American Civil Liberties Union v. U.S. Department of Homeland Security, 738 F. Supp. 2d 93, 110–111 (D.D.C. 2010) (finding that the agency did not sufficiently support full redactions of e-mails and ordering the agency to "re-evaluate this document to ensure that only properly withheld information has been redacted and either make greater disclosure of the content of the e-mail to the plaintiff or provide a more detailed rationale" for withholding text). The fact that courts *can* inspect documents affected by agency redactions and of which an agency denied disclosure does not *require* them to do so. NLRB v. Robbins Tire & Rubber Co., 437 U.S. 214, 224 (1978).

55. See, generally, John Hollister Hedley, "Secrets, Free Speech, and Fig Leaves," *Studies in Intelligence* 41, no. 1 (1998): 75–83, 77–78, 83 (describing CIA's pre-publication review process).

56. Michael L. Charlson, "The Constitutionality of Expanding Prepublication Review of Government Employees' Speech," *California Law Review* 72, no. 5 (1984): 962–1018.

57. See, e.g., Berntsen v. CIA, 618 F.Supp.2d 27, 28 (D.D.C. 2009) (reproducing a pre-publication review provision from an employment contract).

58. U.S. v. Snepp, 595 F.2d 934 (4th Cir. 1979); U.S. v. Marchetti, 466 F.2d 1309, 1317 (4th Cir. 1972). The PRB often holds manuscripts beyond the deadline. A. John Radsan, "*Sed Quis Custodiet Ipsos Custodes*: The CIA's Office of General Counsel?," *Journal of National Security Law and Policy* 2, no. 2 (2008): 201–255, 239 n.121; see, e.g., Jason Vest, "Ex-CIA Officer Heads to Court for Second Time over Proposed Book," *Government Executive*, October 13, 2005. http://www.govexec .com/defense/2005/10/ex-cia-officer-heads-to-court-for-second-time-over-proposed-book/20405/ (describing author's frustration when PRB took 98 days to return manuscript with a long list of redactions). In the period between 2000 and 2007, the number of manuscripts submitted to the PRB increased fourfold, and between 1980 and 2007, it increased twelvefold. Richard Willing, "Spy Books Strain CIA Review Board," *USA Today*, April 30, 2007. http://usatoday30.usatoday.com/ news/washington/2007-04-29-spy-books_N.htm

59. Radsan, "*Sed Quis Custodiet Ipsos Custodes*," 241–242; Scott Shane and Mark Mazzetti, "Moves Signal Tighter Secrecy Within C.I.A.," *New York Times*, April 24, 2006. http://www.nytimes .com/2006/04/24/washington/moves-signal-tighter-secrecy-within-cia.html?_r=0

60. Scott Shane, "C.I.A. Demands Cuts in Book About 9/11 and Terror Fight," *New York Times*, August 25, 2011. http://www.nytimes.com/2011/08/26/us/26agent.html (complaints from former FBI agent about CIA redactions to his manuscript); Laura Miller, "Censored by the CIA," *Salon*, August 31, 2011. http://www.salon.com/2011/08/31/censored_by_cia/ (interview with former CIA agent complaining about intimidation in the PRB review process); Dana Priest, "Suing over the CIA's Red Pen," *Washington Post*, October 9, 2006. http://www.washingtonpost.com/wp-dyn/con tent/article/2006/10/08/AR2006100800764.html (former CIA agent recounting threat of CIA's executive director that the agency would "redact the [expletive] out of your book" because of its criticism of the CIA).

61. Snepp v. United States, 444 U.S. 507, 510 n.3 (1980) (upholding the CIA's pre-publication review process because of the voluntary nature of the secrecy agreement that its employees sign and the agency's "compelling interest" in protecting classified intelligence information).

62. McGehee v. Casey, 718 F.2d 1137, 1141 (D.C. Cir. 1983).

63. Wolf v. CIA, 473 F.3d 370, 378 (D.C. Cir. 2007); Hudson River Sloop Clearwater, Inc. v. Dep't of Navy, 891 F.2d 414, 421 (2d Cir. 1989).

64. Stillman v. C.I.A., 319 F.3d 546, 548 (D.C. Cir. 2003).

65. For example, the *New York Times* obtained an unredacted copy of an internal government history of U.S. efforts to capture Nazis after World War II; the copy revealed significant amounts of information that the Justice Department had redacted in a version it released in response to FOIA litigation. Eric Lichtblau, "Nazis Were Given 'Safe Haven' in the U.S., Report Says," *New York Times*, November 13, 2010. http://www.nytimes.com/2010/11/14/us/14nazis.html?_r=1

66. This can happen with commercial software programs. National Security Agency, *Redaction of PDF Files Using Adobe Acrobat Professional X*, 1. https://cryptome.org/2012/06/nsa-pdf-redaction. pdf; Jaikumar Vijayan, "TSA Document Release Show Pitfalls of Electronic Redaction," *Computerworld*, December 11, 2009. http://www.computerworld.com/article/2521816/security0/analysis— tsa-document-release-show-pitfalls-of-electronic-redaction.html. The problem predates electronic files and redaction; when redaction was on paper, it was sometimes possible to peer past the black mark at the underlying text. Scott Shane, "Spies Do a Huge Volume of Work in Invisible Ink," *New York Times*, October 28, 2007. http://www.nytimes.com/2007/10/28/weekinreview/28shane.html The problem is not unique to American government.

67. Valerie Plame Wilson, *Fair Game* (New York: Simon & Schuster, 2007).

68. Wilson v. Libby, 535 F.3d 697, 701–702 (D.C. Cir. 2008); In re Grand Jury Subpoena, Judith Miller, 438 F.3d 1141, 1143–1144 (D.C. Cir. 2006); Gellman, *Angler*, 360–364.

69. Motoko Rich, "Valerie Plame Gets Book Deal," *New York Times*, May 5, 2006. http://www .nytimes.com/2006/05/05/books/05cnd-plame.html

70. Wilson gives a full account of the PRB process in *Fair Game*, 264–281.

71. Wilson v. C.I.A., 586 F.3d 171 (2d Cir. 2009).

72. Wilson, *Fair Game*, 270–273.

73. Laura Rozen, "Afterword," in ibid., 307–389.

74. Ibid., 319–331.

75. Ibid., 351–352; Joseph C. Wilson, *The Politics of Truth* (New York: Carroll & Graf Publishers, 2004), 239–243.

76. Wilson, *Fair Game*, 392–402.

77. Janet Maslin, "Her Identity Revealed, Her Story Expurgated," *New York Times*, October 22, 2007 http://mobile.nytimes.com/2007/10/22/arts/22masl.html (book review describing dispute with CIA and characterizing the afterword as "fill[ing] in some of the gaps" created by the redactions).

78. Anthony Shaffer, *Operation Dark Heart* (New York: Thomas Dunne Books, 2010). On the book and its author, see generally Scott Shane, "Pentagon Plan: Buying Books to Keep Secrets," *New York Times*, September 9, 2010. www.nytimes.com/2010/09/10/us/10books.html

79. Scott Shane, "Secrets in Plain Sight in Censored Book's Reprint," *New York Times*, September 17, 2010. http://www.nytimes.com/2010/09/18/us/18book.html

80. Ibid.

81. Steven Aftergood, "Behind the Censorship of *Operation Dark Heart*," *Secrecy News*, September 29, 2010. http://fas.org/blogs/secrecy/2010/09/behind_the_censor/

82. Steven Aftergood, "Pentagon Relaxes Censorship of Afghan War Memoir," *Secrecy News*, January 24, 2013. https://fas.org/blogs/secrecy/2013/01/dark_heart_declass/

83. See, e.g., American Civil Liberties Union, "WikiLeaks Diplomatic Cables as FOIA Documents," December 12, 2011. http://www.nfoic.org/wikileaks-diplomatic-cables-foia-documents

84. Mohamedou Ould Slahi, *Guantánamo Diary*, ed. Larry Siems (New York: Little, Brown, 2015).

85. Steven Aftergood, "CIA Classification Practices Challenged," *Secrecy News*, September 24, 2015. https://fas.org/blogs/secrecy/2015/09/cia-complaint/

86. Scott Horton, "The Guantánamo 'Suicides,' Revisited," *Harper's Magazine*, June 2014, 66–67.

87. Deb Riechmann, "Experts: Clinton Emails Could Have Compromised CIA Names," *Associated Press*, June 8, 2016. http://bigstory.ap.org/article/1a737240cf144c728b45ef64e181fi9d/experts -clinton-emails-could-have-compromised-cia-names

88. Michael G. Powell, "Blacked Out," *The Believer*, no. 72 (June 2010): 23–26.

89. Arnold Mesches, "The FBI Files," *Public Culture* 15, no. 2 (2003): 287–294.

90. Jenny Holzer and Robert Storr, *Redaction Paintings* (New York: Cheim & Read, 2006).

91. Jenny Holzer, *Truth Before Power* (Bregenz, Austria: Kunsthaus Bregenz, 2004).

92. Joseph R. Slaughter, "Vanishing Points: When Narrative Is Not Simply There," *Journal of Human Rights* 9, no. 2 (2010): 207–223, 211.

93. Mesches, "The FBI Files," 292.

94. Alex Beam, "Spymasters: Espionage Realist," *Yale Alumni Magazine*, September/October 2011, 43, 44 (characterizing the redactions as a "major conceit" of the novel and noting that Weisberg, the author, made most of them).

95. Motoko Rich, "From Undercover to Between the Covers," *New York Times*, December 22, 2007. http://www.nytimes.com/2007/12/22/books/22weis.html?_r=0 (emphasis added)

96. Trevor Paglen, *Blank Spots: The Dark Geography of the Pentagon's Secret World* (New York: Dutton, 2009); Jonah Weiner, "Prying Eyes," *The New Yorker*, October 22, 2012, 54–61.

97. See, e.g., Warren F. Kimball, "Openness and the CIA," *Studies in Intelligence*, Fall/Winter 2001, 63. https://www.cia.gov/library/center-for-the-study-of-intelligence/csi-publications/csi-studies/studies/winter_spring01/article08.pdf (diplomatic historian arguing for disclosure of past covert actions); N. Richard Kinsman, "Openness and the Future of the Clandestine Service," *Studies in Intelligence*, Fall/Winter 2001, 55. https://www.cia.gov/library/center-for-the-study-of-intelligence/csi-publications/csi-studies/studies/winter_spring01/article07.pdf (retired CIA official arguing against disclosure).

98. The post-Watergate period saw the most extensive disclosures of American covert actions. Kathryn S. Olmsted, *Challenging the Secret Government: The Post-Watergate Investigations of the CIA and FBI* (Chapel Hill: University of North Carolina Press, 1996).

99. 22 U.S.C. § 4351(a).

100. Recent histories of the *FRUS* and the State Department's Office of the Historian are Kristin L. Ahlberg, "Building a Model Public History Program: The Office of the Historian at the U.S. Department of State," *Public Historian* 30, no. 2 (Spring 2008): 9–28; William B. McAllister, Joshua Botts, Peter Cozzens, and Aaron W. Marrs, "Toward 'Thorough, Accurate, and Reliable': A History of the *Foreign Relations of the United States* Series, 2015. https://s3.amazonaws.com/static.history.state.gov/frus-history/ebooks/frus-history.pdf

101. Ibid., 15–27 (describing conflicts over *FRUS* during the Cold War).

102. Richard W. Leopold, "The Foreign Relations Series: A Centennial Estimate," *Mississippi Valley Historical Review* 49, no. 4 (1963): 595–612, 607–609; Page Putnam Miller, "We Can't Yet Read Our Own Mail: Access to the Records of the Department of State," in *A Culture of Secrecy*, ed. Athan G. Theoharis (Lawrence: University of Kansas Press, 1998), 186–210, 189–194.

103. Foreign Relations Authorization Act, Public Law 102-138, § 198, 105 Stat. 647, 685–691 (1991) (22 U.S.C. § 4351 et seq.); McAllister et al., "Toward 'Thorough, Accurate, and Reliable,'" 277–302; see also Philip G. Schrag, "Working Papers as Federal Records: The Need for New Legislation to Preserve the History of National Policy," *Administrative Law Review* 46, no. 1 (1994): 95–140, 139 n.248.

104. President John F. Kennedy Assassination Records Collection Act of 1992, Public Law 102-526, 106 Stat. 3443 (1992). Similarly, Congress enacted the Nazi War Crimes Disclosure Act, Public Law 105-246, 112 Stat. 1859 (1998), to ensure the declassification and release of documents relating to the Holocaust.

105. Public Law 95-591, 92 Stat. 2523 (codified as amended at 44 U.S.C. §§ 2201–2207).

106. On the history of presidential papers before the PRA, see Jonathan Turley, "Presidential Papers and Popular Government: The Convergence of Constitutional and Property Theory in Claims of Ownership and Control of Presidential Records," *Cornell Law Review* 88, no. 3 (2003): 651–732, 657–666.

107. Nixon v. Adm'r of Gen. Servs., 433 U.S. 425, 445–446 n.8, 483–484 (1977) (upholding against constitutional challenge a pre-PRA statute focused solely on President Nixon's records).

108. 44 U.S.C. § 2204.

109. See, e.g., George H. W. Bush, "Statement on Signing the Foreign Relations Authorization Act, Fiscal Years 1992 and 1993," October 28, 1991. http://www.presidency.ucsb.edu/ws/print.php?pid=20152

110. Anne Van Camp, "Trying to Write 'Comprehensive and Accurate' History of the Foreign Relations of the United States: An Archival Perspective," in *Archives and the Public Good*, eds. Richard J. Cox and David A. Wallace (Westport, Conn.: Quorum Books, 2002), 229–246, 241.

111. McAllister et al., "Toward 'Thorough, Accurate, and Reliable,'" 304–326.

112. 44 U.S.C. § 2204(c)(1).

113. Executive Order 13489, 74 Fed. Reg. 4669, January 26, 2009 (Obama's revocation of a George W. Bush executive order allowing former presidents to withhold records as privileged after the twelve-year moratorium with the concurrence of the incumbent president). See generally Laurent Sacharoff, "Former Presidents and Executive Privilege," *Texas Law Review* 88, no. 2 (2009): 301–352; Marcy Lynn Karin, "Out of Sight, but Not Out of Mind: How Executive Order 13,233 Expands Executive Privilege While Simultaneously Preventing Access to Presidential Records," 55 *Stanford Law Review* 55, no. 2 (2002): 529–570, 548–552.

114. Michael Grow, *U.S. Presidents and Latin American Interventions* (Lawrence: University of Kansas Press, 2008), ix–x; Richard H. Immerman, *The CIA in Guatemala* (Austin: University of Texas Press, 1982) 186–201; John H. Coatsworth, "Introduction," in *Bitter Fruit: The Story of the American Coup in Guatemala*, revised and expanded ed., eds. Stephen Schlesinger and Stephen Kinzer (Cambridge, Mass.: Harvard University, David Rockefeller Center for Latin American Studies, 2005), xv. American involvement in Guatemala's internal politics continued into the Clinton administration, as did the CIA's denial and attempted coverup of its involvement in atrocities there. Richard A. Nuccio, "Foreword to the 1999 Edition," in Schlesinger and Kinzer, *Bitter Fruit*, xxii–xxvi.

115. Nick Cullather, *Secret History: The CIA's Classified Account of Its Operations in Guatemala, 1952–1954*, (Stanford, Calif.: Stanford University Press, 1999), 111–113, 119.

116. Immerman, *The CIA in Guatemala*, 4–5; Schlesinger and Kinzer, *Bitter Fruit*, 153–156. For an account of how the CIA and State Department persuaded the *New York Times* to stop reporting on the coup in order to keep the CIA's involvement from Americans, see Harrison E. Salisbury, *Without Fear or Favor* (New York: Times Books, 1980), 478–483.

117. Piero Gleijeses, *Shattered Hope: The Guatemalan Revolution and the United States 1944–1954* (Princeton, N.J.: Princeton University Press, 1991); E. Howard Hunt and Greg Aunapu, *American Spy* (Hoboken, N.J.: Wiley, 2007) 59–84; Immerman, *The CIA in Guatemala*; David Atlee Phillips, *The Night Watch* (New York: Atheneum, 1977), 34–54; Schlesinger and Kinzer, *Bitter Fruit*.

118. Gleijeses, *Shattered Hope*, 4; Coatsworth, "Introduction," xi.

119. One of the earliest critical histories of U.S. involvement in the 1954 coup relied heavily on documents received via the FOIA—although, notably, not from the CIA, which refused to make disclosures under FOIA. Schlesinger and Kinzer, *Bitter Fruit*, xxxvii.

120. State Department Office of the Historian, *Foreign Relations of the United States, 1952–1954, Guatemala*, ed. Susan K. Holly (Washington, D.C.: U.S. Department of State, 2003). https://history.state.gov/historicaldocuments/frus1952-54Guat

121. James X. Dempsey, "The CIA and Secrecy," in *A Culture of Secrecy*, ed. Athan G. Theoharis (Lawrence: University of Kansas Press, 1998), 37–59, 53–55 (on the CIA's interest in openness in the early 1990s).

122. Cullather, *Secret History*, vii–ix, xiv.

123. Nicholas Cullather, "Operation PBSUCCESS: The United States and Guatemala, 1952–1954," 1994. https://www.cia.gov/library/readingroom/docs/DOC_0000134974.pdf

124. Cullather, *Secret History*, iii–xv, xvii.

125. Ibid., 119; Robert Shaffer, "The 1954 Coup in Guatemala and the Teaching of U.S. Foreign Relations," *Passport*, December 2004. https://shafr.org/sites/default/files/Shaffer1.pdf

126. Cullather, *Secret History*, xiv–xv; Press Release, Center for the Study of Intelligence, Release of Records on 1952–54 Guatemala Covert Actions, May 23, 1997 (on file with author).

127. Richard H. Immerman, "Book Review," *American Historical Review* 106, no. 2 (2001): 605 (reviewing Cullather, *Secret History*).

128. Schlesinger and Kinzer, *Bitter Fruit*, 106.

129. Immerman, *The CIA in Guatemala*, 68, 82.

130. Gleijeses, *Shattered Hope*, 7.

131. Stephen M. Streeter, "Interpreting the U.S. Intervention in Guatemala: Realist, Revisionist, and Postrevisionist Perspectives," *The History Teacher* 34, no. 1 (2000): 61–74.

132. Immerman, "Book Review" (complaining of the CIA's "behavior" in refusing to release unredacted versions of classified documents that could conceivably resolve significant historical disputes).

133. Gleijeses, *Shattered Hope*, 3–7.

134. Sharon I. Meers, "The British Connection: How the United States Covered Its Tracks in the 1954 Coup in Guatemala," *Diplomatic History* 16, no. 3 (1992): 409–428, 419, 422–423.

135. Cullather, *Secret History*, 119–123; Schlesinger and Kinzer, *Bitter Fruit*, ix–xi, xxxvii–viii.

136. Central Intelligence Agency, "CIA FOIA—Guatemala." https://www.cia.gov/library/read ingroom/collection/guatemala; State Department, *Foreign Relations of the United States, 1952–1954, Guatemala.*

137. National Security Archive, "Death Squads, Guerrilla War, Covert Operations, and Genocide: Guatemala and the United States, 1954–1999 (Guatemala and the U.S.)," 2000, Digital National Security Archive. http://proquest.libguides.com/dnsa/deathsquads; Bill Clinton, "Remarks in a Roundtable Discussion on Peace Efforts in Guatemala City, March 10, 1999," *Public Papers of the Presidents of the United States, William J. Clinton*, volume 1 (Washington, D.C.: Office of the Federal Register, 2000), 340.

138. On the CIA's mythological status both before and after the mid-1970s disclosure of the checkered history of its covert operations, see Olmsted, *Challenging the Secret Government*, 13–15, 186–189.

139. Timothy Melley, *The Covert Sphere* (Ithaca, N.Y.: Cornell University Press, 2012), 13.

140. Nick Cullather, *Secret History: The CIA's Classified Account of Its Operations in Guatemala*, 2nd ed. (Stanford, Calif.: Stanford University Press, 2006), ix.

141. The CIA's redactions of Cullather's original manuscript literally erased text and left square brackets surrounding empty space; the university press edition repeated this technique.

142. The Guatemala case is not unique. After the State Department refused to allow declassification of certain documents related to British Guiana, *New York Times* journalist Tim Weiner discovered the nature of the classified materials by using open source materials not subject to classification. His investigation revealed the existence of an American covert operation, ordered by President Kennedy, to unseat the nation's democratically elected leader. Tim Weiner, "A Kennedy–C.I.A. Plot Returns to Haunt Clinton," *New York Times*, October 30, 1994. http://www.ny times.com/1994/10/30/world/a-kennedy-cia-plot-returns-to-haunt-clinton.html; see also Colin A. Palmer, *Cheddi Jagan and the Politics of Power* (Chapel Hill: University of North Carolina Press, 2010), 246–269; Stephen G. Rabe, *U.S. Intervention in British Guiana: A Cold War Story* (Chapel Hill: University of North Carolina Press, 2005), 151–173; Tim Weiner, *Legacy of Ashes* (New York: Doubleday, 2007), 191–192, 591–592. This history may have been secret in the United States, but it was widely known in Guiana. Festus Brotherson, "The Foreign Policy of Guyana, 1970–1985: Forbes Burnham's Search for Legitimacy," *Journal of Interamerican Studies and World Affairs* 31, no. 3 (1989): 9–35; Weiner, *Legacy of Ashes*, 592.

143. On the prevalence of open secrets in national security, see Amanda Jacobsen, "Open Secrets in U.S. Counter-Terrorism Policy," in *The Long Decade: How 9/11 Changed the Law*, eds. David Jenkins, Amanda Jacobsen, and Anders Henriksen (New York: Oxford University Press, 2014), 249–268. On open secrets generally and their effects on organizations and society, see Michael Taussig,

Defacement: Public Secrecy and the Labor of the Negative (Stanford, Calif.: Stanford University Press, 1999), 5; Jana Costas and Christopher Grey, *Secrecy at Work: The Hidden Architecture of Organizational Life* (Stanford, Calif.: Stanford University Press, 2016), 40.

144. Dick Cheney, "Congressional Overreaching in Foreign Policy," in *Foreign Policy and the Constitution*, eds. Robert A. Goldwin and Robert A. Licht (Washington, D.C.: AEI Press, 1989), 101–122, 116.

145. David Johnston, "Coverup: Watergate's Toughest Lesson," *New York Times*, February 15, 1998, § 4, 5; Frank Rich, "We're Not in Watergate Anymore," *New York Times*, July 10, 2005, § 4, 12.

146. Peter Baker, "What's Leaking Out of the White House," *Washington Post*, April 8, 2007. http://www.washingtonpost.com/wp-dyn/content/article/2007/04/06/AR2007040601818.html

147. On Cheney and Bush's unpopularity following the end of the Bush presidency, see Lydia Saad, "Little Change in Negative Images of Bush and Cheney," *Gallup*, April 3, 2009. http://www.gallup.com/poll/117250/Little-Change-Negative-Images-Bush-Cheney.aspx; on their more recent unpopularity, see George E. Condon Jr., "Romney Embraces Cheney, Sort Of," *The Atlantic*, July 17, 2012. http://www.theatlantic.com/politics/archive/2012/07/romney-embraces-cheney-sort-of/442 458/

148. See, generally, Jennifer K. Elsea, *Criminal Prohibitions on the Publication of Classified Defense Information*, Congressional Research Service, Report No. R41404 (2012): 26–30 (discussing recently proposed legislation that would expand criminal liability for leaks).

149. On the Obama administration's excessive leak prosecutions, see Adam Liptak, "A High-Tech War on Leaks," *New York Times*, February 12, 2012. http://www.nytimes.com/2012/02/12/sunday-review/a-high-tech-war-on-leaks.html; Josh Gerstein, "Obama's Hard Line on Leaks," *Politico*, March 7, 2011. http://www.politico.com/news/stories/0311/50761.html; Shane Harris, "Plugging the Leaks," *Washingtonian*, July 21, 2010. https://www.washingtonian.com/2010/07/21/plugging-the-leaks/. For an argument about the cyclical, largely symbolic nature of anti-leak campaigns in a political system that requires leaks, see David Pozen, "The Leaky Leviathan: Why the Government Criminalizes, and Condones, Unauthorized Disclosures of Information," *Harvard Law Review* 127, no. 2 (2013): 512–635.

150. Seth F. Kreimer, "The Freedom of Information Act and the Ecology of Transparency," *University of Pennsylvania Journal of Constitutional Law* 10, no. 5 (2008): 1011–1080.

151. One famous example of this phenomenon is the case of the *Glomar Explorer*, a ship that the CIA attempted to use to recover a sunken Soviet nuclear submarine. The CIA continued to try to keep secret the ship's existence despite numerous leaks and front-page stories in major newspapers. See Matthew Aid, "Project Azorian: The CIA's Declassified History of the *Glomar Explorer*," *National Security Archive*, February 12, 2010. http://nsarchive.gwu.edu/nukevault/ebb305/

Chapter 8

1. Floyd Abrams, "The Pentagon Papers a Decade Later," *New York Times Magazine*, June 7, 1981, 25.

2. John T. Correll, "The Pentagon Papers," *Air Force Magazine*, February 2007, 55. http://www.airforcemag.com/MagazineArchive/Pages/2007/February%202007/0207pentagon.aspx

3. See, e.g., David Rudenstine, *The Day the Presses Stopped: A History of the Pentagon Papers Case* (Berkeley: University of California Press, 1996), 329–330; Richard Tofel, "Why WikiLeaks' 'War Logs' Are No Pentagon Papers," *ProPublica*, July 26, 2010. http://www.propublica.org/article/why-wikileaks-war-logs-are-no-pentagon-papers

4. Abrams, "Pentagon Papers a Decade Later"; Tom Wells, *Wild Man: The Life and Times of Daniel Ellsberg* (New York: Palgrave, 2001), 340–341, 514.

5. William L. Lunch and Peter W. Sperlich, "American Public Opinion and the War in Vietnam," *Western Political Quarterly* 32, no. 1 (1979): 21–44.

6. Gabriel Schoenfeld, *Necessary Secrets* (New York: Norton, 2010), 188–189.

7. For a useful and insightful discussion of the problems faced by natural experiments, see Jasjeet S. Sekhon and Rocio Titiunik, "When Natural Experiments Are Neither Natural nor Experiments," *American Political Science Review* 106, no. 1 (2012): 35–57.

8. The Australian political scientist Peter Grabosky reached similar conclusions in his review of five prominent leaks of national security information from the United States (the Pentagon Papers), France, Britain, Switzerland, and Israel. Peter Grabosky, "The Vengeful State: Responses by Democratic Governments to Unauthorized Public Disclosure of National Security Information," *RegNet Working Paper, No. 42*, Regulatory Institutions Network, Australian National University, 2014. http://papers.ssrn.com/sol3/papers.cfm?abstract_id=2482170;

9. WikiLeaks, "Collateral Murder," (Apr. 5, 2010), http://collateralmurder.com/ (also available at https://www.youtube.com/watch?v=5rXPrfnU3G0). A full account of the *Collateral Murder* video and its production appears in Raffi Khatchadourian, "No Secrets: Julian Assange's Mission for Total Transparency," *New Yorker*, June 7, 2010, 40.

10. On the networks to which Manning had access, see Kim Zetter and Kevin Poulsen, "U.S. Intelligence Analyst Arrested in WikiLeaks Video Probe," *Wired*, June 6, 2010. http://www.wired.com/2010/06/leak/. The YouTube video had 15.6 million views as of August 2016. This does not include view counts on re-uploaded versions of the video or versions hosted on other servers. WikiLeaks, "Collateral Murder."

11. David Leigh and Luke Harding, *WikiLeaks: Inside Julian Assange's War on Secrecy* (New York: PublicAffairs, 2011), 116–144; Yochai Benkler, "A Free Irresponsible Press: Wikileaks and the Battle over the Soul of the Networked Fourth Estate," *Harvard Civil Rights–Civil Liberties Law Review* 46, no. 2 (2011): 311–398, 323–330; Tom Lasseter, "Guantánamo Secret Files Show U.S. Often Held Innocent Afghans," *Miami Herald*, April 26, 2011. http://www.miamiherald.com/latest-news/article1938045.html; Charlie Savage et al., "Classified Files Offer New Insights into Detainees," *New York Times*, April 24, 2011. http://www.nytimes.com/2011/04/25/world/guantanamo-files-lives-in-an-american-limbo.html

12. Paul Marks, "Assange: Why WikiLeaks Was Right to Release Raw Cables," *New Scientist*, September 6, 2011. https://www.newscientist.com/article/dn20869-assange-why-wikileaks-was-right-to-release-raw-cables/; Raphael G. Satter, "WikiLeaks Reveals All, Media Groups Criticize Move," *Yahoo! News*, September 2, 2011. http://news.yahoo.com/wikileaks-reveals-media-groups-criticize-move-144202957.html; Christian Stöcker, "A Dispatch Disaster in Six Acts," *Spiegel Online*, September 1, 2011. http://www.spiegel.de/international/world/0,1518,783778,00.html

13. Daniel W. Drezner, "Why WikiLeaks Is Bad for Scholars," *Chronicle of Higher Education*, December 5, 2010. http://chronicle.com/article/Why-WikiLeaks-Is-Bad-for/125628/ (characterizing the diplomatic cables as documents that would have been unavailable to academics for decades). Reuters had unsuccessfully requested information about the attack via FOIA. Dan Murphy, "WikiLeaks Releases Video Depicting US Forces Killing of Two Reuters Journalists in Iraq," *Christian Science Monitor*, April 5, 2010. http://www.csmonitor.com/World/Global-News/2010/0405/Wikileaks-releases-video-depicting-US-forces-killing-of-two-Reuters-journalists-in-Iraq

14. Leigh and Harding, *WikiLeaks: Inside Julian Assange's War on Secrecy*, 110–115; Benkler, "A Free Irresponsible Press," 321–330. For inside accounts of the relationship between WikiLeaks and the newspapers to whom it granted preview access, written from the newspapers' perspectives, see Sarah Ellison, "The Man Who Spilled the Secrets," *Vanity Fair*, February 2011. http://www.vanityfair.com/politics/features/2011/02/the-guardian-201102; and Bill Keller, "Dealing with Julian Assange

and the WikiLeaks Secrets," *New York Times,* January 26, 2011. http://www.nytimes.com/2011/01/30/magazine/30Wikileaks-t.html; see also Javier Moreno, "Why *El País* Chose to Publish the Leaks," *El País,* December 23, 2010. http://elpais.com/elpais/2010/12/23/inenglish/1293085243_850210.html

15. Leigh and Harding, *WikiLeaks: Inside Julian Assange's War on Secrecy,* 116–144; Alexander Star, ed., *Open Secrets: WikiLeaks, War, and American Diplomacy* (New York: Grove Press, 2011), 62–203, 252–328. The State Department releases continued long after the initial wave of disclosures by the major newspapers via news outlets in those countries. Joshua E. Keating, "The WikiLeaks You Missed," *Foreign Policy,* July 1, 2011. http://www.foreignpolicy.com/articles/2011/01/01/the_wikileaks_you_missed (describing releases about Thailand, Haiti, India, Pakistan, and other nations).

16. Lasseter, "Guantánamo Secret Files"; Savage et al., "Classified Files Offer New Insights into Detainees."

17. Immediately after the first major document release regarding Afghanistan, Chairman of the Joint Chiefs of Staff Admiral Mike Mullen declared, "Mr. Assange can say whatever he likes about the greater good he thinks he and his source are doing. . . . But the truth is they might already have on their hands the blood of some young soldier or that of an Afghan family." Greg Jaffe and Joshua Partlow, "Joint Chiefs Chairman Mullen: WikiLeaks Release Endangers Troops, Afghans," *Washington Post,* July 30, 2010. http://www.washingtonpost.com/wp-dyn/content/article/2010/07/29/AR2010072904900.html. Less than a week later, the Pentagon press secretary stated in a press conference that WikiLeaks "has already threatened the safety of our troops, our allies and Afghan citizens who are working with us to help bring about peace and stability in that part of the world." U.S. Department of Defense, "DOD News Briefing with Geoff Morrell from the Pentagon on Wikileaks," August 5, 2010. http://www.fas.org/sgp/news/2010/08/dod080510.html (transcript of press conference by former Pentagon press secretary Geoff Morrell). Military officials continued to press such claims months later. See Hearing to Consider the Nominations of: Honorable Michael G. Vickers To Be Under Secretary of Defense for Intelligence; and Dr. Jo Ann Rooney To Be Principal Deputy Under Secretary of Defense for Personnel and Readiness Before the Senate Committee on Armed Services, 112th Cong., 2011, 10–11. https://www.gpo.gov/fdsys/pkg/CHRG-112shrg74537/html/CHRG-112shrg74537.htm (testimony of acting Under Secretary of Defense for Intelligence Michael G. Vickers, agreeing that WikiLeaks' disclosures endangered individuals who were cooperating with the American military and have damaged the military's ability to recruit intelligence assets).

18. Ron Moreau, "Taliban Seeks Vengeance in Wake of WikiLeaks," *Daily Beast,* August 1, 2010. http://www.newsweek.com/2010/08/02/taliban-seeks-vengeance-in-wake-of-wikileaks.html

19. Jeanne Whalen, "Rights Groups Join Criticism of WikiLeaks," *Wall Street Journal,* August 9, 2010. http://online.wsj.com/article/SB10001424052748703428604575419580947722558.html

20. Joshua Foust, "The Assange Leaks," *Columbia Journalism Review,* July 26, 2010. http://www.cjr.org/campaign_desk/the_assange_leaks.php

21. Ibid.

22. Adam Weinstein, "WikiLeaks' Afghan Documents and Me," *Mother Jones,* July 26, 2010. http://www.motherjones.com/mojo/2010/07/wikileaks-afghan-documents-and-me-source

23. Ibid.

24. Haig v. Agee, 453 U.S. 280, 308–309 (1981) (refusing to extend First Amendment protection for disclosure of an intelligence operative's identity); see also Near v. Minnesota, 283 U.S. 697, 716 (1931) (noting that the First Amendment would not protect disclosure of troop movements).

25. *In the Matter of U.S. vs. PFC Bradley E. Manning, August 19, 2013, Afternoon Session Transcript.* https://freedom.press/sites/default/files/08-19-13-PM-session.pdf

26. Ibid.

27. Daniel S. Markey, "Will WikiLeaks Hobble U.S. Diplomacy?," *Council on Foreign Relations*, December 1, 2010. http://www.cfr.org/publication/23526/will_wikileaks_hobble_us_diplomacy .html

28. Ibid.

29. Robert Burns, "Are Risks from WikiLeaks Overstated by Government?," *Salon*, August 17, 2010. http://www.salon.com/2010/08/17/wikileaks_risks_overstated/; Bradley Klapper and Cassandra Vinograd, "AP Review Finds No Threatened WikiLeaks Sources," *Yahoo! News*, September 10, 2011. http://news.yahoo.com/ap-review-finds-no-threatened-wikileaks-sources-074530441.html; Deb Riechmann, "Coalition Informant Plays Both Sides of Afghan War," *Huffington Post*, June 7, 2011. http://www.huffingtonpost.com/huff-wires/20110607/as-afghan-coalition-snitch/

30. Paul Lewis, "Bradley Manning Trial: Six Things We Learned," *The Guardian*, August 21, 2013. http://www.theguardian.com/world/2013/aug/21/bradley-manning-trial-six-things; *In the Matter of U.S. vs. PFC Bradley E. Manning*.

31. Charlie Savage, "Gates Assails WikiLeaks over Release of Reports," *New York Times*, July 29, 2010. http://www.nytimes.com/2010/07/30/world/asia/30wiki.html?_r=0 (internal quotation marks omitted)

32. Adam Levine, "Gates: Leaked Documents Don't Reveal Key Intel, but Risks Remain," *CNN*, October 17, 2010. http://www.cnn.com/2010/US/10/16/wikileaks.assessment/index.html?hpt=T2

33. Ibid.

34. Daniel G. Arce, "WikiLeaks and the Risks to Critical Foreign Dependencies," *International Journal of Critical Infrastructure Protection* 11, no. 1 (2015): 3–11 (noting that information released by WikiLeaks about infrastructure abroad listed as vital assets under the Critical Foreign Dependencies Infrastructure did not result in any increase in terrorist attacks or activities).

35. *In the Matter of U.S. vs. PFC Bradley E. Manning*, 39–40.

36. The United States emphasized its efforts to mitigate in its sentencing argument in the Manning trial. *In the Matter of U.S. vs. PFC Bradley E. Manning, August 19, 2013, Morning Session Transcript*, 9–17. https://freedom.press/sites/default/files/08-19-13-PM-session.pdf

37. Letter from Harold Hongju Koh, Legal Adviser, U.S. Department of State, to Jennifer Robinson, Attorney for Mr. Julian Assange, November 27, 2010 (hereinafter Koh Letter). http://media .washingtonpost.com/wp-srv/politics/documents/Dept_of_State_Assange_letter.pdf

38. Mark Landler and Scott Shane, *New York Times*, January 6, 2011. http://www.nytimes.com /2011/01/07/world/07wiki.html

39. Ibid.

40. Jose de Cordoba, "U.S. Ambassador to Mexico Resigns Following WikiLeak Flap," *Wall Street Journal*, March 19, 2011. http://online.wsj.com/article/SB10001424052748704021504576211282 543444242.html. The U.S. ambassador to Mexico was not the only diplomat who was forced to resign or was reassigned as a result of leaked cables. Leigh and Harding, *WikiLeaks: Inside Julian Assange's War on Secrecy*, 225.

41. "Ecuador Expels US Ambassador over Wikileaks Cable," *BBC News*, April 5, 2011. http:// www.bbc.com/news/world-latin-america-12979967

42. Mexican president Felipe Calderon pushed for the ambassador's firing, claiming that the cables harmed U.S.–Mexico relations, but it is unclear whether his efforts reflected his sincere conclusion about the disclosure's effects or if instead they were aimed at a domestic audience as he prepared for a contested reelection campaign in 2012. De Cordoba, "U.S. Ambassador to Mexico Resigns"; Mary Beth Sheridan, "Calderon: WikiLeaks Caused Severe Damage to U.S.–Mexico Relations," *Washington Post*, March 3, 2011. http://www.washingtonpost.com/wp-dyn/content/ article/2011/03/03/AR2011030302853.html. On the thawing of relations with Ecuador, see Bureau of

Western Hemisphere Affairs, "U.S. Relations With Ecuador," U.S. Department of State, last updated August 31, 2016. http://www.state.gov/r/pa/ei/bgn/35761.htm

43. Koh Letter; "Remarks to the Press on Release of Purportedly Confidential Documents by Wikileaks," U.S. Department of State, November 29, 2010. http://www.state.gov/secretary/2009 2013clinton/rm/2010/11/152078.htm (transcript of press conference by Secretary Clinton in which she complained that WikiLeaks "undermines our efforts to work with other countries to solve shared problems" and characterized the leaks as attacking "the international community—the alliances and partnerships, the conversations and negotiations, that safeguard global security and advance economic prosperity").

44. George Packer, "The Right to Secrecy," *The New Yorker*, November 29, 2010. http://www.new yorker.com/online/blogs/georgepacker/2010/11/the-right-to-secrecy.html; James P. Rubin, "The Irony of Wikileaks," *New Republic*, December 1, 2010. http://www.tnr.com/article/politics/79531/the-irony -wikileaks-american-diplomacy-hard-left

45. See, e.g., Samuel Witten, "The Effects of WikiLeaks on Those Who Work at the State Department," *Opinio Juris*, December 18, 2010. http://opiniojuris.org/2010/12/18/the-effects-of -wikileaks-on-those-who-work-at-the-state-department/ (providing an extensive discussion of the effects of WikiLeaks on State Department employees by a former deputy legal advisor and principal deputy assistant secretary of state for population, refugees, and migration)

46. See, e.g., United States v. Reynolds, 345 U.S. 1, 10 (1953) (stating that government can protect information under the state secrets doctrine if it can show "there is a reasonable danger that compulsion of the evidence will expose military matters which, in the interest of national security, should not be divulged"). Under FOIA, courts give "substantial weight" to government officials' affidavits regarding the threats to national security that agencies foresee if they are forced to disclose requested documents; under these circumstances, FOIA exemptions 1 (for properly classified information) and 3 (for information specifically exempted by Congress in other statutes) apply. Halperin v. CIA, 629 F.2d 144, 148 (D.C. Cir. 1980). On judicial deference to executive branch claims of national security, see David E. Pozen, "Deep Secrecy," *Stanford Law Review* 62, no. 2 (2010): 257–339, 304–305.

47. "DOD News Briefing with Secretary Gates and Adm. Mullen from the Pentagon," U.S. Department of Defense, November 30, 2010. http://archive.defense.gov/transcripts/transcript. aspx?transcriptid=4728 (hereinafter Gates News Briefing) (transcript of press conference); but see Marc Ambinder, "WikiLeaks Did 'Significant Damage' to Diplomacy, State Official Says," *National Journal*, December 2, 2010. http://www.govexec.com/defense/2010/12/wikileaks-did-significant -damage-to-diplomacy-state-official-says/32859/ (quoting an anonymous State Department official disagreeing with Secretary Gates's statement, arguing that the disclosures are "going to complicate U.S. diplomacy and international cooperation for a long time after the headlines stop").

48. "Clinton: WikiLeaks Won't Hurt U.S. Diplomacy," *CBS News*, December 2, 2010. http:// www.cbsnews.com/stories/2010/12/01/world/main7105891.shtml (quoting Secretary Clinton as saying that at the OSCE meeting, "I have not had any concerns expressed about whether any nation will not continue to work with and discuss matters of importance to us both going forward"); see also Leigh and Harding, *WikiLeaks: Inside Julian Assange's War on Secrecy*, 245–246 (describing the State Department's retreat from its complaints about WikiLeaks' dire effects).

49. Mark Hosenball, "US Officials Privately Say WikiLeaks Damage Limited," *Reuters*, January 18, 2011. http://www.reuters.com/article/2011/01/18/us-wikileaks-damage-idUSTRE70H6TO20110118

50. Hamish Barwick, "WikiLeaks a Boon for US Government: Former Obama Campaign Adviser," *Computerworld*, June 8, 2011. http://www.computerworld.com.au/article/389459/wikileaks_ boon_us_government_former_obama_campaign_adviser/; Gideon Rachman, "America Should

Give Assange a Medal," *Financial Times*, December 13, 2010. https://www.ft.com/content/61f8fab0 -06f3-11e0-8c29-00144feabdc0; James Traub, "The Sunshine Policy," *Foreign Policy*, December 10, 2010. http://www.foreignpolicy.com/articles/2010/12/10/the_sunshine_policy. This observation has been shared by at least one assistant secretary of state. U.S. Department of State, *Internet Freedom: Promoting Human Rights in the Digital Age—A Panel Discussion*, March 4, 2011. http://www.state .gov/g/drl/rls/rm/2011/162490.htm (quoting Assistant Secretary of State Michael Posner, who, after complaining about the disclosures, proudly stated that "one of the salutary aspects [of the diplomatic cable disclosures] is it does reveal the inner workings of a government that's actually paying attention to human rights every day")

51. Gates News Briefing.

52. Joshua Keating, "Why the Snowden Leaks Will Have a Bigger Impact Than WikiLeaks," *Slate*, October 24 2013. http://www.slate.com/blogs/the_world_/2013/10/24/reports_of_nsa_spying _on_france_and_germany_why_the_snowden_leaks_will_have.html

53. Kim Zetter and Kevin Poulsen, "U.S. Intelligence Analyst Arrested in WikiLeaks Video Probe," *Threat Level*, June 6, 2010. http://www.wired.com/threatlevel/2010/06/leak/

54. Jim Garamone, "Officials Condemn Leaks, Detail Prevention Efforts," U.S. Air Force, November 29, 2010. http://www.af.mil/News/ArticleDisplay/tabid/223/Article/114848/officials -condemn-leaks-detail-prevention-efforts.aspx; Adam Levine, "Previous WikiLeaks Release Forced Tighter Security for U.S. Military," *CNN*, November 28, 2010. http://www.cnn.com/2010/US/11/28/ wikileaks.security/; Ellen Nakashima and Jerry Markon, "WikiLeaks Founder Could Be Charged Under Espionage Act," *Washington Post*, November 30, 2010. http://www.washingtonpost.com/wp -dyn/content/article/2010/11/29/AR2010112905973.html; Alasdair Roberts, "The WikiLeaks Illusion," *Wilson Quarterly*, Summer 2011. http://wilsonquarterly.com/quarterly/summer-2011-a-changing -middle-east/the-wikileaks-illusion/

55. See, e.g., Christopher Beam, "Unfair Share," *Slate*, November 29, 2010. http://www.slate .com/id/2276188/; Joseph Straw, "WikiLeaks' Information-Sharing Fallout," *Security Management*, March 1, 2011. https://sm.asisonline.org/Pages/WikiLeaks-Information-Sharing-Fallout.aspx

56. *The 9/11 Commission Report: Final Report of the National Commission on Terrorist Attacks Upon the United States*, authorized ed. (New York: Norton, 2004).

57. Massimo Calabresi, "State Pulls the Plug on SIPRNet," *Swampland*, November 29, 2010. http://swampland.time.com/2010/11/29/state-pulls-the-plug-on-siprnet/; Felix Stalder, "Contain This! Leaks, Whistle-Blowers and the Networked News Ecology," *Eurozine*, November 29, 2010. http:// www.eurozine.com/articles/2010-11-29-stalder-en.html; Joby Warrick, "WikiLeaks Cable Dump Reveals Flaws of State Department's Information-Sharing Tool," *Washington Post*, December 31, 2010. http://www.washingtonpost.com/wp-dyn/content/article/2010/12/30/AR2010123004962.html

58. See generally Patrick McCurdy, "From the Pentagon Papers to Cablegate: How the Network Society Has Changed Leaking," in *Beyond WikiLeaks: Implications for the Future of Communications, Journalism, and Society*, eds. Benedetta Brevini, Arne Hintz, and Patrick McCurdy (London: Palgrave Macmillan, 2013), 123–145, 134–136. For example, the Information Sharing Environment, a government entity built from defense, intelligence, homeland security, foreign affairs, and law enforcement agencies, "provides analysts, operators, and investigators with integrated and synthesized terrorism, weapons of mass destruction, and homeland security information needed to enhance national security and help keep our people safe." ISE, "What Is ISE?" http://ise.gov/what-ise

59. See, e.g., Phil Stewart, "Analysis: WikiLeaks May Set Back U.S. Intelligence Sharing," *Reuters*, November 29 2010. http://www.reuters.com/article/2010/11/29/us-wikileaks-intelligence-idUS TRE6AS67F20101129

60. Calabresi, "State Pulls the Plug On SIPRNet"; Beam, "Unfair Share" ("The scandal will

probably have all kinds of chilling effects"); Jaikumar Vijayan, "WikiLeaks Incident Shouldn't Chill Info-Sharing, Ex-CIA Chief Says," *Computerworld*, August 4, 2010. http://www.computerworld.com/article/2519866/security0/wikileaks-incident-shouldn-t-chill-info-sharing—ex-cia-chief-says.html

61. See, e.g., Aliya Sternstein, "Countering WikiLeaks Could Stifle Information Sharing," *Nextgov*, November 29, 2010. http://www.nextgov.com/nextgov/ng_20101129_9475.php; Vijayan, "WikiLeaks Incident Shouldn't Chill Info-Sharing."

62. *Information Sharing in the Era of WikiLeaks: Balancing Security and Collaboration*, Hearing Before the Committee on Homeland Security and Governmental Affairs, 112th Congress (2011) (statement of Patrick F. Kennedy, Under Secretary of State for Management, U.S. Department of State). https://fas.org/irp/congress/2011_hr/infoshare.pdf; Gates News Briefing. For an argument that the information sharing that developed after the post–9/11 reforms was ineffective, see Amy B. Zegart, *Spying Blind: The CIA, the FBI, and the Origins of 9/11* (Princeton, N.J.: Princeton University Press, 2007), 186–188.

63. Glenn Greenwald, "What WikiLeaks Revealed to the World in 2010," *Salon*, December 24, 2010. http://www.salon.com/news/opinion/glenn_greenwald/2010/12/24/wikileaks

64. See ibid.; Greg Mitchell, "Why WikiLeaks Matters," *Nation*, January 13, 2011. http://www.thenation.com/article/157729/why-wikileaks-matters (listing eighteen "revelations," concerning events from all over the world); Joshua Norman, "How WikiLeaks Enlightened Us in 2010," *CBS News*, December 31, 2010. http://www.cbsnews.com/news/how-wikileaks-enlightened-us-in-2010/ (providing a list of "the more impactful WikiLeaks revelations . . . , grouped by region," that the author describes as having "many major implications for world relations"); Rainey Reitman, "The Best of Cablegate: Instances Where Public Discourse Benefited from the Leaks," *Electronic Frontier Foundation*, January 7, 2011. https://www.eff.org/deeplinks/2011/01/cablegate-disclosures-have-furthered-investigative

65. See, e.g., Peter Beinart, "Why the WikiLeaks Drama Is Overblown," *Daily Beast*, November 28, 2010. http://peterbeinart.net/why-the-wikileaks-drama-is-overblown/; Leslie H. Gelb, "What the WikiLeaks Documents Really Reveal," *Daily Beast*, July 25, 2010. http://www.cfr.org/intelligence/wikileaks-documents-really-reveal/p22691; Andrew Sullivan, "The Starr Report of American Foreign Policy?," *The Atlantic*, November 29, 2010. http://www.theatlantic.com/daily-dish/archive/2010/11/the-starr-report-of-american-foreign-policy/179234/

66. Floyd Abrams, "Why WikiLeaks Is Unlike the Pentagon Papers," *Wall Street Journal*, December 29, 2010. http://www.wsj.com/articles/SB10001424052970204527804576044020396601528

67. Ibid.; Beinart, "Why the WikiLeaks Drama Is Overblown"; Sullivan, "The Starr Report of American Foreign Policy?"

68. Abrams, "Why WikiLeaks Is Unlike the Pentagon Papers."

69. The polls have generally not asked about the public's interest in and knowledge of the substance of the disclosures themselves. Instead, the questions are posed in a manner similar to much of the public debate surrounding the site—as a meta-conversation about WikiLeaks' significance as an institution and idea.

70. Pew Research Center for the People and the Press, "Mixed Reactions to Leak of Afghanistan Documents," August 3, 2010. http://www.people-press.org/2010/08/03/mixed-reactions-to-leak-of-afghanistan-documents/ (finding 47 percent of those questioned believed that the release of the State Department cables harmed the public interest and 42 percent believed that it served the public interest, while 63 percent said they had heard a little or nothing at all about it).

71. See, e.g., *60 Minutes* and *Vanity Fair*, "60 Minutes/Vanity Fair Poll," conducted December 17–20, 2010. *CBS News*. http://www.cbsnews.com/htdocs/pdf/february_final_edition.pdf (finding that 42 percent of respondents were not sure what WikiLeaks was, while only 9 percent con-

sidered it a "good thing" as opposed to "[d]estructive, but legal" (23 percent) or "[t]reasonous" (22 percent)); Meredith Chaiken, "Poll: Americans Say WikiLeaks Harmed Public Interest; Most Want Assange Arrested," *Washington Post*, December 14, 2010. http://www.washingtonpost.com/wp-dyn/content/article/2010/12/14/AR2010121401650.html (discussing poll in which 68 percent of respondents believed the disclosures harmed the public interest, and 59 percent thought Assange should be prosecuted for releasing the diplomatic cables); CNN and Opinion Research Corporation, "CNN/Opinion Research Poll," conducted December 17–19, 2010. http://i2.cdn.turner.com/cnn/2010/images/12/30/rel17n.pdf (finding that 77 percent disapproved of all of the disclosures, and only 20 percent approved); Pew Research Center for the People and the Press, "Most Say WikiLeaks Release Harms Public Interest," December 8, 2010. http://people-press.org/report/682/ (finding that 60 percent believed the release of the State Department cables harmed the public interest); Steven Thomma, "Poll: People Behind WikiLeaks Should Be Prosecuted," *McClatchy*, December 10, 2010. http://www.mcclatchydc.com/news/crime/article24603949.html (reporting that 70 percent of respondents thought the leaks had done more harm than good, and 59 percent thought those responsible should be prosecuted)

72. CNN and Opinion Research Corporation, "CNN/Opinion Research Poll." But see "60 Minutes/Vanity Fair Poll" (finding that although more Republicans knew about WikiLeaks than Democrats or Independents, more of them considered the site "[t]reasonous" and fewer of them considered it a "good thing" than Democrats or Independents).

73. Mark Jurkowitz, Tom Rosenstiel, and Amy Mitchell, "A Year in the News 2010: Disaster, Economic Anxiety, but Little Interest in War," *StateoftheMedia.org*, January 11, 2011. http://www.stateofthemedia.org/2011/mobile-survey/a-year-in-news -narrative/#disaster-economic-anxiety -but-little-interest-in-war

74. Roberts, "The WikiLeaks Illusion."

75. On the Tea Party, see Jill Lepore, *The Whites of Their Eyes: The Tea Party's Revolution and the Battle over American History* (Princeton, N.J.: Princeton University Press, 2010); Kate Zernike, *Boiling Mad: Inside Tea Party America* (New York: Times Books, 2010).

76. To explain the minimal effects from these disclosures, one could claim that the media, government, and major corporate interests have actively and apparently successfully worked to distract attention from WikiLeaks and to destroy its credibility. See, e.g., Kevin Gosztola, "Reflecting on the Afghanistan War Logs Released by WikiLeaks One Year Ago," *Dissenter*, July 25, 2011. http://dissenter.firedoglake.com/2011/07/25/reflecting-on-the-afghanistan-war-logs-released-by-wikileaks-one-year-ago; Glenn Greenwald, "The Leaked Campaign to Attack WikiLeaks and Its Supporters," *Salon*, February 11, 2011. http://www.salon.com/2011/02/11/campaigns_4/; Glenn Greenwald, "The Nixonian Henchman of Today: At the NYT," *Salon*, October 24, 2010. http://www.salon.com/2010/10/24/assange_2/. Evaluating this claim is beyond the scope of this book, although the cruel conditions of Bradley Manning's confinement during his pretrial detention, as well as the disclosure that several private data intelligence firms planned technical and public relations attacks on WikiLeaks and its supporters complicate any effort to simply dismiss the claim as a conspiracy theory. Steve Ragan, "Data Intelligence Firms Proposed a Systematic Attack Against WikiLeaks," *Tech Herald*, February 9, 2011. http://www.thetechherald.com/articles/Data-intelligence-firms-proposed-a-systematic-attack-against-WikiLeaks/12751/; Editorial, "The Abuse of Private Manning," *New York Times*, March 14, 2011. http://www.nytimes.com/2011/03/15/opinion/15tue3.html. Yochai Benkler offers a nuanced version of this claim as part of his broader description of the incumbent mainstream media's "battle" against the "networked fourth estate." Benkler, "A Free Irresponsible Press," 396–397 (criticizing "the ability of private infrastructure companies to restrict speech without being bound by the constraints of legality, and the possibil-

ity that government actors will take advantage of this affordance in an extralegal public–private partnership for censorship").

77. Mark Landler, "A Wartime Leader Ends a War He Never Wanted," *New York Times,* December 8, 2011. http://www.nytimes.com/2011/12/09/world/middleeast/president-obama-ends-a -war-he-never-wanted.html (noting the political and policy-related reasons for troop withdrawal).

78. Peter Baker, "With Pledges to Troops and Iraqis, Obama Details Pullout," *New York Times,* February 27, 2009. http://www.nytimes.com/2009/02/28/washington/28troops.html

79. Mark Landler and Helene Cooper, "Obama Will Speed Pullout from War in Afghanistan," *New York Times,* June 22, 2011. http://www.nytimes.com/2011/06/23/world/asia/23prexy.html?_ r=2&pagewanted=all

80. Nikolas Kozloff, "WikiLeaks Cables: The Great Equaliser in Peru," *Al Jazeera,* June 2, 2011. http://www.aljazeera.com/indepth/features/2011/06/2011627179165204.html. The cables also caused some momentary embarrassment but no apparent significant and lasting damage for the Indian prime minister. Rama Lakshmi, "Publication of WikiLeaks Cable Leads to Calls for Indian Prime Minister's Resignation," *Washington Post,* March 17, 2011. https://www.washingtonpost.com/world/ publication-of-wikileaks-cable-leads-to-calls-for-indian-prime-ministers-resignation/2011/03/17/ ABNssFj_story.html

81. Lisa Lynch, "The Leak Heard Round the World: Cablegate in the Evolving Global Media-scape," in *Beyond WikiLeaks: Implications for the Future of Communications, Journalism, and Society,* eds. Benedetta Brevini, Arne Hintz, and Patrick McCurdy (London: Palgrave Macmillan, 2013), 56–77.

82. Angelique Chrisafis and Ian Black, "Zine al-Abidine Ben Ali Forced to Flee Tunisia as Protesters Claim Victory," *The Guardian,* January 14, 2011. http://www.guardian.co.uk/world/2011/ jan/14/tunisian-president-flees-country-protests

83. Public Library of US Diplomacy, "Cable 08TUNIS679, Corruption in Tunisia: What's Yours Is Mine," *WikiLeaks.* http://wikileaks.ch/cable/2008/06/08TUNIS679.html

84. TuniLeaks. https://nawaat.org/portail/tag/tunileaks/; see also Sofiane Ben Haj M'Hamed, "How WikiLeaks Rocked Tunisia," *Institute of War and Peace Reporting,* July 6, 2011. http://iwpr.net/ report-news/how-wikileaks-rocked-tunisia (explanation by translator of the WikiLeaks' Tunisian cables of WikiLeaks' influence in the country). The TuniLeaks site was itself part of Nawaat.org, a Tunisian-based blog collective that, in March 2011, won a Google-sponsored prize awarded by the group Reporters Without Borders for its coverage of WikiLeaks. Matthew Campbell, "Tunisian Revolt Bloggers Win Google-Sponsored Web Freedom Prize," *Bloomberg,* March 11, 2011. http://www .bloomberg.com/news/2011–03–11/tunisian-revolt-bloggers-win-google-sponsored-web-freedom -prize.html

85. David D. Kirkpatrick, "Tunisia Leader Flees and Prime Minister Claims Power," *New York Times,* January 14, 2011. http://www.nytimes.com/2011/01/15/world/africa/15tunis.html?page wanted=all&_r=0; Tom Malinowski, "Did WikiLeaks Take Down Tunisia's Government?," in *Revolution in the Arab World: Tunisia, Egypt, and the Unmaking of an Era,* eds. Marc Lynch et al. (Washington, D.C.: Foreign Policy Magazine, 2011), 57–58; Sami Ben Hassine, "Tunisia's Youth Finally Has Revolution on Its Mind," *The Guardian,* January 13, 2011. http://www.guardian.co.uk/commentis free/2011/jan/13/tunisia-youth-revolution

86. Robert Mackey, "Qaddafi Sees WikiLeaks Plot in Tunisia," *The Lede,* January 17, 2011. http:// thelede.blogs.nytimes.com/2011/01/17/qaddafi-sees-wikileaks-plot-in-tunisia/; Issandr El Amrani, "Twitter, WikiLeaks and Tunisia," *Arabist,* January 15, 2011. http://www.arabist.net/blog/2011/1/15/ twitter-wikileaks-and-tunisia.html

87. Leigh and Harding, *WikiLeaks: Inside Julian Assange's War on Secrecy,* 247–249.

88. "Introduction to Chapter 2" of Lynch et al., *Revolution in the Arab World*, 41; Hamza Hendawi, "Egyptians Denounce Mubarak, Clash with Riot Police," *Boston.com*, January 25, 2011. http:// archive.boston.com/news/world/middleeast/articles/2011/01/25/egyptians_denounce_mubarak_ clash_with_riot_police/

89. Simon Mabon, "Aiding Revolution? Wikileaks Communication and the 'Arab Spring' in Egypt," *Third World Quarterly* 34, no. 10 (2013): 1843–1857.

90. Ibrahim Saleh, "WikiLeaks and the Arab Spring: The Twists and Turns of Media, Culture, and Power," in Brevini et al., *Beyond WikiLeaks: Implications for the Future of Communications, Journalism and Society*, 236–244. Some commentators have identified more conventional effects that WikiLeaks could have on democratic elections in Kenya and Peru, predicting that the information from some released cables, along with the opinions of the cables' diplomatic authors, would persuade voters to vote against certain candidates. Juan Arellano, "Peru: WikiLeaks and the Presidential Campaign," *Global Voices,* March 5, 2011. http://globalvoicesonline.org/2011/03/05/peru-wikileaks-usa-and-their-effect-on-the-presidential-campaign/; Murithi Mutiga, "Leaked US Cables Likely to Shape 2012 Campaigns," *Daily Nation,* March 5, 2011. http://www.nation.co.ke/News/ politics/Leaked+US+cables+likely+to+shape+2012+campaigns+/-/1064/1119772/-/wedgtu/-/. In addition, several days after the beginning of the crisis at several nuclear power reactors in northeastern Japan that followed the March 2011 earthquake and tsunami, WikiLeaks released diplomatic cables via the British newspaper *The Telegraph* reporting warnings that Japan had received about significant safety problems at Japanese reactors, especially in the event of an earthquake. Steven Swinford and Christopher Hope, "Japan Earthquake: Japan Warned over Nuclear Plants, WikiLeaks Cables Show," *The Telegraph*, March 15, 2011. http://www.telegraph.co.uk/news/world news/wikileaks/8384059/Japan-earthquake-Japan-warned-over-nuclear-plants-WikiLeaks-cables -show.html. This classic whistleblowing act could allow the Japanese public to hold their national government, regulators, and industry actors accountable for their actions (or inaction). Whether they did so, or whether the disclosures were necessary to stir public dissatisfaction, is and will be difficult to prove. But the fact that WikiLeaks could supply these cables on a just-in-time basis illustrates the profound nature of the site as a resource for the public and as a threat to government secrecy. It is important to note, however, that WikiLeaks' and its supporters' claims about the site's positive externalities are not uncontested. Dan Murphy, "Julian Assange: The Man Who Came to Dinner, the Man Who Saved Egypt," *Christian Science Monitor*, July 5, 2011. http://www.csmoni tor.com/World/Backchannels/2011/0705/Julian-Assange-The-man-who-came-to-dinner-the-man -who-saved-Egypt; Dan Murphy, "Tunisia: That 'WikiLeaks Revolution' Meme," *Christian Science Monitor*, January 15, 2011. http://www.csmonitor.com/World/Backchannels/2011/0115/Tunisia-That -WikiLeaks-Revolution-meme

91. *Universal Declaration of Human Rights*, G.A. Res. 217 (III) A, U.N. Doc. A/RES/217(III), Art. 19. http://www.un.org/en/documents/udhr/index.shtml ("Everyone has the right to . . . seek, receive and impart information and ideas through any media and regardless of frontiers").

92. John Oliver, *Last Week Tonight*, episode 32, April 5, 2015.

93. Glenn Greenwald, Ewen MacAskill, and Laura Poitras, "Edward Snowden: The Whistleblower Behind the NSA Surveillance Revelations," *The Guardian*, June 11, 2013. http://www.the guardian.com/world/2013/jun/09/edward-snowden-nsa-whistleblower-surveillance

94. Annual Gallup polling did not detect a significant change between July 2009 and July 2010 in response to questions asking about how "things are going for the United States in Iraq" and whether the United States "made a mistake in sending troops to Iraq"; other polls similarly found little change in American attitudes toward the war and occupation after the WikiLeaks' releases. "Foreign Affairs: Iraq," *Gallup*. http://www.gallup.com/poll/1633/Iraq.aspx; "Iraq," *PollingReport.com*.

http://www.pollingreport.com/iraq.htm (collecting results of longitudinal polling about Iraq). The Pew Research Center found a gradual decline in support for the war and its outcome, especially between 2012 and 2013 (two years after the WikiLeaks' disclosures) but no profound difference that could be traced to the leaked video or documents. Pew Research Center, "A Decade Later, Iraq War Divides the Public," March 18, 2013. http://www.people-press.org/2013/03/18/a-decade-later-iraq-war-divides-the -public/

95. See, for example, Barton Gellman, "Edward Snowden, After Months of NSA Revelations, Says His Mission's Accomplished," *Washington Post*, December 23, 2013. https://www.washington post.com/world/national-security/edward-snowden-after-months-of-nsa-revelations-says-his -missions-accomplished/2013/12/23/49fc36de-6c1c-11e3-a523-fe73f0ff6b8d_story.html; Alan Rusbridger and Ewen MacAskill, "Edward Snowden Interview—The Edited Transcript," *The Guardian*, July 18, 2014. http://www.theguardian.com/world/2014/jul/18/-sp-edward-snowden-nsa-whistle blower-interview-transcript

96. Jay Rosen, "The Snowden Effect: Definitions and Examples," *Press Think*, July 5, 2013 (with frequent subsequent updates). http://pressthink.org/2013/07/the-snowden-effect-definition-and -examples/

97. Drew DeSilver, "Most Young Americans Say Snowden Has Served the Public Interest," *Pew Research Center*, January 22, 2014. http://www.pewresearch.org/fact-tank/2014/01/22/most-young -americans-say-snowden-has-served-the-public-interest/ (finding that Americans' opinions are divided over whether Snowden's leaks served or harmed the public interest)

98. Orin Kerr, "Edward Snowden's Impact," *Washington Post*, April 9, 2015. http://www.wash ingtonpost.com/news/volokh-conspiracy/wp/2015/04/09/edward-snowdens-impact/

99. "Majority Views NSA Phone Tracking as Acceptable Anti-Terror Tactic," *Pew Research Center*, June 10, 2013. http://www.people-press.org/2013/06/10/majority-views-nsa-phone-track ing-as-acceptable-anti-terror-tactic/; Lee Rainie and Mary Madden, "Americans' Privacy Strategies Post-Snowden," *Pew Research Center*, March 16, 2015. http://www.pewinternet.org/2015/03/16/ Americans-Privacy-Strategies-Post-Snowden/

100. Ellen Nakashima and Barton Gellman, "As Encryption Spreads, U.S. Grapples with Clash Between Privacy, Security," *Washington Post*, April 10, 2015. https://www.washingtonpost.com/world/ national-security/as-encryption-spreads-us-worries-about-access-to-data-for-investigations/2015/ 04/10/7c1c7518-d401-11e4-a62f-ee745911a4ff_story.html

101. Keating, "Why the Snowden Leaks Will Have a Bigger Impact Than WikiLeaks."

102. Daniel Castro, "How Much Will PRISM Cost the U.S. Cloud Computing Industry?," *The Information Technology & Innovation Foundation*, August 2013. https://itif.org/pub lications/2013/08/05/how-much-will-prism-cost-us-cloud-computing-industry; Gerry Smith, "'Snowden Effect' Threatens U.S. Tech Industry's Global Ambitions," *Huffington Post*, January 1, 2014. http://www.huffingtonpost.com/2014/01/24/edward-snowden-tech-industry_n_4596162 .html; Electronic Frontier Foundation, "Who Has Your Back? Protecting Your Data from Government Requests—2016." https://www.eff.org/who-has-your-back-2016; Patrick Lane, "Data Protectionism," *The Economist*, November 18, 2013. http://www.economist.com/news/21589110-global -computing-cloud-geography-will-matter-more-data-protectionism

103. Russell Brandom, "Microsoft Offers Overseas Data Storage in Response to NSA Concern," *The Verge*, January 22, 2014. http://www.theverge.com/2014/1/22/5335434/microsoft-offers-overseas -data-storage-in-response-to-nsa-concerns; Stephan Dörner, "For German, Swiss Privacy Start-Ups, a Post-Snowden Boom," *Wall Street Journal* (Blog), August 20, 2014. http://blogs.wsj.com/ digits/2014/08/20/for-german-swiss-privacy-start-ups-a-post-snowden-boon/

104. Steve Holland and Anthony Boadle, "Obama: U.S. Will Probe Reported NSA Spying on Brazil, Mexico," *Reuters*, September 6, 2013. http://www.reuters.com/article/2013/09/06/us-usa-se curity-snowden-brazil-idUSBRE9850F720130906

105. Timothy B. Lee, "The President Is Wrong: The NSA Debate Wouldn't Have Happened Without Snowden," *Washington Post*, August 9, 2013. https://www.washingtonpost.com/news/ the-switch/wp/2013/08/09/the-president-is-wrong-the-nsa-debate-wouldnt-have-happened -without-snowden/; Matt Sledge, "Edward Snowden Vindicated: Obama Speech Acknowledges Changes Needed to Surveillance," *Huffington Post*, January 17, 2014. http://www.huffingtonpost .com/2014/01/17/obama-edward-snowden_n_4617970.html

106. Mattathias Schwartz, "Who Needs Edward Snowden?" *The New Yorker*, May 28, 2015. http://www.newyorker.com/news/news-desk/who-needs-edward-snowden; Jennifer Steinhauer and Jonathan Weisman, "Battle Lines in G.O.P. Set Stage for Surveillance Vote," *New York Times*, May 30, 2015. http://www.nytimes.com/2015/05/31/us/surveillance-vote-in-senate-is-tangled-in-gop -debate.html?_r=0

107. Eyder Peralta, "As Congress Haggles over Patriot Act, We Answer 6 Basic Questions," *NPR*, May 19, 2015. http://www.npr.org/sections/thetwo-way/2015/05/19/407667776/as-congress-haggles -over-patriot-act-we-answer-6–basic-questions

108. For a summary of the changes, see Jodie Liu, "So What Does the USA Freedom Act Do Anyway?" *Lawfare*, June 3, 2015. https://www.lawfareblog.com/so-what-does-usa-freedom-act-do-anyway

109. See, for example, Rainey Reitman, "The New USA Freedom Act: A Step in the Right Direction, but More Must Be Done," *Electronic Frontier Foundation*, April 30, 2015. https://www.eff .org/deeplinks/2015/04/new-usa-freedom-act-step-right-direction-more-must-be-done; Trevor Timm, "Our Statement on Congress Passing the USA Freedom Act, the NSA 'Reform' Bill," *Freedom of the Press Foundation*, June 2, 2015. https://freedom.press/blog/2015/06/our-statement-congress -passing-usa-freedom-act-nsa-reform-bill

110. Edward J. Snowden, "The World Says No to Surveillance," *New York Times*, June 4, 2015. http://www.nytimes.com/2015/06/05/opinion/edward-snowden-the-world-says-no-to-surveil lance.html

111. Jeremy Herb and Justin Sink, "Sen. Feinstein Calls Snowden's NSA Leaks an 'Act of Treason,'" *The Hill*, June 10, 2013. http://thehill.com/policy/defense/304573-sen-feinstein-snowdens -leaks-are-treason

112. Steven Aftergood, "Leaks Damaged U.S. Intelligence, Official Says," *Secrecy News*, February 17, 2015. http://fas.org/blogs/secrecy/2015/02/leaks-damaged/; Tim Risen, "NSA Chief Mute on Spyware, Critical on Snowden," *US News.com*, February 23, 2015. http://www.usnews.com/ news/articles/2015/02/23/nsa-chief-mute-on-spyware-critical-on-snowden; Mark Hosenball, Matt Spetalnick, and Peter Apps, "The 'Snowden Effect': US Spies Say Militants Change Tactics," *Reuters*, June 25, 2013. http://www.reuters.com/article/2013/06/26/us-usa-security-tactics-idUS BRE95P00R20130626

113. Caleb Garling, "Stewart Baker Calls Out Cyber-Surveillance Myths," *Wired*, June 2015. https://www.wired.com/brandlab/2015/06/oh-kiss-ass-thats-not-true-stewart-baker-calls-cyber -surveillance-myths/; Stewart Baker, "Is Snowden a Spy?" *Washington Post*, May 11, 2014. https:// www.washingtonpost.com/news/volokh-conspiracy/wp/2014/05/11/is-snowden-a-spy/

114. David Ignatius, "Edward Snowden Took Less Than Previously Thought, Says James Clapper," *Washington Post*, June 5, 2014. http://wpo.st/7rfq1

115. Amy Davidson, "Don't Blame Edward Snowden for the Paris Attacks," *The New Yorker*, November 19, 2015. http://www.newyorker.com/news/amy-davidson/dont-blame-edward -snowden-for-the-paris-attacks

116. Benjamin Wittes, "What Role Did Encryption Play in Paris?" *Lawfare*, November 16, 2015. https://lawfareblog.com/what-role-did-encryption-play-paris

117. Mike Brunker, "Snowden Leaks Didn't Make Al Qaeda Change Tactics Says Report," *NBC News*, September 16, 2014. http://www.nbcnews.com/storyline/nsa-snooping/snowden-leaks-didnt-make-al-qaeda-change-tactics-says-report-n203731

118. Cora Currier, "How the NSA Started Investigating the *New York Times* Original Warrantless Wiretapping Story," *The Intercept*, June 26, 2015. https://firstlook.org/theintercept/2015/06/26/nsa-started-investigating-new-york-times-original-warrantless-wiretapping-story/. The original *Times* story was James Risen and Eric Lichtblau, "Bush Lets U.S. Spy on Callers Without Courts," *New York Times*, December 16, 2005. http://www.nytimes.com/2005/12/16/politics/bush-lets-us-spy-on-callers-without-courts.html

119. Ariane Cerlenko, "CI-030-05 Close Out for 'Bush Lets U.S. Spy on Callers Without Courts,'" December 19, 2005. https://s3.amazonaws.com/s3.documentcloud.org/documents/2110724/nsa-report-on-nyt-warrantless-wiretapping-story.pdf

120. Ibid.

121. I use the term *threaten* with the caution the term implies. But few would have anticipated that just a few short years after WikiLeaks leaked the Manning files that someone else would produce another massive leak of more highly classified documents. Snowden's brazen willingness to publicly accept responsibility, alongside the fast and easy ability that the Internet affords for the global dissemination of information, may be as rare as Ellsberg's megaleak proved to be in the decades following it. And of course WikiLeaks' technological innovations (to the extent that there were any) could prove only as successful as the material to which it had access, which required the luck and courage (if one sees it as such) of Bradley Manning. To the extent that the U.S. government can keep future Chelsea Mannings and Edward Snowdens from having access to or being able to download such a trove of digital files, or can plausibly threaten her or him with life imprisonment or lifelong exile, then WikiLeaks' "threat" may not be so great. I thank Steven Aftergood for this insight.

122. My thanks to David Pozen for identifying this point.

Conclusion

1. See, e.g., Susan Willis, "Empire's Shadow," *New Left Review* 22 (July–August 2003): 59–70 ("*West Wing* narratives are indeed liberal fantasies"); John Podhoretz, "The Liberal Imagination," *Weekly Standard*, March 27, 2000, http://www.weeklystandard.com/the-liberal-imagination/article/12329 (describing the series as "nothing more than political pornography for liberals, made up of equal parts of longing for and rage at Hollywood's not-so-obscure object desire, William Jefferson Clinton").

2. On *The West Wing*'s enormous success with elite liberal audiences, see J. Elizabeth Clark, "The Bartlet Administration and Contemporary Populism in NBC's *The West Wing*," in *The Contemporary Television Series*, eds. Michael Hammond and Lucy Mazdon (Edinburgh: Edinburgh University Press, 2005), 224–242.

3. Mark Fenster, "Designing Transparency: The 9/11 Commission and Institutional Form," *Washington and Lee Law Review* 65, no. 4 (2008): 1239–1321.

4. Mark Fenster, "The Informational Ombudsman: Fixing Open Government by Institutional Design," *International Journal of Open Governments/Revue Internationale des Governments Ouverts* 1 (March 2015): 275–296; Daxton R. Stewart, "Evaluating Public Access Ombuds Programs: An Analysis of Experiences in Virginia, Iowa, and Arizona in Creating and Implementing Ombuds Offices to Handle Disputes Arising Under Open Government Laws," *Journal of Dispute Resolution*

no. 2 (2012): 437–505; Daxton R. Stewart, "Managing Conflict over Access: A Typology of Sunshine Law Dispute Resolution Systems," *Journal of Media Law and Ethics* 1, no. 1 (2009): 49–82.

5. Steven Aftergood, "An Inquiry into the Dynamics of Government Secrecy," *Harvard Civil Rights–Civil Liberties Law Review* 48, no. 2 (2013): 511–530, 527–528; Steven Aftergood, "Reducing Government Secrecy: Finding What Works," *Yale Law and Policy Review* 27, no. 2 (2009): 399–416, 407–408.

6. Shirin Sinnar, "Protecting Rights from Within? Inspectors General and National Security Oversight," *Stanford Law Review* 65, no. 5 (May 2013): 1027–1086; Ryan M. Check and Afsheen John Radsan, "One Lantern in the Darkest Night: The CIA's Inspector General," *Journal of National Security Law and Policy* 4, no. 2 (2010): 247–294.

7. Dawn E. Johnsen, "Faithfully Executing the Laws: Internal Legal Constraints on Executive Power," *UCLA Law Review* 54, no. 6 (2007): 1559–1612; Neal Kumar Katyal, "Internal Separation of Powers: Checking Today's Most Dangerous Branch from Within," *Yale Law Journal* 115, no. 9 (2006): 2314–2349; Gillian E. Metzger, "The Interdependent Relationship Between Internal and External Separation of Powers," *Emory Law Journal* 59, no. 2 (2009): 423–458.

8. Judge Richard Posner, among others, made this argument in a series of books critiquing the commission's proposals to reorganize the intelligence community. Richard A. Posner, *Countering Terrorism* (Lanham, Md.: Rowman & Littlefield, 2007), 144–145; Richard A. Posner, *Uncertain Shield* (Lanham, Md.: Rowman & Littlefield, 2006); Richard A. Posner, *Preventing Surprise Attacks* (Lanham, Md.: Rowman & Littlefield, 2005). I discuss this criticism of the commission's prescriptions in Fenster, "Designing Transparency," 1307–1313.

9. The concept itself dates back at least to the Pentagon Papers era. Harold Edgar and Benno C. Schmidt Jr., "The Espionage Statutes and Publication of Defense Information," *Columbia Law Review* 73, no. 5 (1973): 929–1087, 1045 n.450; Louis Henkin, "The Right to Know and the Duty to Withhold: The Case of the Pentagon Papers," *University of Pennsylvania Law Review* 120, no. 2 (1971): 271–280, 280.

10. Public Law 114-185, § 2(1)(D)(2), 130 Stat. 538 (June 30, 2016) (amending 5 U.S.C. § 552(b)(5)).

11. Executive Order 13526, § 3.3(a), 75 Fed. Reg. 707, 714 (December 29, 2009). As ever, this disclosure mandate is limited by enumerated exceptions that are largely related to national security and diplomacy, but in order to invoke an exception to declassification, the relevant head of the agency that had classified the information must "clearly and demonstrably" show the danger of disclosure. For a summary of the Clinton program, see Amanda Fitzsimmons, "National Security of Unnecessary Secrecy? Restricting Exemption 1 to Prohibit Reclassification of Information Already in the Public Domain," *I/S: Journal of Law and Policy for the Information Society* 4, no. 2 (2008): 479–524, 486–487.

12. Executive Order 13526, §§ 3.3(j), 5.3.

13. 44 U.S.C. § 2204 lays out the staged lifting of restrictions of public access to presidential documents after the conclusion of a president's final term.

14. Steven Aftergood of the Federation of American Scientists has provided the most informed coverage of ISCAP and the National Declassification Center, which oversees the mandatory declassification program, and he often reports on their successes and shortcomings. For examples of his mixed though generally positive reviews, see Steven Aftergood, "December 2013 Declassification Deadline Passes—And?" *Secrecy News*, January 14, 2014. http://fas.org/blogs/secrecy/2014/01/declass-deadline/; Steven Aftergood, "Declassification Advances, but Will Miss Goal," *Secrecy News*, July 20, 2012. http://www.fas.org/blog/secrecy/2012/07/miss_goal.html; Steven Aftergood, "NARA Proposes New Rule on Declassification," *Secrecy News*, July 11, 2011. http://www.fas.org/blog/secrecy/2011/07/nara_declass.html

15. On Committees of Inquiry, see Sebastian von Münchow, "Security Agencies and Parliamentary Committees of Inquiry in Germany: Transparency vs. Confidentiality," *Connections* 12, no. 4 (Fall 2013): 51–73. On the failure of congressional intelligence oversight, see Amy Zegart, *Spying Blind: Congress and the United States Intelligence Community* (Stanford, Calif.: Hoover Institution Press, 2011).

16. As Kathleen Clark's study of the NSA's wireless wiretapping program shows, even a complex, overlapping accountability "architecture" can fail to provide timely information when the state coordinates and concentrates its effort to maintain secrets. Kathleen Clark, "The Architecture of Accountability: A Case Study of the Warrantless Surveillance Program," *Brigham Young University Law Review* no. 2 (2010): 357–419.

Index